I

"Reading Robert A. Boomsma's story imparts more than just an inspiration about how much one person can accomplish in life's journey by Trusting Him. It is a matter of trying to comprehend how a dozen lives could be embraced within a time period that follows his adventures from Al Capone's street in Illinois to murderous alleys in California, from the jungles of Indonesia to the wastelands of Mongolia, from China to Cuba, from places that many of us strain to locate on a map. Put it bluntly: compared to Bob Boomsma, Rambo was a softie. Motorcycles, manhunters, cobras and mosquitoes from Jurassic Park—mosquitos uruses—blood sucking beetles, drunk pilots, guns, girls, mayhem and murders, and let us not forget Boeing, Burroughs, Komodo lizards the size of station wagons, Dinky, the Gecko of Biak, and a partridge in a pear tree—everything imaginable and quite a bit that is not. All of which can lead to what Boomsma rightly characterizes as PCSS—Post Cultural Stress Syndrome. How did Bob make it through all this and much more? Trusting God. There is no other way. A forty-five-caliber pistol pressed against your skull? Trust God. Defending yourself against a machete-wielding gang with a penknife? Trust God. And write about it all in an account that concludes wonderfully with his "favorite messages and mottos learned along the journey." Prepare to be amazed, humbled, wiser, and most of all, inspired by the life of an extraordinary individual whose accomplishments often dwarf our understanding but not our appreciation of Bob Boomsma's amazing journey through life made possible only by Trusting God."

—Marvin Folkertsma, Lifelong friend,
and retired Political Science Professor

"Having known Bob, and his lovely wife Estella, for more than 30 years now, I considered it a special honor when Bob asked me to write a few words here by way of introduction. This book contains Bob's story, as told from his own perspective. Upon reading it, one thing that jumped out from the pages was that here was the story of a man who took on every life challenge with courage and with faith.

Surely, that was also my personal experience with Bob, and this is what always made my regular encounters with Bob something to look forward to.

I have always believed, and still firmly believe today, that living life to the fullest, taking risks, courageously choosing the road less travelled, and especially not letting myself be constrained by fear, but move forward in faith, trusting God to show the way forward, and, most of all, loving the people God places in my path, would be a source of life, of strength, and of health for me. It would strengthen my immune system, invigorate my T-cells, and raise my serotonin levels. And it would make my life happier and more fulfilled.

But not every experience was mine to experience. Some of it I experienced through other people. When Bob told me, often in exquisite detail, about his travels, his adventures, his numerous contacts throughout the world, it was as though it was made possible for me to visit those places, experience those adventures, and meet those people vicariously.

It is my hope and desire that by reading this book, you, too, will experience some of Bob's adventures vicariously, and that, in doing so, your immune system will be made stronger, and you will be able to tackle your own life challenges with greater vigor and courage.

Perhaps more than anything, it is my hope and desire that you will come to see Bob's God more clearly. That you will come to trust that God in the same way Bob trusted God, in a way that empowered Bob, and can also empower you. For there is no end to the ways God can be a source of strength to those who trust Him.

Thanks, Bob, for being that person in my life for more than 30 years."

—Dr. Gary Voorman

"When I read this memoir from lifelong friend Bob Boomsma I was flooded with wonderful memories. We have been close friends for as long as I can remember. I remember worship at Arcadia Christian Reformed Church, Arcadia Christian School, numerous camping trips and his wonderful parents, lovingly called "Uncle Art" and "Aunt Alice". It was clear from an early age that God had blessed Bob with incredible people skills so it was no surprise at all to me that Bob could defuse a potential knife fight with a well-timed piece of comedy. Bob could go into any social setting with strangers and emerge with friends for life. Like his dad, Bob has always been a great storyteller, a skill on full display in this memoir.

"Trusting Him" could be easily read on one level as a collection of incredible adventures, some of which would have made Indiana Jones turn in his fedora. But that misses the point. The title says it all, "Trusting Him." Bob heard the call of the Lord and turned his back on a lucrative career in banking and venture capital, stepping out in faith to follow Him wherever He would lead. What followed was faithful service to His Kingdom and confirmation time after time that God is faithful to his servants. Perhaps you are wrestling with a call from the Lord. Read this memoir prayerfully and go. God will never let you down."

Thomas G. Bakker, Esq
Lifelong friend and retired Attorney-at-Law

"There is tremendous power in a life story and great inspiration in a biography. The Bible says that God gives us these stories as an example (1 Corinthians 10:6) and for encouragement (Hebrews 12:1). This was true in the Bible and is still true today. Robert Boomsma's book 'Trusting Him' provides us with examples of faith and encouragement to trust God. With each story he tells, we have a concrete guide as to how to follow God and why to follow God. We highly recommend this book.....it will increase your 'trust quotient'!!!"

—Drs. Glenn and Kimberly Gunderson

"I know the plans I have for you says the Lord. They are plans for good and not for evil, to give you a future and a hope."

Jeremiah 29:11 TLB

TRUSTING HIM

BY

ROBERT A BOOMSMA

TRUSTING HIM

PERMISSIONS

All Bible verses are quoted and noted as follows, and given gratis permission, since less than 25% of this publication, and less than 500 scriptures, are taken from the following Bible versions:

KJV – King James Version, Cambridge: *Scripture quotations from The Authorized (King James) Version. Rights in the Authorized Version in the United Kingdom are vested in the Crown, Reproduced by permission of the Crown's patentee, Cambridge University Press.*

NKJV – Scripture taken from the New King James Version®. Copyright © 1982 by Thomas Nelson. Used by permission. All rights reserved.

NIV – New International Version, Biblica. *Scripture quotations taken from The Holy Bible, New International Version® NIV® Copyright © 1973 1978 1984 2011 by Biblica, Inc. TM Used by permission. All rights reserved worldwide.*

TLB – The Living Bible, Tyndale House. *Scripture quotations marked (TLB) are taken from The Living Bible copyright © 1971. Used by permission of Tyndale House Publishers, Carol Stream, Illinois 60188. All rights reserved.*

NASB – Scripture quotations taken from the New American Standard Bible®, (NASB®) Copyright © 1960, 1971, 1977, 1995, 2020 by The Lockman Foundation. Used by permission. All rights reserved. www.lockman.org"

Amplified Bible – "Scripture quotations taken from the Amplified® Bible (AMP), Copyright © 2015 by The Lockman Foundation. Used by permission. www.lockman.org" Scripture quotations taken from the Amplified® Bible (AMPC), Copyright © 1954, 1958, 1962, 1964, 1965, 1987 by The Lockman Foundation. Used by permission. www.lockman.org"

TRUSTING HIM is a Fictionalized Autobiography – *"Mostly a truthful telling of the author's experience with sections fictionalized to "protect the innocent", filling gaps where memory fails, and occasionally rearranging events for maximum narrative effect."* https://www.bing.com/search?q=Definition+of+Fictionalized+Autobiography&cvid=277f3.

ISBN 978-1-64184-631-8 (Paperback)

JETLAUNCH

This book is dedicated to Jesus Christ my Lord and Savior.

Jesus said, "I am the resurrection and the life. He who believes in Me, though he may die, he shall live. And whoever lives and believes in Me shall never die. Do you believe this?"
John 11: 25-26 (NKJV)

"I am with you always." Matthew 28:20 (NKJV)

"Let God have your life. He can do more with it than you can. God commands us to be filled with the Holy Spirit and if we are not filled, it is because we are living beneath our privilege." D.L. Moody

ACKNOWLEDGEMENTS

I would first like to thank my wife Stella for her encouragement to write this Memoir of my life. For her consistent support, her ongoing prayers and patience during the many days and nights of being a writer's widow while I pounded out pages in my self-exiled office. Stella, you have always been the most understanding, gracious woman I have ever met. I will always need your love to keep my thoughtlessness on a leash.

Gratitude to my Mom and Dad who imparted strong Christian values, passing on their life's lessons, and the surrendered life in Christ with verbal illustrations and by demonstration.

Much appreciation to Dr. Gary Voorman and his wife Lois for over 30 years of friendship and Godly mentoring. Gary, I have thoroughly enjoyed our many breakfasts, lunches, and dinners over these many years, as well as your supernatural ability to always quickly see the heart of the matter. I fully expect we can and will continue this tradition. It means a great deal to me, and to Stella, who always greatly enjoys the godly wisdom both you and your bride of 70 years have provided.

Also, a special thanks to Pete and Carol Beckendam for their encouragement to "push through" in writing my story. Pete has since gone on to glory. I will always remember his determination to attend our 50th wedding anniversary gathering, even the day after his final radiation treatment.

James Greenelsh, Videographer, often a travel companion and always a friend. God Bless you for your outstanding work in producing videos and spirit-led songs for ministry. Thank you for letting the Lord use your exceptional talents for bringing beauty and life to God's work in the world.

Dave and Kathy Wimbish, thanks so much for your patience with me with the original editing. Your input and suggestions in my rough draft are much appreciated.

Debbie O'Byrne at JETLAUNCH, thank you for your remarkable cover design. You are especially gifted.

Also, special kudos to Teri Kojetin at JETLAUNCH for her expertise and special gift of patience given her by God in working with me for the hours necessary for making final changes. Thank you, Teri, job well done.

Thanks to Bram Pieters, miracle man, and friend. By God's intervention, I had literally bumped into Bram in a college hallway the day I decided to flee and forget about going to college at all. You actually got angry at me for making that decision. You were right. Everything in my life since then, the people I met everywhere and anywhere around the globe, anything that was accomplished probably would never have happened if it were not for your intervention. Thanks Bram, for getting angry with me and pushing me in the right direction; God's direction for my life.

Thanks also to my God-kids for teaching me more about God's love for us all.

And most of all, my heart is filled with gratitude and thankfulness to Jesus Christ who has forever been at my side through every experience, always protecting, guiding, and providing what was needed. I love you Lord.

FOREWORD

I have always admired those who seem to know, at a relatively young age, what they want to be when they grow up. Some receive their calling early, knowing they want to be a fireman, a cop, a lawyer, or doctor. Sometimes in young children we can see early how their calling and God-given gifts lay foundations for their life's work. For my younger brother Roger, it was clearly his destiny to be a soldier. As kids, we often played cowboys and Indians, but more often, we were soldiers playing at war. He could be seen wearing a belt canteen, helmet, and backpack and carrying the latest toy rifle available. Chess was one of our favorite games, as well as staging historic battles with his toy soldiers.

My Uncle John, mom's older brother, the call would be a pastor. At six years old he was standing on a wooden box and preaching to the neighborhood kids. Even after retirement, he and Aunt Sarah traveled the country in their 80's as Uncle John filled in as interim pastor for congregations that were looking for new full-time pastors.

My Uncle Hank, Mom's younger brother, was a salesman for Swift Meat and later Carter Ink, Inc. In the summer months our family often drove to Illinois for a few weeks to visit family. I frequently traveled with Uncle Hank from downtown Chicago to Peoria making sales calls. He was one of my favorite uncles and was loved by all of his customers. I am sure some of these early life experiences and his gifts influenced my life.

I was not so sure what to do with my life. I just wanted to be a businessman. As a child, how do you play businessman?

You can't. But I could dress like one. Consequently, like Uncle Hank, I always wore a suit and tie when in public and sometimes even at home on Sunday. Well, that was only the first part of the journey. God has such a wonderful way of bringing us along in seasons of life that prepare us for the next. Like Moses, King David, Samuel, and so many others in the Bible. We are all being prepared for where God wants to take us, and for the task he has for us. God directs us to new levels one step at a time, placing the right people, the right opportunities, at the right intersection of our lives, at the right time to take us to the next level. It is up to us to make the choice. It all comes down to our choice, and always has ever since Adam and Eve in the Garden.

I have a very vivid memory of sitting around the table after dinner for our family evening meals together. When I was 16 my Dad asked me what I wanted to do with my life. I told him I didn't really know yet. He responded that he had no doubt I was capable of being anything I wanted -- "but if you let God guide you, you will be, and do, whatever He guides for you." All kids imagine a life of great adventure, but I could not have envisioned how adventuresome the journey would be.

God has a plan for our lives. We all have the freedom to choose. If we choose to follow Christ, we will see His Plan unfolding in our lives, so His Purpose is accomplished.

"For I know the plans I have for you, says the Lord. They are plans for good and not for evil, to give you a future and a hope." (Jeremiah 29:11 TLB)

TABLE OF CONTENTS

PART I

1

CLOUDS

The morning was clear and mild as I climbed aboard a single-engine four seat Cessna 206 at our flight operational base in Wamena, Irian Jaya -- not far from Papua, New Guinea.

Traveling with me was my videographer and friend James Greenelsh and his wife Elizabeth. We were on our way to visit a remote indigenous tribal group which ten years earlier had been cannibalistic headhunters in the jungle highlands, 300 miles north of Wamena in West Papua New Guinea. After all the video gear was loaded, James and Elizabeth took their seats in the rear and I settled in the co-pilot's seat putting on headphones to communicate with the pilot. An hour and half later we flew into one of the many canyons in the area. Steep mountains rose up on each side of us to a height of five thousand feet above us and extended below us for another 3,000 feet.

We had to trust the pilot knew he was entering the correct canyon. If not, we weren't going to make it back to Wamena later in the day -- and maybe not for several days. If it's a blind canyon, there will be no turning around to fly out. The steepness and narrowness of many of these canyons doesn't allow for a small plane to climb over them or turn around. The only alternative is to set the plane down in thick tree-top jungle canopy. In so doing, assuming you survive the crash, you must radio your position, climb down 100 feet or more to the jungle floor, and then wait for help to arrive. As we flew deeper into the canyon, I finally saw a short, uphill, grassy landing strip on the side of a mountain. This was not going to be a run-of-the-mill landing. The plane banked at about 40 degrees, leveled out, and immediately the wheels touched the rough lower portion of the runway. Once safely on the ground, the pilot powered uphill to the top and turned the plane around, facing downhill for a takeoff later. I wasn't sure why he turned the plane around, but three hours later, I was glad he did. It saved us a great deal of time when we needed to make a speedy escape.

No buildings or man-made structures were anywhere in sight. As we unloaded our video equipment, a native suddenly appeared out of nowhere. He was quite short; I'd guess somewhere around four foot six and nearly completely naked except for a long gourd covering his penis. He carried a bow, some arrows, and an eight-foot-long blow gun with a rather large bone protruding through his nose. Suddenly, I was hit by the reality of just how remote we actually were. Neither he, or anything in the surrounding area looked like southern California or anywhere in the United States. I was thinking of Alice and kept looking for the rabbit hole we surely must have fallen into.

The native was the chief of the local tribe and would guide us across a narrow path along the side of a mountain to his village three miles away. How he knew we were coming is a mystery. There is no radio communication with anyone on the ground, so my guess is he saw the plane coming up the canyon and ran the three miles to the grass runway. I noticed that, even at an altitude of 8,000 feet he wasn't even close to being out of breath, despite having run three miles.

The chief seemed like a pleasant fellow, and hurriedly guided us down the lower end of the runway to a narrow foot trail. I began to wonder why he was in such a hurry and, knowing he was formerly a cannibal, was hoping he wasn't hungry.

We followed him as he took us down the trail, through thick jungle and other areas devoid of trees, across small rushing streams and rivers, some of which we could jump across and others we traversed on a single wet, moss-laden 8-inch diameter log. Some of these crossings reminded me of a water slide at a water park; they were very slick from water running down them 365 days a year. If you slipped off the log, you could easily slide 50 feet on smooth stone that looked as shiny as any backyard pool slide. If you started sliding, there was absolutely nothing to hang on to. At the end of your slide was a 2,000-foot vertical drop toward a river in the canyon below, which from this height looked about the size of a piece of string. It would definitely be an e-ticket ride to certain death.

After climbing under, across and over fallen trees for the next three miles, we finally came into a clearing where a small village stood. Several huts were visible behind a circular fortress-type fence. The fence was 10 feet tall and made of tree trunks 5 to 8 inches in diameter. The temperature was around 65 degrees, and everyone was naked. The women wore only a small piece of jungle twine around their waists. I had no idea of its purpose, other than perhaps a form of jewelry. The women carried their smallest children on their shoulders.

The villagers all seemed friendly as they came out to greet us, jumping up and down and waving spears and blow guns above their heads. A fire was burning in the center of the village. Everyone appeared to be happy and welcoming, but I admit that I was thinking, "*We can't go back now, and even if we could, I couldn't outrun them and can't fly the plane.*" I didn't see any black pots big enough for any of us to fit in, so was slightly relieved. I looked around for some sort of barbeque skewer but saw nothing. Again, I was relieved; so good so far.

The chief invited us to dance with them around the fire, linking arms around each other while chanting some sort of mantra in their native tongue. Communication was naturally very rudimentary with many hand gestures in an attempt to understand one another. They offered us food from their meager supplies. We declined as politely as possible as no one was especially tempted by the choice of lizards, frog intestines and charcoal baby birds.

We had been there for nearly two hours when the pilot suddenly stood up, stared down into that 2,000-foot canyon and said, "We have to go! NOW." The firmness in his voice convinced us he was quite seriousness. Thick clouds were quickly rolling in above and below us.

Not needing any extra motivation, I led the charge back across the three-mile stretch to the plane, with several tribal warriors running alongside and behind us.

As I ran, I found myself wondering how a kid born in Chicago, raised in the northeast suburbs of Los Angeles, a banker and venture capitalist in a big city, could possibly find himself in such a primitive and remote part of the world.

It's a story not so much about me, but about the God who promises us, *"For I know the plans I have for you, says the Lord. They are plans for good and not for evil to give you a future and a hop."* Jeremiah 29:11 TLB

At many junctures in my life, when I came to a crossroads and wasn't sure what to do or where to go, God was there with His plan. He led me into places I never would have gone if left to my own devices. He filled my life with amazing adventures, prosperity, and hope.

It's only right that I should share with you what God has done for me. After all, I know for certain that He has great plans for all of His children, if we'll only follow His leading, we can enjoy an abundant life full of His joy.

As the Bible tells us, "In his heart a man plans his course, but the Lord establishes his steps." (Proverbs 16:9)

This is the story of what happens when we learn that His plans for us are always better than our plans for ourselves.

2

THE EARLY YEARS, SOUTH CHICAGO

I'm pretty much a product of Middle America. My Dad was born and raised on a farm 80 miles south of Chicago and ten miles west of the Indiana border. He had eight brothers, six half-brothers and four full brothers, and one sister. My paternal grandfather, Nick Boomsma, migrated to Illinois in the late 1800's from the province of Friesland in the north of The Netherlands. He was 20 years of age when he came through Ellis Island and settled near Wichert, Illinois, where he leased a farm. Wichert was a tiny town, consisting of a Claussen pickle storage warehouse and a small general store with dirty hardwood floors. At the front of the store was a wooden cracker barrel filled with unpackaged single soda crackers.

At the rear of the store, a tiny, barred window served as the Wichert Post Office. A few years after Grandpa's arrival from the "old country," he married his first wife, Anna, also from Holland, who gave grandpa six sons. One died when he was a year old and another, Neil, was killed at age 18 because he was the only witness to a murder. Witchert had no police station, the nearest being in Momence, some 15 miles away. Neil was shot in the back of the head from a passing car on a remote dirt country road after leaving his girlfriend's house. Thieves and murderers were rarely caught in those days, living out their lives in the same area where they committed their crimes. No one was ever brought to justice for killing Neil.

His mother, Anna, also came to an untimely end. A lightning bolt struck the farmhouse, traveled through the wiring, and exited a light switch, killing her instantly. Most homes in those days were new to electricity and weren't grounded as they are today. Grandpa Nick remarried a year later to Mary Balder, also from the Netherlands. Grandma Mary gave Grandpa Nick five additional sons, one of which was my dad, and a daughter, my Aunt Jeanette, whom everyone called Sis. Many years later Grandma Mary was also struck by lightning that entered the house through the very same light switch. She survived, but the right side of her face was paralyzed, and she lost the sight in her right eye. She wore a white bandage over the eye as long as I knew her. It needed to be treated daily with some sort of salve for the next 40 plus years. The older she got, the more the right side of her face began to droop from facial nerves and muscles no longer connected. Still, she lived to 90 with no one ever seeing her unhappy.

Grandpa Nick was a short, wiry guy, only 5'4" and strong as an ox. The family story has it that an uncooperative donkey once kicked him in the head, knocking him unconscious for a few minutes. After regaining conscious, he walked around to the front of the donkey and hit him in the nose so hard the animal fell to the ground unconscious. The donkey got back on his feet a few minutes later. Grandpa always said they got along fine after that saying he was proud to have knocked some sense into him. I cannot attest to the accuracy of the story, but I heard it more than once from a few uncles. Surely there must be some truth to it. And, knowing Grandpa Nick as I did, I never had any trouble believing it. He was tough but had a big heart of gold towards everyone and had everyone's respect...even donkey's.

Farmhouses in those days were often crudely built. Dad always said you could shoot wild turkey through the cracks in the wooden plank walls. In winter, they sometimes woke up with two inches of snow across their beds. Grandpa Nick was not rich in land, but he was rich in the sons, much needed to help with planting and harvesting crops. It also meant there was little time for formal education. Many of Grandpa's sons never made it past middle school. Nonetheless they all did well for themselves and four became entrepreneurs, running their own successful businesses.

My dad's natural gifting was mechanics. He was always able to fix or make almost anything. His auto repair gifts came in quite handy, especially when the crops had to get to market in downtown Chicago, some 80 miles north. The family's old used Model T truck often broke down on the way and Dad had to fix it with whatever tools available. He was often gone for two or three days, coming back to the farm looking like he had been through a war. He spent a lot of time searching junk yards for spare parts and occasionally would have to dismantle the engine or transmission before he could even get back to the farm.

When gone over a weekend, he would stop in Roseland to attend church on Sunday at one of three Christian Reformed Churches there. He would take his Sunday suit and tie, clean up with a sponge bath and shave in a gas station bathroom before attending. It was at one of these services that he met my mother. Love blossomed over many weekend trips to the city after Dad bought his first car. They married in October 1940 and soon rented a house on Wallace Street in Roseland. I came along five years later, in May of 1945. My dad was with Mom in the hospital when I was born and said he knew immediately I had Grandpa Nick's fighting spirit. When the doctor picked me up by the ankles and slapped me on the rear, I peed on the doctor before crying. Not sure how true that story is either, but Dad always laughed to the point of nearly choking when he told it and I always got a tremendous kick out of watching him laugh about it.

LIVING ON THE SAME STREET AS AL CAPONE.

Our home on Wallace Street was a two story with two bedrooms, a living room and a bath downstairs, and another bedroom, small bath, and a living area upstairs. My parents rented the upstairs to a bookkeeper whose real name I don't remember. At age three I just called him Moze. He was a nice old man who became somewhat of a third grandfather to me. We lived on the same street as Al Capone, but eight miles south. I had a Dalmatian dog and together we had much fun together playing in the vacant lot next door.

Dad and Mom moved when I was four years old so Dad could start his own mechanics garage in Hammond Indiana. We moved in with Mom's parents, Grandpa Harry Olthoff and Grandma Rika while Dad built his customer base. Their home was a large Victorian style house with one-bedroom downstairs and five bedrooms upstairs – and only one bath on the main floor.

Grandpa Olthoff was a drafting engineer who designed heavy manufacturing equipment which placed him solidly in the upper middle class.

In those days, it was a Dutch custom to polish the brass doorknobs once a week. All bedsheets were ironed after washing with a hot plate type iron, and the house was thoroughly dusted every other day. We never sat in the living room because that was only used for guests after church on Sunday. The formal dining room was never used either, except for special occasions and guests for large dinners on Easter, Thanksgiving and Christmas dinner. Food preparation for Sunday meals was always done on Saturday because cooking on Sunday was considered working and not keeping the Sabbath. On Sunday morning, Grandpa prepared toast, milk, coffee and peeled hard boiled eggs made the day before and stored in the new Ice Box. The kitchen was exceptionally large and that's what served as today's version of a family room with games and Bible study done around a large kitchen table able to sit eight people. Meals always began with prayer and after meals the reading of the Bible and closing with prayer.

The iceman came every other day to deliver a big block of ice. If he had an extra one, he gave it to me and my first girlfriend, Bobo, who lived one house over. In the summer, we took turns pushing each other up and down the sidewalk on that block of ice until all that remained was a little thin slab. Bobo's mom and dad went to high school with my mom, so they were like family. Two of Grandpa Nick Boomsma's sisters had also migrated from Holland and Aunt Aggie and Aunt Dora had moved to the suburbs and lived on the same street and attended the same church as we did. At age four I often walked to my Aunt Dora's house for my daily piece of candy. I always loved Aunt Dora, not just because of the candy, but because she was always so warm and welcoming. In later years, my wife and I always made sure to visit her when in Chicago.

Grandpa Olthoff was what might be called "an early adapter." When the new dial telephones became available, he got one. When ice boxes gave way to refrigerators, Grandma had one (so much for pushing Bobo up and down the street on a block of ice). When pedal sewing machines gave way to electric, Grandma had one. When new steam irons came along, Grandma had one. I remember there was a coal bin in the basement. The coal truck came every so often to dump a load down the outside coal shoot and into the basement bin. When Oil heating came along, Grandpa was one of the first to make the conversion.

FILLING A NEED / FINDING A SOLUTION

So, there I was, living in the same house with a dad who could fix or make anything, and a grandpa who could design anything on paper using his logarithms books for mathematical finite computations. At age five, I watched an interesting project unfold between Grandpa Olthoff and my Dad.

Grandpa, the drafting engineer, was naturally accustomed to designing first on paper before starting a project no matter how small. Dad could see a project in his head and know what was needed to accomplish the task. Grandma wanted a glass shelf above the bathroom sink for holding small items from hairbrushes to shaving cream and cosmetics. Grandpa went to work at the kitchen table with his drafting equipment, compass, T-square, and logarithms handbook. Dad stood at the bathroom sink with his tape measure, screwdriver, and hand drill, went to a glass cutter and bought a small, beveled piece of glass and had it installed by the time Grandpa finished his drawing.

The two men laughed about that for years – speaking of which, years would pass before I realized my dad's mechanical abilities weren't transferred into my gene pool.

Fast-forward 18 years, a few years after I married my wife Stella, it occurred to me that, being the son of man who could fix anything, I should be able to fix the broken steam iron. It only took five minutes to take it apart but two hours trying to put it back together but always seemed to have one part left that did not fit anywhere. I decided to abandon the project and go buy a new iron, but before I could get my keys and get out the door, Stella had already put it back together. It worked fine with no leftover parts lying around. I still take appliances apart and easily find the broken part, but Stella always puts them back together. I did, however, inherit my dad's ability to diagnose a mechanical problem with a car engine. He could easily define a problem by putting a wooden handle screwdriver on the engine block and listening. It always told him where to start. Being able to diagnose problems has served me well in business and missions work over the years; whatever the challenge, it doesn't take me long to identify a problem and introduce a solution.

In March of 1949, my little brother Roger came along. When Mom changed his diapers, it was my job to carry them to the toilet for pre-soaking before entering Grandma's new washing machine, the kind with the crank roller on top for squeezing water out for the rinse. I had no choice in the matter and did so with my right forefinger and thumb holding my nose. There was no such thing as Pampers or Huggies in those days.

Two of the things I remember most about those two years with Grandma and Grandpa had to do with faith. I will never forget the sight of Grandpa, sitting at the kitchen table in his solid oak armchair smoking his pipe or cigar (much to Grandma's dismay) and reading his Bible, undaunted by anything going on around him. The second powerful memory is walking to church with him on Sunday mornings. He was always the first to rise and dress for church. I was second because I would walk to church with him. He liked to be there early and served as either a deacon or elder for 60 years. Grandpa was a quiet, soft spoken man who listened intently, always knowing how to answer a man using the Bible as his foundation. Later in life this verse from Isaiah 50:4 (KJV) would become one of my favorites.

> *"The Lord GOD hath given me the tongue of the learned, that I should know how to speak a word in season to him that is weary..."*

On Sunday, I always sat next to Grandpa on the end of the pew on the right side of the church about mid-way down towards the pulpit. Harold Hoekstra was the organist, and oh my, what an organist he was! He had a lot of organ to work with. It was a four manual with big bass pipes, horns and flute pipes framing the entire large arched area across the width of the church behind the pulpit. It's where my love for the pipe organ first began. Two songs that I remember most are *"It Is Well with My Soul,"* and *"How Great Thou Art."* When we sang those songs, I'd look up at Grandpa and could see the blood vessels in his neck bulging as he gave it everything he had. To this day, when these two songs are sung in church, I can never actually get the words past the lump in my throat and tears in my eyes. I'm immediately transported back in time to the age of four and still vividly see him singing his heart out. It brings tears even now as I write this. I learned so much from Grandfather Olthoff's always-peaceful spirit and manner, his steadfast faith in God's Word, and his ability to stand strong on God's Word in all circumstances.

HUBCAP CLEANER EXTRAORDINAIRE

At the age of four I often spent time at dad's shop in Hammond Indiana, just across the Indiana state line. When I wasn't across the alley climbing on top of a little shed and watching the world go by, I was helping dad. While he was wrestling engines and transmissions out of cars, I walked around with a little red rag, cleaning hubcaps and wheels. When the cars left the shop and headed out into the snowy, salt-laden streets, customers always had the cleanest wheels in town.

Dad's shop was part of a building owned by his older half-brother, Uncle Sam, a body, fender man and paint man by trade. The building had four sections with four different large garage doors. The front was a show room where Uncle Sam sold Crosley's, a small car much ahead of its time, but they never sold very well. The second section was the body and fender portion, the third a paint shop where Uncle Same did the car paint work. The fourth section was Dad's mechanic shop.

Uncle Sam was a large heavy-set tall fellow with an unusual gift. He loved to play the piano, but never had a lesson and didn't know how to read a single note. Yet he could hear a song once and play it flawlessly from memory. His favorite were the old Hymns, "How Great Thou Art, What a Friend We Have in Jesus, It is Well with My Soul, Amazing Grace, I Need Thee Every Hour" and literally hundreds more.

What I remember most about him, was his purchase of a three manual theater pipe organ from a movie theater in Hammond just down the road from his shop. It took nearly two years for him to install it in his home. All bass and mid-range pipes in the basement, tweeters, strings, and brass sections in the attic. The console was in a glassed-in porch at the front of the house. He'd play it for hours at a time. When he opened it up full throttle the whole house could feel like it was in an earthquake. Everything shook, dishes rattled in the kitchen, picture frames danced on the walls. The organ could be heard three miles across the corn fields. It's probably when I first developed my love for the organ.

The winters were hard on Dad. He developed rheumatism from working under cars on a roller creeper on cold winter days. In an effort to solve the issue he and his brothers spent a weekend with picks and shovels digging up the concrete floor to install a hydraulic hoist. It made a huge difference for him, but after two years, Dad still didn't like working on cars dripping with ice and snow.

Every other weekend on Friday night we would drive south on Route 1 to visit my grandparents in farm country and attend Sunday services at the Reformed Church in Wichert Illinois. By now, my grandparents had sold their farm and moved into a small two-bedroom home next to the church where he served as janitor, getting to know the pastor better than most of his congregation. Grandpa still grew the most amazing food in his half-acre garden, filled with every kind of vegetable and fruit imaginable. In summers, we would sit around the yard eating watermelon and cantaloupe straight from the garden, not to mention delicious, sweet corn and sweet potatoes for dinner. On late Sunday evening, we drove back to the Chicago suburbs. I often fell asleep watching the telephone poles appear and disappear into the darkness behind my backseat window.

In February 1952 we moved to the warm weather of California. There were some sad moments as I would miss my grandparents, neighborhood buddies and my good friend Bobo. Her real name was Phyllis, but at age three I could not say it properly and just called her Bobo. The nickname stuck through all of her life, but later was shortened to just Bo by her siblings. We wrote letters to each other for a few years, but eventually lost contact when Bobo's family moved to Montana where they purchased a motel on an island between two rivers. Several years later her father bought a Christian bookstore in Guam and moved the family there. I didn't see her again until 40 years later when both of our families became members of the same church in Ontario, California.

3

CALIFORNIA BOUND

In February 1952, my parents packed our two-door 1946 Chevrolet Arrowline and we headed west on Route 66 to California. The car was loaded high and tarped with a luggage carrier on the roof. Following behind was Dad's youngest brother, my Uncle Hilbert in his new 1952 Ford half ton pick-up. The truck was loaded with whatever furniture it could hold from the open tailgate and above the cab and tarped for bad weather. I was six years old and brother Roger was two.

For much of the trip, Roger and I rode with great excitement in Uncle Hilbert's new truck. Back in those days, Route 66 was just a two-lane road. Passing slow trucks and cars took skillful timing and good old straight six-cylinder engine power with a full load of all your belongings. It was the middle of winter and there was snow in some areas, but nothing too serious to deal with.

We took our time stopping at various interesting sites like Carlsbad Caverns in New Mexico, Meteor Crater in Arizona, and a few Indian reservations. At the Meteor Crater, Roger wanted to know who dug such a big hole and why. In the Carlsbad Caverns the National Park guide said they would turn out the lights for a couple of minutes to have everyone experience what total darkness was like, asking all parents to hang on to their children. Apparently, Roger didn't get the memo. After about 30 seconds he yelled out, "Who turned off the lights." As a young adult, I would think back to that and wonder how anyone could live in spiritual darkness without knowing the truth of God and His Word. I still wonder today. There are so many people who suffer from anxieties about so many things when they don't have to.

We arrived in Southern California on a Friday evening, staying in a small motel in Monrovia. We didn't have a home lined up and lived in the motel for two weeks. On Sunday, we went to what would become our home church for many years to come. On Monday, Dad went to work in Temple City and Roger, and I came down with the mumps. Dad worked at a private garage in Temple City and spent the late afternoons looking for a house to rent. The owner of the garage quickly became known to Roger and me as Uncle Gordon. A Signal gas station was in front of the garage on the corner of Las Tunas and Golden West and was owned separately by Uncle Jim. Neither were actually biological "uncles," but we soon thought of them as such and this would be the case throughout our lives. We all attended the same church on the corner of Baldwin and Lemon. After two weeks, we moved into a small two-bedroom house in San Gabriel where we stayed for nine months until Dad bought a home on Golden West Avenue in Arcadia, exactly two miles north of Uncle Gordon's garage.

During the summer, I spent many days at the garage with Dad. We would run to the garage in the morning, run home for lunch, then back to the garage until closing time, and then run back home for dinner. Eight miles daily after Dad was removing and repairing engines and transmission in between. Like his dad the farmer, a strong boundless energy man.

One day a few years later Uncle Gordon moved his garage eight blocks west to Las Tunas and Alessandro across the street from Ray Youmans Chevron station. A friendly wager was made to the four mechanics on duty by a Snap-On-Tool man as to who was the strongest man. Someone called my dad into the wager. They had a five-gallon bucket filled with old spark plugs. It looked quite heavy to me, but Dad was confident he could lift it, telling them to put a two-barrel carburetor, a generator, and a starter on the pile.

He picked it up with the pinky of his right hand, lifting it to his mid-thigh below the waist. Everyone else could barely lift it off the ground with a full hand. Dad won the wager.

CALIFORNIA GRADE SCHOOL DAYS

I started first grade at Arcadia Christian School (ACS) a week behind schedule after my mumps disappeared. I had actually already completed first grade at Roseland Christian grade school in the Chicago suburbs and was already halfway through the second grade. But schools in California had a different system so I had to take the second half of the first grade over again. The school had just two-rooms and one was used for storage. There were eight rows with six or seven kids in each row with each row representing a grade, first through eighth. The teacher, Mr. Boreman, had also migrated from Chicago and had been my mother's elementary school teacher, which didn't offer me any special advantages.

He was a serious-minded no-nonsense fellow with a balding head and a small, closely clipped grey mustache, definitely old school in his teaching style. I can only remember him smiling a few times in the six years I attended there. Getting your knuckles rapped with a ruler was an acceptable response for misbehavior. Yes, in those days, discipline was transferred from parent to teacher during school hours. Imagine that!

Shortly after I started school, Mom and Dad bought a used piano, insisting I take lessons. The lessons didn't last long, with six hours of homework every night assigned by Mr. Boreman. The school board comprised of twelve men from our church including my dad, Uncle Gordon, and Uncle Jim and nine others had a meeting and decided that the homework was excessive; kids didn't have time to be kids. Mr. Boreman changed his teaching style to accommodate the board's request, but I never got back to the piano lessons. That was unfortunate because I enjoy playing the piano. I still can't read a note but love to play a little my ear making things up as I go. The piano, full pipe organ and a trumpet (which my brother played) are my favorite instruments.

I walked to school since we lived only three blocks away. Nope, can't claim I walked three miles to school in two feet of snow and blizzard weather. However, my dad really could make that claim.

Then there was Pauline, an 8th grader. Because I was a new kid and a first grader, she was extra kind and friendly towards me, taking me under her wing. As far as I was concerned, she was downright beautiful. Both Roger and I always wanted a sister but never got one. I adopted Pauline and she adopted me. Her dad, Earl, owned a chicken ranch in El Monte and was the regular school bus driver. My dad was responsible for keeping the old bus running in tip top condition as well as occasionally serving as substitute driver for the bus route. Even though I lived only a few blocks from school, I often chose to ride entire bus route just to sit next to Pauline, who fortunately lived at the last stop.

During that first half year of school in first grade, both Roger and I came down with the chicken pox, causing me to miss 10 days of school and a lot of homework. This was before Mr. Boreman toned down his heavy homework assignments. I thought I would never catch up vowing to never again miss another day of school or so much as even an hour. And I never did throughout grade school, high school, and college. I finished six years at Arcadia Christian with A's and B's. Getting a "C" had tremendous consequences. Social promotion was a nonexistent term in educational in those days. If you flunked out you went to summer school, all summer, to catch up. If that didn't work, you stayed behind a year and suffered the emotional consequences.

BLOODY MONDAY

One of my strangest experiences at the new school came shortly after my arrival. Some of the first graders and a few of the fourth graders just had to see what the new kid was made of. One day at recess they all lined up in a row to fight me. They actually came at me one at a time rather than all at once. (Well after all, they were from Christian families, so I guess they thought this was the appropriate method to test my resolve). I stood my ground as one after another put up their fists, and one after another they went down with one punch to the nose. None of them came close to hitting me, and after four knockdowns that was the end it. The remaining three in line opted to pass on their turn. Apparently, I earned my way into the circle. Mr. Boreman went through a lot of cotton balls that day dealing with bloody noses. We all got along fine after that. I guess it was just a guy thing.

THE GUMBALL CAPER

My dad was always a quiet man. He listened intently, and then went right to the point in his response, often using a parable or metaphor to drive home his point.

I was ten years old at the time and Mom sent me to the market for a couple of items she needed for baking. She was always well known and appreciated for her master baking skill which one day led her to be the head baker at Arcadia High School. On my way out of the store I saw a gumball machine. I inserted a penny, turned the dial, and out came my treat. But the dial didn't stop at the top like it was supposed to. I turned it around the dial once more and it dropped another gumball. I kept turning the dial until I had filled my pockets. Wow! I had hit the jackpot with 180 gumballs. I went to a cashier and asked for a paper bag, which she kindly provided. I promised myself to come back the next day and empty that machine again. When I got home, I put all the gumballs in a large, red Rubbermaid cookie jar. Mom noticed and asked where all the gumballs came from. I told her my jackpot story, and she said, "Your father will be interested in hearing that story."

When Dad came home, he quickly noticed the jar on the kitchen counter, looked inside and asked Mom why she bought so many gumballs. She suggested he talk to me.

When he did, I told him my story with great excitement and that I had enough bubble gum for six months of chewing if I used one a day and three months if I chewed two a day.

He then asked me, "Suppose you bought $2 worth of candy at your favorite store, paid with a $5 bill, but the cashier gave you $4 in change. What would you do?"

"I'd keep it. It's his mistake not mine."

"But that would be dishonest, and you'd really be stealing that extra dollar you know belongs to him." *(He raised his voice on the word know).* I could see where this was going. He had exposed, in my heart of hearts, what I knew was right and I had just painted myself into a corner.

"Yea" I said sheepishly.

"Would you just steal candy off the self, hide it in your pocket and run off?"

"No, of course not."

"Then this isn't really any different, is it?"

I tried to sidestep the question by saying, "But this is just a machine."

A frown crossed his brow followed by a cold stare.

"Okay, I got it." What I hadn't counted on was what he said next.

• • •

Dad told me as soon as school was out the next day, I was to go back to the grocery store, find the manager's office and return the gumballs. The following day I was miserable just thinking about what I had to do after school.

Walking to the store that afternoon I was thinking that I'd probably be arrested and sent to jail, and then Dad would be sorry and have to spend more money to bail me out. Still, I did as directed, taking my bag of gumballs to the manager's office. He looked kindly at me and said, "Well, I appreciate your honesty, but I want you to keep those 180 gumballs because we can't put them back since you've already handled them. But I want you to give me your word you'll not do it again." I gave him my word.

Then, much to my surprise, he asked if I wanted a job opening boxes of canned goods and stacking shelves. I didn't take the job because I was already mowing the lawns of several widows in our neighborhood. But I had learned an important lesson: Honesty really is always the best policy. There are ways that dishonesty can sneak into everyday life unnoticed if one is not mindful.

Dad being a mechanic, it was a common occurrence to have someone from church pull in the driveway while we were having breakfast on Saturday morning to ask, "Art, what do you think that pinging noise is in my engine" or "I can't seem to get it in gear as easily as I once did."

They always wound up joining us for breakfast, or at least a cup of coffee and one of mom's famously delicious homemade pastries. If it was a simple fix, he took care of it on the spot. If it wasn't so simple, he told them to bring it to the shop on Monday morning. As a result, we got to know our various pastors, church members and neighbors fairly well over the years. Everyone who received a simple fix wanted to give him a $5 or $10 bill, but Dad always refused.

CHECKERS: ANOTHER LIFE LESSON

Sunday afternoons, Dad always wanted to play me in a game of checkers. It was as predictable as the sun rises. I didn't care much for it because I always lost. Dad would never let me win. This went on for few months until one day I finally determined to beat him. And I did. I was ecstatic. He asked me what made the difference between all those other games I had lost and finally winning this one. At first, I thought maybe he just let me win, but then realized he wouldn't do that. He patiently waited for my response. Finally, I said, "I guess the difference was my attitude and determination about winning this time."

He smiled and said, "You changed your attitude, which helped cement your resolve to overcome the situation; and that, Bob is one of the keys to success that will serve you well in any situation of life. Your attitude will always affect your ability to resolve, to either overcome an obstacle or let it overcome you." That lesson, along with my observations of his wisdom over the years made a lasting positive impression on me.

Dad was never one to worry. He was a student of cause and effect. He was not just interested in finding the broken engine part, but what caused it to break. If he couldn't easily determine the problem with all his mechanical experience, he went to bed that night with a prayer, asking the Lord to help him find the answer. And, without fail, he always woke up the next morning with the solution. My observations of his natural inclinations of looking for cause and effect was a great lesson for me in my study of sociology in college and later in sales and fundraising with regard to understanding people and uncovering their motivations. His "resting in the Lord" taught me how to bridge the difference between the natural God-given talents we are born with and the leading of the Holy Spirit.

When Dad was in his early 60's he started thinking about retirement. Everything was changing. Uncle Gordon had moved his family and business to Bellflower. Dad stayed with the new owner at the same location for several years. Later when the new owners switched to a Honda motorcycle shop, Dad went to work for a Chevy dealership in San Gabriel where they followed a manual stating the time it should take for every repair. He felt that was fine for the standard items but didn't allow for what caused things to break in the first place. Now he was paid according to what the manual dictated, even if it took longer to find the real cause.

Advanced diagnostic machines now determined the same things he used to find by just listening to an engine. He disliked spending more time in the classroom learning about computers than working on cars. Still, his reputation and natural abilities somehow kept him ahead of the ever-encroaching technology curve.

BONANZA & HOSS CARTWRIGHT'S WINNEBAGO

Dan Blocker, who played the role of Hoss Cartwright on the TV show Bonanza, owned a Winnebago motor home that nobody could seem to fix. After spending inordinate amounts of money, and visiting several mechanics across Los Angeles County, no one could seem to solve the problem. Blocker was told that he should seek the help of Art at the Chevrolet dealership in San Gabriel. If he couldn't fix the problem nobody could. Dad, with his cause and effect approach, was able to fix it once and for all. Before long other Hollywood actors, directors and stunt men where bringing their broken vehicles to Dad. He probably could have started his own shop at that point, but retirement was on his radar screen.

During my teens, Dad and I often arm wrestled. For me, it was pretty much a hopeless situation to be going up against a guy who could pick up a bucket weighing 150 pounds with his pinky. One day at age seventeen, I finally beat him. It gave me mixed feelings; on one hand, I was almost euphoric, but also sad because I knew while I was peaking in my strength he was on the downside of his.

4

GOOD NEIGHBORS –
BAD NEIGHBORS

Shortly after we moved to our home in Arcadia, new neighbors moved in next door. Bill and Gwen Wuille were wonderful people. Better neighbors just didn't exist. They had one son and two twin girls. We all got along beautifully, and they became like an extension of our family. There was no fence between our homes and Roger and I often played between yards. In their back-yard were two beautiful plum trees which produced wonderful juicy fruit. During the summer months, Roger and I spent many hours sitting in those trees eating all the plums we could reach, always with our neighbors' blessing. A few years later their family outgrew their two-bedroom home and moved to a larger house on Daines Dr. in Temple City. They remained friends and several years later attended my wedding.

After they moved a wealthy older widow moved in next door. She seemed nice, but we never got to know her as she died a few months later. She left the house and a beautiful original, like new 1954 Cadillac Deville to her son Clark, along with what must have been a great deal of money. Clark soon moved into the house with his wife Irene, son John and baby daughter Susan. Clark quit his job as a machinist and never worked again. And thus, began a ten-year odyssey that would end in tragedy and became the first nationally publicized child abuse case in U.S. history.

It didn't take us long to figure out there was something wrong in that house. Every day, little Susan, about two years old, was put in a playpen in the front yard early in the morning and was kept there until sunset. No one came to check on her or feed her. She had no human contact whatsoever all day long, no matter how cold or hot the weather was. John, around age seven at the time, was also locked out of the house, spending the whole day on the small, raised back porch landing leading into their kitchen which faced our driveway and our kitchen window.

He attended school as required by law, but when he came home, he was not allowed in the house until long after dark. After the police were called by my dad and several of our neighbors, they finally came to investigate the situation, but they said that as long as the children were being fed and the son was in school they couldn't do anything. All our neighbors nearly begged for something to be done, but the situation went on and on – and now Clark resented everyone, and us, for calling the police.

GROWING UP UNDER THE GUN

Our houses were separated by our driveway, and their back door was only 40 feet away from our kitchen window, giving us an easy view of what was going on. Clark then put up a chain link fence on the property line, stopped watering the lawn and cut down all those beautiful plum trees. It didn't take long for the property to look like a desert wasteland. The children were now kept inside, except for John, who was let out to attend school.

Over the next ten years, Clark could be seen at his back-door window holding a 1911 model .45 caliber semi-automatic hand-gun. He yelled obscenities at my brother and me every time we rode our bicycles in and out of the driveway. My mother wasn't immune to the vulgarities either. Every time she walked out the door to go for something at the grocery store, or hung laundry outside, she was bombarded by the same crass language.

The verbal abuse, along with the ever-present handgun, naturally created deep concern, especially for my mother who was worried about her boys.

Dad called a family meeting to make sure we all kept our cool and the situation didn't escalate into a disaster. He asked my brother and me if we understood the word "escalate" and made sure by explaining it, then laid down his rules of non-engagement. We were to go on with our normal lives and not live in fear. We were not to pay any attention to Clark or reply negatively to the obscenities he yelled at us and were also echoed by his son John. Dad also told us that we should never place one foot on their property and be especially careful not to cut corners when we were going in and out of our driveway on our bikes. Mom and Dad also concluded the meeting by telling us we should pray for them, which we did often when we sat down for the nightly family dinner and then gave a scripture verse. It was probably the first time I had heard 2 Timothy 1:7 (KJV) *"For God hath not given us the spirit of fear; but of power, and of love, and of a sound mind."*

We rarely saw Clark's wife Irene. It seemed that she, too, was not allowed out of the house except to walk two blocks north to the grocery store with a little red wagon for the weekly groceries. This soon changed as groceries began being delivered to the house and we didn't see Irene for many years. She, too, was a prisoner. Clark walked to the market every other week for his liquor supply. The Cadillac was never driven. We also never saw little Susan again, but we did hear her crying, and sometimes screaming. We learned later that she had been locked in a bedroom closet facing our driveway. It was terrifying to hear, especially for my mom, who was home during the day. I remember coming home from school and could tell Mom had been crying. She wanted so badly to storm that house and rescue the little girl.

In spite of the whole frustrating situation in not being able to do anything about it, we did our best to live life in a normal fashion. The real tragedy would come 10 years later and continues to this day.

A MURDER AND SUICIDE

My parents were on an extended trip to Canada at the time, and I was a recently married college student who stopped by their house after classes to water the lawn, bring in the mail, and do the gardening.

One afternoon, as I drove down the street, I noticed police cars everywhere. Police were going in and out of our neighbor's house and the Los Angeles County coroner's van was parked in front. I drove into my parent's driveway to the back door, where I was invaded by six TV reporters who shoved their microphones in my face and asked if I knew the neighbors. I did of course, but at that point I didn't know what had happened and chose to say nothing; besides their pushiness irritated me. I turned away and walked into the house.

In turning on the TV the news was broadcasting on every station. It seems that Irene had finally escaped two days earlier by calling a cab when Clark was out on one of his booze runs. She had fled to her sister's house in San Gabriel.

Clark was distraught, not because his wife had left, but because he knew she would tell the real story to the police. It turned out there was a dirty secret none of us neighbors knew about. It seems a third baby had been born during the years they lived next door. The child had some sort of physical abnormality that caused her to cry incessantly. Clark couldn't stand it. He taped her mouth shut, placed her in an old dresser drawer in the garage on the opposite side of the house and left her there to starve to death.

Knowing this would be exposed when his wife left, he told his son John to sit on the sofa while he placed a plastic cover on the living room floor, then laid down on the cover, and, with his son watching, blew his brains out with that 45-caliber pistol he had been frivolously pointing at us all for the past ten years.

John, who had graduated two months earlier from Temple City High School, quickly left town and we never saw him again. We later heard from his mother that he was working for a house painter somewhere in Ohio. His sister Susan was now in her teens but had the mind of four-year-old and was not able to feed or dress herself.

The situation turned out to be the first officially known case of child abuse and neglect of its kind in the United States. Years later, we learned from Irene that Susan eventually did learn how to feed and dress herself, at the age of thirty-five.

Irene also became a ward of the state and was allowed to see her daughter only once a month for only a couple of supervised hours at a time. Stella and I received phone calls from her on various occasions long after we had moved 25 miles east of Arcadia. She would sometimes talk for hours.

Underneath all the agony Irene had endured for all those years, she was by nature a friendly and neighborly lady who was, like the rest of her family, imprisoned by fear of her husband Clark. We saw her phone calls as a cry for any sort of normalcy in her life. A woman drowning in a sea of abnormality, desperately looking for a life raft in a ten-year storm-tossed sea of agony, fear, and grief. We always listened intently when she called, often for two or more hours at a time. Today, 50 years later, it still somewhat haunts me when I wonder if we could have done more in helping her find a life raft in her last remaining years. It brings tears to this day.

5

COPING WITH BELITTLEMENT

By the time I finished the sixth grade in Christian school, the school board decided to cut seventh and eighth grades due to a lack of new students. I would now be attending public school, going from a tiny school with fewer than 35 students to a large public school with 600 students in just the seventh and eighth grades. It was somewhat overwhelming at first, but I adapted well and especially enjoyed the increased competition. My first year in P.E. class I broke the school record for the 50-yard dash.

GAME CHANGERS

Three important things happened to me that first year of public school. One would define me for the next four years. The second and third would influence my life forever and especially the fourth event. The very first day of school we had to fill out several forms. Coming from a small school I had never filled out a questionnaire in my life. To me, this was like a test; a test the first day? I just got here. In one section I totally misunderstood the question and the following day the Vice Principle, a stern-looking woman came into the class to discuss the forms we had filled out and the various mistakes made. For some reason she singled out my mistake for an exercise in belittlement.

Being the only Bob in the room, I shrunk down into my seat, trying to disappear from view like a fast melting ice cube. Everyone laughed. The only redeeming factor was that because I was a "newbie" many of the kids didn't know who I was anyway. All of them had come from 3 different grade schools and didn't know everyone either. Nonetheless I felt totally humiliated. I'd been shot down, emotionally crashed and burned. My self-image took a nose-dive into the dark forest of rejection. For the next five years, I did my best to hide in the back of the room in all my classes, keeping my mouth shut, never volunteering to answer any questions even if I knew the answers, and always praying the teacher would never call on me.

Four years later in the tenth grade, a very savvy teacher recognized the "image" problem and drew me out of my shell. Thanks to this astute kind, caring women, fear was replaced with self-confidence and a boldness that would one day place me before captains of business, congressmen, senators, foreign ambassadors as well as some of the wealthiest people in the US, Asia, and Europe.

The second life-changing event was a Heidelberg Catechism class at Arcadia Christian Reformed church. At the age of 12, I was required, as all of my church friends were, to attend the class every Tuesday evening. It was a "rite of passage" to help kids pass through a doorway in becoming young Christian men, well-versed in the theological doctrine of the Calvinist Reformed tradition. I wasn't so sure it was really necessary. After all, I had been to six years of Christian school where we had to memorize six verses of scripture every day in daily Bible class. Wasn't that enough? Well, no. The class turned out to be another game changer because it was there that I came to realize that the Bible was indeed the Word of God, inspired by the Holy Spirit over more than 1,500 years, and written by dozens of different men who all said God is Love. How could that be unless the Holy Spirit had inspired the authors? When we came to 2 Timothy 3:13-17 (NKJV), especially verse 16, I could feel instantly that something had changed in my heart and knew for certain that the Bible was indeed the "inspired" Word of God.

> "But evil men and impostors will grow worse and worse, deceiving and being deceived. But you must continue in the things which you have learned and been **assured** of, knowing from whom you have learned them, and that from childhood you have known the Holy Scriptures, which are able to make you wise for salvation through faith which is in Christ Jesus. **All Scripture is given by inspiration of God, and is profitable for doctrine, for reproof, for correction, for instruction in righteousness,** that the man of God may be complete, thoroughly equipped for every good work."

I was immediately convinced the Bible was the absolute true Word of God. But even so, at the end of the eight-week class it was generally expected that all the "graduates" would make a confession of faith the following Sunday morning. I now believed the Bible was in fact God's inspired word but wasn't sure what it meant to confess Christ as Lord of my life. I also felt that any confession of faith made at this point would be somewhat phony, just because that's what was expected. I opted out of that next Sunday morning service and ceremony. My parents were surprised and disappointed. When I explained my view, it seemed baseless until such time as I really understood what accepting Christ meant in my heart. They understood and didn't want to force me into anything I wasn't ready for in my heart. We had a discussion about *free will* and what that meant.

It wasn't until five years later, when Stella and I went on a date to a Billy Graham Crusade at the Los Angeles Memorial Coliseum, where we both completely surrendered our life to Christ. Stella and I were sitting with my dad in the bleachers and my mom was singing in the choir. It was a wonderful joy-filled night for all of us when Stella and I went forward.

THE REMARKABLE MR. SCHMIDT

My eighth-grade homeroom teacher was a remarkable man. Mr. Schmidt was born totally blind, and yet, it seemed there was nothing he couldn't do. He had a beautiful German Shepherd guide dog always at his side safely directing him.

Despite his disability it only took him one day to learn everyone's name and where we were all seated. His wife drove him to school every day and he learned somehow that my dad was a mechanic. I didn't know until many years later that he had asked my dad to teach him how to do a brake job on his own car. Mr. Schmidt sat next to my dad on a small rolling cart used for such work, feeling with his hands every tool, part and action needed and learned it in two hours. My Dad tested Mr. Schmidt knowledge when Schmidt wanted to do his own car. He did it perfectly down to the last detail. He truly was an amazing man and all his students greatly respected him.

The third life-changing event during my seventh-grade year came as an answer to prayer. I have an idea that this prayer, at this young age, was ignited by the catechism class. I remember asking God that when the time came, I would like three things in a wife. I wanted her to be a Christian, pretty, and smart. Within a few weeks of that prayer I met Stella. She may have sensed something too, because she wrote in her diary, *"When I get married, I want it to be someone just like Bob"* I didn't know about her diary entry until we had been married for several years.

Stella and I didn't start dating until our senior year of high school, but I was watching her the whole time since the seventh grade. Our ninth-grade English teacher, Bob Wicks still remembers how I was constantly looking at her across the room. Mr. Wicks told me 40 years later that he always suspected that we would marry someday. We sent him an invitation to our 50th wedding anniversary dinner party celebration but he was unable to attend. He did however send the heartwarming note below:

Dear Bob and Stella,

I am both pleased and honored that you have included me in the invited guests to your Fiftieth Anniversary celebration. While I won't be there in physical attendance, I will be there in spirit. I have never known a couple who so completed the lives of each other as you both do. It would be flippant to wish you another fifty years, but I can honestly wish that your religious views are correct and that you will be together forever. That would be wonderful.

It is hard to believe that it was fifty-six years ago when you were both freshmen in the class of a first-year teacher who was feeling his way into the craft. It was wonderful students like you that first year that educated and encouraged me -- more than you know, and I am eternally grateful.

I wish you both a joyful celebration and continuing joy in your lives. Thank you for all that you have given to me and others throughout your lives. – Bob Wicks

God bless good teachers. I didn't know what his religious views were when Stella and I were in his class, but I believe, he does believe, and we I pray for him often. In his class he made sure part of our assigned reading was the King James Version of the Bible which he considered to be one of the most elegant pieces of literature ever written. I have always appreciated Mr. Wicks for his openness, honesty and "push the envelope" spirit. Remember, this was a public school. There was an approved list of literature English teachers had to adhere to and the Bible wasn't on the list. That didn't matter to Mr. Wicks. I have since worn out two King James Versions, still my favorite, but also use the NIV Study Bible.

The fourth game changer was when Ray Terhorst, who lived around the corner from me, and I rode our bikes to Monrovia for a report project for a social studies or world history class, to visit Upton Sinclair. I think we were about 13 or 14 years old at the time. Ray and I just decided we would just go knock on his front door for an interview.

He was the author of 100 books and won the Pulitzer Prize for Fiction in 1943. He was an outspoken socialist and ran unsuccessfully for Congress as a nominee for the Socialist Party and also a Democratic Party candidate for Governor of California during the Great Depression and was defeated in 1934 elections.

He welcomed us into the inner sanctum of his office, cluttered with books and articles spread all around the room. I certainly don't remember the whole conversation but do remember having an icky feeling when leaving. I didn't realize it at the time as my political DNA was not yet fully formed, but this visit certainly helped finalize my anti-socialist/communist views.

During this same time, I also met other lifelong friends; like Marv Folkertsma who attended our church and lived around the corner from me. Marv and I stayed in touch over the years. He became an outstanding professor, author of several textbooks and a few novels as Dr. Marvin Folkertsma, with an exceptional career as professor of political science for nearly 40 years. In my second career in fundraising for Missions I would always stop by when in Western Pennsylvania to spend a weekend before hitting the road again. I got to know his four children and all of which came to refer to me as Uncle Bob. I love those kids and have enjoyed watching them grow into outstanding adults. Marv and his wife Andrea are remarkable parents.

MAKING UP FOR LOST TIME

I mentioned earlier, Stella and I did not start dating until our senior year in high school. But that year, we saw each other every Friday, Saturday, and Sunday night. She was a flag girl, so our first date had to be after the football game. We went to a coffee shop in West Arcadia, and after we were seated, I realized that I had left my wallet at home. I had only 87 cents in my pocket. Panic! I could only hope she wouldn't order too much. Fortunately, she didn't. She ordered French fries, which left me enough for a cup of coffee. We shared the fries. Whew! After we were married, I trusted her completely with the management of all income and investments. She's more than an excellent money manager; a true Proverbs 31 wife. And she even provides me with a decent weekly allowance.

Our dates rarely found us at the movies. Most of the time we were visiting the sights around Los Angeles, talking, and finding our way to areas we had never been before and then looking for another way home without Rand McNally or retracing our steps. I didn't know it at the time, but that exercise would serve me well all across southern California and came in very handy with future employment. It would also set a pattern we both loved, traveling around the country by car. Considering work and vacations, there isn't much we haven't seen, having driven back and forth across the U.S. at least 35 times and in business flying across 50 or more times.

In high school, Stella was always busy with something. In addition to being a flag girl, she was involved in modern dance, ballet, synchronized ballet swimming, was swim princess, took Dale Carnegie courses, John Robert Powers Modeling School, and still maintained a 4.0 grade point average. Her picture was often in the local paper for one thing or another throughout our high school years. She was actually the fifth child born to her mom and dad. Her mother had four miscarriages before Stella made her appearance. Stella was special and her parents were determined to make sure she had every opportunity to achieve success and become a lady of refinement. All of her special training came in handy as my wife years later when she and I dined with and became friends with some of the wealthiest people in the country though my work as a fundraiser, as well as people of political power like congressmen and senators. She surely was my crown.

My own high school years were much less illustrious. I was on the track team, took woodshop, disliked any advanced math, but somehow maintained a 3.0 grade point average. During my sophomore year I went to work after school and spent the summer months working for an insurance broker in Arcadia who was our "good neighbor" living next door before the bad neighbor.

This brings me back to that wonderful teacher who helped me overcome my poor self-image. Up until I enrolled in her sophomore high school class, I had always been insecure because of that belittling experience in seventh grade. But at the beginning of that year, she had each student stand before the class to tell something about him or herself. When my turn came, on the second day, I felt like a leaf in a windstorm, totally out of control. To keep my perfect attendance record I couldn't pretend to be sick and stay home that day. I was trapped. The walk from the back of the class to the front felt like a mile hike, in slow motion. I felt like I was heading for the gallows. I told the class I was working for an Insurance Broker, what my responsibilities were after school and during the summer months. Many guys in high school didn't have such responsibilities. Most who had a job washing dishes in a restaurant, ushering at the local theater, or pumping gas. The teacher was fascinated and asked more questions. The more she asked, the more comfortable I became, spending nearly forty minutes in front of the class and far beyond the allotted ten minutes. Like the waves on the beach, confidence flowed in, fear flowed out like the tide. I was definitely feeling better about my confidence level. My self-image seemed to pole-vault over the bar of fear. I have thought about and been grateful for that teacher and her encouragement ever since.

"For God hath not given us the spirit of fear; but of power, and of love, and of a sound mind." 2 Timothy 1:7 (KJV)

POOPER SCOOPING DAY

Prior to working for our neighbor, the insurance broker, I work for a fellow from our church who was, shall we say, at the bottom end of the dairy business. He made big money and so was able to pay well. He asked if I wanted an after-school job driving a skip loader tractor, scooping up cow maneuver into a dump truck for delivery to Bandini fertilizer processing plant in Santa Fe Springs. Surely a smelly job, but one that paid fifty dollars a day for a couple hours work. I showed up for work after school the following day at the designated location in South El Monte where my employer was waiting for me. He was sitting on a skip loader parked in a small cow corral with several cows milling around a large pile of cow dung. Standing on top of the pile was a much larger cow. It was, of course, a bull.

As my tractor lesson began, the owner accidentally slammed into a large concrete post while in reverse, breaking off a connecting rod for the scoop. It would take a couple of days to have it re-welded, so that was the end of work for the day. I headed home, walking across the barn yard. That's when I heard a loud snort coming from the top of that manure pile. I turned to see that bull was watching rather intently as he moved one of his front hooves as if he were digging a hole. To me, that looked a lot like those bulls in a ring down in Tijuana. He suddenly came thundering down that mound of cow dung like he had a string of firecrackers tied to his tail heading straight toward me. I ran across the barnyard as fast as I could, hitting a seven-foot-high slatted fence and with one leg on the bottom rail and my left hand on the top one, bounded over. The neurotic bull hit a 4x4 post just as my feet hit the ground on the other side. My car was parked 100 feet away, but I kept running. I probably broke my seventh grade 50 yard-dash school record. I approached my car wondering if the bull would breach the fence and was about to put a massive dent in the side door of my car. Thankfully, the fence held. The last my employer saw of me that day was my taillights as I burned rubber heading in the opposite direction. Consequently, that was the end of my less than distinguished pooper-scooper career. Our neighbor the insurance broker hired me the following week. I was grateful.

I relayed the story at the dinner table that night. My dad having grown up on the farm, busted out laughing, discharging his mashed potatoes across the dinner table. My mom was leaning over, spooning her soup, when some of dad's potatoes hit her smackdab in the middle of the forehead. I'll never forget the shocked look on her face. We all had a good laugh about it for years, always teasing Mom that she should wear a helmet and face shield whenever she made mashed potatoes in case Dad should unexpectedly bust out laughing.

A week later my new boss, neighbor Bill, the insurance broker, hired me and asked me to deliver some important contracts to San Bernardino for signing. He gave me the keys to his brand-new Ford Falcon. It was a hot day and by the time I had gone about half-way, the car was starting to overheat. I watched the temperature gauge as it continued to move toward the red. My internal anxiety gauge was also rising as I didn't want to get stranded in the middle of nowhere without help. In those days there was nothing but sandy grape vineyards most of the drive and not much of anything else past Ontario. Thankfully, I made it to San Bernardino, but on the way back in the late afternoon, the outside temperature was even hotter. The engine temperature was nearing the danger point. I had learned from Dad to always keep an occasional glance at the dashboard gauges, so I turned off the air conditioning to save drag on the engine and exited the freeway at Peck Road heading north hoping for a gas station. Whew! I had made it back to civilization.

The last thing I remember was seeing the right rear tailgate of a Mel's Auto-Supply pickup truck turning left in front of me. I quickly swerved to the right to avoid him but had no time to see if the lane next to me was clear. It wasn't. My left front fender hit the right rear tailgate of a pickup in front of me, spinning it into the oncoming lane where it was hit by a large truck and trailer gravel hauler, cutting the pickup in half up to the firewall. While that was going on, I was hit from behind by another gravel truck that sent me spinning into oncoming traffic.

Consciousness returned when a fence post and a small sapling tree were coming at me. I mowed them both down under the car and finally came to a stop about a foot from some one's living room picture window. The left front fender and wheel of my bosses brand new Falcon, up to the hood, were completely gone, yet the hood did not have a single scratch. It looked like someone had surgically removed the left from wheel and fender. It was a miracle no one was killed. I was the only one hurt. The police officer on the scene who took the report said I'd better get to a doctor because my left ear was almost severed. That's when I noticed that my left shoulder was covered with blood. By this time, my Dad arrived and took me to the emergency room at the Temple City Medical Center where the doctor quickly stitched my ear back together. Dad later said it was a good thing the driver-side window was open at impact, because the glass at the bottom of the door was crushed so fine you could roll it into a snowball, and the doctor would have been picking glass out of my face for a month.

After school the next day, I drove my car to the office, wondering if a job awaited me. As I sheepishly walked into the office with my bandaged ear, everyone cheered and clapped. They even had a cake for me with a message on a 3x5 card stuck on top. *Bob, congratulations: You survived your first and hopefully last accident."* I was stunned. My boss came up to me and said, "Don't worry about the car. We're in the insurance business you know! We're just glad you're all right."

After cake and punch he did something that caught me totally off guard. He wanted me to take another set of contracts out to Redlands. I hesitantly said Okay, but I'd better take my car.

He knew I was understandably hesitant, but he also knew I had to get back in the saddle immediately or I might never conquer my fear. He handed me the keys to his personal family car a one-year-old Oldsmobile station wagon.

"I can't. I'll just take my car." He insisted I take his car and I finally gave in. I will always be thankful for his trust, kindness, and graciousness. What a blessing to have such a good neighbor and an understanding boss. I made the trip to Redlands without incident and "road confidence" returned. We remained friends for years to come and he and his family were at our wedding four years later.

STELLA, WILL YOU MARRY ME?

Stella and I had been dating for two years and at the ripe old age of eighteen I asked Stella for her hand in marriage. She accepted. Her parents felt it was better to wait until we had completed at least two years of college and Stella entered nursing school at Pasadena City College (PCC).

I tried college for one semester, but didn't much care for it, you know, because I already knew everything at that age. I opted out and went to work...much to the dismay of my parents. My jobs always paid well and looking back it's easy to see they were all part of God's plan for my life. It would have been difficult to handle any of my subsequent jobs without the experience gained in the previous one. I learned much about the Lord, the people he had placed in my pathway, and about myself.

There was that promise again: *"For I know the plans I have for you, says the LORD. They are plans for good and not for evil, to give you a future and a hope."* Jeremiah 29:11 (TLB)

Stella liked college, but not nursing school. She changed her major to business and graduated with honors and went on to shine in the business world where she always had favor with her superiors. While in college she also entered the Tournament of Roses Parade competition for the Rose Queen and made it to the last 39 out of 400 contestants.

DUTY CALLS – CALLING THOSE THINGS WHICH ARE NOT AS THOUGH THEY WERE.

It was during this time a dear friend; Jack Van Z and I became friends. We were both ushers in our church and we both loved to drive. One night after church we decided to take a little drive. We had no particular destination in mind and just kept driving and talking as Jack drove. Six hours later we found ourselves in San Francisco, had breakfast and headed back south arriving in time to be at our respective afternoon swing swift jobs. Two years later I asked him to be in my wedding which he was not able to attend since he had joined the U. S. Marine Corp. a year earlier, entering a special program designed to train him as a helicopter pilot after boot camp. In return for his pilot training, he had to agree to serve for 4 four years with the Marines.

Jacks parents and mine were good friends and often were at each other's homes for dinner or coffee after church and Jack was often at our house. Dad and Mom were very fond of Jack, considering him as a member of the family. While Jack was in pilot training, we started calling him Captain Jack every time we saw him, believing he would surely attain the rank of Captain. And he did achieve the rank of Captain. After returning from Vietnam he continued his service in the Reserves for nine years and reached the rank of Major.

6

SOMETHING OLD, SOMETHING NEW

We planned our wedding for a couple of months after Stella graduated from college. Ed, my future father-in-law, and I were standing in his driveway talking about the wedding Stella and her Mom were planning. Our conversation happened to be under Stella's open bedroom window, which we hadn't noticed. Ed said he didn't know weddings were so expensive. It was going to cost him six thousand dollars before it was all said and done. He joked that he should have just given me $100 and a ladder. I told him, "Make it a three thousand, I'll bring my own ladder, and we'll both be ahead three thousand bucks." Suddenly, Stella's voice was loudly heard from her bedroom window, "I heard that."

As it turned out, Ed gave us his 1958 Chevy a few weeks later. My dad rebuilt the 283 cubic inch V-8 engine. I had the interior completely reupholstered and with a new paint job everything was ready for the wedding.

GREETINGS FROM UNCLE SAM

We were scheduled to be married on August 28, 1965, but all of that changed on August 1. On that Saturday morning, Stella and I went to the jewelers in Temple City to pick up our wedding rings. The wedding dress had already been received, flowers and photographer chosen, and dates locked in. All five bridesmaids had their gowns, five guys had their tuxedos ordered and invitations to 400 people would be mailed on Monday. Jack Van Z was to be one of my groomsmen but the week after he had completed his helicopter pilot training, he was off to Vietnam. To replace him it was suggested Bob Shepersky, one of Stella's cousins would be a good choice since he was always special to Stella. He accepted.

We drove back to Stella's house to drop her off before I went on with additional errands. As I pulled into my future in-laws' driveway, Lillian, Stella's mother, came running out the front door. She had received a call from my parents saying my draft notice had just arrived in the mail and I was to report to Fort Ord for boot camp on August 28. Everything changed in an instant. Now what? Considering what was going on in Vietnam at the time it was pretty much a certainty I would be heading to southeast Asia after boot camp.

I decided it would be a good idea to take a drive and rethink this whole thing. What was I going to do now? After a couple of hours, I returned to Stella's house with my decision. We would have to delay the wedding for a year or until after my military hitch was over. However, her dad had a different idea. While I was out driving around, Stella and her Mom went shopping and purchased a simple white shift dress.

Ed felt we should get married before going off to war, a common occurrence for his generation in World War II. His brother, Rev. Roger Sawyer, was at the time, a Methodist pastor of a large church in Las Vegas. The suggestion was to drive to Vegas that afternoon, obtain a marriage license on arrival and have Uncle Roger marry us in the Methodist church after his Sunday morning service the next day. We would then have a celebration dinner at one of the hotel casinos before driving back home on Sunday afternoon. Ed had relayed the idea to my parents who were already packing an overnight bag. "Okaaaay," I said.

A couple hours later all six of us piled into Ed's new Bonneville heading for Vegas. We were all back home late Sunday evening and dropped my parents off at their home. Stella and I were standing in her parent's kitchen looking at each other and wondering what just happened. Stel turned to her mother and said, "Now what do we do?" Her Mom laughed and said, "Anything you want to."

Stel and I got in our '58 Chevy and headed out for a one-night honeymoon. I had to be back at work the next afternoon for the swing shift at 3:30 at the aluminum factory. We stayed at a local Best Western, across from the Santa Anita Racetrack. The following afternoon I dropped her off at her parents' house before going to work. The following day I moved into the Sawyer home sharing Stella's bedroom and her single bed. It was cramped, but that was just fine with me.

A week after our Vegas trip, my boss, whom I affectionately called "Chief," asked me what I was doing about my pending wedding. The Chief was in the Army Reserves as a Lt. Colonel. I related the Vegas story and he asked if I had notified the draft board. I told him no, since I was already drafted and due to report to Fort Ord on August 28. He said it could make a big difference, and I was required to notify the Selective Service if there was any change in my status. The following day I visited the draft board and they immediately reclassified me from 1-A to 4-A. The Chief may have saved my life for the second time in suggesting the draft board visitation.

The 4-A status lasted two and a half years until I was drafted again just two months after my brother Roger was killed in the Tet Offensive. (More about that later.) My draft status was again set at 1-A. My parents told me I was an adult and could make up my own mind regarding what to do, but it was clear they were very concerned they could easily lose their only remaining son with the buildup of troops being sent after the heavy losses suffered during the Tet Offensive. Having seen firsthand their emotional frame of mind with the loss of my brother just three months earlier they wanted me to file for Sole Surviving Son. I did and thus ended my affiliation with the military.

After discussing the matter with our parents and respective pastors, we decided to go ahead with the originally planned large wedding for August 28. I moved back into to my parents' home. Stella and I prepaid for a fully furnished apartment across from the Santa Anita golf course and moved in after our "second honeymoon."

We were married at the Temple City Methodist church. Our guest list was extensive, with four hundred invitees filling the pews on a 105-degree day. The receiving line in the social hall was four hours long. After the reception, we had a second reception at Stella's parents' home for family members, uncles, aunts and cousins and close friends from both sides of the family, over 100 people filled their back yard. By late afternoon, the temperature had cooled off. Thank God.

The following day we left on our honeymoon for Clear Lake, one hundred and fifty miles north of San Francisco where we had reserved a Hotel suite overlooking the lake. I didn't tell Stel until we got home from our honeymoon that I was unemployed, having been fired the day before our wedding for a series of incidents I had no control over. The perfect storm so to speak. Again, "unplanned" events inserted into our life. But, once again, "God had a plan."

CONGRATULATIONS! YOU'RE FIRED.

At the time of our marriage, I was working for an aluminum extrusion company in San Gabriel just down the road from the San Gabriel Mission. My job included driving a large heavy-duty forklift and keeping two large extrusion furnaces supplied with round aluminum billets. The billets were stacked in banded bundles weighing one or two tons each. My job was to transport them from the supply yard outside and place them on a downward gravity fed ramp. I cut the bands to let them roll down toward the furnace entrance where they would role one by one into the furnace to be extruded into various forms for window and door frames.

When the finished products come out of the ovens they are moved along by long rollers to a cutting station where they are cut to meet customer specifications. After cutting they are stacked on a long movable table on wheels with large steel "I-beams" separating the various sizes. I used the large forklift to move these heavy tables into a 60-foot-long baking oven. There were a number of other tasks and activities that kept me more than busy.

Normally, there was a second forklift driver, whose job was to stack the finished buddle products for shipment the following day. Unfortunately, he was out sick, so it fell to me to handle both jobs, jumping back and forth between my forklift his smaller one.

The smaller forklift was missing the rubber covering on the clutch leaving only bare metal. My shoes were wet from the heavy rain going in and out of the plant all night long for billets and emptying a large scrap loader into a semi-trailer. It kept me quite busy trying to do both jobs having to move fast to keep up with the production flow. If I didn't, half the plant would be standing idle. Yep! You can see it coming, but due to my hurriedness, I didn't.

While I was moving a finished bundle for the next day's shipment, my foot slipped off the bare metal clutch pedal, causing the forklift to surge forward right in front of the night manager's office where he was sitting there doing paperwork. The tongs on the forklift went thru the plywood wall into his desk, sending him, his desk and chair flying across his office to the far wall. My lower jaw must have dropped to my belt buckle. So did his.

To say the night supervisor looked totally shocked is an understatement. Once he saw the look on my face and realized what had happened, he busted out laughing. I was relieved that he wasn't injured. He was a nice fellow and we always got along. But he couldn't save my job no matter how hard he tried. The next day, he had to explain to his boss in the front office what happened. I was fired the following afternoon when I showed up for work. Our wedding was the following day. Not wanting to cause Stella any anxiety for our wedding day, I thought it was best not to mention it until after our honeymoon.

After our ten-day honeymoon, we returned home, broke and with no jobs. Fortunately, we had already paid the first month's rent on our apartment and had four weeks to find work. While we were gone my brother and our parents had taken the wedding gifts and stacked them in our apartment. There were hundreds of thank-you notes to write, but first there was the challenge of finding work.

The Miracle in the factory -- *"He shall give his angels charge over thee, to keep thee in all thy ways."* (Psalms 91:11, KJV).

Although I didn't plan to spend the rest of my life working in a factory, I disliked losing that job. I enjoyed it, and it was here that I witnessed another miracle in my life.

One night I had some extra time and was helping the fellow who works the saw, cutting the newly extruded aluminum to meet customer size specs. I didn't really know him as my job was always too busy and at lunch break, he was always by himself. He was cutting several window frames pieces while I was at the other end, some 30 feet away, holding them firmly in place as he pulled them through for cutting. On one section, he pulled so strongly it jerked them from my hands, causing several of them to fall to the floor bent and unusable. Several pieces were now nothing but scrap metal. I walked up to him at the cutting saw and said, "This reminds me of something my dad always said, 'Haste makes waste.' I didn't mean it as a criticism, but that's the way he took it. I didn't realize at the time, but this fellow had a hair-trigger temper. Had I known this the comment would have never left my lips.

The factory was always a very noisy place. I looked across the 40-foot section of roller table toward the Chief who was in charge of both ovens and all the orders to be filled. He was a tall, thin man about 6' 4" -- a full-blooded Cherokee Indian with red skin and high cheek bones and penetrating eyes under heavy eyebrows. If he were to wear an Indian head dress, had war paint on his face and came riding in on a Pinto horse, he would be an imposing figure you wouldn't want to meet at the Little Big Horn.

In spite of his imposing stature, he was an amiable fellow and we got along very well. He was in the Army Reserves and had the rank of Lieutenant Colonel. As I looked at him, I shrugged my shoulders and mouthed, "I'm sorry." He smiled and yelled "It's okay." Then suddenly, his mouth opened, his jaw dropped, and his face turned almost white.

A second later I felt like someone had flicked a finger on the back of my head, like my dad used to occasionally do when I was a little kid getting too fidgety in church. I turned around and saw that my co-worker had a 4-foot-long steel I-Beam which he had used to hit me in the back of the head. He was about to swing it again as I faced him. I quickly reached for a similar beam to defend myself. Before I could fight back, the Chief came all the way across the 40-foot-wide table and grabbed the I-beam.

"You don't want to tangle with him," he said. "He's irrational. I'm afraid HE WILL KILL YOU." Apparently, they had had trouble with this fellow before and the Chief knew it was better to walk away from the situation. I took his advice and dropped my steel beam.

The Chief asked if I was all right, and I answered, "Yeah, just fine, why?"

"He hit the back of your head with a steel beam like he was swinging a bat. I thought he had surely killed you."

"I'm fine," I said.

Now I knew that old saying about Dutchmen being hard-headed must have some truth to it. In reality, I was sure an angel had protected me. Later, after calming down, I remembered, "*The angel of the Lord encampeth round about them that fear Him, and delivereth them.*" Psalm 34:7, KJV. Being fired a few months later on the eve of our wedding, was, in my opinion, the Lord's further deliverance from what might have been another encounter with death.

WHAT IF??

At the time of my draft notice on August 1, President Johnson was sending more troops into the battle for South Vietnam. I was pretty sure that's where I was headed. . .and perhaps would have been involved in the first major and devastating battle between the United States Army and the North Vietnamese (NVA) (People's Army of Vietnam-PAVN), in the *Battle of Ia Drang Valley*. Why did I now sense that possibility? First a little history.

The battle was comprised of two main engagements. The first involved the 1st Battalion, 7th Air Cavalry Regiment and supporting units, flying into a hot battle zone via helicopter taking place on November 14–16, 1965 at LZ X-Ray, located at the eastern foot of the Chu Pong massif in the central highlands of Vietnam. The battle was documented by Morley Safer in the critically acclaimed book "We Were Soldiers Once and Young" by Harold G. Moore and Joseph Galloway. In 2002, Randall Wallace, son of a Presbyterian minister and director of *Brave Heart, Pearl Harbor, Secretariat,* made a movie entitled *We Were Soldiers* about the battle of Ia Drang landing zone LZ X-Ray. The movie starring Mel Gibson as Major Harold Moore in command of the 1st Battalion, 7th Air Cavalry Regiment in 1965. Joseph Lee "Joe" Galloway an American newspaper correspondent and columnist was there to record the event. Galloway is a former Military Affairs consultant for the Knight Ridder chain of newspapers and was a columnist who often worked alongside the American troops he covered. As a journalist, he was awarded a Bronze Star in 1998, for carrying a gravely wounded man to safety while he was under very heavy enemy fire in 1965 Battle of Ia Drang Valley. (Source: Wikipedia)

So, what did this battle have to do with what may have happened? Well two months before, when the Cherokee Chief saved me from doing battle with those steel I-beams, he told me he was about to enter the Vietnam War too. As a Lieutenant Colonel in the reserves he would be joining an Air Cav regiment, and if I ever got drafted, he wanted me to be in his unit. He said that anybody who had a head as hard as mine, and who was as ready to take on an enemy as I was, *'I want him in my unit.'* I didn't think much of his comment at the time, probably because I was thinking more about my upcoming wedding and had not yet been drafted. The war was the furthest thing from my mind in August 1965 ...until the morning of August 1st.

I don't know what happened to the Chief. I said my goodbye's the night I was fired for driving the forklift through the wall. I often wonder if he survived the Ia Drang Valley battle or was ever even in that battle. The survivor statistics were staggering at the time. After the war, it was discovered that both sides had deflated their losses and inflated their kill numbers. Generally speaking, the U.S. military confirmed losses of 305 killed and 524 wounded and claimed 3,561 NVA killed and more than 1,000 were wounded during engagements with the Cavalry Division troops. According to ARVN intelligence sources, each of the three NVA regiments' initial strength was 2,200 soldiers. No matter what the final statistics, it was an intense battle that claimed many lives on both sides.

Major Harold Moore and the 7th Air Calvary won the battle of Ia Drang Valley, and subsequent battles. However, Moore knew at the end of the battle what the Viet Cong were willing to sacrifice many lives, and the American military was not prepared for what would ensue. Galloway immediately knew it would be a costly war that we had no hope of winning without paying a terrible cost. (Source: Wikipedia)

7

STELLA'S WITNESS FOR CHRIST AND LEARNING TO LET GO AND LET GOD

A day after returning from our honeymoon, Stella found a job at Burroughs Corporation in Pasadena and began working in their library. She proved to have superb administrative skills. Thus, she was quickly promoted to what was then called Mahogany Row, to serve as administrative assistant to the Vice President of Research and Development. Within a year her witness had led her boss to Christ. She was also chosen to model the new B-4700 mainframe computer in the *Wall Street Journal* (*Oct 28, 1971*), which her boss had designed. I was immensely proud of her!

However, her witnessing fell on deaf ears and stony ground with another fellow who also worked as an engineer at Burroughs. He was a Muslim who frequently passed through her office to see her boss. His name was Sirhan Bishara Sirhan. If only he had listened to what Stella had to say. But he didn't, and on June 5, 1968, he shot and killed Robert F. Kennedy in the kitchen of the Ambassador Hotel in Los Angeles. The shooting occurred just 100 feet from where Stella and I and two other couples had celebrated our prom dinner in May of 1963 five years earlier.

Meanwhile, I was anxious to find a job, but there weren't many options for a man without a college degree. But in going thru my business card file I came across the name of a former boss at the Rocky Mountain wholesale drug company where I had worked briefly just after high school. On the back of his business card he had written a note saying that if I ever wanted to come back, a job was waiting for me. When I called, he asked, "When can you start?" I told him I would be there in 30 minutes.

He put me to work delivering over-the-counter items to drug stores, large discount chain store pharmacies like White Front and other chain drug stores delivering morphine, and other expensive drugs to hospitals across Los Angeles county.

I left for work every morning at six and was fortunate to be home by midnight after driving 400 miles back and forth across the county. I ate three fast-food meals a day and spent most of my time sitting behind the wheel of a Dodge van. I swelled up to 265 pounds in nine months and frustrated that I got to spend so little time with my bride.

Stella longed to provide a home-cooked meal and eat together like normal families. I did too. One night I called and told her that I'd be home early -- around 9 p.m. To my surprise she had prepared an entire meal of potatoes, vegetables, and meatloaf. Of course, I had already eaten two hamburgers with large fries a few hours earlier but didn't want to mention it. As I stood watching her serve the meal, somehow the meatloaf slipped out of the loaf pan, slid across the floor right between my legs and finally came to a stop when it hit the living room carpet. Surely, she was going to cry after spending all that time preparing the meal, but she didn't. Instead, we both busted out laughing, and that marked the beginning of a lifetime of laughing together. From then on, we developed the habit of laughing at life's mishaps and misunderstandings both small and large.

Meanwhile, my weight kept going up. I went to see a weight-control doctor who was a noted specialist in the field. On the first visit, he provided a special diet and a pill to be taken daily in the early afternoon. Over the next month, I lost 65 pounds. The weight was coming off so fast I had to buy new trousers every week. The doctor gasped in shock when he saw me after the first month. Although my heart checked out okay, he told me I had to slow things down. But 30 days later, I had lost another 45 pounds, bringing my weight down to 155. I was climbing the walls with energy to spare and lay awake much of the night, eager to get back on the road the following morning. I felt great and took on additional stops in my routes. I was now covering nearly 500 miles a day in my deliveries. We didn't know it until a couple of years later, but those little pills were actually "uppers." Apparently, doctors could prescribe them in those days for weight control. Fortunately, I had been taking them for only those two months with no apparent damage, other than not being able to sleep much, with my mind and insides constantly running at 160 mph inside.

DANGEROUS CARGO

While I enjoyed working for the drug company, it came with a certain risk. The van I drove was unmarked, but it didn't take long for drug addicts to figure out my scheduled arrival at various drug stores and hospitals. Being extra vigilant became a natural instinct after the first incident when I noticed someone coming up alongside the driver side of the van as I parked in front of a White Front store for delivery of Morphine to the pharmacy. He had a rather large hunting knife in his right hand. I waited for him to get to the door and quickly opened it knocking him down. The knife flew out of his hand as he was knocked unconscious. I tied his hands behind him with my belt and called the police from a nearby phone booth. Yes, there were pay phones in those days. You know, those little glass booths where Superman changed into his cape. When the police arrived, they took him away in handcuffs. After that incident I always kept a baseball bat in the van.

GRANDPA NICK WEARS HIS SUNDAY BEST.

In 1967, Stella and I bought a new Pontiac LeMans and made the trip back east to visit some of our relatives who couldn't attend our wedding, especially my Grandpa Nick and Grandma Mary. Grandpa couldn't pronounce Stella's name properly and always called her Salla. Perhaps it was the Dutch Friesland accent. He knew English but always spoke in Dutch. Grandma died several years later, but Grandpa remained in his home. It was decided by all the brothers and Sis that he needed to have a housekeeper come in the evening to cook meals and once a week to clean the house. She was an elderly widowed black woman named Bessie, a delightful caring woman who became an incredibly good friend to my grandfather over the coming years. She eventually moved in and occupied the second bedroom.

I don't know how their conversations ever developed because Bessie surely didn't speak Dutch. Somehow, they were able to communicate and Grandpa developed a great fondness for her, and especially her southern cooking.

My Uncle Nick, one of Dad's younger brothers always stopped by Grandpa's house every morning before taking his daily gladiola flower sales route to Chicago. Grandpa, of course, would have been in his garden since sunup. They would always have coffee, toast, and fruit from Grandpa's garden together before Uncle Nick headed for downtown Chicago. But one morning when Uncle Nick drove up to the house, he didn't see Grandpa anywhere in the garden. Puzzled, he went inside, but didn't see him in the kitchen or living room.

He called out, "Pa, where are you?"

"In here, Nicky," replied Grandpa, his voice coming from his bedroom. Uncle Nick found Grandpa lying on his already-made bed, dressed in his Sunday best suit with white shirt and black tie, complete with polished shoes. Uncle Nick was stunned. "Pa, what are doing in bed dressed in your suit?"

Grandpa replied, "Nicky, it's time for me to go home and I didn't want to be a bother, so I put on my suit to make things easier." He explained "I've been waiting here for you because I want to make sure you tell all the boys and Sis how much I love them. You'll tell them, won't you Nicky?"

"Well okay, Pa, I'll tell them, but they already know that. I'm confused. Where are you going?"

"It's time for me to go home," Grandpa answered. "This is the day and time. Please be sure to tell everyone I love them. I love you Nicky."

With that said, Grandpa crossed his arms over his chest, clasped his hands together, closed his eyes and died. Uncle Nick checked his pulse and pressed his ear to his chest to listen for a heartbeat. There was none. Uncle Nick sat there and cried for quite some time. He said Grandpa had the most peaceful look on his face he had ever seen. Next to him on the bed was his well-worn Bible. Tucked inside at John 3:16 was his Last Will and Testament, written in his own hand on plain white paper in his native Friesland language. Grandpa left his house, the furniture and all his cash to Bessie. She lived there the rest of her life and many family members stayed in contact with her until her death many years later, always treating her like a member of the family.

8

FIRST BANKING JOB

In February of 1966, we moved into a rental home in Arcadia on Palm Drive. It was owned by a close friend of my dad with whom he had served many times over the years as deacon and elder at our church. The house was one bedroom, bath, large living room with fireplace, large kitchen, and a glassed-in sun porch across the back, with a large private yard totally shaded by a large tree. Compared to our apartment, as nice as that was, it was a mansion, and only $100 a month for the 10 years we lived there. What a blessing!

It was also the year a young 20-year-old from the suburbs, where there was no crime, learned what it's like to work in downtown Los Angeles where there was crime. In the three years of working at 1st and Main St., I was witness to two murders, three police shooting, one suicide, one gun fight between a thief robbing a hotel accountant, then randomly blazing his way out of the hotel firing two 45 semi-automatics wildly in all directions, (one bullet parting my hair before ducking behind a parked Yellow Cab), running past my crouching position as I watched the police kill him a half block away. The thief had viciously shot to death the hotel accountant. Then there were those two or three times per month attempted mugging of my person by intoxicated winos.

All of this was just part of my first banking job in the mailroom at Security National Bank in downtown LA. Fortunately, I didn't have to do much mail sorting. Within two months I was in charge of taking a step van to the Los Angeles Post Office Terminal Annex building, along with 150 keys to open corporate lock boxes. It was a great way to start the day providing opportunity for breakfast at famous Philippe's before returning to the bank.

A few months later I was promoted to picking up the daily deposits of North American Rockwell and delivering them directly to the Federal Reserve Bank in downtown Los Angeles. Their deposits were often in the multi-millions and had to be at the Federal Reserve Bank by 3 p.m. daily where they were time-stamped to get the interest float clock started. I picked up the checks at the Security Bank branch office in Torrance and was usually there by 1:30 just in case the checks were ready early. Many times, they were not ready until 2:40 or 2:45, leaving me just 15 or 20 minutes to get to the Federal Reserve Bank on Olympic Boulevard downtown LA. I rarely took the I-10 freeway, instead choosing surface streets and even alleys if need be to make the deadline. I never got a speeding ticket, but on a few occasions the time stamp read 2:59 and 30 seconds.

Being at the Federal Reserve Bank every day gave me an opportunity to get to know many of the Brinks, Loomis, and Dunbar armored truck drivers. It also gave me access into the basement where once a month all the old paper money was taken out of circulation to be burned; millions just going up in smoke. It was painful to watch.

THE BRINKS ARMORED TRUCK CAPER

One day after leaving the Federal Reserve I found myself behind a Brinks truck heading north on Grand Street. The street was under major repair and quite bumpy. Suddenly, much to my surprise, the back door of the Brinks truck flew open and a sack full of paper money bounced out! I stopped, grabbed it, and threw it next to me on front seat, while honking my horn and flashing my headlights to get the guards' attention. Soon, another bag of money fell out, which I also picked up. Finally, at a stop light, I was able to pull up along-side on the passenger side and got the guard's attention, frantically waving my arm and honking my horn. I held up one of the money sacks, clearly marked Federal Reserve Bank, smiled, and pointed to the back of their truck. The color quickly drained from the guard's face. He jumped out as I handed him the two sacks.

"Were there any others?" he asked.

I told him no and that I had left the loading dock right behind them.

"Thank you, thank you, so much; you saved our jobs. You won't mention it to anyone will you?"

"I won't say a thing. Don't worry about it." He told me there would have been around a million in total cash in both bags.

From that day on there were always fresh donuts waiting for me in the security guard's lounge at the Federal Reserve Bank, courtesy of the Brinks boys. My diet was well underway by this time so I couldn't eat them, but it was a nice gesture. It also concluded my career as Butch Cassidy.

CHAUFFEURING THE PRESIDENT AND CEO

When Security Bank began its merger with Pacific Bank in San Francisco, Frederick Larkin, the President and CEO of Security Bank, took many flights from LAX to Northern California.

I was chosen to be his chauffeur for the trips to LAX. He was a friendly fellow not given to arrogance or snobbishness like I imagined a President and CEO of America's seventh largest bank might be. I got to know him well as he sat in the back seat of the large black stretched Lincoln Continental Town car. After our first few trips, he sat up front in the passenger seat. On one of occasions he asked me what I planned to do with the rest of my life. At 22, I still wasn't sure but told him it wasn't going to be driving. He said good and encouraged me to get back to college. A couple of weeks later I started taking night classes. I will always be grateful to him for his mentoring and encouragement.

Even though I was out of the office most of the time, there was a constant irritation in the office. The manager of the mail department was a middle-aged Irishman who drank constantly from his pocket flask and hidden bottles in his desk. By 10 a.m. he smelled like a brewery. He just didn't like me and was constantly yelling at me about something.

The tension between us blew up one day when he called me to his office and came across his desk at me barking so loudly the whole office could hear. I got up out of my chair and barked back at him just as loudly, leaving his office as he yelled "You're fired!" To my astonishment, fifteen other mailroom employees dropped what they were doing and yelled, "If Bob goes, we go." I had no idea how to respond to this unexpected solidarity. With fifteen people ready to walk out, he turned and slammed his office door behind him cursing and swearing. It was gratifying to know that my co-workers of every nationality and ethnic background were friends beyond what I had realized. The storm having passed, we all went back to work.

NEWS FROM OVERSEAS

In April of 1968, after returning from my daily trip to the Federal Reserve, I received a message from the assistant mailroom manager, Jessie, telling me I needed to get to my parents' home as soon as possible. I was sure something terrible had happened. I left immediately.

9

CRUSHING NEWS
FROM VIETNAM

I left the office immediately running the five blocks to my car, praying silently that brother Roger had not been killed. The drive home out of Los Angeles on the I-10 east was absolute insanity, driving like a madman hitting speeds over 100 mph. Guardian angels must have been working overtime that afternoon. It was a miracle there wasn't an accident or a trail of Highway Patrol cars chasing me.

Arriving at my parents' home I slid the car sideways into Mom and Dad's driveway with the rear of my 58 Chevy nearly broadsiding the palm tree at the driveway entrance. The street was already filled with cars and people from church. Stella had come from work in Pasadena and greeted me in the kitchen to tell me my brother Roger had been killed. From the day he enlisted in the Marines, we naturally knew this was a possibility, and especially since that night six weeks ago when we took him to Norton Air Force Base in San Bernardino, the night he left for Vietnam. Now, despite all our prayers and hopes for his safe return, our worst fear had become a staggering reality.

I lost my cool and punched my fist into Mom and Dad's refrigerator door, bestowing a huge dent in the center. The living room was full of people from church, so I headed to the den at the rear of the house. Dad followed me and there we hugged and cried on each other's shoulders.

After composing myself the best I could, I went to the living room and knelt down by Mom who lay on the couch crying uncontrollably. She grabbed my neck and I started crying with her. Later I learned the family doctor had given her enough tranquilizers to bring a horse to its knees, none of which had any effect on her. The following two weeks were filled with immense emotions and emptiness as we waited for Roger's body to arrive from the battlefield. The funeral would present another huge emotional reality.

Major Cshick was the Marine Corps designated representative from the Pasadena Marine Corps recruitment Depot. He had just returned from Vietnam and this was his first home assignment to bring the news of Roger's death to my parents.

At the time Mom was working at Arcadia High school as a baker, employing her baking talents with special desserts and lunches for the teaching staff. She was always home by 3:30 and sat by the living room picture window going through the day's mail. That's where she was when she saw the green Marine car pull up in front of the house. Two Marines got out and came to the front door. We had always heard that if one military officer came to your door it meant your loved one had been wounded. If two came it meant there had been a death. I can't imagine what went through her mind that day, and what has gone through the minds of tens of thousands of mothers throughout history. Tears still come to my eyes when watching the movie, *Saving Private Ryan*. I am especially moved by the scene where the Army Captain and a chaplain step out of a military car to inform the mother that four of her five sons had been killed in battle during World War II. The feeling must have been similar for my mom.

As mentioned earlier, Roger had always been a soldier. As kids, we played Cowboys and Indians like so many boys, but most of the time he and I were playing soldiers. Behind our house there was an abandoned 25-acre chicken ranch which made a perfect location for hiding and ambushing each other. We didn't realize it back then, but it was an early signal of what would become Roger's early and strong calling to fulfil his destiny as a warrior.

Unbeknownst to our parents, both of us had become very proficient with our BB guns and we often stalked and shot at each other on that abandoned chicken ranch. At the end of each battle, we had little red pelts on our legs and rear-ends. Even though we wore light-weight plastic helmets and ski goggles, our one rule was to never intentionally aim at each other's head. In real war, there were no such rules. Roger was killed instantly by a sniper's bullet to the head. If it had to be, there was some comfort in knowing he didn't suffer. The moment I heard of his death, I remembered what he said to me one weekend a few weeks after he had finished boot camp. I picked him up for a weekend pass from Camp Pendleton while he was in jungle warfare training. He told me he was now a gunnery sergeant, but the life expectancy in a firefight was 30 seconds and I should not mention it to Mom and Dad. I never did. He was quite proficient with an M-60 machine gun and a BAR (30 caliber Browning Automatic Rifle). The statistics for life expectancy were accurate. His life's journey ended during the Tet Offensive on April 13, 1968, seventeen days after his 19th birthday.

Like me, Roger attended Temple City High, where he learned to love and play trumpet as well as football, his two favorite activities. He was excellent at both, and we spent every Friday night in the football stands to watch him and his teammates clobber the opposing team -- most of the time. When Dad realized Roger was serious about playing trumpet, he bought him a special trumpet, one of only 100 made in France. At the time, Herb Alpert, the Tijuana Brass, Bert Kaempfert and his Orchestra and Al Hirt were extremely popular. Roger never had to be told to practice. It was just the opposite. He was determined to conquer Al Hirt's high "C." He would practice until his lips bled, much to mom's horror. One day when he was carrying his trumpet home from school and a couple of elderly widows down the street from us were out working in their front yard. When they asked what instrument he played, he proudly proclaimed, "The trumpet, would you like me to play for you?" Yes, was their immediate reply.

He ran home, got the records he used for accompaniment and spent two hours entertaining them. None of us in the family knew about it until those two widows attended his funeral at our church. They wept as they told us what he had done.

Both Roger and I were always defenders of those who couldn't fight for themselves. Dad always told us not to go looking for trouble and to never hang out with the wrong crowd. If bullied, turn, and walk away. On the other hand, if someone needs help, do your best to come to their aid.

FOURTEEN GANG BANGERS AGAINST TWO

In one such incident, Roger and one of his friends drove to an all-girls softball game to watch the girls play on an independent no school related baseball field. They were the only two guys in the bleachers to cheer them on. In the other bleachers were fourteen Mexican guys rooting for their girlfriends. The other guys did not much like the fact that their girls were losing. What no one knew was that all fourteen guys were members of a local gang. Eventually, they ran out on the field and started beating up all the girls on Temple City's team. Even though fourteen against two is a considerable imbalance, Roger and his buddy didn't hesitate. They grabbed a couple of baseball bats to even the odds and jumped into the fray. The brawl did not last long. When it was over, all the gang members were sprawled unconscious across the infield with various broken bones. Unfortunately, before the fight ended, the pitcher on Roger's team had been severely beaten. She spent the next five years in a wheelchair paralyzed from the neck down and died five years later. After that incident, I have to admit I was temporarily prejudiced against Mexicans, but a number of years later God would cleanse my heart of that prejudice in a way I would never have expected. He did that by prompting Stella and me to seek legal guardianship of a twelve-year-old girl who was illegally in the U.S. from Mexico. After liberating her from a gang-infested area in Carlsbad we became her legal guardians. We can all be prejudiced toward many things in life, but there is a vast difference between prejudice and discrimination; prejudice is an attitude, discrimination is an action. God had a plan and removed those negatives from my life with an action.

THE TET OFFENSIVE

Roger arrived in Vietnam in early March 1968. His letters home could never mention exactly where he was, but we learned later he and a company of Marines were in a small village on the South China Sea called Phou Bai, a short distance from Hue. We were told that his entire company had been overrun and killed by two regiments of Viet Cong. I learned from one of Roger's best friends some 40 years later via declassified documents that this was not an accurate portrayal of the events surrounding his death. My Mom and Dad never knew the true story having passed away before the documents were declassified.

The real story became clear in 2019 when a US Marine Captain made a visit to Vietnam with a small group of surviving siblings. He became interested in the specific battle of the 27th Marines during the Tet Offensive. His research among declassified documents revealed the battle raged for three days. Roger was most likely killed sometime between 7am and 2pm April 13th 1968. Roger's "B" company was pinned down by heavy enemy fire much of that time along a bend in a river along Hwy 1 defending the only fuel pipeline flowing into Hue. Company A was southwest of their position and was trying to reach them when they too came under heavy fire and consequently couldn't reach Company "B" until after they had been overrun.

The 27th regiment of the 1st Division, including companies A, B, C, & D took a combined KIA rate of 65%. The 27th was the only Regiment to be removed from action after 7 months (Feb to Sept) in the war because of the heavy losses. The remainder of the 27th fought on until Sept 1968 when the survivors of the

27th were flown back to the U.S. All other Marines and Army troops had to serve a full year.

My research revealed a thought-provoking statistic. In World War ll the average time a soldier was actually in a heated battle was 4 days a year. Most soldiers were away from home for four years, but actually only in heated battle 16 days of battle in that time. In Vietnam, the average actual time spent in heated battle was 128 days per year with their length of service set at only one year. It certainly helps explain why so many Vietnam vets have suffered from PTSD. A staggering statistic in comparing the two wars leaving us with an inexplicable truth; in peace time, sons bury their fathers. In war, fathers bury their sons. As long as there are wars it will unfortunately always be the same.

It took two weeks for Roger's body to get to our local mortuary. The Major told us we had the right to unseal the casket but urged us not to do so since he had been shot in the head and that would not be how you would want to remember him.

Stel and I stayed at Mom and Dad's house during the two weeks we were waiting for Roger's body to arrive. I remember waking up every morning and thinking this was all a dream and when fully awake realizing it wasn't. I still have that dream once in a while even now 50 years later.

After Roger's casket arrived, his funeral service was held at our Christian Reformed church on Baldwin Avenue and Lemon in Arcadia. The church seats around 375, but hundreds more showed up, including many from Temple City High School and many more from surrounding high schools who played football against Temple City Football team. The church quickly filled up as did the social hall with another 175. After that, speakers were installed outside the church to accommodate the overflow crowds on the lawn. After the ceremony, the procession to the grave site at Rose Hills in Whitter stretched for four miles.

The next few months were the worst for all of us. After nearly three weeks, I finally returned to work. My drunken boss, (the same fellow who tried to fire me) had been calling my parents' home as early as the first week of our ordeal, wanting me to get back to work. I told him that would not be happening until we received my brother's body, and the funeral was over and not one day before. When I did return to work, he never said a word. He had no empathy, only a dirty look.

Shortly after Roger's funeral, Major Cshick gave us lifetime passes for the Rose Parade, which could be viewed from the Marine Corps Recruitment Depot on the corner of Colorado and Sierra Madre. It's there the parade turns north, and floats are parked for a few days for post-parade viewing. The Depot is also where the Grand Marshalls get off their floats. We took advantage of his kindness for several years, and that is where we met John Wayne and Bob Hope, who served as Grand Marshalls in separate years. But the real praise came several years later when Stella ran into Major Cshick and his wife at the traveling Vietnam Wall, when it was set up in the Temple City Park. I was out of town on a business trip at the time, but the Major told her that he and his wife had become Christians as a result of watching how our family handled Roger's death. God brings good from bad even in the worst situations. *And we know that all things work together for good to them that love God, to them who are the called according to his purpose." Romans 8:28 (KJV)*

A couple years after Roger's death, I asked Mom and Dad why we all did not stand more adamantly against his joining the Marines. I certainly wished I had, knowing it still would not have made a difference since Roger was so determined. Dad said, "First, he was of age and was free to make his own decision. Secondly, your mother and I spent our lives instilling correct values in you guys. How could we now abandon those same values for our own personal gain."

Not long after Roger died, a remarkable incident happened one night when I stopped by my parents' house after work. I was taking care of the house and yard for them while they were on an eight-week road trip with their camper trying desperately to retrieve some normalcy in their lives.

Clark, the same neighbor who always cursed and swore and pointed his handgun at us, came out of his house, begin scuffling his feet around in the dust in his back yard as if he were looking for something. I was watering some newly planted Gardenia's about 30 feet from him on our side of the fence.

He finally meandered to the fence and in a very humble tone of voice said, "Bob, I was sorry to learn that Roger had been killed. He was a fine boy. I often saw his picture in the Saturday paper after the Friday night football game."

I thanked him for expressing his feelings and to my amazement, we talked about all sorts of things for the next two hours. I was astonished to learn how well read he was. Finally, he said he had to go back inside. "Good talking to you," I said. He replied, "I enjoyed it, too."

That was first time in 10 years he had talked to anyone in our family, other than yelling profanities at us. It was also the last. A few weeks later he was dead from a self-inflicted gunshot wound to the head from the same handgun he had used to threaten us for all those years.

BACK TO COLLEGE FOR A FEW NIGHT CLASSES

About this time, Stella and I started talking about my going back to college. Three months later I quit my job at the bank, sold our new 1967 Le Mans, (sigh), bought a new VW bug to save on gas, and returned to school. In college, I had a very well-paying part-time job which nicely paid for school and allowed me to feed my habit of buying new cars. I began by taking a couple night classes.

ZERO TOLERANCE

Having finished a mid-term exam early one night I was walking back to my car in the west parking lot. I heard a noise that sounded like a muffled scream. The parking lot was full of cars and very dark not having many streetlights in those days. In walking towards the sound, I saw a guy attempting to rape a girl between two cars. He was trying to lift up her skirt while holding his hand over her mouth. As I was quietly approaching, he hit her in the side of the face attempting to silence her. Filled with instant rage I grabbed him by his hair with my left hand, yanking him backward and formally introduced him to my right fist. Having absolutely no tolerance for sexual crimes against women, I punched him again and again and again. After the first blow he never knew what hit him.

In turning my attention to the girl, she seemed somewhat conscious, but not totally. She was dazed, partly because the blow to her face and probably partially in shock. It did not seem a good idea to let her drive herself home. I wanted to get her parents phone number and get to the pay phone on the corner a block away. As she became more coherent, she gave me her parents phone number while we walked to the phone booth a half block away. I made the call. Her father answered. I explained his daughter had been attacked in an attempted rape. She was fine, the offender was unsuccessful, but she was probably in shock and would most likely have a black eye by morning from a blow to her face. My suggestion was for me to wait with her until they arrived so one of them could take her home and the other drive her car. Her father was understandably filled with anger wanting to do further damage to the offender. I explained the assailant was still lying unconscious where I re-decorated his face.

They lived nearby and arrived ten minutes later. The girl ran into her father and mother's arms sobbing. Her father turned to me and asked where the guy was. After showing him, he said, "I see what you mean. He's still out cold. I'm angry enough to want to continue the beating, but I can't. I'm a cop so I'll need to call for an ambulance to make sure he gets to a hospital." The word "cop" had me concerned. I asked him for a favor to please keep me out of this. He said, "Don't worry, I will. You saved my only daughter, and I will always be grateful. A report will be made, and I'll say my daughter was feeling ill and her mother and I came to pick her up when I found this fellow and called for an ambulance." Then he surprised me by asking me for a favor: "I sometimes have to work the swing or night shift, and that concerns me because I wouldn't be able to pick her up after class. My wife is nurse and sometimes also works swing or graveyard shifts. Would you be willing to meet her at a prearranged location every night after class for the rest of the semester making sure she gets safely to her car?" I told him I would be glad to. We exchanged phone numbers and he called me a few times during the remainder of the semester to thank me again. On one of those phone calls he later told me the culprit had been arrested once before for attempted rape but was never convicted for lack of a witness who could identify him. He checked with the hospital and learned he had survived the beating. I was relieved. His injuries included a broken nose, three missing front teeth, seventeen stitches to his face and two cracked ribs. He was 24 years old and released from the hospital a week later.

I appreciated the parent's gratitude and especially their verbal containment on the matter. Whoever he was, his parents, or someone else in his family might have easily contemplated having me arrested and/or sued.

The victim married a few years after graduating with honors from college. Stella and I received a wedding invitation but were unable to attend as we were scheduled to be out of town.

I only told that experience three times in the last fifty plus years. On one occasion I was criticized for not having him arrested. I explained my desire for no involvement was based on any further reprisals. Too often, even back then, Good Samaritans could easily be cast as the bad guy. Today, for Good Samaritans it is a hundred times worse. The Bible tells us this would be the new reasoning in the last days; good would be proclaimed bad, and bad would be asserted as good. Upside down and reversed. Police going to jail for upholding the law, criminals set free. It's not even ignorance gone to seed. Ignorance has taken root. Absolute foolhardiness! Another Bible prophecy has certainly come to pass.

I further explained, "My thinking at the time was if the culprit immediately paid severely enough for his crime he would think twice before committing the same offense again. Moreover, if I had run to the nearest phone booth for help, (there were no cell phones) it would have been too late to save her. She might have been killed by the time help arrived. Besides, would you feel the same if it had been your daughter?"

When I see a violent crime being committed, especially against someone unable to defend themselves, I must act. To do nothing is to condone and partner with evil. It is beyond my comprehension to even think of doing nothing.

In the Bible, mercy does not precede judgment, judgment precedes mercy. Christ brought spiritual mercy to mankind, but that did not negate facing consequences. Micah 6:8 (KJV) tells us, *"He hath showed thee, Oh man, what is good; and what does the Lord require of thee, but to do justly, and to love mercy, and to walk humbly with thy God?"* Lesson learned. I gave as much mercy as possible under intense rage and anger.

My chosen field of study was Sociology. A year later, one of my textbooks related the story of Kitty Genovese. On March 13th, 1964 she was stabbed outside the apartment building across the street from where she lived in Queens New York. The attacker stabbed her twice, stole her purse, drove away, returned ten minutes later, raped her, and stabbed her several more times while 37 people heard her screams for help and did nothing. It became known in psychology and sociology studies as the "Genovese syndrome."

Under current law in California, (October 2020), assault with a deadly weapon, date rape, selling children for sex, domestic violence, exploding a bomb, shooting into a house with intent to kill or injure people, raping an unconscious person and beating a child so savagely it could result in coma or death, are all considered "none-violent offenses." As of this writing in several states, there is no "bail" law, which California wants to make permanent on a ballot Proposition in the November 2020 election. There have already been several incidents reported that some offenders are committing criminal acts, blatantly stealing from department stores, including acts of violence, and are being caught three or four times in the same day and released with no Bail.

I have to ask myself how would I respond to the same situation in today's world? My response would be close to the same. First, use my cell phone for a 911 call. Secondly, intervene any way possible to prevent any harm to the victim until help arrives.

10

AN OLD MAN GOES TO COLLEGE

When I went to register as a full-time student, the first thing noticed was how young all the kids seem to be. I was 22, they were 18. I felt like I didn't fit into this picture. Stella and I were nearly at the registration desk when I turned around and walked away telling Stel I felt like an old man next to all these young people.

She understood and didn't debate the matter. At the end of the hallway we came face to face with a good friend, Bram Pieters. Bram grew up in the then-Dutch-held territory of Bali, Indonesia. His wife Nellie was in my church youth group and I had known her since our early teenage years. I told Bram how I felt, and he actually got angry with me. "How do you think I feel. I'm six years older than you, and I already have a mechanical engineering degree from The Netherlands which is absolutely of no value in the U.S., I have to start from scratch in my education --right down to taking beginning English and Math."

He had a good point. I turned back toward the registration desk and signed up as a Business major with Psychology as a minor. God's timing is always perfect, providing the right people and the right time to guide us down the path He has chosen for us.

WHAT SHALL IT PROFIT A MAN?

The first day of class, the professor began with, "As you begin your business career this is what you need to build into your brain. There is nothing, I repeat NOTHING more important than this one thing. I repeat, NOTHING, more important than this one word." He turned and wrote the word PROFIT in huge letters on the black board.

My spirit and stomach felt like it had been turned inside out. It affected me like the fingernails scratching on a chalkboard. I just couldn't let this go, and raised my hand to say, "But it seems to me if you don't take care of your employees, you'll always be scratching for profit with an inordinate amount of turnover. That will directly affect your bottom line, not to mention individual creativity."

"Ah," he said. "Ladies and gentlemen, we have in our midst a union man."

I pushed back saying, "Whoa! Whoa! You're making a huge assumption there, Kemosabe. Quite the contrary; I'm a union's worst nightmare. I have nothing against profit, for without it nobody wins. I'm simply saying that if you don't take care of your employees, profit ratios are negatively affected as well as individual creativity -- not to mention the negative by-products that can infect the whole company when managers feel like they have no value. They need to feel they have an investment in the game. Without it they're just employees and will sooner or later find another place to contribute. High employee turnover is expensive."

The bantering back and forth continued for 15 minutes. Which one of us came out on top is probably open to debate, depending on your viewpoint, but it was entertaining for the rest of the class. One thing was certain. I didn't exactly endear myself to the professor nor did I care, having already decided to change my major. After class I headed to the administration building and changed my major to Sociology with a minor in Psychology. I had no intention of going on for a master's or PhD and consequently had no idea how to make a decent living with a BA in Sociology. But at least it was more closely aligned with my inner heart which, until that morning, had eluded me.

The exchange with the professor that morning would be a prelude for an entire career of always challenging and questioning the status quo. Pushing the envelope to find new and better ways of doing things in the business world. Later in the non-profit arena it had become part of my DNA. I guess it was always so, even as a kid, but now I was in full recognition of it. It also got me in trouble from time to time. I became a change agent and that's when you realize there are many people who don't like change, from timid souls to narcissistic controlling bosses. They want and relish your creativity but only if you use in it within their framework.

To change my major, it was necessary to speak to the career guidance counselor, who happened to be the same one I had in high school, and who had now moved to college level. Since it had been nearly five years since I'd graduated from high school, he felt I needed to make up several pre-college courses to bring me up to date in math and the sciences. Bless his heart. If I had listened to him it would have taken me six years to graduate instead of three-and-a-half. I thanked him for his suggestions and immediately circumvented all of them by signing up for every advanced class I could find. I never had any trouble, with the exception of Algebra, and for that I hired a tutor. The age difference with other students was no longer a hindrance to my psyche as I had once imagine because there were several guys who had made it back from Vietnam in once piece and were now picking up the pieces of their lives by going back to college.

ANOTHER MIRACLE

"I will go before you and make the crooked places straight..."
Isaiah 45:2 (NKJV)

My first year of college, Stella and I believed we could make it through four years on her salary. But we also knew it would help with the cost of books, gas, and pocket money if I had a flexible part-time job that wouldn't distract from study time.

The plan was to carry as many units per quarter as possible and finish in less than four years. The first quarter of college I bumped into a friend from high school, Al Whitehouse, who was just back from Vietnam. He suggested I would make a good salesman. It sounded good to me being a people person. His cousin worked at Pacific Outdoor Advertising, which, at the time, seemed to own half of all the outdoor billboards in Southern California. They had just four openings for college students only, and Al had just been hired. His cousin worked for Pacific Outdoor and there were 200 guys vying for the other three openings. I asked him if he would put in a good word for me. The next day I got a call from his cousin for an interview, and two days later was hired.

The job was a simple one. I worked two nights a week of my own choosing, driving two separate routes to check billboards for wind damage (called flag damage) or burned-out lights, either fluorescent or incandescent, fill out a half page report on each one and turn it in at headquarters near downtown Los Angeles at the end of the night. At first each route took five and half hours, but because I knew the city so well was able to shave off an hour and a half by learning shortcuts in the routes and even using back alleys to avoid heavy traffic areas.

My weekly paycheck for eight hour per week was nearly what my wife made per week for 40 hours. Since I didn't want to use my good car for these routes, I purchased a used 1962 Impala Super Sport which served me well for four years. During those four years I never saw the fellow who hired me. Every Thanksgiving a huge turkey was delivered to our house and a large ham every Christmas. As was explained to me at the beginning, upon graduation I was expected to surrender the job for another college student, which I did the week of graduation. Often it just comes down to who you know.

LOCKING HORNS WITH LIBERAL PROFESSORS

One of my sociology professors was quite adamant in his belief that if we change a poor man's surroundings by providing better housing, etc., he will automatically change his attitude. He might as well have waved a red cape in front of a bull, and I was happy to be the bull. I told him he obviously had never been to Lake Shore Drive in Chicago where tens of millions of dollars were spent constructing beautiful two-and three-bedroom high-rise apartments overlooking Lake Michigan. Three years later they had become high rise crime ridden vertical ghettos. Apartments had been totally destroyed by bullet holes and sledgehammers poking holes through walls. I argued with him by saying, "Change a man's heart and he'll change his own environment." It would take too much to relay the entire conversation, but I'm sure I won that one. And again, the class was fascinated by the interchange of conflicting opinions.

I suspected he might want to get even with me on the final exam when we were expected to compute a complicated one-half-page long math formula to determine the standard means in a research project. I had just received a new Brothers calculator for Christmas. Back in the day, portable calculators where somewhat bulky, though still easy to place in a briefcase. For most college students they were unaffordable. In class I sat by the window which had an electrical outlet. I plugged in my calculator and went to work on the formula. He came up to me and whispered, "You can't use that in this class."

"Why not?" I replied.

He said, "It isn't fair to the other students who don't 't have one."

There he was again, waving that red cape in front of me. I whispered back by saying, "Well, that's not my problem. If they want one, they should buy one." He went on whispering something about equality and fairness. I asked him if he thought it was fair to take up so much of my time since we only had 50 minutes for the exam. Besides, I said, "If this is not permitted then show me where it's written. I saw nothing in your class rules, or the college rules for that matter, forbidding the use of calculators," and continued with the computations.

I was the first to finish and was sure I had aced the answer and told him when placing my exam on his desk that I was prepared to defend my position in the dean's office if the test came back with anything less than the appropriate grade for the work done. My thought was a rear-guard maneuver in closing the back door on any potential reprisals. I also added a sincere compliment stating I felt he was a good teacher and enjoyed his class, but I have a natural dislike for anything that smells of socialism. We have to know our rights always remembering to express them respectfully; something that was still in fashion in those days. And, oh yes, I received an A.

11

INDEPENDENT THINKERS WANTED

Before graduation I had seven weeks in between quarters before taking one final four-unit course needed to graduate. We decided to take the opportunity for an extended vacation. After graduation there certainly would-be little time for a vacation of that length.

Our trip took us first to Vancouver Island, British Columbia, and across what was then Canada's first transcontinental highway. It was only a two-lane highway much like the original Route 66. We stopped for a couple days at Lake Louise and continued east across to Thunder Bay at the top of Lake Superior, finally crossing back into the U.S. at Mackinac Bridge in Michigan, touring the Grand Hotel on Mackinac Island.

We spent a couple days with Marv and Andrea Folkertsma, in Michigan where Marv was working on his Master's degree in Political Science, toured the Henry Ford museum and Thomas Edison's workshop, and visited family in Chicago before heading down to Tennessee and finally home on good old Route 66. After returning home from our seven-week trip I finished the last four units needed to graduate with a B.A. in Sociology. Having made the Dean's List and graduated with a 3.8 GPA, I was gratified it was all over.

Having already sent out 100 resumes to various large corporations across the country, applying for a position in human resources. I received a whopping three responses to come for an interview. One from Seagram's 7 on the east coast, one from Newport News Ship Building in Newport News, Virginia, and one from Georgia Pacific Lumber in the City of Industry, CA. Since never being a drinker, and especially so having married a Methodist, and didn't want to move to the east coast to sell whisky or build ships, Georgia Pacific lumber became the only option.

In my interview, they asked me to take a long multiple-choice psychological test, which to me, was mind-numbing. Six hours of multiple-choice questions that drove me nearly senseless. My thought during the test was maybe I should start drinking and take that Seagram's interview. The questions were, as I recall, overly inquisitive and downright nosy; if married, how often do you have sex; do you eat eggs; how often; how many times do you urinate a day, etc, etc, etc. After six hours and 200 more questions of similar nature I began writing answers to such urination questions, as "Depends on how much water I drink." When I handed in my test to the General Manager of the plant, he laughed and said, "You're the kind of independent thinker I'm looking for. Can you start tomorrow?" I was there at 8 am the following morning.

The Georgia Pacific office was a wholesale distribution center with its own warehouse and sales force. My goal was to become an outside salesman. The customary training prior to achieving this goal was two weeks working in the warehouse to learn the various types of lumber, two weeks riding along on the truck and trailer deliveries learning where the customers were located, one year as an inside desk sales rep, and finally a territory for outside sales in two years.

After the first two training segments, I asked the General Manager why we had so much "pecky-cedar" fencing in the back of the warehouse, taking up about a quarter of the available warehouse space. He explained that before he came there was a period where it was a popular selling item and his predecessor had over-ordered from the mill. The demand dropped and the inside sales reps weren't making enough money on it to bother with. I said, "So if we could use that space for more profitable lumber, we would improve sales and naturally the bottom line. Just tell me what we paid for it from the mill and I'll unload it for a nice little profit, and we'll have the space for profitable lumber. But please, if I can unload all that pecky cedar fencing for at least a small profit, you have to put me on the inside sales desk, agreed?" Two days later the cedar fencing was gone, a small profit was made, and I had a desk with the other five inside salesmen nearly a year ahead of schedule. A few weeks later, I sold several tons of teak wood to the US Navy for their Ice Crushers, at the time based in Long Beach and Seattle. The General Manager approached me and said, "So, when do you want to start as an outside salesman?"

LOOK OUT! SHE'S NOT LOOKING

A couple of weeks later I was going to a late lunch with one of the salesmen. I was driving a new car purchased during my last two years in college, a 1972 Chevy Vega. Don't laugh. It served me well and gave me 35 miles per gallon on our trip across Canada. It was a small car built low to the ground with the hood being much lower than most cars. While driving on a wide four-lane street with almost no traffic, I saw a group of young high school age girls talking on the corner on their way home from school.

Suddenly one of them dashed into the street in front of me. I hit the brakes hard, but the low front bumper hit her behind the knees flipping her up onto the hood and rolling her into the windshield. At that point, she wasn't actually injured. When the car came to a screeching halt, she rolled off the hood and hit her head on the pavement. I turned off the engine, turned on the emergency flashers, secured the emergency brake and rushed to her aid, as did my passenger. She was conscious and wanted to get up, but there was a pool of blood on the asphalt underneath her head. I told her not to move until an ambulance arrived. A woman who lived in the corner house witnessed the accident and brought out a blanket which I used to cover her. The police were there in minutes, quickly followed by an ambulance which took her to a nearby hospital.

In the meantime, a police officer asked me for my driver's license. That's when reality of what had just happened hit me like a ton of bricks. I started shaking so badly I couldn't get my license out of my wallet. The cop tried to calm me down. "Everything will be all right. The woman who witnessed the accident told us it happened so fast you had no choice. You did everything right. The skid marks have been measured and we know you weren't speeding."

I wasn't convinced. "Her head is what concerns me, with all that blood."

"The doctors will take care of her," he insisted. He helped me get my license back in my wallet, as I asked what hospital she was going to. My fellow salesman and I drove to the emergency room immediately to see how she was doing. The doctor said she had a fractured skull and would have a terrible headache for a few days but after all the test she should be fine. By now I had lost my appetite for lunch. We returned to the office and I went to see the General Manager to explain why we had been gone so long. He could see I was struggling and suggested I go home for the rest of the day and take tomorrow off if I needed. The following day I learned the young girl was home from the hospital. I sent her a bouquet of flowers with a note saying how sorry this had happened. A week later her mother said she was back in school and was doing well. What a relief!

BURROUGHS CORP.

As it turned out I never took that outside sales job with Georgia Pacific. A few weeks earlier I had tapped into Stella's connections to do some networking at Burroughs Corporation for a sales job. In fact, I had already interviewed for a sales job at the Santa Ana office, but had been turned down leading me to take some resolute action to get it the job. I resigned from my job with the lumber company.

The General Manager of Georgia Pacific threw a going-away party for me, presenting me with a 10 Year Georgia Pacific tie clip for being there all of ten weeks. I thanked him and said, "But I thought there was supposed to be a gold watch at retirement, you know, something like a Rolex." He laughed and said, "We're gonna miss you." The whole lumber experience was most valuable. Even though unknown to me at the time, it was part of God's plan. It taught me how to communicate with people on the phone and how to get appointments with financially powerful people – skills that were extremely valuable for me years later in both sales and Christian mission work years later.

I had the first interview with Burroughs at their Santa Ana sales office. It didn't go quite the way I expected. Josh, the branch manager, was a refined southern gentleman from Shreveport Louisiana. I liked him immediately and believed the feeling was mutual. He noticed I had no accounting experience or accounting classes among my college courses and said it would be difficult for me to sell accounting computers without it. I respectfully replied that I understood and liked people and they seemed to like me, which was probably the most important characteristic in any selling environment. The accounting I could learn along the way. He agreed that people skills were especially important, but not enough to overcome my lack of an accounting background. I was naturally disappointed but left the interview determined to take my case to a higher authority. After all, I had resigned from Georgia Pacific so was unemployed.

After some research I learned that a fellow by the name of John was the District V.P. and Sales Manager for the eleven western states at Burroughs. His office was on Wilshire Boulevard, near Beverly Hills. The next day, after my disappointing interview with Josh, I was at John's office at 8 a.m., dressed in one of my best suits, asking for an appointment for a sales position. His secretary told me his schedule was full, but she would try to fit me in. At 5p.m. I was still sitting in the waiting room lobby.

The following morning, I was back at 8 a.m., asking for a few minutes with him. Her response was the same. Another day passed and I still hadn't had as much as a glimpse of him. The third morning I was back, right on time at 8:00 am. Apparently, he had noticed and asked the receptionist who I was. When she told him, I was looking for a sales position he said, "Send him right in. Anybody that tenacious with the guts to go to the top man, I want to meet him." I told John about my conversation with Josh four days earlier and he agreed with my perspective. He called Josh on his speaker phone and said, "Bob Boomsma is here with me. He'll be in your office tomorrow morning at 8 a.m. and I want you to hire him." Josh said, "Yes sir." Thus, began the second phase of my sales career.

Persistence consists of charging forward even when you hear that negative voice behind you saying, "Quit! Give up! It will never happen." Instead, we need to pretend not to hear it and just keep going. If I recall correctly, it was Napoleon Hill who said, "The majority of men who meet with failure is because of their lack of persistence to create new plans to take the place of plans that fail." And, I think Winston Churchill said something like, "Success is staggering from one failure to another without losing your enthusiasm." But Jesus said it this way after His disciples asked him how they should pray, giving them the Lord's prayer and following it with these words in Luke 11:9 -10 (NKJV), *"So I say to you, ask, and it will be given to you; seek, and you will find; knock, and it will be opened to you. For everyone who asks receives, and he who seeks finds, and to him who knocks it will be opened."*

WORK? LET'S PLAY GOLF!

The following morning, I was in Santa Ana at 8:00 am. Josh smiled and said you are a tenacious fellow and that he probably underestimated me. He was not upset for having gone over his head to a higher authority and praised me for my action. "It's what any great salesman would do." Josh introduced me to the sales manager, a crusty chain-smoking fellow named Bill with a great sense of humor. His first question to me was, "Do you golf?"

"Well, not really," I said. "I took a class my last quarter in college and did a nice job bending the coaches 5 iron. I don't even own any clubs."

"Well on your way home tonight stop at Roger Dunn's up the street and buy a set. We're going golfing tomorrow." I thought, "I'm going to like this job. It's only my first day and I'm going golfing with the sales manager."

That evening, I bought a complete set of Jack Nicklaus Golden Bears with bag, a box of balls, shoes, tees, glove, and a couple of golf shirts. I thought it best to stay in the middle price range just in case this was not my game. After all, I had heard many chokes about golf like "Cro-Magnon man walked the earth beating the ground with sticks; today we call it golf." Perhaps so, but on day two of my second job out of college I had already spent more than I had earned.

The following morning, I went with the sales manager and the top salesman for the branch to play 18 holes. The first four holes went pretty well for a guy who had absolutely no idea what he was doing. On the fifth tee, I felt a solid connection with the ball but didn't see where it went. I asked the other two guys if they saw where it landed. There was no reply. I asked again while frantically surveying the fairway for my ball. Receiving no response, I asked again but heard only uproarious laughter. When I turned around, I saw both of my partners lying on the ground laughing so hard they could barely catch their breath. Apparently, I had scooped up the ball with my lofted wedge iron and sent it flying high into the air over our heads and behind us. The ball rolled down a hill onto the seventh green and into the cup. It was my first hole in one – just the wrong hole!

And I wasn't done yet. On the 15th tee, I sliced the ball sending it flying at about 100 mph, two feet off the ground. It rocketed toward a canal running parallel to the fairway and struck a duck peacefully swimming down the canal. The ball hit him in the back of the head killing him instantly. The last thing that duck saw on a bright sunny day were stars. I've been duck hunting with a 12-gauge shot gun and didn't hit a single duck. I do however own the bragging rights for getting my first duck with a golf ball.

On the remaining three holes, other golfers could see this guy driving around in his golf cart with a dead duck lying on the platform next to his golf clubs. I gave the duck to the guy in the starter's office who said he'd take it home for his wife to cook for dinner. So ended my first day of work at Burroughs, my first official golf excursion as well as second "unofficial" duck hunt. One might say, getting two birds with one golf ball.

CONQUERING FEAR

Burroughs training began with selling several different models of simple four-function and programmable calculators. If you could sell them, they figured you would be ready for in-depth training on the bigger computers. After a couple days of practice in the office on the programmable calculators, I was ready to hit the road. Or so I thought.

I drove to a light industrial manufacturing park. There were blocks and blocks of businesses. An indispensable goldmine of calculator opportunities. A cornucopia of possibilities. I decided to walk door to door carrying two basic types of calculators. I boldly walked up to the front door of the first building, and then a thought hit me, "What if they're not interested and say go away." How would I get passed any of the flack catchers or that nasty sign on the front door that said, "No Solicitors" in big, bold, letters?

Fear washed over me like a gigantic wave on the north shore of Hawaii's big island. Confidence washed away like a tide. The fear of rejection is a salesman's worst nightmare. I felt like the apostle Peter stepping out of the boat on a storm-tossed sea, and like Peter took my eyes off Jesus.

I walked back to my car and decided to find a restaurant and have a cup of coffee. Surely, I could find the "delete fear" button somewhere in my mind. I was still sitting there at noon thinking about it, so decided to have lunch. At 3 p.m. I was still drinking coffee and still firmly in fear's grip. After several more cups of coffee, and several trips to the restroom, it was finally time to go home. Whew! The end of my first day in sales. Now I was really worried and wondering how I was going to earn a living if fear continued to hold me captive. The second day was the same as the first. Fear had progressed into teetering on the cliff of depression. That night brought tossing and turning until I finally took my dilemma to the Lord.

"Lord, I need help in overcoming this paralyzing fear." Immediately, a scripture popped into my mind. *"For God hath not given us the spirit of fear; but of power, and of love, and of a sound mind."* (2 Timothy 1:7 (KJV)

Soon another verse came to mind, Joshua 1:8: (KJV) *"This book of the law shall not depart out of thy mouth; but thou shalt meditate therein day and night, that thou mayest observe to do according to all that is written therein: for then thou shalt make thy way prosperous, and then thou shalt have good success."*

I meditated on those verses until I drifted off to much-needed sleep. The following morning, in spite of not getting much sleep, I felt renewed. Refreshed. Eager to tackle the day. Fear had been swept away with the flood of God's Word.

My first stop that morning was at the same front door where the lightning bolt of fear struck me on that first day. The "no solicitors" sign still dominated the glass door. I ignored it. Once inside, I received a warm greeting from a middle-aged woman, the office manager, who treated me to a cup of coffee and a sweet roll. We had a great visit, and I demonstrated a programmable calculator that caught her attention. I left with a signed contract for six of the most expensive programmable calculators available at that time. Confidence returned. Fear became a small object in my review mirror. The wall of fear had collapsed like the walls of Jericho by trumpeting God's Word the night before.

God has a tender, loving affection for his people. He doesn't want us to be discouraged but to learn from it. God's compassions towards his family infinitely surpasses that of the most loving of parents toward their children. Psalm 63:8 (NIV) says it so clearly, *"My soul clings to you; your right hand upholds me."*

12

LISTENING!

"A soft answer turneth away wrath:
but grievous words stir up anger."

Proverbs 15:1 (KJV)

A few weeks later I introduced another valuable lesson from scripture. It's called "listening." James 1:19 (KJV) tells us *"...let every man be swift to hear, slow to speak, slow to wrath;"*

I was calling on the president of a regional bank with 12 branches in Orange County. When I sat down in front of his desk his voice changed from mild and soft-spoken to excessively loud, somewhere just short of a P.A. system at a Friday night high school football game. My first thought was, he must have had a Dr. Jekyll and Hyde switch somewhere in his head.

He angrily told me that eighteen months ago he ordered several models of our "P" Series comptometers from Burroughs and still hadn't received them. He even swore at me, telling me he hated Burroughs Corp and would never ever buy another one of our products. This went on for about ten minutes. He ranted. I listened, and occasionally repeated what he had just said to let him know I heard him and was listening. Finally, I said, "Well I certainly don't blame you. Considering your situation, I wouldn't buy from us either, or I probably wouldn't even allow another Burroughs salesman in my office. I'm terribly sorry you had this happen, and unfortunately it's all because of no toilet paper." He looked at me like I had just dropped in from outer space. "Have you lost your marbles?"

"No sir," I said. "It's true. All these "P" series (a manually and electrically assisted 10 or 12 column ledger comptometer) are made in Scotland by an assembly line comprised mostly of women who went on strike 18 months ago because there was no toilet paper in the ladies' wash room."

"Are you pulling my leg?"

"No sir, that's the honest truth."

He busted out laughing. We talked and laughed together for another 30 minutes about various cultural idiosyncrasies around the world, after which I walked out of his office with an order for 12 more "P" series ledger units in addition to his original order of eight. Once again, I had learned the truth of scripture: "A soft answer truly does turn away wrath."

Burroughs did not send people for any intense six months training program until they knew they had sales ability. My first serious training exposure involved learning how to push the right buttons, and in what order, how to do demonstrations, various presentation styles, and how to write software. I also learned how to fix the hard wiring inside a computer, which to me looked a little like what I imagine the back side of the cockpit control panels on a Boeing 737.

The training took place at the Pasadena Hilton Hotel, along with thirty other new guys and four women. Even though Stel and I lived nearby in Arcadia at the time, none of the trainees were allowed to return home at night or even for weekends for the next six weeks. They took good care of us in terms of providing three meals a day at the top floor restaurant overlooking all of downtown Pasadena. If so desired, we could have Peking duck every night with all the trimmings. And many of us did. Breakfast was buffet style with anything available one could imagine. Lunch was the same. On weekends we had little free time, having to complete weekend homework assignments that we would be tested on Monday morning.

My roommate at the Hilton prison was John Mayo Balfour, also from my sales branch in Santa Ana. I had become good friends with John who turned out to be the great grandson of John Mayo Balfour who founded the Mayo Clinic.

John and I weren't about to leave our brides for a six consecutive weekends, so every other weekend we took turns sneaking out to go home. On alternate weekends we had our wife join us for a weekend at the hotel. On one such weekend Stel and I were fascinated to watch the filming of a scene for a movie starring Van Johnson they were shooting in the Hilton lobby. I don't remember the name of the movie but do remember thinking I was glad not having to make a living repeating the same lines over and over for 30 different "takes." No offence intended Van.

John and I quickly learned that he wasn't really a salesman and I wasn't a software programmer. As part of our training, we were tasked with writing a small computer program. The test came when I fed the program into the computer. For the first few minutes nothing happened. John and I waited patiently to see if the computer would produce the "hoped for" reaction, a simple paragraph with an easy math computation. It didn't work. The computer made bizarre noises, began spewing out reams of perforated computer paper with all sorts of gibberish on it, belching smoke as it struggled to understand the instructions I had given it. The only way to stop the computers neurosis was to pull the plug. It gave a final hiss and groaned with what seemed to be a sigh of relief. John couldn't stop laughing. I watched in horrified disbelief, thinking I would have to pay $12,000 for the expensive computer's replacement. As it turned out, I wasn't the first salesmen lacking the gift of programming and didn't have to pay for it. It wasn't really broken, just confused, like me. The fact was, John wasn't a salesman, but was a fairly decent programmer. This spawned an idea for me in how to get through the software programing portion of this class. I made a deal with him, suggesting he write my software programs for the class and I'd give him credit for some of my sales when we got back to the branch. That would give him time to figure out where he best fit at Burroughs. The agreement worked magnificently! We both felt that we had been blessed to have been placed together at the beginning of this season of our journey.

STRIKING A DEAL AND HITTING THE ROAD

Computers were classified as Group I, ll, III IV or V depending on the model and complexity. Group l were calculators of all kinds. Salesmen didn't like selling Group l because there was very little commission. And yet, they had to fulfill their assigned quotas. Since I was not eligible for commissions until training was competed, this presented another opportunity. I approached all the salesmen in the branch and told them I'd make their goals in Group l if they let me go anywhere in their territory to get the sale. They would get the commissions and the referrals for any Group II, III, IV and V computers I uncovered. This was particularly attractive to them because the end of the fiscal year quotas for Group I were quickly approaching with little time left to fulfill them. It was an offer they couldn't refuse. I hit the road and roamed freely throughout Orange County as far south as San Diego.

In the narrow hallway leading to the salesmen's office, often called "the bull pen," the branch manager had placed a large sheet of graph paper with everyone's name and the number of Group I units needed to be sold, including my name.

Every day I came back to the branch and made a red mark an inch wide by my name for the number of units sold that day. In two weeks, the red mark was at the top of the graph paper. In the third week, I just kept extending the red mark right off the graph paper and up the wall to the ceiling. Two weeks later it was across the ceiling and going halfway down the other side of the narrow hallway.

About that time a young very well dressed fellow from the head office in Detroit, Jerry, came through our office. He had been selected to start and manage the new Los Angeles financial branch, designed specifically to target banks, savings and loans, stock and bond houses and insurance companies. He was also given authority to pick the best salesman from all product groups from any branch in the United States. Jerry saw the graph in the hallway and told Josh, "I want this fellow," to which Josh replied, "You can't have him." Two days later I was driving to my new office at the newly established Los Angeles financial branch just off Wilshire Boulevard near Beverly Hills.

My new boss was one of Burroughs top salesmen in the country. He was very professional, smooth, soft spoken, sincere, and polished in his manner, dress, and presentation. I was honored he had chosen me and thought I could learn much from him. And I did. He promoted me to Group 1 Product Manager on my first day at the new office. My desk was sitting next to some of the best computer mainframe salesmen in the country, men Jerry had chosen to comprise his financial branch. Jerry immediately took me under his wing, and I began traveling with him up and down the state. He did the major presentations on mainframe computers that I hadn't yet been trained on. Although I was mostly a support attendant setting up and designing graphs and charts used for his presentations, I was also learning important points and selling styles. The training also included working a six-day work week and ten-to fourteen-hour days doing presentations with other office colleagues to major banking institutions. It was great training, but the tough part was the many long hours of being on call day and night to service major institutions such as Coast Federal Savings, Home Savings & Loan, and Great Western Savings. I was expected to carry a small tool kit for pulling off the back panels of various computers to do rewiring as needed. It was about this time that I figured out that Burroughs often promoted people so they wouldn't have to pay commissions. The tide of my discontent was quickly rising.

That's when I met Mike, a smart young fellow from Utah who found his way to our Los Angeles financial office. He had no experience in computer sales, but Jerry thought he had potential. After a couple of months, it was easy to see that Mike wasn't happy. One day I asked him why he was in Los Angeles. "You're smart, your dad is an entrepreneur worth hundreds of millions and I think you have the same DNA." He quit a week later and headed back to Utah.

A few months later he called and asked if I wanted to join him in a business deal on a new hamburger franchise he was starting. His grandmother had developed an unusual recipe for deep frying ground beef in a special batter. He bought the recipe from her and opened a small fast-food restaurant called "Batter Burger" in a mall next to an Orange Julius he already owned. I told him it sounded like an interesting opportunity and went into the venture with him. As it turned out it was the beginning of the end of my computer career.

WE OWN YOU!

Two months later Jerry called me into his office and said, "I hear you're selling hamburgers on the weekends." I honestly didn't know what he was talking about.

"Well didn't you buy into some fast-food hamburger deal?"

"Oh that, yes, but I'm not working in a restaurant on weekends. It was only an investment, and in another state."

I was shocked when he said, "You need to know that Burroughs has spent a lot of money on your training. This company owns you, twenty-four hours a day, 365 days a year."

"Owns me?" I asked. "Well you're partially correct. They have spent some money on me, and you have invested time in me, for which I'm very grateful. But to say the company owns me 24 hours a day rubs my fur the wrong way. Foolish me. I thought Feudalism had died in Europe."

I asked him if he knew where I could get a cardboard box.

"There's probably some in the storage room."

I excused myself, went the store room, grabbed a box, went to my desk, filled it with my personal belongings, walked back to his office and said, "I quit," walked out the front door and drove off while everyone watched from the window with open mouths.

That was a Friday morning. When arriving home, the phone rang. It was Wells Fargo Bank asking if I wanted the job. I had actually interviewed for the job a week earlier, but they hadn't heard from me and was I interested. I replied, "Yes, see you 8:00 am Monday morning."

I will always be grateful for my time at Burroughs and what I learned there, but I was not going to work for a company who thought they "owned" me.

A few months later, Mike and I did another deal, this one involving an unfriendly takeover of a profitable drudging and mining company in the southwest. Mike, his cousin and myself bought up all the outstanding stock of the company, becoming the principle shareholders. The books revealed that the other three owners were crooked as a barrel full of fishhooks and they didn't take kindly to our take over. They beat Mike's cousin so bad they nearly killed him, breaking several ribs, a leg and both arms, and fractured his skull. Mike called to warn me they might be headed my way, and that he and his family were leaving town for a while. For a couple of nights, I slept on the living room couch, guarding the door with a 12-guage pump shotgun and a 9 mm Berretta handgun. The bad guys were caught before they made it to California. They were tried, convicted, and sentenced to ten years in a state penitentiary. We sold the company shortly thereafter.

13

A NEW KIND OF BANKING

The truth was I had become increasingly discontented at Burroughs. It was obvious I would never make any real money when they cut you out of the commission on large sales, just promoting your ego with a fancy title. Promotions don't pay the bills. And besides, once again I was tired of never being home for dinner and evenings with my wife.

I heard about an interesting new opportunity at Wells Fargo Bank, a month before my exit from Burroughs. They were looking for either IBM or Burroughs salesman because they were used to building long-term relationships before a sale was consummated. Their new concept was to develop a middle-market banking system to acquire borrowers/customers of closely held medium size corporations. These companies were often neglected by corporate bankers, who focused on Fortune 500 and 1000 corporations. The interest spread on loans for corporate banking was very slim, just tenths of a point for loaning multi-millions and competing with other banks across the country who were getting the same small interest spread for a piece of the action of 500 million plus loans.

In middle-market commercial banking, as it became known, the bank could secure larger yields on loans of all kinds up to $100 million with a 1 or 2 point spread on each loan. To accomplish this, they developed a personal small bank concept with the horsepower of a large bank by giving a commercial banking Regional Vice President loan approval up to $50 million on only his signature, without using loan committees and thereby allowing for fast approval response time. Also, they offered all the services of the larger bank, like international banking services, LC's, trusts, payroll services etc., at the same Regional office. Each Regional Commercial Banking Center would have a team of three or four loan officers working under the Regional Vice President to handle the intricate analysis, but we could respond very quickly to opportunities that the salesmen had dug up by knocking on doors and networking into various closely held corporations. There would no longer be a loan committee based in some far distant location the borrower would never meet.

As salesmen our assignment was to build a trust relationship to the point of securing the audited financial statements, analyze them to determine if they were bankable and be prepared to defend our analysis to the Regional Vice President. If he agreed, the financials were assigned to a loan officer working under his authority for more in-depth analysis.

Up until this point in time, Wells Fargo's market approach was waiting for new business to walk into the nearest retail branch for home and car loans and hoping that would also lead to corporate business. Our job as former long term computer salesmen was being used to locate and build long term relationships in the banking industry, and "bring-in" these larger borrowers into the bank by convincing them we had a new and better approach to banking.

The first regional center was a block off Rodeo Drive in Beverly Hills and operated by Alan Pribble, the first Regional Vice President under the new Commercial Banking banner. All salesmen reported to a separate sales manager.

I was the second one hired for this new experiment. All of us did our best to make it work. And work it did. What a fantastic time we had! I was given a territory that stretched from Los Angeles east to Palm Springs and southeast to Temecula, always staying north east of I-5. A few months later my regional center moved to the One Wilshire building in downtown Los Angeles. I was excited about not having to commute to Beverly Hills for meetings. A year after that I was given a beautiful large office on the first floor of the original General Dynamics building, which the bank had purchased on I-10 and Rosemead Boulevard. A year later a second regional office opened in the San Fernando Valley and eventually eight were established across California.

I started my cold-calling effort with a computer-generated list of cards the bank provided. The only information they had was the company name, address, and phone number – and much of that information was outdated. Companies had moved, presidents and CEOs had left, or the company had been sold. Not much to go on. Building an updated database required honing my administrative and record keeping skills, as well as networking skills, all of which came in handy many years later when entering ministry work in the non-profit sector.

I was the first of the new salesman to land an account for a $500,000 accounts receivable line of credit. I closed the deal just before Christmas of 1976. At the first annual Christmas party in Los Angeles I was the hero who proved the new concept could work. Much attention and "to-do" was given me by the Commercial Banking Senior Vice President from San Francisco. In those days it was a big deal to land an account of that size in the middle market arena, but I didn't think that much about it and already working on another $1 million borrower. All the attention made me nervous. I saw it as the Lord's blessing on my new job and the Lord was confirming his promise in Isaiah 45:2a (KJV), *"I will go before thee, and a make the crooked places straight..."* How could I take credit for it? Admittedly, the praise felt somewhat addicting. I could feel pride rearing its ugly head in the shadow of success. To compensate, I meditated on Proverbs 16:18 (NIV) *"Pride goes before destruction, and a haughty spirit before the fall."* Giving God the glory for successes would be a constant battle over the coming years as pride tracked me like a hungry wolf.

ALWAYS REMOVE THE PRICE TAG

I will never forget the first and second large borrower presentations I made after joining Wells Fargo. The first was a formal presentation to the Board of Directors of a large company. I bought a new suit for the occasion. I was always expressive in my delivery style, using graphs, charts, and other demonstration aids. At the conclusion of the presentation, the board of directors, comprised of men much older and more experienced than I, congratulated me on a wonderful presentation. They immediately made a motion, and everyone voted to accept my proposal.

I was elated. A million-dollar borrower account was quite a feather in my cap. After some of the board members left the meeting, the president of the company came up to me and said, "I see you bought a new suit." "Yes," I said, "how did you know that?"

He smiled. "You forgot to take the tag off the inside of your left sleeve." We had a good laugh about that for years to come. For some years thereafter, whenever we talked, I told him I had bought a new suit and made a point of letting him know the tag was removed.

The second Wells Fargo presentation was quite different, but also very memorable. Again, the room was full of board members for a potential multi-million-dollar corporate account. About a half-hour into my presentation, I started noticing the faint smell of urine. The longer I spoke, the more pungent and noticeable the odor became. I wondered if someone near me at the board table was having some sort of incontinence issue. I knew it wasn't me, so ignored it and concentrated on my presentation. The unusual circumstance continued throughout the meeting. As it turned out, no one in the meeting had a problem. It was preparation for what God sent me to do later that day.

Earlier that day, John, our pastor at the time, had called and asked if I could fill in for him to visit a patient at City of Hope that afternoon. He wasn't sure he could make it because he had another urgent appointment. The patient was a 14-year-old girl suffering from advanced cancer. Her right leg had been amputated a few inches above the knee. She was unconscious when I walked into her room. Her father and mother were sitting at the foot of the bed with tears in their eyes. I didn't know them, and they were not members of our church, or any other church. I introduced myself and prayed with them before laying hands on their daughter and praying for her. Unknown to me, my pastor was able to make it after all, and had quietly entered the room and was standing behind me, also praying. After our visit, and sharing Christ with the girl's parents, my pastor and I walked together through the parking lot to our cars. Pastor John said he had never smelled such a strong urine odor in his entire life. It was so bad he almost vomited. I told him I didn't smell anything out of the ordinary, but I told him what had happened during my presentation earlier that morning. He felt it was the Lord's doing, to help me focus on praying for the girl and ministering to her parents. The girl died within a few days, but I learned a few months later that her parents had accepted Christ.

POISONOUS SNAKES IN A DEPARTMENT STORE?

Another unusual experience while visiting a future Wells Fargo client and president of a closely held corporation. His wife had been shopping at a local department store earlier in the day. She tried on some attractive turtleneck sweaters and bought two of them. While the clerk was ringing up her purchase, she suddenly started feeling sick. By the time she exited the store she was sweating and near vomiting. She called her husband from a pay phone and asked him to pick her up and take her home. Knowing that was very unlike her, he called an ambulance which arrived the same time he did. She was rushed to the nearest hospital where the doctor did several tests asking her what she was doing when she started feeling sick. She mentioned trying on a couple of turtleneck sweaters, and when he looked at the back of her neck, he noticed two small red pin-point puncture marks. Her purchase was still in her possession and had been carried with her into the ambulance. When the doctor unfolded the turtleneck of one of the sweaters, he found three small eggs, one of which had hatched a small rattlesnake. He immediately treated her with anti-venom, and she was discharged a week later. It turned out the sweaters had been imported from a foreign country and some mentally disturbed individual had placed the rattlesnake eggs in rolled-up turtleneck sweaters. When the department store checked the entire shipment, they found rattlesnake eggs in nearly half of the boxes of turtlenecks. The store naturally called other stores in their chain across the country for immediate checks. I never heard if they found any at other stores. That was thirty years ago, but if you think it's a fictional story, it's not. In the evening news on May 22, 2016, there was a similar story when a Lowes in Denver found several Copperhead snakes in a plastic sack of small decorative rocks in their garden section.

The incident reminds us we should always be thankful every day for God's Grace and protection. The Bible tells us in Psalm 91:14 (NIV) *"Because he loves me,"* says the Lord, *I will rescue him; I will protect him, for he acknowledges my name."* and Luke 10:19 (NIV2011) *"I have given you authority to trample on snakes and scorpions and to overcome all the power of the enemy; nothing will harm you."*

ALWAYS GO STRAIGHT TO THE TOP

Another worthwhile skill acquired at Wells Fargo would serve me well in fundraising for ministry was how to get in front of the most important man in the company, the President or CEO. In sales, you always need to get to the fellow who will be making the final decision. To do this, you must first make sincere friends with his secretary or administrative assistant. The operative word there is "sincere." Flattery is not sincerity. Taking time to get to know the administrative assistant as a friend is as important as getting to know the President and CEO.

One of the major challenges I faced at Wells Fargo was that it took all of one week to book appointments for the following week, which meant that I was only in front of the decision maker two weeks out of every month. That's not very effective. At the time my sales manager believed that more calls equaled more closed deals. I felt it was the quality of a call, not the quantity, that would generate the biggest deals and most profit for the bank. For example, one of my colleagues made more calls than anyone else and, in fact, closed more deals. Good for him. But they were all small deals. At the end of the year, he may have brought in forty new customers to my eight. But I had $5 million in new business and he had $1 million. The goal was to have as much of the bank's money out for loans as possible. The sales manager, James, wasn't convinced that I was right, but I was tenacious in staying with my strategy no matter how much he criticized my approach.

Still, I wanted to make myself more efficient and improve the effectiveness of the calls I made. One day I realized that if I could believe God would help me get two weeks a month filled with quality calls; I could also believe it would take me only one day a week to book the following week of appointments. I decided to make Thursday my "appointments day" for the following week. It worked wonderfully.

And, six months after booking that first $500,000 deal, I landed the first $1.5 million unsecured line of credit for a small manufacturing company. I told James, my boss, at the next monthly sales meeting, it would be a great idea to start a program to honor any salesman who reached the next level; say a $5 million club for business closed in one year and then a $10 million club and so on.

He just laughed and said, "Boomsma, that will never happen."

I replied, "Well if you don't believe it, why did you even dream up this concept of having professional salespeople going after middle-market companies. Besides, it calls all of us to stretch beyond our current capabilities -- to keep shooting higher. Everybody will grow beyond their current expectations."

He laughed again, but I knew a cord had been struck. The following year "yours truly" was the first to land $5 million in total new business. James presented me with a plaque in honor of my achievement. The following year, five other guys in addition to myself were presented $5 million plaques and a year later I received the first $10 million plaque.

I also suggested that anyone who hit that mark should also be given an all-expenses paid trip for him and his wife to Hawaii or the Bahamas for a week. But for some reason that didn't catch on. But hey, I tried. Before long, most of us were cashing large regular commission checks three times a year totaling $35 – $50,000 each. Not bad for the late 1970's and early 1980's.

GOING FROM GOOD TO GREAT

After the first few years, I came up with another way to help close bigger deals. By now I was very well known in the banking industry, having appeared in the Wells Fargo annual report for bringing in Ole's Hardware, at the time the largest chain of retail hardware stores in California. I called the President and CEO of Wells Fargo, Carl Reichardt with my idea.

Carl Reichardt took over from Dick Cooley shortly after I joined the bank. Carl was one of many CEO's chronicled in the book "*Good to Great*" by Jim Collins. He is credited with making the right decisions under deregulation that Bank of America and many other banks wouldn't. "Carl's main component was cutting wasteful habits caused by bureaucratic cultures that arise to compensate for incompetence and lack of discipline, which in turn arises from having the wrong people on the bus in the first place. If the right people are on the bus and the wrong people are off, you don't need a numbing bureaucracy."[1] Carl never doubted that Wells Fargo could emerge from deregulation as a stronger company, not a weaker one.[2] He stated simply "There's

---

[1]   Jim Collins – Good to Great – P.132
[2]   Jim Collins – Good to Great – P 128

too much waste in banking and getting rid of it takes tenacity, not brilliance."[3]

Carl was relentless when it came to cutting bureaucracy and waste. "He froze executive salaries, shut down the executive dining room and replaced it with a college dorm food-service caterer; closed the executive elevator, sold corporate jets, removed free coffee from the executive suite, banned green plants from executive suites, requiring a third-party company to come in from outside the bank to water them regularly, threw reports back to people who submitted fancy binders"[4] and a host of other cost-cutting efforts. "B of A headquarters across the street in San Francisco didn't have the discipline to rinse their own cottage cheese and preserved the posh executive kingdom in their imposing tower in downtown San Francisco. After losing $1.8 billion over three years in the mid 1980's, B of A finally made the necessary changes in response to deregulation."

The concept of a Commercial Banking division serving all the needs of middle market industries out of a regional center for business capital and personal needs definitely had Carl's blessing and was generating a great deal more profit than Corporate Banking.

I called Carl to present my idea. Knowing he was obviously a remarkably busy fellow; I suggested the parameters under which we would use his time. Would he be willing to host a private luncheon at his San Francisco office around his conference table for customers that we had already presented our proposal to? It would be a method to personalize and "seal the deal," with him as the head of the fifth largest bank in the world. It would only be for deals we were relatively sure we were going to get, but the extra personal attention would make the customer feel as important as the large corporate borrowers. And of course,

---

[3] Jim Collins – God to Great – P 128

[4] Jim Collins – Good to Great – P. 128

[4] Jim Collings – Good to Great – P.129

they were important. He was elated and loved the idea. In the following years, we closed hundreds of additional millions of dollars in loans with this added tool.

There were now eight of us salesmen covering the entire state with five strategically located regional Commercial Banking Centers. My idea was working better than imagined; a hundred million here and a hundred million there and pretty soon you're talking big dollars. In the eight years of my tenure with Wells Fargo, all of the guys hired from Burroughs or IBM as salesmen did six billion in new business for the bank with an average point spread per deal of two points over prime as opposed to one tenth, or less of a point Corporate banking was getting on large multi-million dollar loans.

HOBOING FOR DOLLARS

One summer vacation Stella and I took a two-week trip to Colorado. It was after the movie, *"A River Runs Through It"* with Brad Pitt. The movie sparked my interest in fly fishing, as it did for many thousands of others. I succeeded in perfecting a fairly good 3-point cast, but never caught any fish -- just tree limbs, causing me to spend an inordinate amount of time climbing trees to unhook my line. Nonetheless, I had fun, always fueled by huge hope. The trip did produce a potential idea in fishing for new accounts for the bank.

The idea came to me when I happened to meet a fellow who called himself a "professional hobo." He explained that he organized professional hobo trips for people who were willing to pay to ride the rails at least once in their lifetime. Basically, hopping a freight train for an experience somewhat similar to Huck Finn floating down the Mississippi River, something I, too, always wanted to do in my youth. He taught his clients how to protect themselves with special goggles to avoid flying debris, how to hop on a slow-moving train without killing yourself, what type of clothes to wear, etc. I spent several hours with him, learning how to be a successful hobo.

How did I put this idea to work for Wells Fargo? I was aware most potential prospects had one of the "Big Eight" accounting firms or one of the five major regional accounting firms doing their quarterly and annual audited financial statements. Many of them also used the same legal firms. I put together a new plan of calling on these accounting and law firms to see if this might be an additional way of acquiring new customers. If I could convince accountants and lawyers that our banking approach was well suited for their clients, they could do much of the pre-selling for me, and at the very least get me in the door. In getting to know accountants and lawyers, I began to see they too had that childhood dream of riding the rails. They were high-powered, hard-working men – but did they really have the dreams of at least trying the free hobo lifestyle for a week of adventure? A Huck Finn experience somewhere deep inside. Only one way to find out. I invited a few of them on a Hobo trip. I did not tell my sales manager about it who would surely think it was a lame-brained idea. My view was it is sometimes better to ask forgiveness than permission. If my idea was right, forgiveness would not be necessary as witnessed by bringing in several new accounts referred to me.

I only did two of these hobo trips, but it was enough to accomplish my purpose. On the first trip we picked up our freight train in Barstow at one of the largest rail freight yards in the country, after our wives (who thought we were all crazy) dropped us off. We never knew where any freight train was going to take us, but we did set the return time to a week or ten days, jumping off the train in a city that had a major airport. We checked in at a nearby hotel for a night to rest, a hot shower, change into clean clothes carried in our backpacks, and catch a flight back to LAX or Ontario the following day. On a subsequent trip with a different group, we left from Seattle and jumped a train which took us to Denver, by far the most beautiful scenic ride. We always rode empty box cars which provided shelter from wind and bad weather. On one occasion, we were discovered by railroad cops who could easily see from our dress of designer jeans and sunglasses that we were not typical hobos but just out for the experience. They let us go without any hassle, reminding us to be extra cautious. In the days of the depression and dust bowl era, railroad cops were much tougher and known to severely beat hobo hitchhikers, sometimes to even to death.

It was a tremendous bonding experience for all of us. And, as I suspected, my professional hobo friends were soon referring me to their major corporate clients leading to a cornucopia of new major accounts even after leaving the bank.

An Offer from Retail Banking

My exposure one year in the annual report for landing the Ole's Hardware account led to an offer from within the bank from the regional vice president of Retail Banking for California, located on the same floor as our Regional Commercial Banking headquarters on Rosemead and the I-10 freeway. The retail Regional Vice President wanted to hire me away from Commercial Banking to bring in new business for all the Southern California branches. She worked hard at trying to entice me away from commercial banking, even bringing in the Executive Vice President of retail from San Francisco in an attempt convince me with all kinds of promises.

My meeting with him was interesting. I don't remember exactly what I said but the conversation resembled more of a chess game. I love a good chess game. His ego led him to believe he could make short work of this by convincing me to make the switch. I told him that the Wells retail banking format had nothing to offer that was any different than any other bank in town, whereas commercial banking was changing how banking was done and therefore had much more to offer as witnessed by our successes, which was highly publicized throughout the bank. He said, "Well that's what we want you to do for retail; increase the profit spread." I replied, "I'm already doing that for retail. When we book a multi-million-dollar commercial borrower, that money flows through a nearest retail bank. Additionally, retail also benefits because payroll account balances are also held there, not to mention car and boat loans for the company's management and their employees, etc. Meaning your branches are getting a couple of days' worth of float on millions of dollars flowing through a retail branch each month." He countered with an assistant EVP title and a salary which admittedly was attractive. But my heart just was not in it. Titles don't generally impress me. Besides, I knew there would be far too much politicking involved. Nonetheless I had a great time with our discussion volleying back and forth but was pleased to stay with commercial banking.

CALLING THOSE THINGS WHICH ARE NOT AS THOUGH THEY WERE.

In late 1979 the prime Rate reached 21.5 percent and didn't start dropping until September 1981. The prime rate is the interest rate charged by banks to their best customers. The rate is almost always the same among major banks. Essentially it was the base rate on corporate loans posted by at least seven of the ten largest U.S. banks.

In mid-December all the salesmen and loan officers were present for our monthly meeting at the commercial banking headquarters in downtown L.A. Everyone was downtrodden, depressed, and worried. As a new group at Wells, we all had been doing an outstanding job, but the high prime rate could possibly throw the whole concept in the compost pile. I didn't say much until someone asked me, "Bob, what do you think?" I was much more optimistic than anyone else and replied, "I think it will be my best year yet." Some laughed and said I must be smoking something. "Look," I said, "Companies will still have to borrow to keep funding their business cycle. Business is still going on like it always has. They'll undoubtedly pass the cost on in their products and services, which won't be good for the consumers and obviously inflation will be an issue. But in the end, the prime rate will drop back to normal levels, probably sooner rather than later."

It turned out I was correct. The prime rate stayed unusually high most of that year and into the next before dropping back to normal levels. What amazed everyone at the end of the year was that I had booked more business than the previous two years combined, and a great deal more than anyone else standing there that day.

100-MILE BICYCLE RACE TO PALM SPRINGS

One of the very first accounts I brought to Wells Fargo was Hooker Industries, manufactures of racing headers for drag racing and NASCAR events to increase engine horsepower. It was impossible to be at any racing event anywhere in the country without seeing their logos on cars. Being a car enthusiast, I always knew about them, so gave them a call. The timing was perfect as they were already thinking about making a banking change. They liked what I had to say. It was the beginning of a friendship that extended beyond my Wells Fargo days.

The company was birthed by Gary Hooker in his garage many years earlier. He and his good friend Dave Spangler built it into a phenomenally successful brand. Both Gary and Dave were super sportsmen, incredibly disciplined and competitive in all aspects of their personal lives as well as business. They often competed in the annual Hawaiian Triathlon and always placed in the top 10 to 15 percent of competitors. For them, canoeing from Newport Beach to Catalina Island and back was a fun relaxing afternoon. Gary was an ultra-marathon runner in those days. He sometimes ran from Newport Beach all the way to his office in Ontario, and then back again at the end of the day. As our friendship developed, it didn't take long for them to get this slightly plump overweight banker to start riding a bike, something I hadn't done since I bought my first car at age16. One afternoon they invited me to join them in a bike ride from their office in Ontario to Palm Springs. They said it was a nice, "easy" 100-mile ride. I had my doubts about that word "easy." I showed up with the only bike I still owned, a 35-pound Schwinn Varsity. They of course, were professional cyclists, with bikes weighing far less than half what mine did, with Sew Up tires and light-weight titanium shafts. Dave and Gary knew I probably wouldn't make it all the way to Palm Springs, suggesting that if I made it as far as the San Gorgonio Inn in Banning, they would pick me up on their return. If I didn't make it to Banning, I was to wait for them at Taylor's Bar and Grill at the entrance to San Timoteo Canyon.

The three of us left Ontario on Brooks Street, headed up to Fourth Street, and then east paralleling Interstate 10. By the time I had gone four blocks they were long gone, nowhere in sight and already miles ahead. About 12 miles into the ride it started to rain. Not just a drizzle. A soaking downfall that continued for the next two hours. It was winter. Wet and shivering I continued, finally arriving at Taylor's Bar and Grill at 9:00 p.m. It had taken me eight hours to go halfway. I was tired, hungry, wet, cold, and totally exhausted and just wanted to go home, sit by the fire with some hot chocolate.

Gary and Dave finally arrived to pick me up at 1 a.m. They had made it to Palm Springs in a little over three hours. They had been lying around a hotel Jacuzzi drinking beer (to replace the carbs they had burned), while I was grinding out the miles in my tennis shorts and tee shirt with icicles hanging from my nose. Now that they had arrived at the bar, I was hoping we would head home. Not so. Apparently, they still needed to replace more carbohydrates with several rounds of beer. One would think that drinking beer since four in the afternoon would leave them three sheets to the wind. But in all the years I've known them, I've never seen them under the influence.

The grill portion of the bar was closed, and I'm not a beer drinker, but they did have Coke. I guzzled four of them sitting there until they showed up at 1 a.m. I learned the same storm that brought rain to me had dumped three inches of snow in San Timoteo Canyon. The snowfall was not much of a disadvantage for them. They made it to Palm Springs in three hours and 25 minutes, only 16 minutes slower than their best time in perfectly good weather. The bar closed at 2 a.m. and I finally got home at 3:30 a.m. A fun afternoon for them. Not so much for me!

They called the following week and asked me to meet them at a Buds bike shop, where they'd get me fitted for a proper bike. They told me the next race to Palm Springs was a month away, and "We expect you to be there." I wound up ordering a $1200 ten-speed Masi Racing bike and discovered the right equipment does indeed make a world of difference.

The next race a month later I made it all the way to Palm Springs, placing seventh out of the 45 contestants who had been invited. Some riders several miles behind me had to deal with another issue. A swarm of bees attacked them, eliminating many contestants with several winding up in the hospital after colliding with them; some with being stung by 20 or 30 bees in San Timoteo Canyon. I finished the 100 miles in 5 hours and 30 minutes, averaging a little over around 18 miles an hour. After making it to Palm Springs, I was so pumped (no pun intended) I wanted to keep going. For all those who successfully finished, we had a great time the rest of the weekend at our hotel, telling stories about our ride. No trophy. No prize. Just bragging rights that you finished.

I have to admit, when the euphoria dissipated, sitting on that little narrow two-by-four racing seat for five hours was most uncomfortable. There wasn't a single comfortable chair in our house for several days.

The next invitation from Dave and Gary was a rowboat trip from Newport Beach to Catalina Island using a professional one or two-seater rowboat like often scene at Harvard University rowing team. I said thank you, but no thanks. We had several bike races after that, and they also introduced me to Malcolm Smith of off-road racing fame.

Dave is still a serious professional bike racer, holding numerous national records. He no longer rows to Catalina or participates in triathlons in Hawaii but is a serious driver for Team Vesco. In August of 2016, they took aim at their goal to reach 500 miles per hour in a wheel-driven car in hopes of breaking their current world record of 458 mph set in 2001. A couple years ago Dave was hoping to break the 500 mph and hitting over 400 mph when the drive shaft flew apart, causing a tire to blow. He was able to keep control of the car and safely brought it to a stop. The team began redesigning the drive shaft and getting ready to try again for the record. Their wheel-driven car is vastly different than the jet powered thrust-driven cars. As of this writing in mid-June, hotels have been booked a year in advance for both the Nevada and Salt Lake Utah, side of the competition on the Salt Flats. I was hoping to attend Speed Week in August one of these years as Dave tells me he will see to it I get observation time in the Pit Crew as they prepare for their next record-breaking attempt. On October 2nd, 2018, Dave was able to break Team Vesco's former record of 493 mph hitting 503 mph.

I also knew of another record-breaking fellow in the Riverside area, Malcolm Smith and asked if Dave and Gary would introduce me. Maybe he too was looking for a new banker.

14

MOTORCYCLE MAN

Malcolm Smith is best known as an "off road" racer of both motorcycles and off-road cars and trucks in races like the Baja 500 and 1000. Several documentaries have been made of his races. In watching these films it's always easy to tell who's winning. Malcolm is miles out in front with an easy, relaxed style to his driving/riding over some of the roughest roads on the North American continent and the world.

I got to know Malcolm when helping provide him with an unsecured line of credit at Wells Fargo for his motorcycle accessories distribution company in Riverside. It was about the same time I got interested in motorcycles.

Malcolm is a six-time winner – three times on a motorcycle and three times in a car – of the Baja 1000, the off-road racing's version of the Indy 500; a four-time winner of the Baja 500; a two-time winner of the Mint 400; and a two-time winner of the Roof of Africa Rally, also winning the Paris-Dakar Rally in 1987 and the 1987 Rallye de l'Atlas in Morocco in an off-road dune buggy. I could go on and on, listing all the gold medals and first-place trophies he has won, including the European Cross-Country event, considered to be the Olympics of motorcycling. Malcolm's talent on two wheels earned him a co-starring role in Bruce Brown's 1970's classic motorcycle epic, *On Any Sunday*, with Steve McQueen. The notoriety that followed the movie lifted him to legendary status. Yet his demeanor and "Aw Shucks," attitude is what contributed most to his folk hero status.

Malcolm served as a consultant for Range Rover of North America's Great Divide Expedition. This was the first-ever continuous journey by motor vehicle along the Continental Divide in the rugged Colorado Rockies, a 14-day 1,000-mile trek through North America's most vigorous terrain. Touring Colorado's Rockies is second nature for Smith, who has been a trail leader in the famous Colorado 500 motorcycle ride for more than a decade. When he is not racing or riding, he splits his time between Malcolm Smith Motorsports in Riverside and his Sunshine Ranch, high in the mountains of Colorado. *(Source: Wikipedia)*

When he first built his Colorado home, he invited me to check it out on a trip Stella and I were making to Colorado. We did. It was a beautiful home tucked in the pines up against BLM land and overlooking a gorgeous meadow with grazing Deer and Buffalo. Absolutely relaxing.

His newest endeavor, Malcolm Smith Adventures, Inc. grew out of numerous requests to lead motorcyclists on tours of the Baja peninsula, traversing some of the legendary Baja 1000 trails. With the help and advice of his wife Joyce, he introduced "Malcolm's Seven Days of Baja." This annual charity event has grown to include 75 riders and support crews and has spawned several smaller rides in North and South America. To date, the annual Six Days of Baja ride has contributed over $250,000 to his orphanage in Baja. In 1995 he and Joyce took interest in the then fledgling orphanage at Valle Trinidad in Baja Mexico. Today, this incredible facility, nestled high in the Baja Mountains is home to more than 50 children. Many who have "graduated" from the orphanage have built successful lives and careers. *(Source: Wikipedia)*

Back in my banking days, Malcom organized and hosted an annual motorcycle ride from Southern California to the Laguna Seca Raceway near Monterey, California, for a group of 50 or so of his close friends and suppliers, including his banker – yours truly. I invited Darrell Gilman, a friend, Army veteran, and excellent mechanic from high school, to go with me. Along with 50 other bikers, we cruised on Highway 101 up to Route 126, across to California's scenic Route 1 and up to Monterey.

It was on that 25-mile-stretch on Rt 126 across to the coast that I realized I probably should have a bigger motorcycle. Darrell was on his 1200 cc BMW, while I rode my Honda CB 900 cc. The Ninja type bikes took off with throttles wide open and quickly disappeared over the horizon. The cross-country stereo equipped 1200 cc Gold Wing Aspencades cruised behind us.

I was zipping along at 120 mph when Darrell pulled up alongside me, smiled, and took off like he had a Tomahawk missile strapped to his bike. I was already at full throttle, and praying that no cows, deer or even a ground squirrel would be admiring greener grass on the other side of the road. At these speeds, the consequences could be a lot more disastrous than just road rash. After all, a squirrel or deer could be seriously injured.

I rendezvoused with Darrell where the 126 meets Route 1. The remainder of the ride was speed restrained as we traveled along the winding mountain road with 800-foot drop-offs onto rocks along the Pacific Ocean below. Not a location to be rubber-necking scenery. Darrell and I spent three days at the races with the group before heading home late Sunday afternoon via Salinas and Route 101, stopping for dinner at the famous Anderson's Pea Soup restaurant in Buellton. My bike might not have been the most powerful, but it was wonderfully comfortable. After saying goodbye to Darrell at his home in Temple City, I headed east toward home on the 210 Freeway, enjoying the ride so much I kept going all the way to Victorville -- another 75 miles before turning back and arriving home at 2 a.m. A couple of years later, after purchasing a new Kawasaki 1100, I had a much shorter ride that wasn't so great.

KISSING THE MOUNTAIN – ANGELIC PROTECTION

After learning how to handle my new, more powerful Kawasaki 1100 motorcycle and with Stella riding on the back, we took a ride with our Pastor John and a few others from our church. On one ride up to Crestline and down the other side of the mountain we had a slight mishap on a narrow two-lane road. It had rained the day before and the center of the road had some pea gravel residue. I wasn't in a low enough gear, moving too fast on tight curves and was frightened by the amount of pea gravel in the middle of the road. I was concerned about slip-sliding and laying the bike on its side with both of us underneath the bike with some serious road rash. Centrifugal force drove me into the oncoming lane just before a sharp curve. At the same time, a large, bob-tail truck was coming around a curve heading right at us. If I cut back into the correct lane too sharply, I would hit the pea gravel and wind up underneath the truck. If we made it past the pea gravel, I may have avoided the truck, but because of our speed would have gone over the cliff behind the truck. The only option was to take a rocky drainage ditch on the left which ran along the mountainside of the road. We slid into the ditch and scraped along the side of the mountain -- finally coming to a stop when our front wheel hit a large three-foot diameter cement drainpipe that went under the road. The side luggage bags were scratched, the frame that holds them was bent and our helmets were damaged from hitting and scraping the granite side of the mountain.

My ego was dented, but at least our heads weren't. I couldn't hear Stella shouting Jesus's name throughout the ordeal but was glad she did as angels surely saved our lives. The front tire was half flat and the front forks was slightly bent. Riding the bike home was a little like trying to steer a wild galloping 1,000-pound Buffalo. I have never ridden a 1,000- pound-buffalo, but you get the point. It was hard work for the 80-mile trek home.

Two months later the bike was completely repaired, but not my ego or my fear. It was the last time Stel would ride with me, and if it were not for our motorcycle-riding pastor it would have been my last ride as well. Pastor John called after learning my motorcycle was repaired to tell me that he and I were going for a ride on the very same mountain road. I hesitated. Actually, I greatly hesitated, wavered, hemmed, and hawed -- fumbling around for any excuse I could find. He wasn't buying it and told me that I couldn't let fear stop me from doing what I loved. Knowing he was right, I jettisoned the fear and agreed. This time I paid more attention to my speed and gearing. We had a wonderful ride and my fear evaporated like the morning fog.

FIRE! FIRE!

I was driving my company bank car out to Ontario to make a call at Hooker Industries office. It was 1:30 in the afternoon and the traffic on I-10 was fairly light. Suddenly, near the Dudley off-ramp, a car in the slow lane directly across from me hit what looked like a foot-long piece of 2-inch lead pipe. The pipe bounced up under the car and punctured the gas tank and exploded. The passengers were a Hispanic family -- a father, his seven-year-old son sitting directly behind him in the back seat, and his wife, seated in the front passenger seat. The father pulled over to the side of road, jumped out and grabbed his son from the back seat. Because traffic was so light, I was able to cut across all lanes without hitting anyone and pulled over ahead of the burning car. Grabbing a blanket from my trunk I rushed to the passenger side of the vehicle. The door was jammed tight.

By now the flames had traveled from the gas tank along the right inside of the car and raced forward toward the panicked wife in the front seat who was in shock and unable to open the passenger door.

I gave it a hard yank, with one foot braced on the side of the car. Thankfully, the door opened and I thru the blanket on her right arm and shoulder to smother the flames. Within seconds another car pulled to the shoulder behind the burning car. The driver was a nurse on her way to work at Pomona Valley Hospital just a few miles away. It turned out that she was a burn nurse and had her trauma kit with her. As I gently and cautiously helped the injured woman out of her car, the skin from her right arm came off like melted butter.

At that moment, a fire paramedic unit also pulled up having just returned from another call and quickly extinguishing the fire and began helping the burn nurse. The father and son were unharmed. Since everyone was in good hands, I stepped aside and continued to my appointment.

I have a habit of never wearing a suit coat while driving, and this day was no different. After arriving at Hooker Industries, I put my coat on and went to my meeting. Two hours later, I drove back to my office at Wells Fargo and went directly into a meeting with my regional vice-president to discuss my conversation at Hooker Industries.

I took my coat off for the meeting and someone noticed I had black soot and pieces of something hanging from the left upper sleeve and back of my shirt. They were pieces of the lady's skin that had come off when helping her out of the burning car.

The next day there was an article in the local Daily Bulletin newspaper mentioning the accident. The woman had been transferred to the Sherman Oaks burn ward. She received third degree burns on her right arm, shoulder and face and was expected to fully recover. What an amazing set of miracles the Lord provided for this family -- with a skilled burn nurse and fire paramedics pulling up behind them within minutes after the accident. For them, as with us, I thought *"I will instruct thee and teach thee in the way which though shalt go: I will guide thee with mine eyes."* Psalms 32:8 (KJV)

FROM MOTORCYCLES TO HORSES

One of the most fascinating accounts I brought to Wells was a fellow by the name of Albert Yank, a humble and distinguished gentleman of remarkable integrity. I grew up three blocks from the Santa Anita Racetrack in Arcadia. My first, second and third visits to the thoroughbred racetrack came at the age of eight, when everyone went there to take a little pink sugar cube to be immunized against polio. To a child, it was like a scene from a science fiction movie where the country had been invaded by space aliens. It was frightening to see long lines of parents and children with worried long faces waiting to get their pink sugar cube of hope.

My fourth visit, 35 years later, was quite different. This time, I was there to make a large profit for the bank, and of course, for myself. Albert was considered to be, by everyone in the thoroughbred horse racing business, the best blood stock agent in the world. Anyone who was in any way associated with thoroughbred racing knew Albert. I had heard, through my networking grapevine, that he couldn't get more than a $75,000 line of credit from Bank of America. I called him suggesting I'd like to talk about his business to see if we could do something better for him. As a blood stock agent, he would travel the country and world studying the blood lines of the most winning horses in history. Armed with this information, he could predict which horses would win which races at racetracks like Santa Anita, Belmont, Hollywood Park, Saratoga, Pimlico, and which ones would most likely make it to the Kentucky Derby at Churchill Downs.

I studied with great interest his track record (pun intended) and discovered that he was, indeed, extraordinarily effective at what he did. He lived in a large old green Victorian house just east of the Arcadia Methodist Hospital. In the coming year, I was a guest at his home to play backgammon with other players and clients of Albert, such as Berry Gordy, the founder of Motown records, and Nelson Bunker Hunt, who was at the time one of the largest thoroughbred horse owners in the country. Years later, Hunt's fortune collapsed after he and his brothers tried but failed to corner the world silver market. When I knew him, he was one of the wealthiest men in America with several winning thoroughbreds. Hunt had a heart for God's Kingdom work and was past Chairman of the Board of the Bible Society of Texas and a contributor to youth Campus Ministries.

It was sad watching what happened to him. The government took him to court and seized nearly all his assets, leaving him with just enough to live on. He was a very amiable man and I liked him. In his later years, I visited him in Dallas when fundraising for missions. He reminded me somewhat of Winston Churchill in appearance, but without the cigar. He had a tender heart and loved giving to Christian endeavors.

My first meeting with Albert lasted for three hours. I asked for his past ten years of financials, a list of references, which read like the Who's Who of Hollywood from actors to directors and producers, as well as corporate executives from major Fortune 500 and 1000 companies. A few days later, after analyzing the financials, I offered him a *suggestion*.

"We'll dip our toe in your thoroughbred pond by starting you out with a $500,000 line of credit, secured by some of the thoroughbreds you own personally, and we'll go from there. You teach us the horse business and we'll teach you the banking business."

He was elated as no bank in the state, let alone the country, would give him a chance to prove himself, which as far as I was concerned, he had already done if any bank just took the time to do their research.

I had a helpful tool in my bag of bank goodies. My Regional Vice President loved horses and, in fact, owned one -- not a racehorse, but more a Saturday afternoon riding horse. He agreed with my assessment and approved the loan. A couple of weeks later we concluded the deal. We took our time in the analysis as this was a first deal of its kind for any bank including Wells. The next thing we knew we were being invited to the same dinner parties as Albert's clientele. When Albert threw a party for his clients it was a star-studded event equal to Hollywood's famous after-Oscar parties. On one occasion, at Hollywood Park in Inglewood, he had an authentic Arabian tent constructed that would seat over two hundred of his customers. A delicious middle eastern meal was served while everyone reclined on pillows around traditional Arabian low tables.

Stella was always invited to these events, as were the wives of all his clients. A couple of hours before the dinner was scheduled, all the wives received a dozen long-stem red roses delivered to their homes by chauffeured limousines, which then drove the invitees to Hollywood Park. Stella and I were seated with Jack Klugman, from the TV series "*The Odd Couple*," Lee J Cobb, and E.G. Marshall from one of my favorite classic movies "*Twelve Angry Men*," and Jayne Kennedy, actress, model and sportscaster. At the table across from us was Berry Gordy, founder of Motown Records, along with many other corporate moguls and others who had some interest or connection to thoroughbreds. A year later, Alan, my Regional Vice President at Wells, and I were Albert's guests at Churchill Downs for the Kentucky Derby, where we saw and met many other owners and famous horse trainers. Not long after this we were financing stud fees of famous stallions that had won the best races in the country. It was amazing to learn that some people would pay upwards of $250,000 to breed their mares with famous winning stallions with no guarantees of success.

Equally fascinating, and yet sad at the same time, were the immaculate horse barns paneled in various expensive highly polished woods from around the world and clean enough that you could almost eat off the floor. These multimillion-dollar horses had their own teams of caretakers, the equivalent to butlers, looking after their every need. Frankly, the horses lived better than most people, and several levels above the poorest in our country. The bank never lost a dime in the thoroughbred business, making loans totaling tens of millions. I stayed in touch with Albert for many years after leaving the bank and Stella and I visited his ranch in the Riverside County California a number of times after he retired. He stabled his own horses there, as well as a number of celebrity horses.

MILLER'S OUTPOST

On my visits to a potential new account, I noticed a huge, unmarked building along I-10, just west of the Ontario Airport. In checking it out, I discovered it was the main warehouse a head office for Miller's Outpost, a large fast growing retailer of blue jeans, shirts, blouses, socks, belts, etc. for men and women, especially teenagers. The company was phenomenally successful. A couple of days later I called to get an appointment. The business was owned by two brothers, David, and Lou Miller. I was not able to get the business for the bank, but it was a captivating meeting which offered up some worthwhile points of wisdom that led to their success.

They took me through their entire warehouse, consisting of several acres of merchandise under one roof, with none of it staying in inventory more than 12 to 14 days. It was awe-inspiring. The operation was so expansive we toured it in a golf cart. The most interesting portion was actually going through their front office. All those working in accounts receivable and payables were girls 17 to 18 years old. They had just graduated from high school, but there they were working as buyers, writing checks for millions of dollars' worth of merchandise every couple of weeks.

I suggested they were sort of young to be handling that amount of their money. One of the Miller brothers said there were two reasons for this: "First, they don't know they can't do the job because no one ever told them they couldn't. Second, because they are just out of high school, they know instinctively which styles will sell and which ones won't. We trust their instincts."

The response greatly impressed me. It was more evidence that when young people are raised in a positive environment, believing they can do anything because they've never been told they "can't," and you pay them above the normal salary, you've got a fortune in human assets. It was another proof for my argument with my socialistic college professors. The soil that nourishes a "can-do" attitude with the freedom to pursue dreams, leads to great accomplishments. Contrast that with those who are raised in the negative environments of broken families, many of which are constantly told they'll never make it and never encouraged to believe in God or their God-given gifts. They eventually come to believe only in their worthlessness. Naturally, there are always exceptions to this where single mothers and fathers have inspired their offspring to great heights in many fields from industry, medical, education and political arena. Unfortunately, it's not the norm.

SWIMMING IN DOUGH

About this time, my research showed me that Ontario California was the home of a major above-ground outdoor swimming pool manufacturer. I made a cold call. And that's where I met another amazing man by the name of Dave Nelson, a remarkable fellow of integrity and discipline in all aspects of his work and personal life. The company was actually owned by a holding company in New York, but Dave ran and had total authority for the manufacturing of Doughboy above-ground pools. He was almost uncanny in his ability to predict future sales year after year when any number of variables could easily upset his predictions.

If memory serves me correctly, Doughboy's fiscal year began September 1, at which time Dave started buying his raw materials, steel, PVC and all the necessary raw components needed for the manufacture of these well-known pools. He spent millions to bring these resources to Ontario, where the pools were manufactured. The trick was that retail pool sales in the United States don't start until May of the next year when retail stores start considering how many they needed to order for the coming summer months. If it snowed in Spring -- which it sometimes did in various places around the mid-west and east coast in early or even late spring, fewer pools were ordered. By then, Dave had already spent millions on raw materials. If sales were flat, he'd be stuck with inventory with the company left holding the debt on his line of credit used to finance the business cycle, and that would affect what he would have available to borrow for the next coming year. The cycle was similar to a farmer who had a bad crop year but without government subsidies to cover shortfalls. Dave had no safety net.

When I first contacted him, he was looking to make a banking change so he could obtain a better cost of funds. Timing is everything. After collecting his audited financial statements for the past ten years, I easily determined he paid his annual accumulated bank debt on August 31 every year without fail. He was just the kind of borrower I was looking for.

Dave and I became good friends. He was also a pilot and owned and flew his own plane, a single engine Moonie 231 Turboprop equipped with every possible type of flight instrument one could imagine. I remember flying with him for lunch one day to Catalina Island and noticing that the cockpit resembled that of a major commercial airliner. The Catalina small craft airport runway from the air and with the early afternoon sun easily resembles the landing approach on an aircraft carrier, with a drop off cliff of several hundred feet at the end of the runway. After lunch we flew over the end of that runway. The canyon below had three destroyed airplanes piled up from engine failures on takeoff. Dave said that's what happens when people falsify records to the FAA and don't do regular maintenance. I already knew that he was the kind of guy who paid close attention and kept accurate records.

Dave often flew commercially back and forth to the parent company in New York. He told me that on one occasion he was standing in line at the airport in Ontario, California when he began to feel he shouldn't be on the flight. By the time he got to the gate he decided to follow "his instincts," turned around and went home. Four hours later, the plane crashed just outside of Chicago, killing everyone on board.

"Wow!" I said, "That was the Holy Spirit speaking to you. You would be dead now if it weren't for the Holy Spirit speaking to you." I don't think he understood what I was talking about at the time and pretty much let my response drop into the "I'm not sure abyss."

In February of 2014 I called him at home to catch up. It had been 30 years since we originally met. We talked for nearly 90 minutes by phone and reviewed some of the good times of the past, including the subject of the flight that crashed in Chicago. This time he seemed to agree with my comment about the Holy Spirit protecting him. I was pleased to learn that he "got it." I know we will see each other at the Lord's Banquet table. We still get together for lunch from time to time as schedules permit. I enjoy reconnecting with special people from the past.

BEEP! BEEP! THE ROAD RUNNER (DIGOUTIUS-HOT RODIS)

One of the extra exciting perks of meeting and befriending interesting people was being invited to participate with them in their side interests and hobbies. I could probably write a separate book on many of these exploits. One such adventure was Bonsai Running. One client was almost a fanatic at this illegal sport, where participants build their own fiberglass European style race cars. These vehicles are low to the ground fast cars that look a lot like Lamborghinis, Lykan Hypersport, Bugatti Veyron Super Sport, or a Lamborghini Reventon, and many other styles -- but with their own specially constructed engines with fiberglass bodies capable of 300 miles per hour.

The idea was to put the car in an enclosed trailer, tow it out to an isolated desert location where you can find a 20 mile-stretch of straight, flat deserted road with no obstructions, like dead animals, debris, or crossroads. Once the road was clear, the car is unloaded from the trailer, and with full open throttle try to break your personal fastest speed record. There was nothing official, and certainly nothing legal about this type of racing. Again, bragging rights only.

On one occasion, we hit 250 miles per hour on the first run and 275 on the return. Certainly, the fastest 20 miles of road I'd ever traveled. Fortunately, we encountered no Highway Patrol officers who probably couldn't have caught us anyway. At the end of the run it was time to re-trailer the car and head back to the barn. Anyone who happened to be standing along the road in the middle of the desert at 3 a.m. probably would have reported a low flying UFO. In this case, we were the UFO. Thankfully, we saw no one on the road.

FORMULA ONE RACING

On another occasion, I was given the privilege of driving a Formula One race car owned by a client I had brought into the bank. My exciting excursion took place at the original Ontario Motor Speedway. My customer was testing a new modified engine with his driver. After they finished, he asked if I'd like to drive the car. I hesitated. (It was a fake hesitation on my part. I really did want to drive the car – but I was apprehensive because I knew we were talking about a $250,000 piece of machinery. He insisted. Having no choice, I "gave in" taking the first couple of laps slowly to get the feel of the car and track. But as I passed the pit area, he was gesturing for me to let it rip. I did, hitting 200 mph on the straightaway. What a thrill. Another "E" ticket ride. I have always had a need for speed. The speeding tickets I've signed over the years will attest to this. For much of our married life, Stella always said my right foot had not yet received salvation. These kinds of opportunities weren't helping. But now, all these years later, in my age of better wisdom, my right foot has joined the rest of my body for salvation.

Back in those days, it was natural for me to say yes when another of my clients with a drag-racing hobby, down a quarter mile strip, asked if I wanted to try a test run of his top-fuel dragster. After the usual response, "No, I better not," even while I was thinking Yes! Yes! Yes! Just pry me into this thing and "Where exactly is the parachute release on this thing." A burnout for traction, and down the strip I went.

As before, I took it easy on the first run, then let her rip on the second, hitting 169.64 mph in 7.856 seconds. Not exactly "Big Daddy" Don Garlits or Kenny Bernstein, the first to break the dragster 300-miles-per-hour speed record in 1992, but not bad for a novice who had just stained his underwear when struggling to pull the parachute release.

The engine had 2,000 horsepower. A little more than my Chev 8-cylinder Impala, but pretty mild by today's style dragsters with top fueler nitrogen dragsters having 6,000 horsepower, and some as much as 10,000 horsepower. Today's top fuelers can reach 100 mph in 8/10 of a second, topping out at 386 mph in 3.8 seconds on a drag strip that's only 1,000 feet long, instead of the traditional quarter mile. Nonetheless certainly another "e" ticket ride.

BUCKS FOR PALLETS

Another one of my clients was a closely held company that made and refurbished pallets in Fontana right alongside the I-10 Freeway. It was a smaller company, but exceptionally profitable and was my first $500,000 deal for Wells Fargo mentioned earlier. When I met with them, on a Friday morning, I discovered that the company was a wonderful family-run operation and very profitable. They were unhappy with their current bank and had three written offers sitting in front of them from banks that wanted their business. They were ready to make their choice that same afternoon. I was able to convince them to give me a chance to compete and would come back by Monday afternoon with a better deal. They agreed to delay their decision. I collected five years' worth of financial statements, quickly reviewed them. The rest of that afternoon and on Saturday I spread their statements and came up with a significantly better cost of funds, plus other services they weren't currently getting. My RVP agreed and prepared the documents. At noon on Monday, as promised, I showed up with a written proposal. After reading it and asking questions for clarification, they said, "You've got a deal." The following day, we wrote a check for $500,000 to cash out their current bank and gave them an unsecured credit line for the same amount with a much better cost of funds.

The family quickly became fast friends inviting me to use their second home at Big Bear Lake anytime.

One of their great hobbies was deep-sea sports fishing. Every year they provided a four-day deep sea fishing trip into southern Mexico angling for Yellow Tail for all their employees and their banker. The boat was chartered out of Newport Beach and included staterooms and bunks with three full meals a day. I attended every year --- even after I learned that greasy eggs and bacon for breakfast doesn't mix well with rough seas. I had never before had a problem with sea sickness but on one particular trip I was feeding the fish last night's dinner. Still, we always had a great time and got to know many of the employees, which were like family to the company owners. And I would tell my former business professors, all the employees had been there for 30 years and had been well taken care of with ESOP choices.

DONUTS TO DOLLARS

I was basically a middleman salesman for Wells. My job was to convince potential clients how impressive our concept was, collect and analyzing their financial data to see if they were bankable, then sell our regional vice-president on the idea it was a good deal to offer the potential customer a multimillion-dollar line of credit.

On one such call I met another fellow of remarkable integrity who was not able to move forward because of his past history. Bill had built a small chain of twelve Mexican upscale dinner restaurants which he franchised. To get into the next restaurant he planned to build, he asked an investor for $100,000 up front to get the project started. When the building was finished, he would pay for the kitchen equipment and lease the building and equipment to the new franchise owner. However, the existing franchisee's organized among themselves and conspired against him, deciding they were going to take over and refused to pay what they owed him on the remaining property and equipment. He was forced to declare bankruptcy, losing the company, his home, as well as all the money from those who had given him upfront good faith money for future slots in the franchise.

Like any good entrepreneur, he bounced back with another plan. He borrowed $5,000 from a friend. He used the money to start a donut shop at a crucial intersection near a freeway leading into Los Angeles to catch the morning rush hour traffic. He was in his shop at 3:00 a.m. every morning, making fresh donuts, rolls, and coffee to catch those jammed in rush hour traffic. He was still there making fresh donuts for those caught in the evening rush hour. In my opinion, they were the best donuts you could buy anywhere.

The new venture was phonemically successful. Three years later he had 35 locations in Southern California. By now, Bill realized he could make more money by placing his donut shops on the corner of strategic intersections and building "L" shaped strip malls to go with them, and leasing to a major anchor tenant, such as a chain supermarket or drugstore. Soon, he was making more money in real estate than his already profitable donut shops.

He was now looking for a $10 million line of credit to expand his business. He told me his story in our first meeting and mentioning that when his donut shop chain had become successful the first thing he did was go back to all the investors who had lost money in the Mexican restaurant franchises repaying their losses, using a higher interest rate that was called for in the original contract. In cases where some of the investors had died, he hired a private detective to locate their children and paid them back all the losses suffered by their parents.

I knew that every other bank in town had already turned him down because of his bankruptcy records. I also knew this would be a battle for me with the bank, but Bill's story made me determined to do my best for him. I called him once a week to give him the latest news – good or bad – and to tell him not to give up, as I was still in his corner. After several weeks, it looked pretty hopeless. I decided to go over the head of my regional vice-president in trying to get the job done.

I called Carl Reichardt, the president and CEO of Wells Fargo, explaining Bill's story, especially the part about going back to all those who had lost money in his original venture, and even hiring a private investigator to *"make right"* the debt. I told him that Bill seemed to me to be exactly the type of customer of integrity the bank would want. He agreed and called my regional vice-president and told him to make the deal work. Two weeks later I called Bill and told him we would have the paperwork ready for his signature in two days for a $10 million line of credit. He was elated.

But for me the victory marked the beginning of the end of my eight years at Wells, but not because I had gone over the head of my regional vice-president, who was also good friend.

EXCUSE ME! WHAT DO YOU MEAN I'M FIRED?

The donut deal actually closed on December 27th just four days before the end of the year. In January of every year the sales manager would ask each salesman to project how much business he would bring in during the coming year. For this particular year, I had projected $12 million in new business, and up to December 27th I had brought in only $3 million. This made the sales manager nervous. Actually, furious was more like it. He had promised his superiors in San Francisco a certain number, which all the salesmen would produce as an aggregate total. Without my donut deal that number would not materialize, especially since the other salesmen were also behind their projections. With my donut deal, our division would be over the projected total. I had saved the day. Nevertheless, a few days into the start of the new year, the sales manager told me I was fired. My regional vice-president told him he was making a gigantic mistake, but he didn't listen.

I was in shock but decided not to contest it because there were other ominous dark clouds forming on the horizon. The clouds came in the form of the executive vice-presidents within the bank's home office in San Francisco. It turned out that salesmen in our Commercial Banking division were making more money than they were, and it made them green with envy. For the last several years of my tenure they had been complaining to everyone above them that this was not fair. Richardt told them it should not make any difference since the salesmen were bringing in tens of millions in profit to the bank and therefore had earned their large commission checks. Nonetheless, the EVP' laments eventually prompted changes in the compensation program. We could no longer expect a new company car every other year, which was not a big deal to any of us. Then the commission structure was slowly whittled down to the point where it no longer made sense to go after the larger deals -- which always took longer to close than smaller ones. The amount of compensation no longer made it worth the effort it took to land the bigger deals, my favorite area. As far as I was concerned, after eight years it was time to move on to something else.

The regional vice-president had given wise counsel to my sales manager, who was fired six months after I was terminated. He wound up at Crocker Bank and tried to start the same program there. Six months later, Wells bought Crocker and he was out of a job.

Psalm 31:15 (NKJV) describes it very well for me, *"My times are in Your hand; Deliver me from the hand of my enemies, and from those who persecute me."* And II Chronicles 20:15b, NKJV *"...Be not afraid nor dismayed...for the battle is not yours, but God's.*

I will always grateful and thanking God for very fulfilling life chapters with Wells Fargo as well as the many lasting friendships made there, many of which have been retained through the years.

15

THE NIGHTMARE YEARS

In 1967, two years after we were married, Stel and I decided (okay, I decided) to buy our first new car. I preferred a 1967 Chevelle Malibu SS with a 396-cubic inch engine, but the price was more than I was willing to pay. Today that same car in mint condition would be worth twenty times the original amount. Still, there was no way I could spend that much money, no matter how much I loved cars. Being the son of a mechanic, who never thought buying a new car was a good idea, I struggled with the decision. After all, Dad only payed $6,000 for his first home. In the end, my practical side kicked in, (well a little bit), and we decided on a new 1967 Pontiac Le Mans, purchased at a Santa Monica dealership.

Fifteen years later, and thoroughly into my Wells Fargo career, we started investing commissions in limited partnerships. We had an unsecured line of credit for $500,000, (from another bank, with additional unsecured lines totaling another $500,000, and I was writing checks for $100,000 without batting an eyelash. We had joined an investment group consisting of 1,600 investors, the majority of whom were Christians with a collective purchasing power of $165 million in cash liquidity aside from other non-liquid assets. The general partner was involved in all the partnerships, putting together deals consisting of 35 people each from within the 1,600 people in the larger group. He had financial planners, an office staff who were also investors in many of the deals. All of that was fine, or so we thought. There was never any hint of impropriety on the part of the general partner, and we checked him out thoroughly for several months before joining the group.

However, we learned too late, when there are that many investors involved, it only takes one unsatisfied investor who thinks he's been cheated to take it all apart. One boll-weevil can ruin the entire cotton crop and our crop was about to be obliterated.

There was immediate cash available to take advantage of deals that often came up quickly. For example, we heard about 100 acres of raw land that was for sale in the Temecula area, a section of Southern California that was in the path of phenomenal growth. Raw land can be a very risky investment unless the investor/owner is also a developer or working with someone who can make the TI improvements like electricity, water, sewers, streets, and curbs. As a group, we never got into land development.

But, in this case, before purchasing the land, we learned via the networking grapevine that a major oil company was also planning to buy the property, so it became a quick turnover for us since there was already a hot buyer. We bought it before anyone else for $10 million, with a double escrow, selling it 90 days later for $20 million.

Shortly after that venture, we bought a 10-story office building in Whittier after the developer went bankrupt. The building was a finished shell but as yet with no tenant improvements. We bought the building at an enormous discount and immediately started securing 10-year leases signed by doctors, dentists, attorneys, etc., and building out the tenant improvements to their needs. A year later with a 95% occupancy rate with signed leases for 10 years we sold the building for a handsome profit.

One of the more entertaining and fun investments was the purchase of a 172 – foot yacht, the sister ship to John Wayne's *"Wild Goose."* Like John Wayne's boat, it was originally a mine sweeper in World War II before being converted into a pleasure yacht. It was in excellent shape and had five staterooms plus quarters for a crew of ten. Before buying it, we checked with the Coast Guard and learned it wasn't a sea-worthy vessel and therefore couldn't be taken beyond the breakwater of Newport Harbor. This fit our purpose quite well. We paid $500,000 for it and rented it out for corporate dinner parties, holidays, weddings, and weekends which provided our investment return the first year. We sold the yacht a couple of years later for $3 million.

DISASTER STRIKES.

Not every deal was successful. There was one real estate deal that caused some investors to lose money, but not because of any wrongdoing on anyone's part in the partnership. The general partner wanted to make up some of their losses and saw an opportunity on another troubled real estate deal. He had an opportunity to make some cash on the purchase and immediate sale of an apartment complex by a developer in bankruptcy. Like the ten-story office building, we could purchase the property for 30 cents on the dollar and immediately sell to a well-known developer. The opportunity would first be offered to all those who were losing money in the former deal. Sounds like a Ponzi scheme, but it wasn't. I was helping out and had just come from the San Fernando Valley with a signed agreement for the deal.

When I walked into the general partner's office, I was greeted by several California DOJ agents, all armed with handguns and wearing badges on their belts. All the employees were locked in the board room. No one was allowed to leave until they sorted out "who was who" and their position in the company. I was asked if I was an employee or investor. Even though I was not an employee, they still searched my briefcase, and detained me for two hours before I was allowed to leave. Thus, began a five-year nightmare, but one that ultimately gave us greater trust in the Lord and taught us lessons we never could have realized in college at three times the tuition cost.

It all started when a disgruntled investor had contacted the California DOJ because he felt there was fraud involved on the part of the general partner. All the partnership's assets were frozen immediately and thus everyone's invested dollars. This went on for two years to supposedly protect us as investors. The "authorities" tried to prove fraud while sorting out the many partnerships representing $165 million. When they couldn't, they started selling everyone's assets for fifty cents on the dollar to pay for their investigation because after two years the state would no longer provide the funds for a small army of investigators to proceed. They never found any fraud. When they figured they were finally finished with their investigation, and selling our assets to feed their investigation, the investment company had no choice but to declare bankruptcy. The bankruptcy court started selling what was left of our investments for 20 cents on the dollar. All the investors, in hundreds of partnerships, were left to defend themselves in their own various partnerships. In our case, Stella and I were forced to employ six different law firms in the six different partnerships we were involved in at the time. By then our personal loss exceeded $500,000. Since I was fired by my sales manager at Wells Fargo and thus had no income, we were paying $10,000 dollars month in attorney fees with money borrowed from our bank credit lines, plus the mortgage payment on our own house and normal monthly expenses like buying groceries, the light bills, water, etc.. The debt hole was getting deeper every month. It was like trying to repair a sinking ship in the middle of a typhoon.

ALL THIS AND LIBERACE TOO

One of the investments we were trying to salvage had to do with the Liberace home in the Hollywood Hills. A famous house that had the grand-piano shaped pool in the back yard. Stel and I were the major partners in the investment. Liberace had died some years earlier and donated the house to the Los Angeles Civic Opera who wanted to liquidate it. A fellow wanted to buy it but couldn't qualify for a bank loan. He heard about our investment group and contacted us for a hard money loan. We obtained a bank appraisal which came back with a value of $3 million. There were no liens or debt on the property, and we felt safe securing our position with a 1st Trust Deed and loaned him the $500,000 to purchase it from the opera company. Stel and I had the largest portion at 20% of the loan amount into the investment.

Three months later the borrower had not made a single payment. We filed loan default documents, recorded with the city and county and sued in civil court to claim the property.

As it turned out, the borrower – I'll call him Sam -- never intended to pay us. We pursued him in court for three years, all the time incurring additional attorney's fees. He had an unscrupulous attorney who worked with him as a partner. When we filed our civil action, his partner/attorney would file delaying motion to drag the whole process on. This went on for those three years. We learned that Sam had taken ownership of six other homes in high-value areas of the Hollywood Hills and other expensive areas, -- using the same tactic with other private investment groups. Eventually, the investors would be overburden with attorney fees leaving the investors no choice but to walk away declaring a loss. Once a court action was dropped, Sam acquired the property by default, sometimes selling it for the appreciated value and splitting profits with his corrupt attorney. In other situations, they retained these mansions for rental properties giving him and his attorney millions in assets on their financial statements. We were determined to fight on no matter the cost.

However, each time we thought we were close to winning our court case, Sam and his attorney would do something that was totally illegal by throwing half the house ownership into a dummy corporation out of state. We spent months running down their delaying tactics. Finally, four and a half years into the case, our adversary did something none of us expected.

Congress had just passed an addendum to the Rico Act designed to seize Mafia loan sharking. While the law had the right intent, it was poorly written. Ten percent interest rate was now illegal for private lenders, even though banks do it all the time with credit cards. The law was so loosely written that it snagged many private lenders in the net meant for the Mafia. Such was the case with our loan.

The day after Congress passed the law, all of us in the investment partnership were served with a lawsuit. Sam was suing us for $20 million dollars under this new law grandfathered into the Rico Act. We were now fighting on two fronts, civil court for our original loan, and federal court to defend ourselves against this new federal law. Our attorney informed us this would cost us $100,000 just preparing for a trial in the federal court. All of us in the partnership were now long past frustration. Anger was now the prevalent emotion, quickly replaced with fear, and soon thereafter depression that our investment would lead to a total loss and then some.

As defendants we had 30 days to respond to the lawsuit. The fear was daunting. While discussing the situation at home one evening, it finally dawned on me. Everything **WE** had built? In all of these ventures, had we really consulted with the Lord – on any of these matters -- or were we just too busy building personal wealth?

That's when it hit me. A spiritual light bulb switched on. A lightning bolt of revelation. This whole five-year ordeal with this fellow was not about the money or personal accumulation of wealth. The lesson to be learned was forgiveness. This whole situation was really about praying for our enemy and his salvation. Does God really mean it when he tells us to pray for our enemies and those who persecute us? Yes, He does.

There was only one problem. I was still so furiously angry. How could I sincerely pray for an enemy's salvation while harboring un-forgiveness, bitterness, resentment so deep it had become hatred? A verse came to mind: *"With the tongue we praise our Lord and Father, and with it we curse men, who have been made in God's likeness. Out of the same mouth come praise and cursing. My brothers, this should not be. Can both fresh water and saltwater flow from the same spring? My brothers, can a fig tree bear olives, or a grapevine bear figs? Neither can a salt spring produce fresh water.* James 3:9-12 (NIV2011)

I had to forgive my adversary. Truly forgive from the heart. Still, I just couldn't bring myself to actually say the words if I didn't mean them in my heart. We prayed. I tried several times to say, "I forgive Sam," but couldn't get the words past the angry lump in my throat. I asked the Lord for help in getting those words out. And He did.

I finally said, "*I forgive Sam.*" The anger left immediately, flooding out of me like water bursting from a collapsed dam. A gigantic weight immediately lifted my shoulders. The weight of bitterness, anger and unforgiveness was gone. I felt free. Free to pray sincerely from the heart. Another scripture verse came to mind as Stel and I continued to pray:

> *"Verily I say unto you, Whatsoever ye shall bind on earth shall be bound in heaven: and whatsoever ye shall loose on earth shall be loosed in heaven. Again, I say unto you, that if two of you shall agree on earth as touching anything that they shall ask, it shall be done for them of my Father which is in heaven."* *Matthew 18:18-19 (KJV)*

Stel and I had agreed in prayer, and in so doing we had loosed ourselves from the chains which prevented the Lord from working on our behalf ...and also Sam's. In Mark 11:25 (NIV) Jesus tells us, *"And when you stand praying, if you hold anything against anyone, forgive him, so that your Father in heaven may forgive you your sins."* We had also loosed our adversary for the Lord to work in his life.

What Sam didn't know, and neither did we, was that our attorney was a former FBI agent, and consequently had access to several avenues of information that other lawyers didn't. None of what he learned could be used against our opponent in our current civil action or in federal court. But the information gained did provide our attorney with the opportunity to drop several hints as to what was known about their current and past illegal activities. The old adage, "Information is power" is certainly true.

When we told our attorney about our epiphany to forgive and pray for Sam, he was horrified. He thought it meant we were opting out of the civil action and capitulating on everything. We explained it was not our intention to bail out of the lawsuit, but we had turned the spiritual corner and now realized there was something much more important than the money and all that had taken place up to this point.

Our attorney was stunned. After all, not many attorneys are used to praying for their courtroom opponents. He was glad to hear we were staying in the fight as we were the financial anchor investor in the case. Since our attorney was Jewish, he was astonished at our epiphanic response. Perhaps he was more familiar with an eye for an eye. But he would soon see the power of forgiveness. He called us exactly a week later to tell us that Sam had called and said he wanted to settle both the civil action against him, and he would drop his federal lawsuit against us. Our attorney agreed, but stipulated that he must pay, not only the principle and interest on the original loan, as stated in the loan documents, but also all our attorney fees for the past five years, as well as pay all the back property taxes that had accrued since he'd been living in the house for the past five years. Ten days later we received a check. I continued to pray for Sam for the next year until sensing a relief in my spirit.

I had actually met Sam personally early on in our dispute. He was an amiable fellow and I liked him as a person, but also knew I could never trust him.

As Dr. Carlton Booth, a professor at Fuller Seminary would say to me some years later, "Bob, sometimes God will allow a Goliath in our life to bring out the David in us."

The whole five-year ordeal not only would reveal many life lessons but would more than prepare us for a much bigger assignment the Lord had for me. One that would take me around the globe more than once.

16

BLACKLISTED

By the time I received the left foot of fellowship from Wells Fargo I was pretty well known in the banking industry, so finding a job took all of one day. I accepted a position as a regional VP of a Finance company (name to remain anonymous) based in Oregon that covered several western states in its business dealings. I was only there for nine months. My geographic area of responsibility was pretty much the same as it had been with Wells.

A finance company does the same thing as a bank, except it lends money to companies that are not yet bankable for any number of reasons. They lend to newly established companies, or ones that have fallen unto hard times usually due to bad management or some catastrophic event. They are sort of in the middle of the money lending business. The next level down are hard money lenders from the private sector lending market where the cost of funds is considerably higher. The next level below that is where the real sharks live.

In my first week of orientation, I asked if we were allowed to refer clients who didn't meet our lending criteria to other lenders who were below us and willing to take higher risk for a higher price loan. "Yes" was the reply and I was given a list of these other approved finance companies. With that I hit the streets and started putting out "feelers" in my banking network. It didn't take long before I had several troubled companies to follow up on and was able to book some good solid business loans.

One such company was a major tennis shoe manufacturer, the ones that made the "black and white high tops" many of us guys wore as kids at one time or another. One day I was asked by the executive vice president (my boss) at this Finance company, how I could find so many deals for them. My simple reply was, "Networking."

The tennis shoe manufacturer had a fascinating story to tell. They had suffered a tragic fire in their manufacturing facility that totally destroyed their building and all their equipment. The company was owned by two brothers. One was an out-and-out optimist, while the other was more of a pessimist. They took me to an abandoned factory they had located they wanted to purchase in starting over. They needed to borrow the money to purchase it and install new equipment. The building was a mess, with all the upper factory windows broken out, very dusty and dirty with holes in the roof and totally empty. But it was much larger than their original burnt and totally destroyed building.

The optimistic brother was excited and could see the possibilities for growth and getting the company back on its feet. The less optimistic brother was just the opposite -- discouraged, depressed, and simply could not see the vision for the future. It reminded me of a psychology study I had read about in college about the two little brothers, one of whom was a pessimist, the other an optimist. The pessimistic boy was put in a room with toys of every conceivable type and told he could play with anything he wanted all day long. Instead, he sat depressed for the entire day and said, "It doesn't matter because you won't let me keep any of them." Conversely, the optimistic boy was placed in a room full of horse manure. His response was, "Wow! With all this manure there has to be a pony in here somewhere" and began digging to hopefully find the pony.

The company had an excellent and profitable record prior to the fire, so I collected several years of audited financial statements as well as the police and fire reports which cleared the company of wrongdoing in the disaster for insurance purposes. All of this wasn't good enough for the president of the Finance Company, who put the kibosh on the deal. So, I recommended the shoe company to another finance company from their list of approved lenders, as I had been told we could do once we had turned down a deal. The president of the Finance Company, who I had met only once the day I was hired, ordered that I be fired for referring the shoe company to another lender. Naturally, I was stunned for getting in trouble for doing something I had been told was normal procedure. The only thing I could figure out was that the president was under pressure for a several-million-dollar loan he had pushed for in Hawaii that had gone bad. My guess was he originally looking for an excuse to make trips to Hawaii on the companies' dime. So, for the second time in less than a year, I was out of work.

The next day, I started calling other banks and finance companies hoping to once again cash in on my good reputation. For the next week, everyone I talked with, informed me that they were told I was a cheat and had taken business away from my former employer and had profited from it by receiving kickbacks under the table.

Again, I was stunned. Kickbacks? You must be joking. It was a complete fabrication and my immediate superior, the executive vice-president, knew it was too, but had to follow the president's demands. The only way this vicious rumor could have been spread so quickly was that the president of the Finance Company was responsible for the character assassination, although I had no idea why, and still don't. A few months later, I ran into the Executive Vice President, who had originally hired me, and he too had left the company, feeling the president had lost his marbles. In the end, the president should have done the shoe company deal. They received financing from the other finance company I had recommended and are still in business today, stronger financially than ever and are once again bankable.

It was a difficult time, but I made up my mind that I was not going to let it get me down. There was no need to be concerned or depressed about what people were saying about me because I understood that God is my defender. There are several stories in Scripture that give us this assurance. The one that sticks out in my mind concerns Miriam, the Prophetess, sister to Aaron. Miriam began to speak against Moses because of his Cushite wife. God came down in a cloud and reprimanded Miriam for speaking against His anointed one, Moses, and when the cloud lifted, Miriam's skin was white with leprosy. Moses pleaded on her behalf, but the Lord replied to Moses, *"If her father had spit in her face, would she not have been in disgrace for seven days? Confine her outside the camp for seven days; after that she can be brought back."* (Numbers 12:14 NIV) Why was God so angry with Miriam? She hadn't lied, or killed anyone, she didn't commit adultery; but she did speak against the reputation of one of God's children, namely Moses.

God takes it seriously when someone tries to discredit or belittle one of His children. He sees what's happening and doesn't sit idly by. People can't keep you from your destiny if you're honoring God. Leave the matter in His hands. In Psalms 105:15, (NIV) God clearly states, *"Do not touch my anointed ones..."* As Christians, we are God's anointed. David clearly understood not touching God's anointed when he was hiding from Saul in the caves and had the opportunity to take Saul's life. God hears every negative word spoken against you and is aware of anyone who has ever tried to hold you back. We must never forget that God is preparing that table for us right now in the presence of our enemies. We also have to remember; some people are never going to like you no matter what you do in trying to win them over. In fact, it could happen that some may have been sent to dislike you.

Judas was sent to betray Jesus. It's interesting to note, Judas wasn't in the upper room when Jesus breathed the Holy Spirit on the other eleven disciples. He was however in the room at the Last Supper when Jesus told Judas to go do what he had to do. Judas didn't have the Holy Spirit and consequently betrayed Jesus. However, Peter also betrayed Jesus just hours later. The difference was that Jesus knew both their hearts. Jesus knew Peter's true heart, aside from the fear that gripped him at Jesus trial, and that was to feed His Sheep. Judas was uncommitted to that effort not having the Holy Spirit and conceded when offered money by the Pharisees to betray Jesus. Another example: if Saul didn't have his prideful dislike of David, David may never have taken the throne. Saul and David were both chosen but for quite different ends. Then there was Pharaoh, King of Egypt and Moses who was chosen by God to lead Israel out of captivity. Pharaoh chose to chase after the Israelites to recapture them. He and his army were destroyed in the parting of the Red Sea. He was chosen by God to drown in that endeavor, and in his finale glorified God. Pharaoh had a choice, actually several choices when doing spiritual battle with Moses. Everyone is not supposed to like you. God is your defender. You don't have to get even. Revenge is not an option for Christians. Romans 12:19-21 (NIV), clearly states, *"Do not take revenge, my friends, but leave room for God's wrath, for it is written: It is mine to avenge; I will repay," says the Lord. On the contrary: "If your enemy is hungry, feed him; if he is thirsty, give him something to drink. In doing this, you will heap burning coals on his head." Do not be overcome by evil but overcome evil with good.*

As the Lord did with Moses, God will vindicate you. We just need to run our race with integrity, joy, and let the negative bounce off us like water off a duck's back. The Lord is capable of defending your reputation. When Jesus was here in the flesh, most of the people who came against him were religious people -- the Pharisees. But Jesus didn't try to change their minds. He didn't spend hours arguing doctrine. He ignored the critics and just ran His race. Jesus was criticized for healing on the Sabbath. He did the right thing, but the Pharisees said he did the wrong thing. No matter what you do, some will never be "for you."

To reach our highest potential we have to accept being controversial. Jesus was the most controversial person who ever lived. Two thousand years later people are still arguing about Him. He had more critics than anyone and He never wasted time trying to convince them who He was, never wasted time trying to payback people for making Him look bad. He never had time for all the pettiness. It should be the same for us. It's a distraction standing between you and your destiny. Use that energy to move toward your God-given dreams. We don't have enough energy to fulfill our purpose, and at the same time defend ourselves against our critics. Whatever emotional energy we're using to answer critics is better spent on fulfilling your God given purpose.

Nehemiah provides another excellent example who understood and used this principle well. He was on a hill rebuilding the Jerusalem wall and gates. Below the hill was Sanballat the Horonite and Tobiah the Ammonite official who mocked and ridiculed Nehemiah and his men accusing them of rebelling against King Artaxerxes, who had actually given Nehemiah permission, even supplying all the materials he would need from his personal forest. *"What is this you are doing?"* they asked. *"Are you rebelling against the king?"* (Nehemiah 2:19b NIV2011). They were trying to deceive and distract Nehemiah to keep him from his purpose.

We can all have people like Sanballat and Tobias in our lives, those that come against us to distract us and get under our skin. I certainly have. It's bait trying to lure us off course. The fight is not trying to straighten them out but to keep our focus and not getting entangled in things that are insignificant. Nehemiah could have come down the hill to argue with Sanballat and Tobias but repairing the wall and gates would not have moved further along. We must ask ourselves, if we argue trying to convince our critics, will we be any further along toward our destiny, our purpose, or just feeding our ego and making our flesh feel good. But we have a defender. *"Be still and know that I am God."* (Psalm 46:10a KJV). Let God fight those battles. God will take care of your critics.

Nehemiah was on the top of the hill. His critics were at the bottom of the hill. Anytime we start answering our critics, we're going downhill to defend ourselves. We're leaving the high place and descend to their level. Like Jesus, do not answer your critics. Stay on the mountain to keep focused on what's really important.

FROM BAD TO WORSE

Speaking of downhill, within a week of finding out that I had been blacklisted, everything started going further downhill. Our investments were failing when the state continued looking into alleged fraud on the part of the general partner. Stel and I were tired, discouraged and decided to take a trip up to northern California where we could breathe deeply the fresh air and enjoy the peaceful calm of the Redwood forest.

At the time, I was Chairman of the Advisory Board of our church. When we called home one afternoon to check messages, a friend also serving on the board, asked us to come back quickly because everything at the church was falling apart. It had become known that our pastor had become involved with woman in the congregation.

We left for home immediately. By the time we got there it was discovered that more than one woman was involved and the whole mess had been going on for a couple years. As a result, the church was splitting. Half the congregation didn't believe the allegations. The other half did. Many of them blamed me because I was close to the pastor. They felt I surely must have known what was going on and should have said something. It was all news to me. Many of our church friends deserted us.

Within a 30-day period, our investments where frozen with lawsuits flying around like vultures over a dead carcass. Our church was in turmoil. Friends not only left us but blamed us for the whole church split. At the same time, I was being blacklisted in the banking industry, out of work, and powerless to find a job in banking. Everything in our lives was falling apart and there was little we could do to stop the slide into this deep crater. It was extremely discouraging to think that everything we had worked so hard to build was sifting through our hands like water. We found ourselves floundering in a marshland of uncertainty.

IN NEED OF A MIRACLES

When in the basement of despair you are more open to hear the Lord's voice and His promises. In this desperate situation, there were three significant miracles and one "confirming presence" that guided me up from darkness and into the light.

The first miracle came while I was making a simple repair in the courtyard leading to our front door. While doing some trimming, I accidently stepped on a sprinkler shrub head covered by asparagus ferns. "No big deal," I thought, "I'll replace it from my parts inventory." That's when I discovered it wasn't so simple. The threaded sprinkler head had snapped off inside an elbow that was close to the concrete walkway. If I wasn't careful, a portion of the sidewalk might have to be jack hammered out just to fix a 25-cent part. That would be expensive, especially for someone who had no income at the time. Without the repair water would be shooting 10 feet in the air every time the computer controller came on. This was now an urgent problem. I had no idea how to get the broken threaded part out of the elbow. We had a dinner date that evening at a friend's home and I was running out of time. The sprinkler would come on while we were gone. Panic quickly overtook me.

Then a thought entered my mind: "*You have a couple of dowel sticks in the garage.*" I searched the garage and found one. It was too big. "*But you have a smaller one.*" In searching further, I found a dowel stick with a smaller diameter, but it was still too big to fit in the broken section of the elbow. "*You can use your pocket-knife and whittle one end down a bit.*" I did until I heard, "*That's enough.*" Then, as I walked out of the garage, I heard, "*Don't, forget the hammer. Insert the dowel stick into the broken elbow, tap lightly three times, and unscrew the broken part.*" It worked like a charm.

After putting in a new thread connector and shrub head I went back into the garage. Then it hit me. Who was giving me those specific instructions? I must have been hearing the Lord.

No, that couldn't be. Why would God, the creator of the universe be talking to me about how to fix a 25-cent part? "Was that you Lord?" I asked in my heart. I distinctly heard a quiet voice inside reply, *"Yes, it is I."* Then the voice said, *"Bob, if you will follow my instructions to the letter, every jot and tittle, like you just did with the broken sprinkler, I will restore to you the years that the Locust hath eaten, the cankerworm, and the caterpillar..."*

I recognized that as coming from Joel 2:25a (KJV). Tears began to stream down my face. I was convinced it was the Lord speaking and was humbled to know that God, Jehovah Jireh, Elohim, El Shaddai, Yahweh-Nissi, the God of the Universe, actually cared enough about me that He was willing to help me with this small sprinkler problem. From that point on my personal relationship with the Lord took a major leap into a deeper understanding of the height, width, and depth of His love.

THE SECOND MIRACLE

The second miracle followed shortly thereafter. Now that God had my attention, I realized where my mistakes occurred. I had forgotten Him in my quest to succeed. Over the years I had drifted into pride, forgetting to give Him the glory for successes -- something I had learned well in Bible Class when I was 12 years old, and now remembering it was not all about me. In reality, I had not built anything. God did. He deserved all the glory.

When we get to heaven, we will throw all our earthly crowns at his feet for only *"Thou art worthy, or Lord, to receive glory honor and power: for you created all things, and for thy pleasure they are and were created."* (Revelations 4:11 (KJV).

After re-discovering this self-buried treasure of my youth, I fell on the floor in repentance, crying, with my face literally in the carpet for several hours. I was overwhelmed by the thought of my selfishness in disparaging Christ's work on the Cross. Where was God in all my self-effort? At the time, all of these setbacks felt like the worst month of my life. In actuality, it was the best month of my life. My spiritual life was being rebooted. Everything that had happened brought me closer to the Lord than I had ever been. "A man's heart plans his way, But the LORD directs his steps. Proverbs 16:9 (NKJV) Thus began my exodus from the wide road, back to the straight and narrow.

"My son, do not despise the LORD's discipline, and do not resent his rebuke, because the LORD disciplines those he loves, as a father the son he delights in. Proverbs 3:11-12 (NIV2011)

"And have you completely forgotten this word of encouragement that addresses you as a father addresses his son? It says, "My son, do not make light of the Lord's discipline and do not lose heart when he rebukes you, because the Lord disciplines the one he loves, and he chastens everyone he accepts as his son, Hebrews 12:5-6 (NIV2011)

There can be no richer blessing than understanding and truly comprehending the height, breadth, and depth of Jesus's love for us. Have I totally arrived at this understanding? I wonder if that's possible this side of heaven. Probably not. But I'm much further along and still learning the immenseness of His Grace.

THIRD MIRACLE

The third miracle began one day just after Stel left for work. She had taken a job at World Vision so we could at least buy food, make the house payment, and stop tapping into our credit lines for at least those items. This day was also a miracle for Stella since she had been on medical leave for several years, recovering from Epstein Bar Virus. After she left the house that morning around 7 a.m., I sat at the kitchen counter on a backless wooden stool with my Bible, pen and a fresh yellow notebook pad, determined to hear and record what the Lord had for me. I decided not to move from that uncomfortable wooden stool until I heard from Him, *"I love those who love me, and those who seek me find me."* Proverbs 8:17 (NIV2011): When we seek, we find. After what seemed like only a couple of hours later, Stel walked in the back door. When I asked her why she was back so soon, she looked at me as if I had lost my marbles.

"What are you talking about? It's 6 p.m."

I glanced at the kitchen clock and saw that it was, indeed, dinner time. Then I looked down at my yellow note pad and saw nearly the entire note pad was filled with writing. The Lord had been revealing his Word to me for the past 11 hours and I hadn't to my knowledge moved from the kitchen counter in all that time. I remember going from scripture to scripture as He connected them together as if sewing a tapestry of knowledge for me. Revelation after revelation, answering questions I had someday hoped to study to find the answers. There were nearly 50 pages of notes as evidence of the value of my alone time with the Lord.

I often wondered why Jesus chose three particular men -- Peter, James, and John -- to go with Him to the Mount of Transfiguration. Was there a special meaning to these particular three men chosen? Yes, I believe so.

John the beloved. At the last supper it was John who rested his head on Jesus shoulder. *"One of them, the disciple whom Jesus loved, was reclining next to him."* John 13:23-24 (NIV2011). John was the only disciple present at the foot of the Cross of Calvary. John was the only one who truly understood how much Jesus loved him. And it was at the cross that Jesus told John to look after his mother. John 19:25-27 (NIV2011) *"When Jesus saw his mother there, and the disciple whom he loved standing nearby, he said to her, 'Woman, here is your son,'and to this disciple he said, 'Here is your mother.'* From that time on, *"this disciple took her into his home."*

John's name means Grace. The New Testament is about God's grace and Love, which is a fulfilling of the Law in the Old Testament.

Peter means the Rock. The Ten Commandments were written on rock, which represents the Law.

James means Replace. The veiled message on the Mount of Transfiguration was GRACE - REPLACES -LAW.

"For sin shall not be your master, because you are not under law, but under grace." (Romans 6:14) Sin is not our master. We are no longer under the law, but under grace. We were held in bondage by the written law." (Romans 7:6) The Law is powerless to overcome sin (Romans 8:3). It could only bring pardon, a state of acceptance with God. The law was only a shadow of the good things to come, not the reality. Jesus did what the law couldn't do. (Hebrews 10:1-4)

Christ is the end of the law (Romans 10:4 (NIV). The law was put in charge to lead us to Christ so that we would be justified by faith. Now that faith has come, we are no longer under the supervision of the law. (Galatians 3:24-25)

So, what was the Purpose of the Law? It was added because of transgressions until the Seed (Jesus) to whom the promise referred had come. Moses was the mediator of the old law. (Galatians 3:19.) Jesus is the mediator of the new covenant. *"For this reason, Christ is the mediator of a new covenant, that those who are called may receive the promised eternal inheritance --now that he has died as a ransom to set them free from the sins committed under the first covenant."* (Hebrews 9:15.) The Law still plays a role, not as a means of salvation, but as a moral and ethical guide, <u>but now obeyed out of love for God and empowered by the Holy Spirit,</u> not human will power. (Rom. 8:4)

Therefore, a fulfillment of Jeremiah 31:33-34, a prophecy of the New Covenant. Fulfilled literally means *fully met.* (Matthew 5:18, NIV2011) *"For truly I tell you, until heaven and earth disappear, not the smallest letter, not the least stroke of a pen, will by any means disappear from the Law until everything is accomplished."* It was all accomplished when Jesus said on the cross, *"It is finished."*

THE ROSE OF SHARON

The gracious peaceful confirmation of God's presence during this tumultuous time of our lives came one night after we had gone to bed. We still hadn't forgotten the many legal entanglements of the past several years. As Stella and I lay in bed, I suddenly noticed a very slight sweet smell, a smell that quickly intensified. The only way to describe it is that it was like the smell found in the refrigerated section of a large flower shop -- where one can almost taste the many fragrances of all kinds of flowers at once. Imagine that same smell multiplied by 1,000 times and you will begin to imagine what the fragrances we smelled was like wafting across the bedroom as we lay there. I asked Stella if she was awake and if she also smelled the aroma. She did. I mentioned to her that it was surely Jesus. "It reminded me of the Rose of Sharon spoken of in the Song of Solomon, *"I am the rose of Sharon, The lily of the valleys."* (Song of Solomon 2:1-2, NASB77)

Our storm was not totally over, but the following morning we looked up references to the Rose of Sharon and found a verse that would help sustain us in the coming months. *". . . "for the LORD hath comforted his people, and will have mercy upon his afflicted."* (Isaiah 49:13, KJV)

17

STARTING OVER WITH GOD'S HELP AND A SPECIAL FRIEND

Since there seemed to be no other option after being black-listed, I decided to start my own company. I knew the banking industry and decided to become a money broker, helping companies find needed operating capital from other banks or finance companies. Once again, here is where my networking skills came in handy. I applied for and received a Personal Property Brokers (PPB) license from the State of California.

In two-weeks' time, I had more potential business than I could handle. It was encouraging. Exciting! But potential doesn't pay the mortgage or buy groceries. It would take time before any income flowed out of the other end of the pipeline.

Just before starting a brokerage company I first worked a month or so with a friend, Dick Bahruth, who I first met nine years earlier at La Verne Heights Presbyterian church. We both grew up in Arcadia and started carpooling when I was working for Wells Fargo at One Wilshire and he was working in advertising at Ogilvy and Mather. We had similar approaches to business and still do today 45 years later. We have complimentary styles and often bounce ideas off each other. Dick had also started his own company after leaving Ogilvy and Mather, selling ads in the two magazines he represented. He and his wife Diane started in their garage and asked me to help out by making follow-up phone calls. I don't know how much I might have helped but it was fun working together for a couple of months. Shortly thereafter he rented an office on Bonita Avenue which had an extra office he wasn't using. He rented me the space at a reasonable monthly rate. It was at that point I started my own brokerage company, called Cash Flow International. Dick had contacts that helped me design my logo, letterhead, and business cards. I was off and running. Dick also had recently purchased a new car and was kind enough to sell me their used Camaro which I needed since no longer having a company car. Several months later, Dick's business was growing, and he needed to expand to a larger office space. His rental cost went up and I couldn't absorb the added cost for my portion not having yet closed any business. I moved back into my office at home. I shall always be grateful for his supportive friendship in our lives at a much-needed time.

My networking gifts also led to some investment banker and venture capital opportunities. I met a fellow from India, Mr. Nawal, who was starting a new business importing shrimp from Nigeria. His brother was a member of the Indian Parliament, which at the time controlled most of the shrimp in Nigeria enabling him with easy access to shrimp. He needed to have Letters of Credit (LC's) to have them shipped to Ports in Houston and New York. I was able to get him the LC's and sought to arrange to own a small percentage portion of every shipment coming into the United States. Suddenly, I was in the shrimp business. I did the same with other companies, often finding the venture capital for a fee, but also seeking reasonable equity position. Maybe I was the original Shark Tank -- actually more of a small bass tank. I have zero tolerance for greed. I had become sensitized to greed and backed away if I suspected it was the motivation behind any project.

FROM SHRIMP TO 747 CARGO PLANES

Mr. Nawal and I developed a strong friendship. Several months later he called to ask if I had any contacts in the aircraft industry.

His brother, as a member of the Indian Parliament tasked him with finding two short-fuselage 747's cargo planes which the Indian government would use to transport various parliament members on international flights. They would handle the inside luxurious improvements to their own specifications.

I told him I didn't, but did have a friend, Carl, who owned his own plane and was retired from several years of service with the DEA as well as several years with U.S. Customs. Maybe he could tell us where to start looking.

After contacting Carl, he agreed to make some calls for us. The following day he faxed me a list of several 747 short fuselages cargo planes for sale currently owned by Tiger Airlines. The info included all present locations of 747's for sale, the sale price, flight hours and all flight log records including the last engine overhauls. I almost fell out of my chair. My heart began to pound. A tornado of excitement and expectation filled my office. All of a sudden, I was perhaps in the aircraft brokering business. Even though I had known Carl for a couple of years, he once let me fly his Cessna 152 to Concord, California. And no, I didn't have a license. He was with me and let me do some of the piloting, as we were working on another deal together in Northern California. Carl told me later that he had used his contacts with various U.S. government agencies like the National Security Agency (NSA) to do background checks on Mr. Nawal and myself before getting involve in a deal of this size.

The next step was meet and discuss the fees that would be fair for the three of us for brokering the arrangements. The planes were selling for around $70 million each, depending on their age and flight hours. I checked around and found the average brokering fees for such transactions would be around $10 million. I suggested we divide the money into increments of $3 million each for Nawal and myself and $4 million for Carl since he had found the planes and secured all the records on each aircraft. I relayed this to Carl for his approval and sent broker fees agreements to the Indian government via Nawal which were approved, signed, and faxed back. Carl arranged the locations in two different countries for the Indian government to view the planes, kick the tires, and review all the records. The first inspection would take place a week later at Heathrow Airport in London, the second a week later at Amsterdam Schiphol Airport in The Netherlands.

Once that was set, I arranged a trust account with a New York bank to handle the money transfer from India and the three of us as the brokers of record. This was the easiest deal I had ever done, not to mention the fastest $3 million dollars I'd ever made; a piece of cake, a walk in the park. Everything in my office suddenly had taken on a greenish tint. The sights, smells and sounds of crisp freshly minted $100-dollar bills wafted through my office like an air freshener. The adage of "who you know" is true. So is who you don't know. With that kind of money floating around, a feeding frenzy is sure to develop. Greed lurks in money waters, and vicious sharks were about to tear our catch to sheds.

Three days later I received a call from the New York bank stating they needed to clarify the parties involved because there were now 30 other brokers claiming to be a part of the money transfer from India. I said, "No that can't be, there are only three," and restated our names. To this day I don't know how an additional 30 brokers wiggled their way into the picture. But what I do know is sharks can smell blood from miles away. It's the same with money. I can only speculate there was someone in the bank trust department who contacted another broker in return for a piece of the action. The word got out and all the other sharks sauntered up to the *"something for nothing bar"* claiming to be part of the scaffolding of the deal.

Whatever the case, I wasn't going to represent a welfare benefits program for thieves. I suggested to my other two partners that we pull the plug until we could find out where the leak was and select another bank. Everyone agreed. Nawal notified the Indian government via his brother. I don't know if India ever got the 747's, but we certainly never got $10 million in broker fees. The smell of fresh greenbacks in my office was quickly replaced by smelly rotten fish.

The experience did however provide many valuable lessons about circling sharks, greed and how to exclude them from participating. It helps if you create a major diversion, a fake deal, and sneak in under the wire undetected from another direction. California politicians have been doing it for decades.

The deal wasn't meant to be. Another exercise in "surrender and trust. *"The Lord will perfect that which concerneth me..."* (Psalm 138:8a) KJV

18

AN ANGEL NAMED ALEJANDRA

E arly on in our journey in visiting the darkness of our
financial abyss, Stella and I were sitting in church one
Sunday morning near Christmas time. We both smiled
as we saw all the cute little children walking down the aisles in
all their special new-bought Christmas clothes. The little girls
were all dressed up in their charming dresses. They reminded
me of something I had said to Stella some years earlier: "When
we get through this financial tornado, we need to revisit the
idea of adopting a child." I wrote a brief note on the back of the
church bulletin and handed it to Stella. She wrote "AMEN" and
handed it back. I didn't know she had been praying about this
for number of years.

Exactly 24 hours later we received a call from our good friends
Dr. Frank Goodman and his wife Evelyn, who remembered that
we had once talked about opening our home to children. Frank
and Evelyn were already in their late 60's at the time and had
just taken-in a 16-year-old-girl, Monica, whose mother was an
illegal alien. The woman had five daughters and they were living
in a single car garage in Carlsbad, California. Their mother still
loved their father, but he was serving a life sentence in a Tijuana
jail. The mother would occasionally go down to visit him but
on one occasion she didn't have enough money to hire a coyote
to get her back across the border. As a result, she was stranded
in Mexico for more than three months.

Three of the girls were now in their teens, and Monica had been taken in by Dr. Goodman and Evelyn. They were putting her through her last year at Arcadia high school, and her younger sister Alex, 12 years old at the time, was visiting for the weekend. They wanted to find a home for Alex that would be somewhat near them in Arcadia so she could have at least one sister nearby. Frank suggested we come for coffee that same afternoon to meet her with no expectations suggested or mentioned to Alex by the Goodman's or ourselves.

We visited that same afternoon. It was love at first sight. She reminded me of a beautiful flower growing in an empty vacant lot; lonely, afraid, shy, and frightened of what the future might hold. We knew instantly we would be interested in having her live with us. After visiting for a couple of hours we drove back home, arriving just in time to hear the phone ringing as we entered the house. It was Dr. Goodman. He told us he went ahead and asked Alex if she would like to live with us and she said, "Yes."

Wow! Just 24 hours after I wrote that note on the back of the church bulletin, we now had an opportunity to open our home to a child. We knew instantly this was God's will. We had a great peace about the situation, even though, as of yet, we had no income from my new brokerage business and still living on credit lines for essentials and the mortage.

We decided that since it was December and the school semester in Carlsbad ended in late January, it would be a good idea to have her stay in Carlsbad until then. It would also give us time to figure out how we were going to legally get an illegal alien into our home and our local grade school. None of which we had even the slightest inkling how to do.

SITUATION URGENT

Two weeks later Dr. Goodman called and told us Alex was all alone and one of the other sisters was throwing parties with gang bangers in that little garage they called home. That was a horrifying thought that kept us awake that night thinking about what could happen in such an environment. We were still awake when I finally said to Stella, "Let's drive down right now and get her. I feel the Lord will clear the pathway before us because we already know we are in His Will. He will show us how we're going to get an illegal alien legally into our home and into school, and where the income will come from to support her. This would be a huge leap of faith but one we must take."

We left immediately arriving at the quiet, darkened garage in Carlsbad at 3:30 a.m. When we knocked on the door, Alex answered in a frightened shaky voice, "Who is it?"

We asked her if she wanted to come and live with us starting right now.

"Yes!" she squealed as she ran around the tiny garage cramming a paper shopping bag full of everything she owned. We stopped for an early breakfast on the way home. It was nearly 8:00 am by the time we got home and introduced Alex to her own room down the hall. We were all quite tired and slept till 2 p.m.

Alex had originally come across the border when she was six years old, so she already spoke excellent English. There were no problems whatsoever when it came to communication. But as soon as I got out of bed that afternoon, I started worrying about what we had done. We had no plan. But the Lord did. Exactly how God was going to make this work was a mystery. It was nearly Christmas and school would be starting in mid-January. We had to move quickly, and God gave us a plan that same afternoon.

The following day, we drove to downtown Los Angeles and visited the Child Services Foster Care program. We told the social worker we didn't want to be in the Foster Care program because we looked at this as a permanent situation and didn't want Alex moved around from family to family at the whim of someone else in the bureaucracy. We explained that we wanted a legal guardian-ship classification, outside of the Foster Care program which he said was fine. He handed us 25 pages to fill out, including a floor diagram of our house, the room she would have, our financial statements, income, etc. Since it was lunchtime, he suggested we fill out the questionnaire while he went to lunch. We could go over the paperwork together when he got back.

Now I started to get nervous. Bureaucracies greatly annoy me. They're an incongruity in my cognitive system. We still were asset rich but cash poor living off Stella's income from her administrative assistant job at World Vision, and our credit cards to buy groceries and pay the mortgage. I had several lines of unsecured credit, but my brokerage company had not yet yielded any income. Nonetheless, we knew God was in this and He would make a way.

After lunch, the social worker reviewed our 25 pages. He didn't say a word. He didn't ask a single question. I was delighted there were no questions about the "no income" portion, yet worried that he didn't ask. I kept a calm face and tried to look as perfect and holy as possible. He finally looked up at us and at the same time stamped our application, "APPROVED."

On our way home we visited the central school district office in San Dimas to learn how we could get Alex legally into the local junior high. The counselor told us all we needed was a copy of her school records, Tetanus and TB shots, and the paperwork at least started by our attorney that would prove we were pursuing legal guardianship even though the court date would be several months away. We also learned it was a year of amnesty for any illegal alien who wanted to apply.

The following day we met with our family attorney, who unknown to us, had supported himself by working for Child Welfare Services while attending law school. He knew all the ropes, and in two hours had the paperwork completed and a copy ready for us. We took all the paperwork to the school district and found that her school records from Carlsbad had already arrived the following day. Within three days of coming to live with us, Alex was ready to start school! I was sure it would take us months to deal with the bureaucracy of Los Angeles County. I seemed to have forgotten the Lord could move mountains, and the hearts of all those involved – and He surely did.

After getting the green light for her schooling, we went shopping. Clearly, a paper shopping bag with all the clothes she owned was not going to be sufficient. On the other hand, there was that little fact that we had no income, - except for Stella's secretarial job, and still fighting six partnership cases in court trying to salvage whatever we could of our investments. Despite the income obstacle we were not going to let this child go to school looking like a poster child on the back of a milk carton. We were in -- all the way. In fact, I had already begun thinking about how we could move in the direction of a college education for her once we were out of the financial cavern.

Our shopping spree included several new sets of clothes for school, church, several pairs of shoes and various outfits for other school and social occasions. A little more debt was not going to make much difference at this point.

If you had walked into our house on the fifth day after Alex was with us, you would have thought she had been part of our family for years. This was a match made in heaven. Our first Sunday at church she received a lead part in a play for the coming Easter Program. School also went well, and she quickly made friends with several other girls, many of whom came to play at our house. It didn't take long before we had a house full of happy, laughing teeny boppers playing cards and board games. If someone had painted that picture of our lives a few weeks earlier, I would have said they were silly.

Alex was about a year behind in school because of her original language difference having come to the United States from Mexico at age six. Because I was still building my finance company with an office at home, it was easy for me to pick her up every day from school and begin the process of bringing her up to speed in math, history, social studies and English composition. Twice a week we would stop for a small ice cream cone at the local Baskin-Robbins before getting to her homework. In three months, she had gained that lost year and was actually a year ahead of her classmates. I like to think it was because of my excellent teaching ability. In reality it was primarily because she is highly intelligent and just needed someone for a little "one-on-one" tutoring to launch into her true potential.

On the sixth day after her arrival, I was able to close the first deal under my newly established company Cash Flow International picking up a check for my effort, which coincidentally covered a year's worth of our expenses plus a great deal more. Looking back, "one year's worth" was significant since God had another plan unknown to us, but I had to go through the humbling processes with my business associates which eventually led me into missions. Now, we could start climbing out of the ever-deepening hole of debt -- buying groceries with cash instead of adding to our credit card debt, making mortgage payments, and taking care of other basic necessities. It was the Lord's blessing and confirmation that we had stepped out in faith with Alex.

We were always fascinated by how Alex watched us so closely, especially at the dinner table -- probably because she had never seen what an average family looked like at dinner time. She was used to eating on the run and never much at a table large enough to sit a whole family, let alone having a father figure. She was quiet and contemplative, and I could tell right away she was analytical in her thinking process. She worked hard to succeed in school, but we wanted to make sure she had time to have fun as well. We took her on weekly outings, often including her sister Monica. We visited Disneyland, took a summer driving trip through the Mother Lode gold country of central and northern California, flew to Portland, Oregon to visit our close friends Bram and Nellie Pieters. She had never been on an airplane before, so that was a thrilling experience for her. We also made sure she went to a week of Christian summer camp sponsored by our church. There, she made a profession of faith and received the Baptism of the Holy Spirit.

Some years later, she mentioned how much she always appreciated and loved the way the three of us finished each day by lying on her bed and reading the Psalms, Proverbs and New Testament. We would always ask her what she understood and felt about a particular verse or chapter, and most of the time she was absolutely accurate in her understanding. Thank God. I wanted to do everything possible to make sure she was filled with joy. *"Train a child in the way he should go, and when he is old he will not turn from it."* (Proverbs 22:6, NIV)

THE WISDOM OF A CHILD

Even though Alex was still a child, she exhibited the wisdom of an adult. She always thought things through and was very much a positive influence on her peers. If they were participating in any sort of foolish activity, she simply no longer associated with them. I gave her a lot of credit for natural instinct. She was, and is, a delightful addition and blessing in our lives.

After she had been with us for three months, we learned from Dr. Goodman that her mother had finally made it back across the border. Naturally, she would be worried where Alex was, so he called her to assure her that her daughter was in good hands and living with us.

Although we had never met her mother it was important to us that Alex stay in touch with her, so we set up a time to drive down and meet her. It was a difficult meeting. We told Alex that if she wanted to return to her mother, she should feel free to make that decision, but we were totally committed to her and hoped this would not be her decision. We also felt that if her mother wanted Alex to come home, then we should not stand in the way, even if, as we learned from Alex, she had been verbally abused by her mother. She was in some ways the Cinderella in the family.

In our visit we brought the subject up. Alex's mother said she knew we could give her daughter a far better life than she could as a part-time maid, so it would be up to Alex. She replied that she wanted to remain with us. It must have been difficult for her mother to hear that from her own daughter. Tears came to her mother's eyes and ours as well. We promised we would bring Alex for regular visits. We also wanted her to keep her native tongue, even though she spoke perfect English.

Over the next several months, we made a few trips back to Carlsbad so Alex could stay connected with her mom and other sisters. This also gave us the opportunity to get to know some of her sisters, nieces, and nephews. We soon felt like we had gained an entire family.

Three months after her arrival the Immigration and Naturalization Service granted her full amnesty from the paperwork we filled out three months earlier. After four months we had the court hearing with a judge at Superior Court on the issue of legal guardianship. The judge had several questions for Alex as well as for Stella and me, and legal guardianship was easily granted after a 30-minute hearing with the Judge.

Eventually, all the sisters became legal citizens after Alex did, and today one sister is now a registered nurse.

Alex age 12 when first coming to live with us.

Alex with a few of her nieces

Sister, Monica – Arcadia High school graduation.

Alex one year later in 1987

Board Games with school friends.

Dr. Frank Goodman & Evelyn Alex, Monica, Bob, Stella

L-R Bob, Arcadia Br. Manager, Max Knell President
& Chairmen, Ole's, Miss Rice, V.P So Cal Retail
Banking, Payroll service personnel.

19

THE HEALTHCARE ENTERPRISE

We were following the directions given to me by the Lord that day in my garage.

"And I will restore to you the years that the locust hath eaten, the cankerworm, and the caterpillar...Joel 2:25 (KJV)

We had a new church, new friends, our credit had survived, money was again flowing in, and we had a daughter. There was one more step which the Lord would bring me to, a place which allowed me to fully dedicate the rest of my career towards Him without any hinderance.

A few months after Alex came into our lives, I had arranged some venture capital contacts for four fellows involved in health care. They hadn't been able to find the money needed for what I thought was a good idea. They offered me a partnership in the business, and I folded my company into theirs, moved out of my home office to a new location in Irvine.

The partnership consisted of five guys with diverse skills and talents. One came with experience in the healthcare field as an astute accountant, another had successful sales experience in medical equipment, and three of us had varied experiences in banking and finance.

Their idea was to buy industrial medical clinics, most of which were owned and managed by doctors with little or no business experience. Consequently, most were losing money and near bankruptcy. We would manage the clinics for a fee, bringing them to solvency in return for an equity position, or we would buy them outright at a predetermined level of solvency. Industrial clinics are usually located in or near heavy industrial areas where everything from general flu symptoms to life-threatening accidents requiring serious medical attention. Corporations paid a fee for this health-care service and we arranged for the most seriously injured accident victims to be sent to the nearest hospital, who in turn payed us a referral fee if they were on our approved list.

We discovered there were many young board-certified emergency room doctors who wanted to have their own chain of clinics. We convinced the best qualified of these to join our group exclusively for an equity portion in our company while at the same time receiving their normal doctors' fees. We in turn, would handle all the back-office paperwork, including the doctor's first report which, according to California law had to be completed within 24 hours after a patient was first treated.

Our first test case was with a doctor who had three locations but was quite broke simply because he did a terrible job collecting receivables. Most of his receivables were 120 days or more overdo. Consequently, he never had enough cash flow to pay off his bank loans. His bank was about to foreclose on everything he had, sell his equipment for twenty cents on the dollar and just write off the rest as a bad loan loss. The doctor was also months behind in his workmen's compensation claims with the state, so he wasn't getting any income from that source either, not to mention being over two months past due on his doctor's first report to the state.

We approached his bank and asked them to give us 90 days to bring his billings current and we would guarantee them 100 cents on the dollar to pay his past due loans. In return, we asked for a $500,000 line of credit to buy other clinics in the same financial straits. It was a hard sell since we were a new company, they knew nothing about. But in the end, the potential for recouping their significant losses totaling several hundred thousand dollars -- a huge amount for a small regional bank -- was worth the gamble they decided to take.

Once that was locked in, we went to the local workmen's comp office and told them we wanted them to put in new computers in their local office, directly on-line to our office so we could file workman comps claims immediately as they came in and thereby eliminate another source of delayed receivables. They said it would take months, maybe years, to get approval from the state for computers to streamline the process. We said, "No, you don't understand. We'll pay for the computers and provide the necessary software to put them directly online from our office to your office." It was a done deal.

Ninety days later the bank had all their outstanding loans fully repaid as agreed and they gave us a $500,000 line of credit for the purchase of other clinics.

Unfortunately, the doctor did not keep his end of the deal. He refused to follow up on his promise to make us partners or to sell his clinics to us, which were now once again in the black and profitable. We anticipated his greed would bring such a conclusion. What the doctor didn't know was that our accountant/partner had uncovered many corrupt accounting techniques on his books. He made copies of all these unscrupulous dealings and paperwork showing the dates of all transactions. Basically, an insurance policy for us if his past dealings ever became known to authorities. All sorts of fraud were uncovered, the largest being more than one Small Business Administration loan for $250,000 that was used for exotic vacations, and a trip to Bogota, Columbia. Hmmm? By this time, the doctor had kicked us out of his building, terminating all of us without paying our last several months' management fee.

Despite the doctor's dishonorable conduct, we felt fairly good about things because working with him had given us an opportunity to successfully test our business model and we now had a working line of credit with his bank. We leased a third-floor office in a new office building a half-block down the street and facing his clinic.

One day we received a call from the District Attorney's office asking if we had any past records for an investigation they were conducting on the doctor. We naturally said we did and several years' worth.

The DA wanted to know if they could have them for their investigation. "Certainly," we said. The same afternoon, we handed over boxes of financial records. Six weeks later, we watched from our third-floor office as armed federal agents and local police surrounded his building, handcuffed him, and took him into custody. It would take months, perhaps even years for this to be cleared up so we focused on other clinics for sale. We never heard the final fate of the doctor, but it surely wasn't very good.

SHADY DEALINGS IN BOWLING GREEN

Once word got around that we had access to venture capital for a simple fee, plus a reasonable equity position, other opportunities started coming our way. One came via a phone call from a fellow in Kentucky who was trying to raise money to purchase a golf course near Bowling Green. We never spent our own money to travel out of state for potential deals. If someone wanted to give us a shot at a deal, they paid all expenses, signed an exclusive agreement, and two of our partners would make the trip and initial analysis.

We discussed the possibilities, our fees, and accepted the invitation from the fellow in Kentucky. Two airline tickets were sent by FedEx to our office and it was decided that one of the partners, Phil, and I would make the trip. We arrived at the Bowling Green airport at 2:00 in the afternoon and were picked up by a chauffeured stretch limousine. We were driven directly to the golf course while the client's scantily dressed secretary/girlfriend filled us in on some of the details. The secretary was our first yellow flag.

Once at the golf course we met the prospective client, who walked with us to examine much of the 5,400-yard course. He seemed like a pleasant fellow and a no-nonsense sort of guy. The golf course was well-designed but not in the best shape. The fairways were mostly dry as were the greens. Privately, Phil and I were thinking the same thing; this isn't worth the supposed $20 million he was asking us to find, so this deal must have a lot of padding in it for something else.

GUNS, GIRLS, SNARES AND DECEPTION

After walking the course, we were taken to an upscale restaurant and treated to a large dinner where we got down to business. After dinner, he took us into a swanky hotel downtown for our night stay and for which he was picking up the tab. On the way he had to make a stop as he wanted us to meet another partial partner where we watched a movie in a private home theater entitled "Greed" with Michael Douglas. Afterwards, when we got back into the limo, Phil and I noticed a semi-automatic 9mm pistol lying on the back-seat floor under the front seat. Hmm! That wasn't there before. Second yellow flag.

At the hotel, our client wanted to talk more in the lounge area and have drinks. Phil and I are non-drinkers and just ordered Coca Cola while our prospective client talked on and on about unlimited possibilities for making extra cash above our broker's fees. All of the things he suggested were illegal and worth a long uncomfortable stay in a state penitentiary if discovered. Phil and I were thinking bribery and hadn't forgotten that gun so conspicuously left on the limo floor. We figured the gun was probably placed there to intimidate us with his power. Legitimate businessmen don't intentionally leave guns lying loose in their cars.

By this time Phil and I were both independently thinking of a way to extricate ourselves without causing undue suspicion. A fast explainable get-away was in order (emphasis on fast). At the end of the drinking session, our "host" waved ten girls over to our table from the bar and told us he would send five girls to each of our separate penthouse rooms on the top floor and we could have our pick of them for the night. Phil and I clearly conveyed that wouldn't be necessary as we were both happily married.

Later Phil and I met in my room to discuss how we would extract ourselves from the situation as quickly as possible. We felt we would be threatened if we said we weren't interested. After all, it would not be difficult to find out where we all lived. The next day, the plan was to have additional discussions on our fee and other details at an 8:30 breakfast. Phil and I already knew we weren't going to stay around another day.

We started by checking with the airport to find how early we could get a flight the next morning. Fortunately, there was a 7 a.m. flight directly to John Wayne Airport in Orange County near our office in Irvine. Second, we called our partners and told them to dig much deeper in their research to find out anything and everything they could about this guy. Third, since we were fairly sure this fellow was going to be busy for the night with some of the women, he had offered us, we figured he probably wouldn't be up too early. We had a cab ready to pick us up and take us to the airport at 5:30 am. We were on our flight by 6:30. By the time he woke up we would be somewhere over Texas. We left a hand-written note in a sealed envelope at the front desk telling him about an emergency back home that required our immediate attention and we left earlier that morning and would get back to him by phone. Our self-imposed deportation worked beautifully.

When we got home, our partners told us that our would-be client had served prison time for fraud, writing bad checks, and assault with a deadly weapon. Again, my dad was right. Be careful who you pick as friends – or clients.

The next afternoon, our questionable former client called and threatened to sue us. We told him to go ahead. We reminded him that we had never signed a contract and let him know that we had since become aware of his criminal record. We had just enough information to make it sound like we knew more than we actually did. But then, he didn't know that. We never heard from him again. Checkmate! We did however change our analysis procedures for checking out potential clients, thanking God for lessons learned and His protection.

20

DANGER ON THE 57 SOUTH

Commuting south to Irvine area every morning was not my favorite activity in this new partnership. The trip was long, and traffic was always heavy on the 57 Freeway. One morning, there was a bad pile up in the north-bound lanes. Everyone heading south was rubber necking. I was too, but not so much as to not pay attention to the cars in front of me. Not so for the lady behind me in a smaller car. She plowed into the back of my Mercedes – and the fellow behind her slammed into her. I rushed to her driver side door glancing at my rear bumper as I went. I couldn't see any visible damage to my vehicle, but her car looked more like an accordion than a car. I asked her if she was okay. She was moaning "Oh, my neck!" I couldn't blame her. She had been hit pretty hard from behind and pinched in between two cars. But at the same time, I had the funny feeling that this wasn't going to end here. And I was right.

Despite all the commotion due to the accident on the other side of the freeway, it didn't take long for a CHP motorcycle cop to arrive on the scene. I made sure my side of the story was correctly portrayed for the accident report and called my insurance agent after getting to the office. The CHP officer asked if my car was drivable. I said, "Yes, it appears to be undamaged at least at quick glance." He told me I could be on my way. As it turned out, my car was damaged. It didn't even have a scratch on it, but an inspection a few days later at a body shop revealed that the frame was badly bent. Repairs would cost $3,500. Insurance covered the repairs.

Exactly 51 weeks later, a week before the statute of limitations ran out, a knock on the front door of our home brought another one of those memorable moments. "Are you Robert Boomsma?" Yes, I responded. "You've been duly served," as the appointed Lawsuit server made a speedy retreat off the front porch.

After all the previous lawsuits, I was quickly approaching the point where I would never answer a knock on the front door again. The Iranian woman who had rubber necked her car into mine was seeking $1 million for injuries suffered, medical bills, loss of work and a new car. My insurance agent told me not to worry about it. Nonetheless, I was thinking "The audacity of that woman! She runs into me due to her own negligence, and now she has the nerve to claim it's my fault." I had experienced frivolous lawsuits before and was tired of it. Making money isn't all that difficult, but it's much harder to keep when people know or even suspect you have some. It seemed like there were always dozens of people trying to take it away from you. In this case, I was sure it was an unscrupulous attorney looking for deep pockets.

Over the next few days, resentment took up residence in my thoughts. It didn't take long before bitterness took root, and to make it worse I kept watering the roots with my angry thoughts. "Who does she think she is? I'll show her. I'm going to file a counter suit. I'll fix her."

On Sunday morning we went to church. I didn't hear much of what the pastor was saying. I was continuing my internal resentment rant when I suddenly heard a very loud voice call my name from behind me: "*BOB!*"

Instinctively I jumped and turned around, but we were sitting in the last row up against a wall. I knew immediately this was surely the Lord's voice and He definitely wanted my attention. The voice was loud, firm, but not angry. His voice quickly snapped me out of my spiritual amnesia.

He continued in the softest, most loving voice one can imagine. *"Bob, ...what if you were the only person, I could find that would pray for this woman's salvation, would you, do it?"*

Instant conviction. It's amazing how small you can feel when the Lord catches you red handed. My bitterness was rebellion, plain and simple. I was ashamed in allowing the thorns of resentment to spoil the flower of forgiveness. Forgiveness had been totally bypassed. The feeling was probably much the same as the crowd of "would-be" stone throwers felt toward the women caught in adultery when Jesus said, "Let he who is without sin cast the first stone."

I said under my breath, "Yes Lord, I will pray for this lady." Bitterness and resentment washed out to sea immediately replaced by a wave of compassion and love. Once again, I had allowed compassion and the fruits of the Spirit to be overrun with anger.

Never underestimate the density of men. If that sounds harsh, consider that Balaam had to have a donkey speak to him before he realized the consequences of his own disobedience. We could all mention other biblical characters who had the same slowness of spiritual capacity. I gain some comfort in knowing a donkey wasn't necessary to get my attention, even though I felt like one. Disobedience has consequences. Thank God for his patience.

A couple of months after the accident my insurance company called to say I was right. The Iranian woman had retained a known deep-pockets ambulance chasing attorney. My insurance company's attorneys made short work of the case and no further action was needed. I prayed for the lady's salvation every day for nearly a year before feeling a release.

So, there it was again. Another opportunity to trust the Lord; another opportunity to pray for an enemy; another opportunity for forgiveness. I often feel that the Lord allows us to keep tripping over the same obstacles in our path until we finally learn the lesson deep in our hearts. We stumble. We fall. But we get back up and try again by the Grace and patience of our Lord.

Portia Nelson was an American singer, songwriter, actress, and author, best known for her appearances in the 1950's cabarets.

But she is also remembered for a poem she wrote many years ago -- a five-chapter autobiography that many of us could easily write our name on:

* * *

Chapter One: I walk down the street. There's a deep hole in the sidewalk. I fall in. I'm lost. I'm helpless. It isn't my fault, but it takes forever to find a way out.

Chapter Two: I walk down the same street. There's a deep hole in the sidewalk. I pretend I don't see it. I fall in again. I can't believe I'm in the same place again. It isn't my fault, but it still takes a long time to get out.

Chapter Three: I walk down the same street. There's a deep hole in the sidewalk. I see it's there. I still fall in. It's become a habit. My eyes are open. I know where I am. It is my fault. I get out immediately.

Chapter Four: I walk down the same street. There's a deep hole in the sidewalk. I walk around it.

Chapter Five: I walk down another street.

God loves us. He is patient and kind. He gives us opportunity after opportunity to get things right. Rejoice in His love, mercy, and grace. Proverbs 20:22 (NIV2011) tells us *"Do not say, 'I'll pay you back for this wrong,' wait for the LORD, and he will avenge you."*

In writing, reviewing and discussing my story with Stella for this book, it occurred to us that all true enemies, those who came against us, are now, like the scripture says, "as nothing" -- either dead or in prison (some perhaps only in their minds); or, on the positive side, they have allowed the Spirit of Life in Christ to guide their life. They became friends of Jesus and friends to us. Naturally, we know not all their endings, but we can pray for them and hope.

Isaiah 41:11 KJV *"Behold, all they that were incensed against thee shall be ashamed and confounded: they shall be as nothing; and they that strive with thee shall perish."*

Now that we knew our Industrial health care system worked, we continued to look for other industrial clinics to purchase, including a 99-bed non-profit hospital, of which many were also operating in the red, primarily because they didn't know the ins and outs of Medicare. One of our partners did, as he helped write the Medicare rules and regulations. We were in a good position to expand our presence in medical care.

But at the same time, I was growing restless and feeling like I needed to move on. There were several reasons for this, but the major one was that something in my heart was pulling me in a totally different direction.

21

"I WANT TO GO BACK HOME."

Alex had been part of our life for a year, was now 14 and quickly growing into a young woman. In early December, exactly one year after having met her for the first time, she said she wanted to go back to Carlsbad and live with her Mom. We were shocked! Especially me.

Things had been going so well. I didn't understand how she had come to this change of heart. A tidal wave of emotions stormed through my mind. What did we do wrong? We provided a beautiful place to live. Gave her a room of her own for the first time in her life, provided all kinds of new clothes, took her on trips, sent her to summer youth camp, and provided all these life experiences she probably never would have had. We had invested much of ourselves in this little girl. I spoke to the Lord about it, but I still felt angry and upset. I sat Alex down in her room and said, "Absolutely not. We'll continue to make regular visits to see your mom and your sisters as we always have, but you're staying here with us."

Then, for the first time since coming into our lives she had a temper tantrum. I did not see that coming and thought it best to leave her alone in her room to ponder the significance of her request. I went to my office across the hall to hopefully throw some cold water on my irritated state of mind.

She didn't want to mull it over, having already made up her mind. It was me who had to mull things over with the Lord.

After getting quiet before the Lord, I distinctly heard His quiet, calm voice say,

> *"Bob, you didn't always listen to me either -- but because I have given all my children the freedom of choice, I had to let you make your own decisions, even when I knew you weren't always doing what was best for you. Now you must do the same with Alex."*

That was certainly true, but difficult to hear. After discussing the matter with Stella, I went back to Alex and confessed that I was wrong in trying to force her to stay. If she wanted to go back to her mother and other sisters in Carlsbad, we would support her decision. We all agreed it would be best if she completed the school semester with us until the end of January when she could return. This would be the last Christmas we would have with her. We did our best to make it a memorable one, but deep inside I was a shipwreck of emotions seemingly stranded on a desert island. I had always wanted a daughter, and this wasn't working the way I planned. Hmm? Did I say, "The way **I** had planned?"

When the time came for her to leave it was emotionally unbearable to take her back to Carlsbad. I asked Dr. Goodman if he would be willing. When he came to pick her up, she certainly left with more than she came with and that was fine as long as she would be happy. We too had gained much, maybe more than she had. There were no regrets for the time invested in her life. It was God's assignment for us that year. I just did not expect the nest to be empty so soon. We told her if she ever needed anything, she should feel free to call us and we would still pay for her college education.

Four months passed. We never heard a word from her. On a Saturday, I was again working in the yard and talking to the Lord about how I felt. "Lord, I don't understand why we haven't heard from her. We poured our life into her and surely the course of her life had changed as well, but still, she hasn't called to even say hello."

That's when I heard that quiet voice again, *"Bob, I know how you feel. Many of my children don't call me either."* His words caused a lump in my throat, bringing tears of repentance. Was I guilty of the same thing? That moment moved me into some serious reflection I have never forgotten, and again changed my life as did so many things learned the year we had Alex. Since Stel and I never had children, the past year with Alex had, in more ways than can be counted, changed our entire perspective and our own relationship with the Lord. Most parents have 18 or so years to bring up a child in the way they should go, and we experienced much of the same things all condensed into one year. It was a year of continuous blessings with many of the same experience's parents have. Good times, tense times, ups and downs, exciting, yet oh so fragile when considering the responsibility of the task at hand.

Within a few days after hearing the Lord's response that Saturday afternoon, Alex called. We were thrilled and knew how God feels when His children connect with Him. After what Jesus suffered on the Cross, can you imagine what He feels like when we call him? When we spend time with Him, we are in a real sense worshipping Him. We often think of praising God as just singing in church on Sunday. It is. But it's much more than that and can take many forms. When we enjoy something, a piece of music, a book, or places we have visited where we thoroughly appreciated the scenery, we seem to have an intuitive desire to praise it and share it with others. C. S. Lewis in his book" Reflections *on the Psalms"* suggests *"We* do this because we delight to praise what we enjoy because the praise not merely expresses but completes the enjoyment; it is appointed consummation." (Source: "Reflection of the Psalms" P.81) *(A quote from dear brother Adrian DeVisser, Pastor of Kita Savanah church in Sri Lanka in the book "Eastern Voices" P. 103 Compiled by Asian Access © Asian Access 2017.)*

Alex told us she had been hesitant to call us because she was afraid we might feel that she had just been using us to better herself. We assured her that thought never occurred to us. From that point on, we have stayed in touch via visits, emails, texts and prayer.

We attended her graduation from high school four years later. She attended college at night, and has now earned three AA degrees, one in Accounting, one in Sociology and one in Criminal Justice. She has a natural gift in accounting and has used it well in all of her work positions at Calloway Golf corporate office and Legos home office. Working with troubled youth was always her desire even when living with us at age 13. Three years ago, she accepted a new position overseeing several retirement center locations for a conglomerate holding company with 60 locations in two Western states. Today she oversees locations in central California as well as serving as a consultant for the same holding company. We are enormously proud of her!

In accepting Alex as our own, we were obedient in serving Christ, and serving Him is being submissive. Obedience and submission are praising Him as much as our generosity and loving one another. Hebrews 13:15 (NKJV) instructs us to praise continually: *"Therefore by Him (Jesus) let us continually offer the sacrifice of praise to God, that is, the fruit of our lips, giving thanks to His name."*

Mom & Dad - Bob at 4
months on Wallace St Chicago.

Bob & Grandpa Nick
Boomsma at Reformed
Church in Wichert ILL.

Grandpa &
Grandma Nick Boomsma

A day in the Park in
Roseland ILL with Grandpa
Olthoff and Dad

Bob & Bobo age 4 – Grandpa
Olthoff's backyard, Chicago.

70 years later-Bob & Bobo
10/19/19 at Crosspoint
Christian Reformed Church
50th Anniversary celebration.

Stella -
High School graduation 1963

Bob -
High School graduation 1963

Senior Prom May 1963

ROSE TOURNAMENT FINALISTS—thirty-nine girls, finalists in the 1965 Rose Queen contest, are being screened by the selection committee. Another screening session is scheduled today at the Tournament House in Pasadena. The committee will choose a queen and six princesses for the famed New Year's Day parade. The lucky queen and her royal court will be announced Dec. 1.

Stella in the running from 400 contestants to 39
for the 1964 Rose Parade Queen & her court.

Stella, Modeling new B-4700
for Wallstreet Journal release, Oct.28 1971

Grandpa Nick's Bible

Roger 6 months, Bob 4 years old

Bob (11) Roger (7) Golden
West Ave. Arcadia

Roger playing Marine at age 9

Roger playing trumpet at concert in Chicago -
playing Sinfonies de Fanfares by Rondeau –
Music for Organ & Trumpet.

Roger U.S. Marine Corps   Roger high school graduation.

Roger somewhere near Hue, Vietnam

Sister ship to John Wayne's Wild Goose. Five
state-rooms172 ft. yacht, a converted mine sweeper.

Rented out for corporate dinner parties, holidays,
weddings & weekends

Dave Spangler – Former President Hooker Industries
(Pictures from VescoTeam.com)

Dave has been co-drivers for Team Vesco for many years.
He was able to break their own speed record at 503 mph

Front row left Dave and wife Karen

PART II

22

A NEW CAREER

The partnership with the other four fellows in the health care was no longer working out. I was feeling pulled in a totally different direction. After looking at another industrial clinic to buy, and the possible purchase of a 99-bed hospital, we were all working day and night. I hadn't spent much time with Stella for several months.

Late one afternoon, I headed to her office at Life Ministries Japan in San Dimas to take her out for an early dinner. At the time, she was administrative assistant to the executive vice-president. She was the last one in the office and involved in the completion of a project. I picked up one of the many evangelism magazines in the office and quickly became interested in the articles and the ads. I had never given missions much thought before but was intrigued by the opportunities for businessmen to be involved in a short-term mission trip.

That's when the Lord began to fan embers deep inside of me. Nothing was the same after reading those articles. The next day I told my partners it was necessary for me to take a month off because I felt the Lord leading me to go on a mission trip. At the time I did not know where that might be, so did some research. The partners all said that was fine with them and asked me to share what was learned as they might also be interested in short-term missions' trip.

As the next few weeks passed, I sensed that God definitely had something else for me. The sparks inside had ignited a flame and were burning hotter and brighter. After six weeks, I knew I could no longer remain in the partnership and I submitted my resignation. The next three months I spent most of my time praying and studying the scriptures to seek what God had in mind. I prayed, "Lord what is your will and my purpose from this point forward?"

I admit growing weary during this time and consequently wandered down some side roads thinking I knew what the next assignment was. Up to this point in my life, I thought of evangelism as putting money in the collection plate on Sunday when missionaries came to speak, and then praying, "Thank you Lord for not sending me."

One day I finally figured it out; or so I thought. With my background in finance, banking, and computers sales, I knew there had to be a closely held company that was growing so fast that the owner was having trouble controlling it all. He could probably use a good, strong Christian right-hand man to help him hold up his hands like Aaron and Hur did for Moses in battle. I contacted a search firm in Century City specializing in "presenting" a candidate, revamping resumes, and getting them prepped for the right executive position. It was a specialty head-hunting firm that makes a person look better than he really is. And, surprisingly, they did. I apparently did not know how marketable I was.

My first interview was with a closely held company doing $100 million a year in sales. The three-hour interview concluded with an offer for $350,000 a year salary and stock options after 2 years. A $30,000 per month salary seemed rather good to me. There was only one problem. Deep inside I knew it was not the Lord's will and declined the offer retreating to my prayer room and Bible for what turned out to be another month.

One afternoon I again went to have lunch with Stel at Life Ministries Japan. These lunches were getting to be a most pleasant habit. In the parking lot, I ran into Dr. Ken. He founded

Life Ministries Japan some twenty years earlier. Then a few years earlier, started another Christian outreach recruiting teachers in the United States and Canada to teach English in universities in China as a tent making approach to sharing the Good News.

I had known Ken for several years, and he mentioned that he knew I was no longer associated with my partners and wanted to know what I was planning next. At that point had no idea. He invited Stel and me to an event that same evening at the Pasadena Hilton where they were presenting a program and a short film aimed at recruiting teachers to serve in China. I didn't know anything about China, but he urged us to come to the event as his guests.

We attended that night and sat with four of the twelve board members for the dinner and presentation. After seeing the short film *"China Crossing,"* produced by James Greenelsh, I was hooked.

What a wonderful opportunity to share the Good News. I knew instantly this was where I was supposed to be. After the meeting, Dr. Ken and I talked. He said there were opportunities opening up across China to teach English and he needed fund-raising help so he would have more time to further develop these opportunities. It seemed like a perfect fit for me. I had always felt comfortable dealing with people of great wealth in my previous jobs since graduating from college. He wanted me to start in a week and let's see what happens.

It didn't take long for me to start having second thoughts. It seemed I had just fallen into this. It was too easy, too unexpected. Perhaps I had missed something. Maybe I should continue looking for one of those other massive salary jobs.

That's when the Lord gave me a scripture from Luke:

"I will follow you, Lord; but first let me go back and say goodbye to my family." Jesus replied, "No one who puts a hand to the plow and looks back is fit for service in the kingdom of God." (Luke 9:61-62, NIV2011).

I was convinced. The Lord's voice in that scripture was quiet, but I heard it loud and clear. The path truly is straight and narrow. If you look back when you have put your hand to the plow, how could you ever plow a straight row? *"Because strait is the gate, and narrow is the way, which leadeth unto life, and few there be that find it."* (Matthew 7:14, KJV) There was no reason to look back, even three years later when a secular organization came looking for me with offers that I saw as a test of my resolve to stand firm and stay the course in God's chosen path for me.

THE ENGLISH INSTITUTE

I began working at the English Institute in November of 1988. Since I was the first full-time fundraiser to be out and about the country, other than Dr. Ken himself, they sent me to a one-week fundraising class in Los Angeles. I found it to be of little value. Most of the class was dedicated to raising money for community projects like parks, walkways, green belts with lakes and ducks, museums, etc. None of them were Christian in nature. I'm sure all their examples were nice projects, but nothing even came close to the more eternal needs of those who hadn't yet heard the Good News.

I needed to know which foundations and individuals were among the largest givers to Christian causes. My search led me to a branch library in Santa Ana that was part of a National Foundation Directory in New York and San Francisco. There, I found hundreds of directories, most of which were at least four to six inches thick, containing hundreds of pages full of information on how much they gave annually, what their interests were with years of tax returns. *Oh, Lord. Where do I start?*

What surprised me most of all was that there was no one else looking through this treasure chest of information. What a cornucopia of potential income sources and knowledge. It was like a map to where the gold was buried. And yet, the only other person in the building was a little old lady who was managing the library. I described to her my ministry's goal and mission. She was able to narrow the directories from hundreds to twenty or so. After spending a solid two weeks categorizing and cross-referencing with several other directories, I came up with a list of four hundred foundations that might be interested in helping fund the ministry's work. I prioritized all 400 from A to D, with A being the most likely interested and D the least likely to provide funding.

I started making cold calls to foundations around the United States, presenting my elevator speech in an attempt to obtain a first meeting. As in banking, I quickly learned that an elevator pitch should be strong and interesting enough to capture attention, be no more than 30 to 60 seconds in length, focused on their primary interest and supported by substantial additional research. I also learned that if the potential donor's giving pattern over the last few years didn't contain something somewhat similar to what our ministry was doing, I was wasting my time and theirs by calling them. Keep in mind that I was only calling on Christian Foundations and very wealthy people running their own companies or CEO's of Fortune 500 or 1000 companies who were known to be solid Christians.

The second lesson learned was that in order to get people to open their hearts, I had to open mine first. It was important to share a little of my journey and how it was that I had migrated into ministry from banking after receiving God's call. Generally, when you open your heart to others, they will open their hearts to you with their personal stories.

Some of the people I talked with were also contemplating making career changes as I had done. Consequently, they were not only receptive but anxious to hear my story.

It was at this juncture I realized how the Lord had used our financial difficulties to prepare me for work in ministry missions work. The Lord had indeed lifted us out of the financial abyss in restoring losses and we were better off than before as we had no debt. No money concerns to tether or prevent me from full dedication to the work of raising money for God's work in the world. I was the Lord's free man.

More Lessons Learned

I learned other important lessons as well:

- Speak just enough to tell your prospective donors what is unique about your ministry, and always be an exceptional listener. If you listen closely to their story, you will learn everything you need to know about how to talk to them and what influences their giving.

- After a friendship has been developed, always ask if you can present a written proposal backing up your verbal message. I quickly learned the operative word for a proposal was "short."

- Your proposal should contain nothing that you haven't already said in the process of developing the relationship/friendship over time; the proposal itself just becomes a formality for their records.

Over the next few years, I was always surprised when making joint calls with other supposedly "seasoned" fundraisers in other ministries who never asked the right questions and never really listened. Then they went back to their offices and took three months to write a 40-page redundant proposal. By then the prospective donor had likely begun to lose interest and moved from being a passionate, strong, potential donor to a cold uninterested one.

Most private funding foundations receive hundreds of lengthy proposals every month and most of these go straight into the waste basket.

An Absurd Offer – Beware of Seductions

After three years with the English Institute, I received a call from a large financial institution that wanted to significantly expand its operations in California and several western states. They had become aware of my record with Wells Fargo and asked if I would be interested in an executive vice president position. Besides the title, they offered a $300,000 per year salary. I thanked them and told them I had been out of the financial arena for three years with a new career.

Refusing to take no for an answer, they called back a week later and said they really wanted me to head up this new division and increased the annual salary offer to $500,000. Again, I turned them down. There was no question in my mind that I was where God wanted me. Another week passed. They called again offering $750,000 a year salary plus stock options of another $750,000 per year based on annual performance. I couldn't believe it. I had to give them credit for being persistent. It was difficult for me to imagine I could be worth that much in the financial arena. Nearly $63,000 a month salary sounded absurd, not to mention the stock option. I remember thinking they must have the wrong guy. I thanked them for their offer and said I still must decline as I was now on a totally different path.

I've never regretted that decision. Never once looked back and never doubted if I should have taken the current path. A few years later it was confirmed. The company went bankrupt. Hundreds of their branches in several states disappeared. Hundreds of people were out of work and many others lost a great deal of money.

Thank you, Lord, for helping me make the right decision and staying on Your Chosen_path for me.

And now, thirty years later, my wife says jokingly, it's a good thing she didn't know about it at the time because her check book has no conscience. Stella and I always try to find the humor in situations and her comment all these many years later made us laugh.

Jesus replied, *"No one who puts his hand to the plow and looks back is fit for service in the kingdom of God."* Luke 9:62 NIV

23

GOD REDEEMS

The only thing I didn't like about my new job was the lack of space in the office headquarters. My desk was in an extremely small cubicle that had my elbows bumping the edges. I suggested to Dr. Ken that I could get more done working from my home, just three miles away. This would still allow me to attend meetings as needed as well as Monday morning prayer meetings.

I timed my request after Mr. Weyerhaeuser of Weyerhaeuser Lumber in Washington State came for a visit and remarked that this was not a very good office setting for a fundraiser. Bless his heart.

Several months later while making a presentation to the Weyerhaeuser Board of Directors, I was more or less nailed to the wall by the executive director of the Weyerhaeuser Foundation, whose job it was to pre-screen all proposals and presentations. He had been in that position for a number of years and had become territorial, taking his job too seriously and seemed to believe, at least subconsciously, that the money given was his own, rather than Mr. Weyerhaeuser's. I had seen this before with other executive directors of Foundations. Mr. Weyerhaeuser was not having any of it. I learned a week after my presentation he fired him for his rudeness, arrogance, and unfriendly nature toward me in my presentation at which he was present. God is my defender.

THE GARDNER FROM GOD

My office at home overlooks a courtyard leading to the front door. While making phone calls to set up my first fundraising trip, I saw someone knocking on the front door. When greeting him, there stood a young Asian fellow. He told me he was a gardener looking to expand his business in our neighborhood. As it happened, I was looking for a new gardener and asked him to walk the property with me so he could give me a quote. His price was fair, and I asked him if he could make our yard his first stop every Friday morning. He agreed. Three months later, I was so impressed with his consistency and excellent work ethic I gave him a raise. He seemed astonished and said nobody had ever done that before.

MEMORIES OF VIETNAM—VANS STORY TO ME.

As we talked that day, I learned that his name was Van, and he was from Vietnam. In broken English he explained that he was from a small village near the city of Hue called Phou Bai, located on a small peninsula darting out into the South China Sea.

"I know exactly where that is," I said.

He wanted to know if I had been there.

"No," I said, "but my brother was killed near there in the Vietnam War."

A gloominess darkened his face. He told me he had lost his parents, a brother and many cousins in the Tet Offensive starting in late January and February of 1968. He was seven years old at the time and recalled having nowhere to sleep and nothing to eat.

Along with 45 other war orphans, he stumbled onto a U.S. military base where the Marines shared their "K" rations and provided a safe place for them behind piles of bunkered sandbags. Goose bumps were now forming up and down my arms.

Five weeks before my brother Roger was killed, he called us from Hue, asking us to send a Care package full of non-perishable food once a week. That became the Friday afternoon task for my Mom, Stella, and myself. It seems Roger's Marine unit had taken in 45 young children who had lost their parents, homes, and families during the Tet offensive. Twenty years later, a 27-year-old Van was standing on my front porch. He did not know me. I did not know him. But he never forgot the Marines who shared with him their K rations and American food like peanut butter, canned tuna, Spam, crackers, and other canned foods.

We both stood, quietly together on my front porch, tears in our eyes about our mutual losses in the war.

My brother Roger and his fellow Marines had fed him physically when he was a small lost boy and I knew in my heart God had somehow, all these years later, brought Van to my front door. Only God could orchestrate something like this, and I took it as a sign to take hold of the baton. It was now my turn to feed him spiritually, which I did for the next eight years. Van and his wife (also a survivor from Vietnam) became friends.

Eight years later I found myself complaining to the Lord that I was having no success in reaching Van with the Gospel. He was a Buddhist and overcoming the only thing he knew was difficult. One day I said to the Lord, "If someone else has the assignment to lead him across the threshold to Christ, then okay, I accept that," totally releasing my concerns and laying them at the foot of the Cross.

The very next week I greeted Van as usual when he came on Friday morning. He walked towards me with a determined questioning look on his face and asked if I believed in life after death.

"Van," I said, "that's what I've been sharing with you these past eight years."

He explained his mother-in-law was sick and dying of cancer in Vietnam. His wife was about make the trip to visit her to say her final goodbyes. The desperate situation had prompted his question about life after death which neither he nor his wife had given much thought to before. I suggested Stel and I would like to take him and his wife to dinner the following evening and we could have dessert at our house. He was excited because his wife had always wanted to meet my wife.

In the meantime, Stel went to the Christian bookstore and asked for a Bible in Vietnamese and a children's picture Bible. They had the children's picture Bible in stock, but the owner/manager said he never remembered carrying or ordering any Bibles in Vietnamese. Nevertheless, he agreed to check the storeroom. Upon returning he said, "Well I don't know where they came from because we never order them, but I have two brand new books of John in Vietnamese. Stel said, "I'll take them both, along with the children's picture Bible."

The following night, after dinner at a nearby restaurant and dessert at our house, Stel gave each of them the book of John, in which she had underlined John 3:16. We felt the Holy Spirit telling us not to say anything, but just to give them the two books opened and underlined to this verse. It was miraculous to watch what happened next.

When we handed them the Bibles, their faces were drawn, uptight, and worried, due to their concern about Van's mother-in-law. When they read John 3:16, brightness filled their faces as hope rushed in like a wave. They said in unison, "We believe," and both immediately accepted Christ. We saw on their faces the serenity that can only be seen when Christ enters the heart. Joy and peace filled their faces the very second, they looked up after reading John 3:16. They were like moths instantly drawn to a bright light in the vastness of a dark night.

Van's wife made the trip back to Vietnam two weeks later, and, as we suggested, took one of the books of John to her mother. We learned a couple of months later after her return that her mother was healed, accepted Christ, and led many others in her village to Christ before she died a several years later. She was in her 80's at the time.

I'M AN AMERICAN NOW

One day I suggested to Van that he take the test and become a U.S. citizen, and explained why it was important to do so. Eight months later, he came on his usual Friday morning with an excited look on his face to tell me "Bob! Bob! My wife and I become U.S. citizens." His excitement is hard to describe, but his smile said it all as he beamed with pride from ear-to-ear.

Early in our friendship, I referred Van to several of our neighbors to help him enlarge his gardening business, and all of them hired him. He is busy on our street for several hours every Friday morning and has many other accounts in nearby foothill cities.

On another occasion, I encouraged him to move his young family, then consisting of two boys, from a bad crime area to another safer location and a better school system. I also suggested buying a home instead of renting and paying it off as soon as he possibly could, explaining the interest saved could help pay for his children's college education. He bought a beautiful five-bedroom home. Six years later he again came excitedly on his usual Friday morning, now having two additional children, and said, "Bob, Bob, I pay off house. I pay off house." Focus, discipline, and frugal living reaped excellent results.

TROUBLE AT SCHOOL

One evening I received a call from Van. Immediately I could tell he was upset, and it had something to do with his oldest son, John, now a senior in high school. He said, "Bob, Bob, you know John good boy." *"Yes Van, I know he is. What's the matter?"*

He could barely speak. He wasn't crying, but almost breathless with anxiety. I told him to put John on the phone and let him tell me what was going on.

John explained, "Uncle Bob, my teacher told me I can't graduate in June. I said, "Why? You're a straight "A" student."

He said a new substitute teacher had taken over his class on a permanent basis and she accused him of cheating on an assignment that accounted for 40 percent of his grade for the year, meaning that he would fail. I told him to create an accurate timeline of events leading up to the situation, which we would go over the following night at their home. I also told him to ask for a parent-teacher conference and be sure to mention that your Uncle Bob and Aunt Stella will be coming along with your parents.

The following night, I went over the timeline with John and his parents. The assignment in question was a group project with other classmates and John's portion of the team effort was doing research on the internet. John didn't quote his sources in the footnotes, which the teacher checked and said he had taken verbatim from the internet without noting proper credit. John did not know he was supposed to quote the source. Accordingly, he admitted that he had made a mistake but did not know this was considered cheating. His punishment seemed excessive, especially to his parents who had never received a high school education. They were bursting with pride that their firstborn was supposed to graduate in eight weeks with a "4.0" grade point average.

Going through the timeline John had prepared, I discovered something about the teacher's actions that greatly concerned me. She had called John's mother at her place of employment and left the following message with a receptionist, a total stranger, "Well, you just tell her that she needs to call me at once because her son is a cheat and liar and cannot graduate next month."

John was quite shaken with that statement, as I was. He had always been a perfect student, so we all wondered what motivated such an angry comment. To me, this seemed like a clear case of slander and possibly character assassination. I resolutely determined that I was not going to let her get away with it and was prepared to go as high as the situation might merit, including hiring an attorney if necessary.

The parent-teacher conference was scheduled for two days later. In the meantime, I went to John's mother's place of employment with a deposition document in hand and asked the woman who took the call to write in her own words exactly what the teacher had said on the phone. Two days later I had that deposition in my briefcase for the parent/teacher conference. I wore a pinstriped suit and carried the deposition in my briefcase, pretty much I thought, looking like I was an attorney. I wanted to advocate for John against an injustice, but on the other hand,

I didn't want to ruin the career of young, inexperienced teacher. There must be a way to preserve her career without handicapping her with a black mark on her record from a court case. I had purposed in my heart not to use the deposition unless it was absolutely necessary.

The meeting was held in the vice-principal's office, a middle-aged black woman with a PhD who obviously from her attire and mannerisms was a professional educator. I was impressed with her calm demeanor which radiated a confident wisdom. I felt certain there would be a fair and equitable outcome.

John's parents were looking very confused, and when I looked at John's face, I saw a pressure cooker about ready to blow its lid, not with anger, but tears.

As the conversation progressed, it started to feel as if any real resolution was fading away like the morning fog in San Francisco Bay. My deposition was looking like the only option. I was just about to open my briefcase when this lovely vice- Principal said she would like us to step out in the hallway so she could discuss the matter further with the substitute teacher. We all stood in the hallway for fifteen minutes before being called back in. When seated, I put my briefcase on my lap and started to undo the combination lock.

The vice-principal said the teacher had something she wanted to say. The teacher began with an apology to John and his parents, saying she had made a mistake in calling him a cheat and a liar. I set my briefcase back on the floor beside my chair.

The vice-principal chimed in, "John, you were also wrong in not quoting your sources and not knowing is not an excuse. You will, however, be allowed to wear the cap and gown and partici-pate in the graduation ceremonies with your classmates but will not be able to attend the May Prom dance.

"Furthermore, you will have a "makeup" assignment as follows: You will need to write 10 pages per week for the next three weeks about your experiences here in high school, and with the help of your Uncle Bob for proper English and grammar, you must turn them in to your teacher at the end of each week." I was relieved.

The deposition would not be needed. John didn't care if he was excluded from the prom. He didn't have a girlfriend and wasn't planning to attend anyway.

What did matter was that he had been called a cheat and a liar. For an Asian this is terribly dishonoring. The last thing John would ever do is dishonor his father and mother. Everyone waited for John to accept the teacher's apology and the makeup assignment offer. But John was struggling. His face was turning redder by the minute. He just couldn't seem to get past the fact that his parents might now think of him as a cheat and liar. He bent over in his chair almost like he was about to throw up, his face getting redder and redder. Several minutes of silence passed. John kept saying over and over, "I'm not a cheat and a liar."

Tears began trickling from his eyes like a leaking dam about to burst. I knelt down in front of him and said, "John, the teacher has apologized and admitted she made a mistake in saying what she did. Your mom and dad know you are not a cheat or a liar. An offer has been made. The hand of reconciliation has been extended. They don't have all evening for you to make up your mind in accepting this compromise."

He replied, "I'm not a cheat or liar." I told him, "I know. Your mom and dad know. The teacher and vice-principal know. You did make a mistake, and this will be a powerful lesson for you to remember when you attend college next fall. If you don't accept the apology and makeup assignment you won't be able to wear the cap and gown and graduate with your class. I know that's important to you and especially for your mom and dad. Now please accept the olive branch and let's get to work on that assignment."

To everyone's great relief he finally accepted the offer. We thanked the vice-principal for her mediation, shook hands and left. Stella and I decided to take them all out to dinner. In the meantime, John had walked far across the parking lot with tears in his eyes, still grappling with the thought that his mom and dad thought badly of him. At the restaurant, he still looked sullen and discouraged. I told him again that he was not thought of badly by his parents, or us, and this was the best way out of an error made by both parties. By the time dinner was served he was again laughing and had moved on emotionally.

The next two weeks were quite an eye-opener for me as I read and corrected John's ten weekly pages about his high school experiences. John was always a high-energy go-getter, definitely a Type A personality. Some of the good parts I had already known from his father, who often spoke with pride about John and all his children during his Friday gardening visits. But John had kept secret the many persecutions he had experienced of which his parents knew nothing because he didn't want to worry them.

At one time he considered pursuing dentistry as a profession and went to several dental offices and said he would work for free just to learn as much as he could about dentistry. After 15 dentists turned him down, saying he must be foolish, he finally found one who said you've got a deal.

Later, having changed his mind about dentistry, he took a job at Burger King for some spending money. Within a couple of months, he was made a shift manager and was pulling down more money than any of his fellow students, many of whom were spending their time doing drugs and cheating their various employers to support their habits. One day, John caught a fellow student stealing from the cash register. He told the student to stop immediately and return what he had taken. If he didn't, he would fire him. The young man was stealing for some time to support his drug habit. John caught him stealing again the following day, fired him, and reported it to the owner.

In retaliation the student gathered his friends, spray painted and trashed John's used car which Van had bought for him when he turned sixteen. They further spread vicious rumors around school and continually bullied him. John never said anything about it to anyone. There were other incidents where he was bullied and picked on simply because he was an honest straight-A student who didn't do drugs.

As it turned out, the owner of the Burger King owned four other Burger Kings, and promoted John to area manager, overseeing the food ordering for all of them and keeping the books. He was now making more money in his senior year of high school than anyone else in his class and probably making more than some who had already graduated from college and four to ten years older than he was.

His good looks, honesty, car, and money drew many attractive girls, some of whom were looking for a potential marriage relationship. Others were looking for a "sugar daddy" to support their drug and alcohol addictions. But John wasn't buying.

By the time he completed his two week "make-up" assignment I had become quite impressed with his life story, but especially how he handled persecutions throughout high school as an "Asian outsider." I told him he handled all those incidents like a Christian should, and that I was proud of how he had actually practiced what the Bible tells us to do about praying for our enemies and forgiving those who persecute us, and that I have seen adult Christians who have yet to learn that lesson. He responded, "That's exactly what I did; prayed and forgave them." Remember, this is coming from a 17-year-old high school senior.

I asked him if he learned this from his parents. He responded, "Well, yes in a way. Do you remember that picture Bible you gave my parents 7 or 8 years ago? Well, they put it on the dresser in my bedroom where I picked it up and started reading when I was about eight years old."

In his Vietnamese culture, as the oldest sibling, he is responsible for helping to teach life's lessons to his younger siblings. John became a practicing Christian, as did his two younger brothers and sister.

All of Van's four children went on to earn master's degrees with 4.0 GPA's. John is now working on his PhD. All of them are earning large salaries in various professions, a point of great pride for Van and his wife who were never able to complete their education due to the Vietnam war.

Van's Journey from Vietnam

I often talked with Van about his experiences in Vietnam. He told me that after the war, when he was around 14 or 15, he was imprisoned for two years as punishment for living with U.S. Marines during the Tet offensive. He was beaten at least once a week during this time but was told he would be freed if he admitted that he had lived with the Marines. After several months of abuse, he finally decided to admit that he had indeed lived with the Marines, and the authorities finally released him several months later. He made his way to the coast along the South China Sea finding work as a helper for a fisherman. He saved as much money as he possibly could and after four years was able to buy his own fishing boat and hire a small two-man crew to help him.

All the time he dreamed of finding a way out of Communist Vietnam – and one day He did. When word spread that he was striking out into the open sea. Several others asked to join him. By the time he set sail for the unknown his small boat was completely overloaded with people and their handfuls of personal belongings.

They set out into the South China Sea headed toward Singapore. No maps, no navigation equipment of any kind. Five days out, with no land in sight, a typhoon headed directly toward their small boat. It would surely capsize them, and many on board, if not all, would drown.

Through God's grace, shortly before the storm hit, a large Taiwanese freighter spotted them and picked them up. The typhon hit as soon as everyone was on board and Van's small fishing boat was overcome by a large wave and quickly vanished beneath the raging sea. The freighter was on its way to Singapore where they were dropped off and left on their own.

For the next two years, Van held various jobs to keep himself fed. He lived in empty shipping containers along the docks until a traveling Catholic priest from Phoenix Arizona found him and offered to sponsor him. It took the priest a year to raise the money and complete the paperwork to get him legally into the United

States. When Van arrived, the Priest found him a job mowing lawns. Since Van was more acclimated to high humidity instead of the dryness of Arizona, he headed for Southern California a year later, settling in Pomona where he met his future wife also from Vietnam. Again, he had saved his money and bought a gardening route with the money earned from his Arizona job. A few weeks later, he showed up on my front porch looking to expand his gardening business. God's love and grace had been watching over him long before he understood or heard of Jesus's love for him.

Because Van lost his brothers and sisters in the Vietnam War, as well as many cousins, he thinks of me as a brother. I lost a brother in the same war, at the same time, and now have gained another, plus three nephews and a niece. Only the Lord could orchestrate something like this.

John's High school graduation

Van & family

"God has placed eternity in the hearts of man..." Ecclesiastes 3:11 (NIV2011)

24

FIRST CHINA VISIT

I admired Van for leaving his native home to strike out for a better life. He completely understands how the rule of communism works. When he arrived here, he was obviously a stranger in a strange land, but he adjusted and thrived.

After making my first domestic fundraising trip covering several mid-western states, it was time for me to make my first trip to a land that was strange to me. I would be traveling to China to see the English Institute at work to better explain to potential donors what their donations would accomplish.

The flight to Hong Kong from California took twelve hours. I fell asleep a couple of hours before landing and was awakened by the flight attendant's call to secure seat belts. Minutes later, I looked out my window and straight into the offices of people working in high-rise buildings and close enough to easily determine if they were male or female. The buildings rose into the sky much higher than the plane was flying. Not fully awake, I was sure we were going to crash! And yet, the other passengers, mostly Chinese, didn't seem to be panicking. It turned out that the original, and only Hong Kong airport at that time, was tucked into the only available landing space, requiring an approach that takes the plane between buildings, and requiring a sharp right-hand turn for the final approach. At that point, the plane interacted with some sort of laser beam to guide the aircraft onto the runway. I could breathe again.

Over the next several days, I would be attending the English Institute's annual teacher's conference, which takes place every February. Teachers of all subjects are recruited from across the United States and Canada to teach English and share the "Good News" in universities across China. An Apostle Paul tent making approach. The purpose of these annual conferences was three-fold: (1) Give teachers and their families a break from the stress of being constantly under surveillance by the government. (2) Provide an opportunity for them to find out from other teachers from across China, what techniques were working for them, and (3) Enable the Institute to provide updated information on security and changing political climate depending on what province they were teaching in.

It was always interesting to hear the stories from teachers who were sharing the Good News in a closed country where you could be arrested and expelled for saying the wrong thing. They were highly creative in sharing the Good News in a classroom environment.

I talked with as many teachers as I could, but because they were so busy, most of the interviews took place at dinner, or late in the evening. During the afternoons I had some time and decided to explore the fascinating city of Kowloon, Hong Kong.

SMALL GANG, BIG KNIVES

During these conferences everyone stayed at the YMCA in Kowloon to keep costs as low as possible. With hundreds of teachers and several staff from headquarters, staying in regular hotels can get expensive. Most afternoons, I would go to my room, grab a pair of good walking shoes, and start exploring a block away at the Star Ferry. I worked my way along the harbor, watching people selling their food and goods from their boats which also serve as their homes. I weaved in and out from the harbor to the many small shops that tightly cram the city for miles in all directions. Somewhere between Nathan Road and

Soy Street I had unknowingly wondered into a less than desirable part of town, an area of gang activity and other illegal pursuits.

I was fascinated by a group of young fellows sitting around a small table playing Mahjong, a board game originating in China. The game pieces were all made of jade. There were about ten young men standing around watching two fellows play the game. All of them were wearing sleeveless white under shirts with various dragon-type tattoos up and down their arms. Maybe that should have been a clue to what happen next, but I moved closer to get a better look.

One of the players looked up at me with an incredibly angry expression that could kill. He seemed very annoyed at my presence. I suddenly felt like I had stumbled onto some state secret, or some sort of religious Mahjong High Mass. Before I could extricate myself, "the angry one" jumped up and in a matter of seconds produced a knife, one of those fancy wrist-twisting maneuvers that exposed a 7-inch knife blade. All the others were staring at me to see what would happen next. I figured it was useless to run. Run where? I didn't even know where I was. All I knew was it was a long way back to the YMCA. It was equally useless to stay and fight a guy with a seven-inch knife blade with nine other guys who would surely join in the fray. My only available option seemed to be humor.

I stood my ground, held out my right hand as if to say *"wait,"* while I carefully dug into my pants pocket with my left hand. I pulled out my trusty little red Swiss Army pocketknife, the kind with the toothpick, tweezers, little scissors, nail file, and calmly unfolded the tiny little one-inch blade. I then stood back with my left arm behind my back as in a sword fighting stance, held out my little blade and said with a smile on my face, *"On guard."*

My opponent stood there for a moment with a stunned look on his face, not knowing what to do. His buddies were staring at me with looks that clearly said, "Who is this fool?"

After what seemed like forever, but was probably only 15 or 20 seconds, the angry leader with the knife smiled and broke into laughter. So did all his friends. Situation defused.

They pulled up an orange crate and invited me to watch their game. It is said that music is a universal language. I'm sure that's true, but so is humor -- at least it was this time.

LUNCH ON THE GUANGDONG EXPRESS

After a week in Kowloon, I traveled by train to Guangdong China, up through the New Territories north of Kowloon. The train was an old one but relatively comfortable. It was operated much like an airliner in the sense that lunch was served by an attendant who came through each car with a cart. There weren't many choices. You can have anything you want as long as it's soup with Chinese-made soda pop or water. Remembering not to drink the water, I ordered a Coke. I noticed that it was bottled in China but figured it surely must be produced under the bottling standards of Coke U.S.A. Along with my drink I had a bowl of the "soup of the day." It was reddish rust in color and didn't have much taste. At least it was hot. I learned later that it was coagulated pig blood soup, a delicacy for the Chinese. For me, not so much. After learning what I had ingested and feeling somewhat nauseated, I experienced no ill effects other than an occasional desire to snort. Fortunately, this only lasted for a couple hours.

When I reached Guangdong, the first thing I noticed was the platform was full of poor people trying to sell postcards of the area, and all the postcards were exactly the same.

At the time of my visit, it was a year after the Tiananmen Square student uprising in 1989. Near the train platform there was a picture behind a glass-encased rectangular type bulletin board, the kind you would find on almost any college campus in America. A closer look revealed a picture depicting eight blind-folded students on their knees, hands tied behind their backs. Directly behind them stood eight soldiers with rifles pointed at the backs of their heads. The poster was an advertisement by the government that there would be an execution the following week at the local soccer stadium. All the university students who were "suspected" of being involved in the uprising had been rounded up and would be shot. Just suspected, no trial, no proof. All townspeople in the area were expected to attend. The admission fee equaled a week's pay for most of the local poor people. If they refused to attend, the cost would be deducted from their pay and enforced by the local police. Welcome to Communism.

Most of the students who participated in the demonstrations did so along the coastal cities of China. I talked with many students on this trip at various Universities. Most of them remained on campus for several months after the deadly government crackdown for fear that they would be arrested if they were found in any of the small villages and towns that surrounded the universities. Many reported that they had seen dump-trucks full of students being driven into the countryside. The trucks came back empty. No one ever saw them again.

I'm always amazed how so many people, who are free to vote in our country and other western countries, often support socialistic or Communist regimes. Many of these voters have never visited a Communist country and seen the tremendous poverty, hopelessness and total control of citizens that are produced by totalitarian governments. I like the way Thomas Jefferson stated it: "Tyranny is defined as that which is legal for the government but illegal for the citizenry." Edmund Burke said it pretty well too, "The essence of tyranny is the enforcement of stupid laws." But the quote I like most is from Susan B. Anthony, "Resistance to tyranny is obedience to God." Speaking of senseless laws, as I rewrite this chapter during the Covid-19 pandemic, Wisconsin issued a new law stating that everyone must wear a mask in their own home while "Zooming" for business or church meetings. Ignorance gone to seed comes to mind.

JAMES, THE BUILDER OF MEN AND CITIES.

My next stop on the train trip was Shenzhen. At the time, it consisted of only a few small buildings around the train station, surrounded by small farms and wide-open countryside. A couple years later I would meet and have dinner on Hong Kong Island with James Jihin, (I called him J.J. short) a Chinese born businessmen and a strong Christian. He was the one the Chinese Communist Government had chosen to turn Shenzhen into a metropolis, compete with modern housing, light and medium manufacturing, modern skyscrapers, office buildings and hotels.

For a number of years, J.J. had built many of the newer skyscrapers, apartment buildings and modern hotels in Kowloon and on Hong Kong Island, across the harbor from Kowloon. He was known for his honest business dealings, which attracted the attention of the regime in Beijing. They were looking for a qualified contractor/builder who could be trusted, so it would be okay to use him even if he was a known Christian. The government had economic leverage which they would attempt to use in persuading him.

At the time there was a concrete shortage and many of J.J.'s concrete suppliers in the U.S. and elsewhere couldn't keep up with the demand. J.J.'s numerous construction projects were severely affected by the shortage, costing him thousands of dollars per day as projects sat idle. I remember the shortage well because I had purchased a house in southern California and could not get a brick wall built for lack of concrete. The Chinese government had access through their contacts to fast available supplies of concrete and promised James that if he would design and build Shenzhen, he would have all the concrete he needed to complete his Hong Kong projects.

JJ struggled with the decision for a couple of weeks, having no desire to do business with the Communists. However, on a business trip to Shanghai he felt the Lord tell him to go ahead as a witness of his love for the Lord. Through his business integrity, he would be glorifying his heavenly Father. He called the authorities after his plane landed to accept the offer. He signed contracts two days later in Beijing and the very next day concrete trucks started showing up at all his Hong Kong construction sites.

SPIRITUALLY HUNGRY STUDENTS AND BLOOD THIRSTY MOSQUITOS

During my time in China, I was to spend a week at a university in the rural countryside. I would be staying with a young American couple who had been teaching at the university for a couple of years and living on campus.

On my first night there I had dinner with them and their two small daughters, after which I walked the university grounds adjacent to their campus living quarters. The students were all very friendly, especially the girls who seemed more outgoing extraverts than the boys. The girls all looked more like 14 or 15 years of age instead of 20 or 21. I was aware that many of them were looking for an escape route out of China. It's not uncommon for them to latch on to any foreigner from any country, but especially an American of any age, as a possible ticket out of the country.

During my walk I came up behind one of these young girls practicing her English. She was startled to see an American and quickly asked me to review her English pronunciation. She wanted to know if I was a Christian and went to church and Sunday school. Within 10 minutes, 30 students were gathered around, listening, and asking more questions about churches in America and who Jesus was. Wow! What an opportunity! Their open questions in a closed country caught me by surprise. I could tell by their interest level that this could take some time, so I suggested we move to the lawn area and sit on the grass.

As we did the questions kept coming as fast as I could handle them. A half-circle formed quickly, and our discussion continued well past dark. Unfortunately, mosquitos were also swarming like bats leaving a cave for a night of feasting. Somehow, they seemed to know there was a new source of foreign blood in town. As annoying as the bites were, I felt like the Apostle Paul or Peter expounding on the scriptures in the most careful, common language I could muster. I had to be cautious because I couldn't be sure if someone in the group was a PSA (Public Security Agent). PSA's lived on the campus among the students and there was always at least one in every class. Unless a student knew and told you who it was, you could never be sure. The students asked me to teach them more English in some of their classes the following day, which I was honored to do.

After returning to my hosts' home that evening, we had a cup of green tea together and a good conversation about the joys and hazards of sharing the Good News in such an environment. At 11 p.m. we all pretty much talked out and retired for the evening. After washing up and treating mosquito bites I finally retired to a fairly large extra bedroom and climbed into bed under a mosquito net, exhausted and ready for a good night's rest and quite satisfied I had safely shared a little about the story of Jesus. Happily, I was not joined by mosquitos. Besides, I had already been bitten at least 30 times while sitting on the grass and already looking like small golf balls where bulging from my face and arms. Fortunately, I had received malaria shots from my family doctor before leaving.

It was quiet for about 15 minutes as the construction just outside my second-story window had ceased for a shift change. In China, construction of new buildings goes on 24/7, 365 days a year. The new five-story building going up just 25 feet from my window would contain thirty new classrooms, administrative offices, and dormitories on the upper floors. The temporary construction elevator for hauling bricks and other construction materials to the upper floors, was operated by a very noisy diesel generator below my window.

Most universities in China do not have inside elevators for students and teachers. The dorms are ridiculously small, narrow, and decorated in Spartan fashion, usually containing bunk beds three high on each side of the room to accommodate six students. In the center between the beds is a simple small table where four to six students can eat or study. If all the students are in the same room at the same time, I have no idea how they manage. Dressing in the morning before class takes place in shifts as there is not much room for everyone to be out of bed and getting dressed at the same time. Toilets and showers are down at the end of the hall.

TICKIE TIC, TICKIE TIC, TICKIE TIC, AND COBRAS

As I lay in bed during the quiet 15-minute interlude of construction activities, I heard sounds all around me. It sounded like some sort of little creature crawling across the linoleum floor, *tickie tic, tickie tic, tickie tic.* I tried to imagine what it could be. I was fully aware that there are venomous snakes in China, probably quite common in the huts and mud brick homes in the hinterlands, but not here. It certainly didn't sound like slithering snakes.

I listened more intently as the sound intensified. Whatever it was, their numbers seemed to be increasing. My curiosity finally got the best of me. I grabbed my small pen flashlight, pulled apart the mosquito netting and shined the light in the direction of the strange noise. Some 50 cockroaches about the size of tablespoons were hastily dashing around the floor in search of something to devour. I call them the cheetahs of the bug world. These things were big enough in size and numbers to kidnap me and hold me for ransom. How do I get rid of these things? I'm never going to get any sleep knowing I'm surrounded. They were looking for a meal and I was determined not to be on the menu. On the other hand, there was no way to eliminate them. The diesel motor started up again and drowned out the sound of their movements. Good enough. Besides, cockroaches don't eat people...do they? I've heard rats can, but I didn't see any. The diesel engine actually became a nice background white noise and I soon drifted off to sleep.

The following morning the roaches had vacated. I enjoyed a wonderful breakfast of scrambled eggs, toast and coffee and had enlightening conversation about life in China with my American teacher hosts.

Their day would first begin by boiling water to put in four large thermoses for the day's usage in the classroom teaching the various English classes. I would join them to take over a couple of the classes. The afternoons were spent shopping for fresh foods at the local open-air markets a couple miles away in the village, requiring a walk of four miles round trip. Shopping for fresh food is a daily task as there are no refrigerators. Much will spoil even though it may still be squirming when purchased. By the end of the day I would know how exhausting it is just to survive with the simplest of necessities.

After breakfast, I headed out the front door and down the wide cement steps. The steps were framed with cement handrails on both sides, culminating at the bottom with a large, square, flat concrete post. As I was going down the steps, I was looking across the campus and didn't see the coiled hooded Cobra with raised head perched on the flat landing at the bottom. I was about three feet away when I finally saw him. His evil shining eyes were level with mine as he sat on the post. One bite and serious trouble and pain would have found me.

I froze and quickly jumped to my left about the same time people came out the door and began walking down the steps. I yelled for them to stay to the left as they came down the steps.

A few tense moments later the snake slithered down the post and off into the bushes. No harm done, but I remember wanting to kill it. I just didn't happen to have my 12-gauge shotgun with me.

I taught several classes that day, and felt it went very well even though there was indeed a Public Security Agent (PSA) in every class. The students knew who they were and several of them quietly pulled me aside to identify them for me. Hence, most of my time was spent answering their questions on proper pronunciation of English words, and what life was like in the United States, rather than addressing the spiritual topics they had brought up the day before on the lawn. It was truly a wonderful experience. I think of those students often wondering how they're doing.

A few days after returning home I was asked by Dr. Ken to represent the ministry at a special donor event in Sioux Falls, South Dakota. It turned out to be a shock for me as well as a test of my patience.

DIVISION IN THE BODY?

A number of wealthy donors from across South Dakota had invited several organizations like ours to come and present their ministry work in various countries around the world. Being fairly new to missions I thought to myself, "This is wonderful. I'll get to hear what other ministries are doing and how everyone is working together in our own way to share the Good News.

Up to this point in my short mission's career I found it exciting that so many missions groups were all working toward the same high purpose and all using different formats and approaches. Well, not exactly working together. I guess it was naïve thinking on my part. There is competitiveness and jealousy in the business world and the same is true of the mission world. Not every part of the Body of Christ has realized I Corinthians 12: 25-26, *"So that there should be no division in the body, but that its parts should have equal concern for each other. If one part suffers, every part suffers with it; if one part is honored, every part rejoices with it."* (NIV2011)

Some twenty organizations had been invited, from the larger ones like Campus Crusade to middle size and smaller ones that weren't as well known in the Christian missions' community. We were in a large room lined up and seated on one side. On the other side were several wealthy donors from around both North and South Dakota. We were separated by a large open space in the middle, with a large podium at the head of the room and a projection screen for those who wanted to use a Power Point presentation. Everyone received the same amount of time to present their ministry with time afterwards for Q & A.

I was scheduled as the third speaker in the morning of the second day. My talk went quite well, and so did the question-and-answer part of the program. But sadly, many of my counterparts were not as supportive. They accused the ministry I represented of not cooperating with them in the same countries where they were working. I told them this was because we were engaged in extremely sensitive work in these closed countries. I explained that every mission outreach in the room had created auxiliary ministries, much like corporations have holding companies under one holding company. For instance, Campus Crusade for Christ operates in many closed countries under different names. We chose not to go that route.

I also explained that if the authorities discovered we were working with one of the other agencies in proselytizing within a Communist country it would mean all of us would be kicked out. However, we do tell these same countries we are a Christian organization from the onset, so we don't have to operate under a fictitious name. There is nothing to hide. How many of you operate with the same level of openness? The room was silent.

While I felt fairly good about the way I handled the situation, it was the beginning of a reality check for me that there is jealously among para-church organizations who should be working together, praying for one another, and supporting each other for the glory of God. I will cover this in more detail later, showing how destructive and wasteful this has been in some countries, thereby allowing the devil to walk right in and destroy the foundations of work already accomplished.

I invited Dr. Ted Engstrom to join me on my 1st trip to China who was then serving as our Vice Chairman of the Board & President Emeritus, World Vision. Picture taken at the Emperor's Summer Palace.

Great Wall of China – on my third trip to China, Stella was able to join me to see the work firsthand, including an opportunity to teach English to a class of University professors.

Stella teaching an English class at the Beijing Teachers University.

25

BLOOD SUCKING GREEN BEETLES

After returning from international trips there was not much time to rest. Instead, I'd begin traveling around the United States, meeting with potential and existing donors while everything I had just witnessed was still fresh on my mind. Investors like to know what's going on with their donated money.

In addition to the donors who were CEOs and "Captains of Industry," I often went to visit wealthy farmers owning ten or twelve thousand-plus acres. When I met with these families, I felt extremely grateful for the days I had spent on my grandfather's farm as a boy. Those experiences had instilled in me a love for farming and country life, as well as an appreciation for the hard work that farming entails. I felt completely at home on the farm and connected immediately with prospective donors who made their living from the earth.

I made many of these trips in the fall harvest season because I loved helping with the harvest even though it has changed and modernized a great deal since my boyhood days. It was wonderful to be out in the fresh air with the sights and sounds of my youth. It was a special thrill for me to be driving an eight-row corn harvester. Absolutely exciting to be able to look at the computer screen mounted above the windshield to see the exact number of bushels being harvested per acre. And then there was the stereo music and the air-conditioned cab. My grandfather could not have imagined such a harvesting tool or the cost of one these behemoth machines. I was honored they trusted me to operate these $300,000 pieces of equipment.

Many of the farmers had large families which meant there was not always enough room for me to stay with them in their homes. In one small farming community there were no hotels, so I stayed with one of their cousins by the name of Doris, who owned and operated a beautiful bed and breakfast in town five miles from the farm. Her B&B had six bedrooms, many of which were usually rented out to salesmen calling on farmers. In the morning, all the tenants had a country breakfast together, prepared by Doris in her country-style kitchen. It brought back memories of the big breakfasts I had enjoyed with my grandparents on their small farm so many years ago. It also offered abundant conversations with other fellows from diverse walks of life selling their equipment and seed to farmers.

I always had a great home-cooked dinner at these farms and enjoyed telling them what the ministry was accomplishing and how the Lord was using their donations in the lives of those we were serving throughout Asia.

One night I came back to the B&B later than usual. I climbed the stairway up to my room as quietly as possible. I quickly cleaned up and went directly to sleep without turning on a light. An hour later I was awakened by something pricking the back of my neck. The room was filled with moonlight, so it wasn't really necessary for me to turn on a lamp. I looked at my pillow and saw a somewhat-fluorescent big green beetle. I didn't know until that night that some species of beetle's bite people. With a swish of my hand, I sent the bug flying across the room and then lay awake for another hour wondering if big green beetles in these parts were poisonous. Apparently not since I woke up when the alarm went off at 4:30 a.m. and ready for another exciting day on the farm.

After dressing I noticed that the pillow had a large dark spot that looked like dried blood. I checked my neck with a mirror but found no swelling or redness. I was relieved. My clothes were draped over a rocking chair, under which I noticed that big bug

I had killed during the night. It was flattened and quite dead. I reached for it and found it to be a chocolate mint in a brilliant florescent green wrapper which Doris always put on the pillow after making the room up every morning. The supposed blood on my pillow was actually melted chocolate.

In spite of feeling foolish it was amusing story I related at breakfast downstairs with all the other sales guys. Everyone had a good belly laugh, especially Doris who thought it was a great story for the local newspaper. A month later she sent me a copy of the front-page clipping in the local paper, *Farming News.* The headline read, "LOS ANGELES MAN BITTEN BY LARGE FLUORESCENT GREEN BEETLE WHILE SLEEPING." The headlines garnered great deal of local attention and more laughs. God has a sense of humor. So, should we. I still have that article somewhere in my files.

A $25,000 CHALLENGE WAGER

The farmer I was visiting at the time had come with me on a trip to China to see the work, so he was well aware that I would be asking him for a large gift toward the end of my visit.

To make it interesting, he challenged me in the barn one afternoon. He handed me two farm implements weighing about five pounds each. I don't remember what they were called, but they were used in connecting a tiller-plow to a tractor. He said, "I'll give you $25,000 if you can hold one in each hand, palms down and arms straight out for three minutes. I said, "Wait a minute." I was fairly sure I could do it and knew he had the money, so suggested, "How about if we make it a little more challenging for both of us; how about $50,000 per minute, per arm, for a total of $300,000." He looked a little worried since I had upped the ante so easily.

He said, "And if you can't?" I replied, "If I can't we revert back to the $25,000." His response was "OK! You're on."

When I left the next day, I had a check for $300,000 but could barely lift my arms, let along lift my carry-on luggage into the overhead bin. A female flight attendant did it for me and thereby unknowingly rubbed salt into my humiliating wound by saying, "Nothing to it."

I said, "Yes, but not if you knew what I went through yesterday."

She asked what the story was, and my brief version prompted her to bring me a couple of ice packs. What a sweetheart!

Additional duties for me on the farm included removing new-born piglets from the sow to another pen thereby giving "mom" a few hours to rest. Since sows can give birth to 10 piglets and sometimes more per litter and have two or three litters per year, I knew that poor sow could certainly use a little R & R. My assignment was taking these little screaming newborns by their hind legs, four at a time in each hand, moving them to another location in the barn and taking them back to the mother a few hours later. This particular farm raised pigs commercially, so often had several sows giving birth the same day. It can keep a "piglet transporter" busy for several hours moving them back and forth.

The barn itself was beautiful and newly built with heating and cooling, drains for every stall and plenty of hose bibs for washing the concrete floors several times a day, all of which drained to a central holding pit located outside the barn for sun drying and was later sold for fertilizer production. The outdoor holding pit is pumped out regularly and hauled away by a commercial pig poop removal service. A clever sign on the back of the tanker truck read, "Pig Poop is your Waste, but our Wealth."

If you're a city dweller and never smelled pig waste, you are blessed. The stench is indescribable and overpowering. After only a few hours in that barn, my clothes smelled the same way, and I had to leave the next morning to catch a flight home. There was no way I could pack clothes in my carry-on without stinking up the whole plane. All my other clothes where dirty and with nothing fresh to put on, I sat at the dinner table that evening in a borrowed bath robe while Grandma, who lived with the family, washed all my clothes for the following morning's flight. Thank you again Grandma. I'm sure everyone on the flight would have thanked her too. Quite an interesting trip; bitten by a big green beetle, stinking like a pig, shoulders so sore I couldn't lift my arms any higher than my belt buckle, which by the way, Grandma had to buckle for me that following morning. Very humbling! But then.... I did have that check.

In August 1990 Stella and I celebrated our 25th anniversary by taking a three-week trip to the Hawaiian Islands, spending a week each on the islands of Oahu, Maui, Kauai. We rented a helicopter service for the day flying to the top of Haleakala Observatory and down lava shoots and up to the top to the sound of William Tell Overture, lunch on Black Sand Beach, rented a catamaran with a crew of three to sail to the north end of Maui, snorkeled with Sand Sharks and countless colorful fish, stayed at the Turtle Bay Hilton north side of Oahu where we golfed and rode horseback along the beach. What a wonderful trip. We took another trip to Turtle Bay Hilton five years later after I had conducted a two-week donor vision trip to several provinces of China and Hanoi Vietnam. After calling Stella from Hong Kong with a spur of the moment suggesting she meet me at the airport in Oahu. We arrived within an hour of each other. I was exhausted from the China trip and slept 24 hours straight while Stel floated in the Bay below our room. It was most relaxing.

When I woke up and wondered downstairs to join Stella floating in the quiet Bay, I quickly noticed Hawaii Tropic was holding their annual swimsuit calendar shoot the same week. The scenery had an additional beauty that year....my wife was there.

26

OUTER MONGOLIA

Fundraisers are always busy, at least the best ones are. As a fundraiser, you have the freedom to control your own schedule and are rarely expected to be in the office. At least that's the way it's supposed to work. Not all ministries understand this simple concept. You can't build relationships and raise much money without being on the road visiting donors and continuously visiting new ones. Today, many organizations use only the Internet, long before the Covid-19 Pandemic. Some ministries want the Director of Development, or the VP of Advancement, who may or may not be supervising several others, to be available for endless meetings governing the daily administrative functions. However, a fundraiser managing 250 smaller donors and 150 major donors has plenty of his/her own administrative functions, especially if they don't have a secretary or administrative assistant.

By now I was into my third year as a fundraiser for the English Institute, serving as Foundation Development Manager and also as Director of Development for its Canadian affiliate based on Vancouver Canada. My schedule was demanding, continuously flying to cities throughout the United States and Canada. Fundraising, at its core, is *friendship making*. I always saw it as effort to connect God's people with God's work. The larger the president's vision, the easier it is to portray that vision to donors. A leader who has no vision is a ship without a rudder, drifting anywhere and accomplishing little. Additionally, if a ministry's needs are broken down into small projects you should not be talking to a wealthy individual who has a giving capacity a thousand times greater than your project. Why not? Because that donor is looking for big vision, big opportunities, big long-term plans that have the capability of enlarging the Kingdom. For donors like these, it's almost insulting to ask for a $10,000 gift. He didn't build his company on thinking small. He wants to give money to ministries that think the same way.

At the end of that first year with English Institute, I was planning a major donor trip when I received a call from Dr. Ken asking me to go to Mongolia for a ten-day trip with a man named George Patterson. He was thirty years older than me, and a natural-born apostle, having planted some 300 churches in South and Central America. Dr. Ken asked him to do a special week of training for the four new teachers who would be serving in the newly opened country of Mongolia. Although I didn't realize it at the time, I would be traveling with a modern-day version of an Apostle Paul, both in his faith and demeanor. He was a calm, quiet man who always had the assurance that God was in control of every situation. During this trip, I often thought of the adventures the Apostle Paul had experienced, like being shipwrecked and being bitten by the viper coming out of the fire. There were no fires and no vipers on the trip, but on one occasion the words "plane crash" flew through my mind (pun intended). I would learn from his example and remember, often rejoicing in the words from that familiar hymn, "Blessed Assurance, Jesus is Mine."

Our trip would take us to Khovd, Mongolia, which is so far off the beaten path you feel like you're going to fall off the earth. It is 1,270 miles north of Lhasa Tibet, 200 miles east of Kazakhstan, and several hundred miles south of Siberia. In other words, at the crossroads of "doesn't exist and you can't get there from here." In our letters to donors we often referred to the area as *the ends of the earth.* For geography buffs, Khovd is situated at the foot of the Mongols Altay Mountains on the Buyant River. It has a cold, desert climate, with long, dry, frigid winters and short summers. Several ethnic tribes reside in the area, including the Kazakhs and another seven or so Mongolian tribes. Some of the tribes represent their own nomadic village with their own culture, a slightly different dialect, clothes, dances, songs, ceremonies, and musical instruments.

I really didn't want to go to Mongolia, as I was in the middle of planning a major fundraising trip across the U.S. and Canada. Dr. Ken said I didn't have to go but he thought it would provide an excellent opportunity to see another cultural area of the ministry outreach. He was right of course.

I had a week to unwind my fundraising trip and prepare for Mongolia where it was now the beginning of winter. I was told that because winter was waiting in the wings, combined with the breakup of the Soviet Union -- which once held Mongolia as one of its satellites -- there was some risk that we might be stranded there for the winter if the Russians couldn't get gasoline to the remote region of Khovd. This then was in the back of my mind as I prepared for the trip; the apprehension of being stranded a thousand miles from the nearest airport was a substantial concern.

I decided to cover this risk by taking extra clothes, beyond my normal Spartan packing methods. I would also carry a large duffle bag filled with non-perishable food such as crackers, peanut butter, small lunch size cans of tuna, power bars and anything else I could think of at the time. When I finished with my list, the duffle bag alone weighed 75 pounds. But hey, I was prepared. If stranded at the ends of the earth, I might lose a lot of weight -- which wouldn't really hurt me -- but I could also survive the winter.

In those days there were no direct flights from Los Angeles to Beijing, so the following week I flew to Hong Kong and picked up my connecting flight back northeast to Beijing, staying at the Beijing Holiday Inn for the night and connecting with Ken and George at the Beijing airport the following morning. The flight from Beijing to Ulaanbaatar, Mongolia's capital, was on Russian Aeroflot Airlines. I called it Aero-Flop Airlines because they were always flopping and falling from the skies. In 1973 alone they had 27 crashes killing nearly 800 people that year. It was an interesting plane, but the next hop from Ulaanbaatar to Khovd was even more interesting. (Scary might be a better word). The flight from Beijing to Ulaanbaatar was a four-engine jet much the same size as the original Boeing 707. There were six passengers on board. Ken, George, and I made up 50 per cent of the passenger manifest.

Like most commercial airline carriers there were restrooms front and aft, but all of them looked like and smelled like they hadn't been cleaned since Genghis Kahn. There was so much dried, crusted human waste on the floor the doors were stuck open. I imagined the toilet wouldn't flush anyway as the waste tanks probably hadn't been pumped and drained since Genghis time either. I decided to wait until the two-hour, 753-mile flight was over and we had landed in the capital city of Ulaanbaatar.

The airport in Ulaanbaatar had no ramps or extending arms coming out from the terminal like most modern airports. An old, rusty Russian ladder pickup truck pulled up for deplaning. This was only a few years after the fall of Russia, so I wasn't surprised at the lack of up-to-date equipment. The Russian occupiers had high-tailed it back to Moscow leaving Mongolia even more destitute than when they controlled the country.

Communism and Socialism never produced much for the Mongolian populace, or the people of any other country for that matter. Mongolia was on its own for the first time after 70 years of Communist rule. The authorities had set up a parliament and held free elections, but the Communists remained in control. My experiences there brought to mind a quote from Alexis de Tocqueville *"Democracy and socialism have nothing in common but one word: equality. But notice the difference: while democracy seeks equality in liberty, socialism seeks equality in restraint and servitude."*

At the time of my visit, Ulaanbaatar was a city of 500,000 people. The population of the entire country of Mongolia was only 2 million, with 22 million horses. Consequently, Mongolians are superb horsemen and always have been having conquered more square miles on the earth than the Romans. I don't think anyone knows the Yak population.

The Yak is a long-haired bovine looking creature, much like our domestic steer, but somewhat shorter with lots of long hair covering their entire body. They are found throughout the Himalayan region of South-Central Asia, and on the Tibetan Plateau as far north as Mongolia and Russia. Most yaks are domesticated, and I had the opportunity of riding one on this trip. Yaks are powerful beasts of burden and extensively used the way oxen are used in other parts of the world. They have great value in Mongolia, as are camels. About 75 per cent of the population is nomadic and both animals are used to carry Gers or Yurts (round tent homes) for families, as well as all inside furnishings as they move from location to location while searching for good grazing.

Yurts, as the Russians call them, have been a distinctive feature of life in Central Asia for at least three thousand years. The first written description of a yurt used as a dwelling was recorded by Herodotus, the 'father of history', who lived in Greece between 484 and 424 B.C. He described yurt-like tents as the dwelling place of the Scythians, a horse riding-nomadic nation who lived in the northern Black Sea and Central Asian region from around 600 B.C. to A.D. 300. Mongolians call them Gers and traditional Gers consist of an expanding wooden circular frame carrying a felt cover. The felt is made from the wool of the flocks of sheep and skins of Yaks. It's difficult to find trees anywhere in Mongolia, except in the Alti Mountains. The timber and supporting poles to make the external structure are not found in much of Mongolia these days and are usually obtained by trade.

THE VIEW FROM ABOVE

From my airplane window, Ulaanbaatar looked rather stark. Beneath us were a few four or five story buildings and a large number of Gers scattered around both inside and outside the city limits. The most noticeable and tallest standing structure was a smokestack at the coal-burning power plant. However, they didn't have enough coal to power much of anything unless it was shipped in from Russia, and that didn't happen very often. The area around Ulaanbaatar and stretching for a thousand miles in every direction is a barren treeless desert. It really did look like the end of the earth. My first thought was, *"What am I doing here and will I ever get home from this isolated place."* I felt an over-whelming sense of loneliness. A spirit of depression swept over me like a wave. The next day that feeling would greatly intensify.

The Ulaanbaatar airport was very much a third world experi-ence. The floor was covered with worn-out and torn linoleum, yet relatively clean. We took an old Russian style bus to our hotel, a former Russian military barracks for Russian army officers. The "hotel" was, as you might expect, very Meager in décor, with two bedrooms, one bath and a small kitchen. The water worked only one hour a day, but you never knew what hour. If you were lucky a quick shower might be possible. Quick was the operative word, first because one never knew how long the water would actually be running, and secondly because the water temperature was somewhere around 45 degrees and you wanted to get it over as quickly as possible. Forget hot water.

When there was water in the shower and tub it probably hadn't worked in years and actually offered only a sputtering of rusty water. I opted for a sponge bath if the water in the sink was working. If not, you began to smell like a yak rather quickly. Toilet flushing was dependent on what I called "the water whooshing hour," which naturally remained unflushed if you couldn't hold and time your deposits to match unknown whooshing hour.

After somewhat of a restless night sleeping on a soft bed and hard overly stuffed pillow made of Yak hair -- about the hardness of a cement block -- George and I headed for the airport early the following morning for our 1,000-mile flight to Khovd. Dr. Ken stayed in the area for a fishing trip with local Communist Parliament members.

As George and I boarded our flight the effects of Communist rule were fully evident. The piston-driven twin-prop engine

Aeroflot plane we boarded probably had not been serviced in 10 or 15 years due to a lack of parts and mechanics.

The plane had 120 seats, two on each side of the center aisle. The nose of the plane looked like it had been through an aerial flack attack over Dresden in World War II. George and I walked out onto the tarmac and handed one of our suitcases to a fellow loading the rear luggage compartment and boarded from the rear door and sat about three quarters of the way back from the cockpit on the right side. I kept my 75-pound food duffle bag with me, putting it under my feet and forward as much as possible under the seat in front of me. As we talked, Mongolian passengers kept boarding until all the seats were filled.

Seated in the forward rows were eight German fellows who were heading for the Altay Mountains west of Khovd for a week of hunting Snow Leopards. They had loaded all their high-powered rifles and gear in the rear and had paid $25,000 a person to the government for the right to hunt these rare and protected animals. I'm not a tree-hugger type of guy. I love cats of all kinds, but especially any endangered species like Snow Leopards. If they actually were able to even find and shoot one, they would pay another $35,000 for each kill. The thought horrified me and secretly it didn't endear me to these guys who were rather arrogant to begin with.

Snow Leopards are sometimes called the Ghost Cat because they are very elusive, well camouflaged making them extremely difficult to see, even with high powered binoculars or rifle scopes. They are slightly smaller than the other big cats, but they range in size, generally weighing between 60 and 120 pounds, with an occasional large male reaching 165 pounds. Females are smaller, often less than 55 pounds. The tail is a dominant feature, being quite long and flexible to help them maintain balance while traversing up and down nearly vertical rocky terrain. Their tails are thickly covered with fur, allowing them to be used like a blanket to protect their faces when they curl up to sleep in cold, windy, snowy conditions. Small, rounded ears help minimize heat loss. Their paws are very wide, helping them to distribute their weight better for walking on snow. They are yet another one of God's magnificent creations designed for harsh environments. The closest I ever came to one was a dead one on the return trip from Khovd, killed by one of the German hunters. Fortunately, they had only killed one.

The plane was finally fully loaded. Every seat was taken, but passengers kept boarding. A small Mongolian woman holding a baby motioned that she wanted to sit between George and me. We naturally wanted to be accommodating, especially since other passengers were also making room to do the same in other rows. Having a window seat, I turned my legs toward the window, put up both arm rests and placed my feet on my duffle bag beneath me. George turned his lean 6'4" frame and moved his long legs toward the aisle. When we were finally settled, George's knees where approaching his chest and the woman was sitting between us on the split seats, probably smaller than a 15-inch laptop computer, while holding her small baby in her arms. Did I mention there aren't any safety rules when flying in Mongolia? And no seatbelts either.

Soon, the center aisle leading to the cockpit was filled with people sitting on the floor. Finally, the pilot and co-pilot came on board through the rear door, stumbling their way up the isle trying their best not to step on anyone. They weren't always successful. You could hear grunts as people's hands and feet were stepped on. One of the pilots nearly fell into George's lap as they moved up the aisle. Even more alarming, both pilot and co-pilot had a quart of Russian Vodka they were sipping as they stumbled up the aisle. I know this because I asked a Mongolian fellow in the seat directly in front of me, who spoke fairly good English, what they were drinking. He told me, "Russian Vodka, Mongolian pilots won't fly Russian planes unless they're drunk."

Naturally, I now felt much better. Not being a drinker, I wondered if this might be a good time to start.

Another reason for concern was that the luggage loading continued at the rear of the airplane. How could we possibly take on anymore? It was then I looked out the window and thought

I must be hallucinating. The entire front of the aircraft was up in the air and we were now sitting back into the seats as if we were in recliners.

I mentioned to George, "I don't think this plane is going to even get off the ground. We're way too heavily loaded -- and with two drunken pilots, I'm not sure I even want to be onboard. I think we should get off while we can and maybe wait for another plane." It didn't matter there was only one flight a week, and only if there was gasoline available.

George smiled and, in is usual calm manner said, "It will be fine. The Lord will get us there."

I thought to myself, "I'm glad you're so sure George, but right now I'm feeling solidly in the doubting Thomas camp."

Finally, the loading door was closed and latched leaving us like 130 sardines packed into a can designed for 60 --not to mention the weight of everyone's luggage. The engines wouldn't start. *"Thank God!"* I thought.

Airport workers rolled out a large, four-wheeled generator, and after several attempts the two engines finally started billowing large plumes of black smoke past the windows. After a full-throttle bumpy ride down a short runway we finally lifted off the ground just feet before the runway ended. That's when I started repeating Psalm 91:9-12: (KJV)

"Because thou hast made the LORD, which is my refuge, even the most High, thy habitation; there shall no evil befall thee, neither shall any plague come nigh thy dwelling. For he shall give his angels charge over thee, to keep thee in all thy ways. They shall bear thee up in their hands, lest thou dash thy foot against a stone."

George's calm spiritual demeanor seemed to be transferring to me. I felt a peace as I remembered that the Lord is in control at all times, no matter where we are -- and He holds us in the palm of His hand. Remembering the biblical account of Elisha receiving the anointing from Elijah, I wondered if some of George's mantle had been transferred to me.

Settling in as best we could, with our knees tightly against our chests, I calculated it would take four hours to reach Khovd, assuming of course, we could stay in the air.

An hour after take-off a young woman dressed in a stewardess uniform appeared from behind the curtain near the pilot's cabin. I didn't even know she was on board. She had probably been preparing lunch in the small unnoticed galley. It was a pleasant surprise to learn we were going to get lunch. I wondered how this was going to work with the center aisle full of people. For this flight attendant it was not a problem. She simply threw the box lunches to everyone as far as she could, and everyone passed the box lunch to the seat behind them. She had an exceptionally accurate arm and would make an excellent NFL first-round draft choice.

Lunch consisted of slightly cooked snails, a small, hard, dinner roll with cute little fuzzy green stuff growing on one side, and marginally cooked Kaspischer, an even-fingered Gecko (as opposed, I guess, to odd fingered geckos which *Wikipedia claims don't exist,* yet they list them). But for sure, they were some sort of small lizard. After looking inside, the box I gave it to the woman with the baby, who I was certain would enjoy it more than me. I motioned to her not to eat the furry green roll, but she ate it anyway. Perhaps she was used to it. I held the baby, a cute little girl while the mother ate. She seemed grateful, giving me a big smile, and saying something in Mongolian which I took to mean "Thank you."

I would have grabbed one of my power bars from my duffle bag but couldn't move to reach under my feet. "Oh well," I thought, "I need to lose some weight anyway." I didn't know, that by the time this trip was over, I would lose 25 pounds. I had to use my little Swiss Army knife to punch another hole in my belt so I could keep my pants up. I love that little knife and still carry it with me everywhere. I once had to cut my way out of a jammed airplane seat belt after landing in East Kalimantan on Garuda Airlines.

Shortly after lunch, I looked out the window and noticed that we were, at most, 200 feet above the ground. I thought we must be passing over some sort of plateau. Either that or all the excitement of that well-balanced box lunch, I had not noticed we were losing altitude. Suddenly, the ground dropped out from under us and the plane went into a nose-first dive. All I could see was a very sheer cliff behind us. This could not be normal. We were literally nose diving toward the ground. I thought, "Both Pilots must be passed out drunk, and this is where it all ends." I could almost see the newspaper headlines at home: "*California man dies in Mongolian plane crash – found with knees embedded in his chest.*"

The plane leveled off about 400 feet above the ground, landing a few minutes later on a small dirt road. Everyone started exiting the rear door. I was elated. George was unruffled. We looked at each other and figured my calculations must have been wrong about the estimated four hours to Khovd. I grabbed my food duffle bag and followed George out the rear exit door.

It felt especially satisfying to be stretching, and even better to be on solid terra-firma still in an upright position. We looked around for some sort of terminal building, but there was nothing in sight.

I noticed that just beyond the plane, all the bushes were noticeably more sparse, scattered, and shorter -- being only a few inches tall. Closer in, toward the plane all the bushes were noticeably taller and greener in color. That's when I noticed that nearly all the other male passengers were standing with their backs to the plane and both hands near their private parts. All the women where squatting, facing the plane. Ah Hah! An epiphany. My deductive, lightning-fast brain concluded that we had stopped for a potty-break.

Actually, it was more than that. After a few minutes, an Old Russian gas tanker truck came out from behind a grouping of large boulders, drove up and parked beneath one of the wings, connected a large four-inch hose and began pumping gas. While gas flowed into the airplane, the truck driver and both pilots stood beneath the wing, talking, and lighting up cigarettes. George and I stepped back another hundred feet, prayed and held our breath. By God's grace, there was no explosion, and after 30 minutes or so, everyone re-boarded taking their original seats.

I was right after all about the estimated flight time. We flew another two hours and landed in Khovd mid-afternoon where four American English teachers stationed there were supposed to meet us. We took a short walk across the tarmac, through the dirt floor terminal and out the front door but didn't see any people who looked like Americans. About five minutes later, our hosts showed up in an old smoke-belching Russian army Jeep. They were late because they couldn't get it started.

A young American couple from Colorado and a student from the University of Phoenix stepped out and greeted us. The younger couple made up two of the four teachers stationed here to teach English at the only university for 1,000 miles in any direction. The university student from Phoenix was doing his doctorate work on the flora and fauna of Mongolia and lived in the same building as our teachers.

We piled into the jeep and drove to the Russian-style buildings in a small settlement five miles from the airport. There were only four buildings, former Russian army barracks that were now serving as apartments for a variety of different Mongolian tribes and some Kazaks from nearby Kazakhstan.

By the way, according to Wikipedia, Kazakhstan is the world's largest landlocked country, and the ninth largest country in the world. I never would have guessed. Its territory covers 1,053,000 square miles, is larger than Western Europe and borders (clockwise from the north) Russia, China, Kyrgyzstan, Uzbekistan, and Turkmenistan. The terrain of Kazakhstan is much like Mongolia and includes flatlands, rock canyons, hills, deltas, snow-capped mountains, and deserts.

RUMORS

We first heard the rumors while at the airport waiting for the English teachers to pick us up. A little woman with the harsh, weather-worn face, had apparently started it. She sat behind a tiny window, the only one in the entire airport that was used for checking in for return flights to Ulaanbaatar. She had spread the word she was not going to allow the two Americans to get on the plane for the return flight to Ulaanbaatar next week.

Why she had said such a thing was a mystery to George and me. We couldn't understand why we were hearing this after just landing. After all, we had never met her, so what could we have done to offend her? Perhaps she was a communist and hated Americans? The rumor persisted the whole week of our stay and fueled my concern about being stuck in this remote part of the world all winter long.

I knew there was only one flight a week between Khovd and Ulaanbaatar. If we missed it, we could be stuck here for another seven days or longer. If the truck from Russia didn't show up, maybe all winter. I was glad to have the duffle bag with extra food. Chances were improving it might be needed.

As I mentioned earlier, there were only four English teachers stationed in Khovd, the young couple who had picked us up at the airport, and an older couple in their mid-60's. George stayed with the younger couple in their apartment and I stayed with the older couple. The purpose of our visit was for George to teach specifically on baptism procedure in a country where the water, if you can find any, can be frozen seven months of the year.

Each apartment consisted of a small bedroom, a living area, a bathroom of sorts, plus a small kitchen with a pot belly stove for cooking and heating. Running water worked most of the time with the water coming from deep wells. Showering was a welcome luxury. I slept quite well on the living room couch during my week's visit.

The day after we arrived the first order of business was a visit to the open-air market for food. This provided an excellent snapshot of the various tribal cultures in the area. Particularly noticeable were the Kazakhs. We watched them slaughter a lamb and we walked back half a mile to our apartment as I carried a leg and thigh of the freshly slaughtered animal over my right shoulder. There is no need for refrigerators in the winter months. If you hung your meat on the outside balcony, it would be fine since the daytime winter temperature rarely got much above freezing and sometimes colder.

That afternoon George began his teaching on planting churches and baptizing in unusual environments. After the second day, I felt it necessary to experience the culture and explore the area just in case I had to spend the next six months here. There were children playing some sort of Mongolian game in a large courtyard area between the three now converted Russian army barracks. I had no idea what the game was about so went down to watch. After watching for 30 minutes I couldn't figure out the object of the game. They had a ball about the size of a softball so decided to teach them the game of baseball.

Can you imagine trying to teach children the rules of a western game when neither of us spoke the other's language? It was quite comical, but they seemed to have a lot of fun, and even if we didn't play the game right, we sure laughed a lot. We attracted the attention of several parents and they, too, were having a great time watching. After a few hours it was time for dinner.

The next morning the children were all waiting for me at the entrance to our building. I spent an hour with them before we were off in that old Russian jeep to explore Khar Lake, 80 miles away. It is also known locally as Black Lake because the water often looks black. It's in the Mongolian Great Lakes Depression area and is part of a group of lakes that were once part of a larger prehistoric lake that disappeared 5,000 years ago.

On our return from the lake the jeep broke down. We were still about 70 miles from Khovd. It was going to take at least two and a half days to walk back, which meant we might be spending the winter here after all. Each of us had a liter of water which would have to suffice, and that was about it. If we were not on that flight at the end of the week, assuming it showed up at all, we would indeed be stuck here. I felt like Jonah must have felt in the belly of the whale. Alone!

I was comforted by some research I had done that said Mongolians are a very friendly people. If for some reason, you were stranded in the middle of nowhere you could always get back to Ulaanbaatar by camel, although it might take a couple of months. Whenever you came across a settlement, the people would take you in, feed you and give you shelter for as long as you needed it. Or they would lend you a camel and guide you back to Ulaanbaatar. Any stranger would be accepted immediately as a member of the family. This is true even though most of these people have no conception of where America is located, let alone California. There are no televisions and only a few radios, so they know absolutely nothing about international concerns or politics. They have only one concern. Surviving. Still, despite the comfort that came from knowing that Mongolians are a friendly people, it gets unbelievably dark in the middle of nowhere, and in Mongolia at that time of year it also gets extremely cold at night. And, we hadn't passed any Yurt settlements along the way. Fortunately, our University of Phoenix student had some experience with car engines, and after making an adjustment with a paper clip, screwdriver and some duct tape kept in the jeep, we were soon on our way again.

After returning safely from our Black-Lake excursion, a gift was given to us by one of the Mongolian families living in the same building. They knocked on the apartment door shortly after dinner and carried in a large trunk filled to the brim with dried clumps of Yak dung. I first thought this must have be some sort of joke or perhaps an insult? It was, however, quite the opposite and considered one of the greatest and most valuable gifts one can give a stranger. Yak chips would keep the teachers warm all winter as they burn with the same intensity and length as coal. We all thanked them and invited them to sit down and have some coffee, tea cakes and chocolate candy bar, a real treat for these nomadic people.

I spent two nights living in a Ger with this family 50 miles south of Ulaanbaatar. I was given what some almost consider their national drink, fermented mare's milk, and Vodka. I don't recommend it. One tiny little sip had me exhaling fire. I accepted for the sake of cultural politeness so as not to offend their hospitality. Finishing that small shot glass would have had me leaning against a Yak for two days wondering which way was up.

GLOWING EYES IN THE DARK – HA!

George conducted his teaching in the mornings which left the afternoons free to explore the area's many converging cultures. One evening I got back long after dark.

Keep in mind that there is no electricity. Light at night is by candlelight or Coleman-type lanterns. I now know what the term "pitch black" means. As I climbed four flights of stairs to get to my host's apartment, I discovered that it's even darker than dark in the stairwells, and naturally I had forgotten to take my little flashlight with me on this trip.

The stairs were bare concrete, and they generated a hollow echoing sound. The stairwells were also littered with broken glass. The only employment in Khovd for thousands of miles is a form of rubbing alcohol production. With the fall of Russia, a deep depression swept through Mongolia, and Khovd was hit especially hard. The workers at the plant were, like so many people across the country, were unsure of their future and many of them drank the rubbing alcohol they were producing. It is a complete understatement to say that alcoholism was rampant in Khovd.

As I was slowly making my way up the stairs, I kept stepping on something that crunched beneath my feet. Some of it was glass, but some of it sounded more like Fritos corn chips or potato chips. It wasn't until the following morning that I discovered the stairs were covered with smashed cockroaches. Dead bugs were everywhere. It reminded me of what had happened on my trip to China a year earlier. The roaches weren't the only creature I encountered in the stairwell.

As I reached the second-floor level, something in my peripheral vision caught my attention. As I looked down the hallway, I saw two glowing eyes about two feet off the floor staring back at me. I stared back and immediately thought of a snow leopard. After all, cats see and hunt in the dark. My rational mind knew this was highly unlikely, but at that moment, in the dark echoing stairwell in an unfamiliar country I wasn't taking any chances. Abandoning rational thought, I took off like I had a Saturn rocket strapped to my back. I quickly rounded the corner and shot up the stairs, taking two and three steps at a time.

When I reached the next landing, I heard that "Snow Leopard" cry out, "Baaa! Baaaa!" My leopard was somebody's goat. In case he had any plans to butt me in the butt, I fired the second booster rocket and jetted to the fifth floor, made a quick left-hand turn down the hallway to the fourth door on the left, fumbled for the key in my pocket and quickly opened the door. I listened at the door and heard the goat heading down the stairs and out the front door. The poor thing. I probably traumatized him more than he did me.

I played baseball a couple more times with the children that week -- or to be more exact, something that vaguely resembled a form of baseball with a little football mixed in. Like kids everywhere, these boys and girls loved to run, so once they got their hands on a ball, they took off in any direction. We had great fun together but wished I could speak their language to teach them the real rules of the game.

Toward the end of the week we were able to meet with two non-communist Mongolian Parliament members from the Khovd area, who graciously donated two boarding passes for our flight back to Ulaanbaatar. It was an exceptional gift as they are allowed only two trips back and forth to the capital each year. We hoped this would guarantee our seat for the return trip to Ulaanbaatar, but the rumors persisted. It was rumored the woman behind the tiny little window at the airport was not going to let us on the plane even if we had ten boarding passes. Everyone in the settlement seemed to know about it. Apparently, she had a vast power in her small domain of influence and enjoyed using it.

On the day of our scheduled departure, our host took us to the airport early in the morning. The University of Phoenix student joined us. We reasoned that if we got there early enough and were first in line, we would demonstrate our determination to be on that flight, if of course, the gas truck showed up.

THE CRUSH

For an hour we were the only four people in the airport before other passengers flooded in forming a line behind us.

"Good," I thought. "We have established our place for being first to board." There were no signs indicating gate locations and there were only two doors, one leading to the tarmac where we arrived a week earlier, and one on the other side of the terminal overlooking the runway. Our logical assumption was that the door leading to the tarmac was the one to choose since the only other door didn't even have a place for a plane to park.

Nevertheless, another rumor started that the boarding would be through the "other" door. Everyone reversed direction, facing that door, and leaving us last in line. Twenty minutes later another rumor spread through the crowd that the exit door was the one by the tarmac. Now we were again first in line. This happened two more times. The four of us decided to sit on the floor, hold hands and pray about it. At the time of our visit there were perhaps only 20 to 30 known Christians in the entire country and most likely no more than one or two of them were in the airport with the exception of the four of us. We attracted a lot of attention from the other Mongolian passengers who probably thought we were rather peculiar. As we finished our prayer the plane landed, taxied up on the tarmac and a Russian gas truck pulled out from an unnoticed Russian military Quonset hut and headed for the plane. It looked like we had made the right choice with regard to the door, but it didn't seem to matter. Before we knew what was happening, 30 people shoved their way in front of us, putting us further back in the line, with perhaps 100 people pushing us forward from behind us.

As with our flight to Khovd a week earlier this same plane would also be carrying 130 passengers coming in from Ulaanbaatar, again with 65 more people than it was designed to carry, and all of them were pushing and shoving to get through the entry door to the terminal.

Did I mention there were not yet any orderly systems in Mongolia? It was easy to see what was about to happen...and it did. All 130 people exiting the plane were pushing their way into the airport and colliding head on with all 130 of us who were trying to get onto the tarmac to board the same plane with both groups trying to go thru the same door. The word madness just isn't sufficient to describe the chaos.

The week in Khovd instilled some valuable lessons about missionary's selflessness. Things I read about missionaries, had knowledge of, but never actually experienced personally. Things you know in your head but have not yet traveled to your heart which sometimes can be the longest journey.

I observed how one last remaining Hershey's candy bar, a real treat that takes months to arrive from home, was shared equally with eight people. In fact, if they have any prized possession, from clothing to shoes or special food treats from families at home a world away, they will freely share it with fellow missionaries as well as indigenous friends. My attitude with the 70-pound duffle bag full of food I had been dragging all this time was for **my needs** in case of getting stuck in the middle of nowhere for the winter. My attitude was one of survival and totally only for **my needs**. Jesus sent out His disciples and told them to take nothing with them. He was saying HE would always meet their needs. Shouldn't I be thinking the same way?

Before starting my career in ministry, my background was the competitive world of the main frame computers, business, and banking. Dog eat dog, winner take all, take no prisoners attitudes in highly competitive situations. In my inner heart I never felt totally comfortable in that environment. I did well in it, but some people are destined for this type of life and others aren't. I wasn't. Nonetheless, some of these attitudes tarnished my sub-consciousness thought and I didn't realize it until this trip. I was feeling terribly small and overwhelmingly selfish. Before leaving for the Khovd airport that morning I purposed in my heart to leave a third of my private food stash with our missionaries host at each of the two remaining visits I would be making where they were stationed across Mongolia.

Now at the airport my food bag weighed about 50 pounds instead of 70. However, the Lord wasn't finished yet with his lesson in selfishness. Here, in this remote third world airport another test would come. Was I willing to sacrifice my life to save a stranger! A child?

George and I now had 60 people behind us with another 60 or 70 in front of us. Everyone pushed forward, shoulder to shoulder, packed together so tightly that I could barely hold on to my carry-on or the food duffle bag. At 6' 4", George was standing behind me and nearly a foot taller than I and any of the Mongolian passengers. I told him, "Just hang on to my coat tail and I'll act as a blocker to get us through that door." What was I thinking? Sure, I can handle pushing through 60 men ahead of me with 130 more coming from the opposite direction. No problem. I'm more powerful than a locomotive, able to leap tall building at a single bound and faster than a speeding bullet.

In less than a minute I was exhausted just from the struggle to stay on my feet, let alone push forward against the crowd in front of me. I felt light-headed and knew I was about to pass out. If so, I would surely get trampled in the crush, winding up with legs, arms and ribs broken and perhaps even trampled to death. Fear overwhelmed me. There certainly weren't any paramedics, hospitals or even doctors for thousands of miles.

Then, suddenly, everything came to a halt. The pushing and struggling stopped. Everyone stood motionless, standing quietly, sanely, like someone had hit the pause button on a video tape. I took a deep breath with a sigh of relief.

LET GO AND LET GOD

That's when I noticed a small clearing about five feet in diameter just in front of me. Across this small clearing there was a little Mongolian girl I guessed to be three or four years old. She was undoubtedly the cutest little thing I'd ever seen with large brown eyes. My first thought was, *"What's this cute little girl doing here? If I could barely stand up with all the pushing and shoving, how is she ever going to survive?"* She wasn't holding anyone's hand and seemed to be all by herself, just staring at me with those big brown eyes. It was as if she was talking to me through her eyes; *"I am alone, and I'm scared."*

I couldn't leave her alone in the middle of this chaos. I decided to jettison the food duffle bag in my right hand, reach across the clearing, grab her up with my right arm and hold her as tightly as I could while pulling my carry-on with my left hand. *"Lord,"* I prayed silently, *"Please give me strength to protect her."*

To my right side stood 30 or more people, including Gerry, the University of Arizona student who had come along to the airport to see us off. He yelled, "Bob, throw me your duffle bag and as soon as you get through the door on the other side of the glass partition, I'll throw it back to you."

I didn't know how he could see the little girl through all these people, but it offered a solution for me to help her. I let go of my carry-on bag in my left hand, grabbed the food duffle bag with both arms and threw all 50 lbs. of it over the heads of several people. As soon as Gerry caught it, the maddening crush started again. I grabbed my carry-on, but never got the opportunity to grab the little girl. The next thing I knew, I was through the door and into the small waiting area on the other side of the glass partition. I heard Gerry yell to me as he threw the bag over the partition.

Letting go of my carry-on I caught the duffle bag like a wide receiver for the Green Bay Packers, grabbed the carry-on and found myself flying out the door onto the tarmac. I turned around but George wasn't behind me. A few seconds later his tall gangly frame stumbled out the door staggering to keep his balance. We both looked at each other and agreed that was the most chaotic and exhausting experience we ever had.

I immediately asked him, "What happened to the little girl?"

His answer stunned me.

"What little girl?"

How could he possibly not see her? He towered over everyone else, and he had been standing right behind me.

I said, "The little girl standing in the clearing after all the rushing and pushing stopped."

He shook his head. "There was no calm, no stillness, no five-foot diameter opening, I saw no little girl, just constant pushing and shoving. It was absolute madness.

"But I did see you throw your duffle bag, and I can't figure out how you could throw that heavy thing over the heads of all those people, or why you did it, let alone how you caught it when Gerry threw it back to you."

I realized then that what I had experienced had been a vision. A vision so clear and real it was like having been in a movie. And what happen to those 130 people pushing into the same doorway coming from the tarmac?

The flight back to Ulaanbaatar offered time to reflect on the vision as well as the reasons why the Lord wanted me on this trip:

1. The Lord wanted me to learn more about sacrificial giving; to actually observe firsthand and have the opportunity to make a choice. We can know something intellectually in our head but not yet understand it with the heart in a spiritual sense.

2. He wanted me to learn to really trust Him for my daily needs.

3. I needed to know, deep down in my spirit, that His timing and provision is always perfect.

4. He wanted me to learn that there's more to life than just my survival. It's about sharing my blessings with others.

5. It was about serving, *"And whosoever will be chief among you, let him be your servant; Even as the Son of man came not to be ministered unto, but to minister, and to give his life a ransom for many."* Matthew 20:27-28 (KJV)

In my vision, the little girl represented all of Asia, which at the time was in the midst of a great and uncertain change, especially Mongolia. Many people across Asia are like that little girl. They are afraid of all the political, economic, and social uncertainty. I heard the Lord say, *"Bob, much of your work is to share my love and hope through my Word with those who have hungry hearts. The harvest is great, and the workers are few. Your work is more than connecting my work with my people to finance ministry. Those I have connected you with who have great wealth also need to be ministered to; feed them also."*

Many years later at Pomona Purpose church our pastor gave a sermon on joyful sacrifice in which he offered a quote by J.D. Greer. "Joyful sacrifice is giving up something you love for something you love even more. You rejoice in suffering when you love what you gain through suffering. Suffering is the means by which God has ordained bringing salvation to the world. Life in the world comes only through death." The sermon message was, "Use what God has given you as God wants." The death of self. The crucifixion of the flesh. As John the Baptist said, *"He must increase. I must decrease."* John 3:30 (KJV) I have always said, "All of life is learning how to die to self." I'm still learning.

STRAIGHT RAZORS

After returning to Ulaanbaatar and beginning my second week in Mongolia, I met with people from several other mission agencies who were also working in Mongolia. We often got together in the evening to discuss all the ways the Lord was moving in Mongolia and how everyone could work together. My faith in organizations working alongside each other was being restored from my earlier experience in South Dakota.

During the day, I was guided around the city by a young lady, a South Korean missionary, who had been serving there for the past two years. I had come across South Korean missionaries in other countries. They are awesome evangelists who seem to have a natural gift of evangelism for leading people to Christ.

While we were walking through the city portion of Ulaanbaatar among the many empty shops, I saw in a reflection in an empty store-front window that we were being followed by four young men, commonly known at the time as "hooligans." Remember, this was soon after Russia had abandoned Mongolia as a satellite country. There wasn't much in the way of an organized government and people were hungry and looking for ways to survive. The hooligans were teenagers who had established a reputation for using straight razors to slash fanny packs off of foreign travelers. They normally wouldn't hurt anyone but had become proficient at slicing only the fanny pack from your waist for any cash that might be in it.

I told my companion that I would swivel behind her, facing them squarely and thereby letting them know we were on to them. It worked. They immediately knew their intended caper was over. All of them took off in different directions. It pays to always be aware of your surroundings and listen to that "still small voice in your spirit."

Even though these young men were planning on robbing us, I couldn't help but feel pity for them and ask God to rescue them from their desperation. This was a trying time for many in Mongolia. People were selling everything they had, or the Russians had left behind, to anyone they could find to get money for food.

TEARS CAN CHANGE HUNDREDS OF LIVES.

As mentioned earlier, at the time of my visit there were fewer than 20 or 30 known Christians in all of Mongolia, including an American English teacher I never met but who had been there a year earlier.

A year before my visit to Khovd, the first Christian English teacher, a young man, arrived in this remote region. As he disembarked from the same plane I arrived on, there was a young Mongolian girl of 21 at the airport that day. She watched him and thought he looked like a nice young man. When she saw how radiant and pleasant his countenance was, she determined he must be a holy man. She mustered up the courage to ask him if he would come and pray for her grandmother, who lay dying in her Ger on the outskirts of Khovd. He said he would, and she led him to her family Ger where he knelt down and placed his hand on the grandmother's forehead and began to pray. After a few minutes, the young woman noticed tears rolling down his face. He continued to pray for her for another 15 minutes before standing. The young woman was deeply moved by this young stranger. He had never been there before, didn't know her or her grandmother and yet was totally willing to pray for a stranger to the point of tears. She had to know more about him and about his prayer, so she asked him why he would do this. He replied he was a Christian and began to tell her the story of Jesus and gave her a Bible. She accepted Christ a couple of weeks later and thus became the first Christian in the general area of Khovd.

She told many of her friends about her new relationship with Christ. Two years later she began writing music given to her by the Holy Spirit and playing a guitar. She became the praise and worship leader of the first small church in the Khovd area and later started teaching a women's Bible study group.

When Soviet communism took control of Mongolia in 1920, all religion was immediately banned. When the country re-opened to the outside world in the late 1980's, there were only a few Christians in the entire country. In 1995 there were about 4000 Christians. Today, there are more than 200,000 and approximately 1,000 churches. Hundreds have been trained in pastoral leadership by several different Christian organizations from the United States and Europe. How things have changed for the better since my first trip to this long-suffering country. PTL!

PEOPLE ARE WATCHING US.

The National Security Agency may, or may not, be reading our emails, but God is certainly reading our hearts. Like the young Mongolian girl with the dying grandmother, other people are constantly reading our action, and like the old adage, you may be the only Jesus they have ever seen.

Several years ago, Stella and I were at LAX waiting at our departure gate for a flight to Chicago. As I looked down the long corridor of departure gates, I saw a familiar couple coming toward us. It was our good friends James and Elizabeth Greenelsh who were catching a flight to another city. Their departure gate happened to be across the aisle from ours. James is a videographer, and in the years ahead I would travel over significant portions of Asia for up to a month at a time with James and Elizabeth, making short films about the ministry I was representing. We hugged and briefly caught up with each other as we stood partially out in the busy airport main aisle leading to the many other departure gates.

Soon, it was time for Stella and me to board our flight, so we stood in a circle, held hands, and prayed together. Four hours later, we were standing in the baggage area at Chicago's O'Hare Airport when a woman came up to us and said she had been on the same flight with us from Los Angeles. She was a Christian and was deeply moved when she saw us holding hands and praying with our friends back at LAX. She mentioned that she never seemed to have the courage to freely demonstrate her faith as we had done. As she boarded the flight, she prayed for the courage to share Christ at the first opportunity. She didn't have to wait long. After finishing her prayer, she noticed the young woman sitting next to her quietly sobbing, tears rolling down her face. She asked if she was all right and the young woman shared her heart-rending story. It seems her husband was having an affair and had recently filed for divorce. She listened intently and felt the Holy Spirit rising up inside of her and began to share Christ with her. By the time the plane landed in Chicago the young stranger had accepted Christ. Tears of sadness were replaced with a glowing smile of hope.

Before moving on, I want to share another story I read in Ray Johnston's book *HQ The Hope Quotient*. Ray is a graduate of Azusa Pacific University a short distance from our home. Ray now also serves on the Board of Trustees. He is the founding pastor of Bayside Church in the Sacramento area, a church which he describes as "a church for people who don't like church." In his book he recounts the story of a revival that took place in North Carolina in 1934. Two 14-year-old boys approached a tent meeting, heard the music, and quickly classified it as a church service. They turned around to leave when an usher asked them to stay and led them to two available seats.

The speaker that evening was a little-known gentleman by the name of Mordecai Ham. Ham never received a book deal, never hosted a TV program, or got an invitation to the White House. But at the end of his sermon he gave an altar call, and both of these boys went forward. One of them was a tall, skinny kid named Billy Graham. The boy with him was Grady Wilson. The pair later launched the Billy Graham Evangelist Association, through which Billy Graham spoke to more people about Jesus Christ than anybody in modern history. Grady Wilson served alongside Billy for 50 years, organizing the entire process.

The world impact of those two skinny teenagers became possible because of an usher who encouraged two uninterested teens to stay for the service that evening. God can and will use whatever is needed to build His Church and the gates of hell will not prevail against it. *"And I say also unto thee, that thou art Peter, and upon this rock I will build my church; and the gates of hell shall not prevail against it. Matthew 16:18 (KJV)*

In Mongolia I left the remainder of my food at two stops in other Mongolia areas before returning to Beijing. I bought some Russian made china from an elderly Russia lady just across the border in western Siberia. A whole set of 8 cups, saucers, and dinner plates could be purchased for the equivalent of $10 American dollars. Since that was too difficult to carry home, and with no need for a whole set, I bought just one cup and saucer as a souvenir. My heart went out to her and I couldn't help not paying her the price for the whole set. Tears came to her eyes. People would sell anything to make a few Tughriks.

Gas stop & potty break 500 miles west of Ulaanbaatar, 500 miles east of Khovd and 700 miles east of Kazakhstan.

Gassing up

Welcome home Obe-Wan

Mongolian Yak – not a comfortable ride.

Staying with host family for two days

27

COUSIN JO AND OTHER HEROES

After returning home from Mongolia, Stel and I made a quick trip to Illinois for the wedding of one of my cousins. While there we had an opportunity to meet Johanna (Jo) Boomsma, a third cousin and sister to Rev. Clarence Boomsma, an accomplished and successful preacher, teacher, and author in the Christian Reformed Church in Grand Rapids. Jo had a mission's entrepreneurial spirit about her. At a time when it was not considered appropriate for a single woman to start a ministry, she followed her vision to help the poor in the Appalachian Mountains of Kentucky. She couldn't get any financial support, but she did what she believed God wanted her to do.

I had always heard about her, but never actually met her. She knew about my work in missions, so it was a wonderful visit and time of sharing. Jo was a graduate of Calvin College. It took ten years to get her degree because she had to take time off on several occasions to work to save up enough money for another year of school. *"Every year that I worked I had a different job,"* she told me. *"I learned something else. It all prepared me for this work."* That was Miss Jo, able to look back on her life and see the purpose for what at the time may have seemed purposeless, yet able to see without a doubt the Lord's hand in her life.

After getting her degree she founded Christian Appalachian Homes (CAH) in Inez, Kentucky. She built it into a bustling place, filled with women and children from the nearby towns and "hollers" who had been abused and fled to the safety and shelter they knew they would find at CAH. She was always there to help them.

She spent her life serving others even though she had more than her share of bumps and bruises. She battled cancer for years and endured 13 surgeries. As a young woman she suffered through three years of depression. She never married after the young man she loved, left her for another woman when she was in her twenties.

She talked about what she had learned. *"Persistence is a key down here or anywhere. Don't give up when you have failure. I don't think you ever really fail if you're right with the Lord. Patience, perspective, and priorities are also important words that I live by. But it takes faith. I pray for faith and love."* (Taken from *Phil de Haan - The Calvin Spark - The Magazine for Alumni and Friends of Calvin College.*)

Not long after meeting Cousin Jo I had an opportunity to meet and spend some time with another of God's heroes, U.S. Senate Chaplain Dick Halverson. I had scheduled a fundraising trip to the East Coast, including Washington, D.C., when Bob Foster, Vice Chairmen of the Board for the English Institute, suggested I meet and visit with Halverson, a close friend of his. Of course, I was delighted to do so. Prior to becoming Senate Chaplain, Dick was the pastor of Hollywood Presbyterian Church, as was his successor, Lloyd Ogilvie. We had a wonderful two-hour visit. I was encouraged when he told me that his daily morning prayer and Bible lessons were well attended by many members of both branches of congress.

After a meeting with Billy Graham's wife, Ruth, and an additional meeting with Elizabeth Dole, wife of Senator Bob Dole, who was at the time heading up the Red Cross, I made my first visit to the Vietnam War Memorial, where I had a deeply emotional reaction to seeing my brother's name on the wall. There is something special about that memorial, and many others who have no family connection or name on the wall have said the same thing. I couldn't contain my tears. Since then, I've visited the memorial three additional times and each time had the same deep emotion response. I don't think you never fully get over such a loss. You move on because you must, but the scar tissue is sensitive pain that is always there.

Cousin Jo

Senate Chaplin - Dick Halverson
(Picture: Internet stock)

28

HANOI VIETNAM

An emotional fork in the road came when I was asked to make my first trip to Vietnam with a donor group. Our group consisted of donors and some of our board members. We would be meeting with government officials in Hanoi to sign contracts to provide English teachers in some of North Vietnam's universities. This would be the first of two trips to the Communist country 20 years after the war.

Before the Hanoi portion of the trip would include five days in Beijing China. Stella and I decided that she would go with me for the Beijing portion of the trip, and while I continued on to Hanoi, she would return home. This would be her first opportunity to see firsthand what I had been doing for the last few years.

At 2:30 am, the day we were scheduled to fly out of Los Angeles, I woke up with severe back pain. The pain was so intense vomiting was near. I was barely able to get out of bed to the bathroom. It would be impossible to make a three-week trip to China and Vietnam in this condition and wondered if Stella should still go with the group for the first portion of the trip. I prayed, asking for healing, but mentioned to the Lord I was willing to stay home if that was His Will. I really wanted Stella to have the experience.

Somehow, I drifted off to sleep, waking up four hours later without any trace of pain. I carefully eased out of bed just in case, showered and shaved, still no pain. We headed for the airport at 8:00 and by 10:45 boarded our ten-hour flight to Beijing. By God's grace, I had a pain-free flight and trip.

We all walked through the old original airport in Beijing, carefully observed by soldiers all carrying AK-47's. The airport seemed stuck in the 1930s with its dingy green walls and cracked and faded linoleum floors. We made our way to the basement where we waited for our luggage to come down the old roller wheel ramp. Everyone else's suitcases came shooting down -- but not mine. Stella and I waited, and waited, and waited. By now all the other folks in our group were already upstairs boarding a bus for the hotel. We didn't want to miss the bus so decided we'd come back later to check on my luggage.

I was slightly miffed about the situation, but Stella tried to lighten my distress by saying, "Better you than me." That's why I married you my dear. Your empathy always attracted me. We've laughed about that ever since.

The luggage did not come later that day, or the next day, or the day after that. By the fourth day it was an understatement to say that I was starting to smell like an old goat and taking showers before bed and every morning helped only a little.

During our five days in Beijing, both Stel and I had an opportunity to teach at the Beijing Teachers University. Stella was able to co-teach with Dr. Ted Engstrom who was then serving as our Board Chairman as well as President Emeritus of World Vision. Because we had wealthy donors and board members with us, we were staying at one of the best hotels in Beijing, the Shangri-La with its imported marble floors in the lobby, mahogany lined hallways with a view of Beijing from the 20th floor. Butlers stood in the hallway around the clock -- one for every two or three rooms -- waiting to help in any way necessary.

The morning of the fourth day was truly glorious. At our group breakfast Dr. Engstrom was giving the morning devotion on the faithfulness of God. I had to excuse myself for a few minutes to go back to our room. There I passed a kidney stone almost without noticing. No pain whatsoever.

A knock on the door revealed one of the butlers who handed me my missing suitcase. After another quick shower and change of clothes I enthusiastically rejoined the devotions. It turned out that my suitcase had traveled to Singapore, Bangkok, and Tokyo and finally back to Beijing. My clothes had already traveled further on this trip than I had.

NEGOTIATING FOR A SEAT

A few days later Stella headed for the Beijing airport for her flight back to Los Angeles. The rest of our group caught a flight to Hong Kong where we would catch a flight to Hanoi the following day.

Unfortunately, there was only one flight to Hanoi per day and this one was overbooked. After much confusion and some strong insistent negotiating with Vietnam Airlines we were able to get everyone on the same flight... except one. Dr. Ken, our president, was willing to catch the next flight the following morning but I insisted that if anyone needed to remain with the group it was him. I would catch the following days flight and rendezvous with them in Hanoi later.

While everyone else climbed onto the bus to take them out onto the tarmac for boarding, I remained at the ticket counter to either somehow finagle a seat or at least make sure I was on the next morning's flight. I suggested that since it was only a two-hour flight there must at least be a jump seat available (used by flight attendants during take-off) thereby allowing me to stay with the group. The gate attendant said they couldn't do that as it was illegal. I knew that, but it was worth a try and it gave me another idea; make it so expensive to leave me behind, they would find a seat, even if a jump seat. Thus, I asked them to pay for a first-class hotel room at the Shangri-La Hong Kong, plus a dinner voucher at the best restaurant in town, and $10,000 cash in Hong Kong dollars. They agreed. They were naturally very polite and accommodating for having to leave me behind. After receiving my cash, vouchers, a voucher for a cab and a guaranteed seat for the next morning's flight, I turned and walked away only getting about 50 feet from the counter when the ticket agent came running after me and said, *"Mr. Boomsma, we have found you a seat on the plane with your friends."* I knew they would, after paying out all that money for my expensive overnight stay. I was delighted to fly with the rest of the group but, it hurt, a little bit, to surrender all those vouchers and especially the $10,000 in Hong Kong cash.

The ticket agent took me through the bowels of the airport basement with all of its pipes and steam vents to a waiting bus, one of those low, squatty transport models that can easily pass under the wing of aircraft. The flight was already maneuvering around on the tarmac headed for the runway, but a radio call from the flight agent stopped the plane as my bus approached.

In the meantime, our donors were telling Dr. Ken that it was too bad I couldn't be on the same flight. Ken said, "I'm betting Bob will make this flight. He's resourceful." Someone said, "But we're already underway." Some of the donors made gentlemen's bets with Ken that I couldn't possibly make the flight. Naturally, if Ken was wrong, the ministry wouldn't be expected to pay up, but he figured he'd take advantage of the opportunity. The bet from several takers totaled of $350,000 that I wouldn't make it. About that same time the plane stopped, and my bus pulled up. A pickup truck with a walk-up ladder pulled up to the front cabin door just behind the pilots. I walked up the steps into the plane and called out, "Hi guys." Ken started laughing and telling everyone to pay up. The combined fundraising and contract signing trip was just starting and we had already raised a nice chunk of change.

Once I got inside the plane, the flight cabin door was still open, so I said hello to the pilots as I waited to find out where the flight attendants were going to seat me. I had never had an opportunity before to spend so much time peering into the flight deck, with all the switches, buttons, radar screens, etc. It was quite fascinating and would become more so within minutes. The flight attendant gave me a polite smile and pointed to the flight deck, suggesting I enter the pilot's sanctum. This was a surprise.

As it turns out, there is also a jump seat on the flight deck. It's located behind the co-pilot, mounted on a rail that slides toward the center and slightly forward, settling nearly between the two pilots yet just a little behind them. This was my seat for the entire flight. The Airbus 320, the newest at the time, was owned by France, with French pilots, and leased to Vietnam Airlines.

The Airbus cockpit windows are exceptionally low thereby allowing a great 180-degree view. It was fascinating to watch the take-off, which had already been punched into the flight computer, guiding the takeoff speed, flight route and altitude all the way to Hanoi. The pilots didn't even have their hands on the controls once we lined up on the runway.

Halfway to Hanoi we encountered severe thunderstorms. The pilots decided it was best to fly around them, actually in between two storm fronts to avoid any danger. The interesting part was how they negotiated around the storms. Since the computer was flying a preset course, the pilot simply pulled out a nob button about the size of a man's thumbnail on the top of the instrument panel to disengage the autopilot. He was now flying this monstrous piece of equipment with that small button. He turned the small knob right and then left as we gracefully flew between two nasty looking cloud formations. On the rest of flight one of the pilots was studying from a thick three-ring binder, staying completely away from the controls. He'd occasionally look out the window while the co-pilot kept a lookout for other aircraft. What was in that binder? The newest technical changes for that particular aircraft model. A new volume is issued every week.

The pilots were very friendly, and I even learned a little French, but didn't want to ask too many questions that would pilfer study time or checking for other planes in the area.

Dinner was served and I was fortunate to get the same meal as the pilots. It's better food than what the passengers get. I'm all for that. Keep those fellows happy and well-fed is my motto.

Scars of War in Vietnam

As we entered North Vietnam airspace the residue of war was quite visible. Thousands of bomb craters potted the landscape as far as the eye could see. It looked like an unending sea of bomb craters of all sizes, much like the surface of the moon.

While having the advantage of the best seat in the house, it did mean I missed something else. Since being out of site from other passengers, and consequently also out of sight and mind of flight attendants, I missed that part where they ask passengers to fill out all the paperwork that needs to be completed before landing in a foreign country. When we deplaned and were standing in the customs line, I happened to notice some of my co-travelers had several multi-colored sheets of paper tucked in with their passports, all of which had been handed out by flight attendants and filled out onboard prior to landing. I scrambled through the small third world airport to find the same-colored sheets and quickly filled them out before I got to the window. Whew; made it. Or so I thought. I was missing one particular sheet which would cause some anxiety for me as it was the one needed to get out of the country a week later. I didn't know that at the time. But hey, I was in the country and with our group.

The first thing I noticed were all the soldiers. They were everywhere, and they all looked like young boys of 14 or 15, wearing green military uniforms with sleeves that were far too long. All of them had AK-47's strapped across their chests. The year was 1993, some 18 years after the war ended. I learned later that the average age of 75 percent of the entire population of Vietnam was under 17 years of age, and most of the young girls had been raped by the Communist leaders and soldiers during or after the war ended.

The second thing I noticed is that just-about everyone in Vietnam rides a small motorcycle or moped, and there does not seem to be any traffic laws. Just trying to cross the street is risky business; yet there are very few accidents between mopeds and pedestrians. The streets are filled with groups of small boys and girls all selling the very same post cards. It's their sole means of support. Most of these children are born out of rape situations and abandoned to the streets. The children are all beautiful, especially the young teenage girls. They reminded me of little dainty flowers springing up in the rumble of war. My heart went out to them and I wished it were possible to adopt them all rescuing them their horrible life on the streets.

Before signing the contracts with government officials, we took donors around to various sightseeing venues that had survived the war; the Hanoi Opera House, the single pedestal pagoda, and a tour of Ho Chi Minh Mausoleum, where supposedly Ho Chi Minh's body was on display. We learned via the grapevine, that his body had actually been sent to Russia for a special re-mummification a few weeks earlier, but it didn't stop the government from displaying a wax model lying in a glass coffin. No cameras are allowed, and everyone must walk the high catwalk overlooking the body below with great reverence and in total silence. No one is allowed to speak. There were armed guards with AK-47's every 25 feet to make sure all rules were strictly obeyed. I didn't know it was considered irreverent to be walking with my hands in my pants pockets and was severely scolded by one of the guards.

One place I was anxious to see was the infamous Hanoi Hilton, where American fighter pilots were held after they were shot down. The compound was surrounded by 30-foot-high walls with two large wooden arched doors for an entrance. The doors were open, so I looked into a large hallway and straight across another 30 feet to a second set of large arched wooden doors. Beyond the second doors was the open courtyard where our pilots were held in small, barred cells at ground level. The hallway was perhaps 50 yards long to the left, an equal distance to the right and patrolled by a soldier with an AK-47. I waited until he passed the arched entrance doors and figured it would take him at least 2 minutes to cover the 50 yards before he turned around to make his return trip. Plenty of time for me to dash quickly cross the 30 feet to the second set of arched doors, snap a quick picture, retreat back to the outer street doors, and disappear into the crowed street. I got the picture, but the guard didn't cover his normal 50 yards and started his return march sooner than expected.

I beat a hasty retreat as he yelled at me to stop. I could hear the sound of the bolt clicking on his AK-47 as it echoed down the empty hallway. By the time he got to the first set of arched doors I had disappeared in a sea of people, mopeds, and rickshaws. I've been searching for that picture ever since and still haven't found it; so much for being a photojournalist.

SMUGGLING VIET CONG WAR FOOTAGE OUT OF VIETNAM

On our last day in country, we were scheduled to sign contracts with the Communist government. English teachers would be provided for various universities throughout North Vietnam for the coming five years. We had some time before our afternoon flight, and everyone had various things they wanted to do before we rendezvoused at the hotel. My friend James, our videographer for this trip, had made an unplanned visit to a Hanoi television station in hopes of getting some "B" footage. He met with the station manager and managed to talk him out of several VHS tapes of war footage from the Viet Cong perspective. He wasn't sure whether the station manager was allowed to legally provide these tapes, let alone to an American, but since James was staying in Hanoi for an extra three days to shoot some additional footage, he asked me to smuggle them out of the country. If they learned I had the tapes they could confiscate them, arrest me, or perhaps both.

As I was coming back from one of my own venues, I summoned a rickshaw to take me back to the hotel. It was nearing the monsoon season and the first storm of the year decided to unload its fury while in that rickety rickshaw. A rickshaw does a fine job of covering your head but not much else. By the time I got to the hotel, even with an umbrella, I was soaking wet. I had only minutes to safely stash the four VHS cassettes in the bottom of my carry-on and change my clothes before catching a cab to the airport.

When I got to the airport everyone was pulling out their passports with little blue, yellow, and pink slips of paper and handing them to armed soldiers before entering the gate area.

Most of our group had already been cleared to enter the boarding area while a few others, including me, were still further back in line. When I handed my passport and papers to the soldier, he shook his head no and pointed for me to stand aside as he checked the papers of others going through. I'm thinking, "Now what! How did they learn so quickly about those tapes I have concealed in the bottom of my suitcase? Now I'm going to be arrested and detained, maybe even in Hanoi Hilton or some other equally horrible place." Not exactly what I had in mind as an ending to this visit.

Jan, the wife of Dr. Ken our president, was also along on this history making journey and she noticed I didn't have a small yellow form tucked into the pages of my passport. Now, I at least knew what color was missing a week earlier when we arrived. I quietly drifted away from the soldier looking around the floor for any yellow piece of paper I could find. Finally, and as nonchalantly as possible, I picked one up off the floor while pretending to bend down to tie my shoelaces. It was an old dirty yellow sheet just blowing across the floor. It didn't have the right date on it, or of course, the right name. I stuck it in my passport, pretending to be writing on it and casually tucked myself back into line.

The same guard looked at my collection of colored paper slips and passed me through. The irony is he probably couldn't read English anyway. This is the one time I was thankful for bureaucracy. I was on my way out and so were those VHS tapes, some of which were used a few months later as part of a ministry information video.

"I will go before thee and make the crooked places straight: I will break in pieces the gates of brass and cut in sunder the bars of iron." Isaiah 45:2 (KJV)

View from inside pilots' cabin, Airbus 320 flying into Hanoi

Everything is tight & close in Hanoi. Seconds
before the train comes through people are playing
games on card tables, & children are playing.

Troops marching everywhere.
Mostly young adults.

Only one seat remaining. Seated with pilots in the cockpit.

29

SPIES IN THE CHURCH

After returning from my first trip to China in early 1990, I was asked to speak at a Chinese church in Southern California with a congregation of 400 members. This was a common occurrence in the years to come, but this was the first opportunity to speak at a Chinese church in southern California. By now, I was well versed in writing proposals for donors and also knew what not to say publicly in front of large crowds, especially a Chinese congregation where we couldn't be sure who was in the audience. Speakers from the ministry were never to mention the "M" word (Missionaries).

As I sat next to the pastor on the pulpit that morning, I heard the Holy Spirit tell me there was a spy in the congregation and to be extra cautious about using the "M" word. The "word" from the Holy Spirit was very much on my mind as the pastor introduced me. As I scanned the pews, I was even sure who it was in the front row. Amazing since I didn't know anyone in the church.

The service was in Mandarin and an interpreter was provided. This was a blessing. The interpreter gave me time to consider my next words carefully. After 20 minutes I sat down and was pleased with how my talk came across when the congregation applauded.

The following day, Monday, Dr. Ken returned from China and asked to see me in his office. He told me he had been sitting in a large roundtable meeting in Beijing on Sunday. Sitting next to him was a high-ranking official of the Public Security Agency (similar to our NSA) who had been a friend for several years. During their meeting, the man leaned over and asked Dr. Ken "Do you know a Bob Boomsma?" Dr. Ken replied, "Yes, he works for us in our headquarters office."

"Well, I received a report this morning that he spoke in a Chinese church (mentioning the church name and city) and he said that your organization is sending missionaries to China."

Dr. Ken assured him that was highly unlikely but promised to look into it. I was sure I hadn't used the "M" word, but just to make sure, I returned to the church the following day where I sat with the pastor and board members listening to my informational talk on a tape cassette. I was relieved having not used the "M" word.

Everyone on the church board suspected who the possible spy was and mentioned he was sitting in the front row on the left. The very same person the Holy Spirit had revealed to me in church the day before.

At the time, it was very common for most Chinese churches across America to have at least one spy in the congregation for two reasons; 1) they were still looking for students who had escaped after the Tiananmen Square uprising, and 2) many Chinese businessmen traveled back and forth to China on a regular basis, and the Communist government always kept tabs on them.

The noteworthy consideration for me was that my talk had traveled all the way to Beijing in a matter of hours. As it turned out, the supposed spy wasn't really a spy but a "spy wannabe," a man and his wife, both students at Cal State Fullerton, had a son who had just finished a three-month visit with them. It was during the son's visit that the Tiananmen uprising occurred in China.

The parents saw an opportunity to gain some points with the Chinese government by trading what they thought was valuable information and perhaps get their son back to California on a more permanent visa situation. The church had their suspicions about the couple and decided they would continue praying for them in hopes they would become members of the congregation.

I never heard the final outcome, but certainly was glad I hadn't messed things up for the ministry.

ENCOURAGING WORDS

We all know the importance of encouragement. Encouragement causes us to reach higher. Two of the men who were great encouragers in my life during this time, in addition to Dr. Ken, were Dr. Carlton Booth and Dr. Ted Engstrom, both of whom were on the board of the English Institute. Dr. Booth was a professor at Fuller Seminary. Dr. Engstrom was originally President and CEO of World Vision and was, when I got to know him, World Vision's president emeritus. Both of these men often sent letters of encouragement stating how delighted they were I was on staff and how they not only liked what I did, but how I did it.

Both of men reached out to me during a difficult experience I had with a large Christian Foundation, which for some reason, twice in my mission's career in working for two sperate ministry's, spread rumors, misconceptions and outright lies about me. Both Dr. Booth, and Dr. Ken encouraged me to stay the course and stay on the high road. Dr. Booth summarized it for me when he gave me the words I quoted earlier, *"Bob, sometimes God will put a Goliath in your life, for you to find the David within you."* In this particular situation it was a great encouragement to stay the course.

In the years going forward, I worked for four other Christian ministries, and their words of encouragement often brought great contentment in helping me to stay focused on Philippians 4:8: (KJV) *"Finally, brethren, whatsoever things are true, whatsoever things are honest, whatsoever things are just, whatsoever things are pure, whatsoever things are lovely, whatsoever things are of good report; if there be any virtue, and if there be any praise, think on these things."*

I must give a sincere thank you to Kathy Ross, my first tutor in writing a Christian-based proposal. Kathy, the wife of Dr. Hugh Ross at Reasons to Believe, has a wonderful gift of writing. I knew how to write proposals related to the computer and banking industries but didn't know much about writing proposals for donors in the Christian non-profit sector. Kathy was recommended and she wrote the first one for me thirty years ago. It would serve as a template for the hundreds of proposals I wrote over the years. Her style was informative, concisely organized with brilliant brevity, leaving the reader with a clear perception of the ministry's value to the Kingdom and the request for funds. Many non-profits think they need to write 40 pages. Unfortunately, 95 percent of them are redundant and often end up unread in a wastebasket. Years later, I learned that Kathy graduated from the same high school I did and was in the same graduating class as my brother, who she remembers well.

Psalm 37:3 (KJV) *"Trust in the Lord, and do good, so shalt thou dwell in the land, and verily thou shalt be fed."*

30

CARPE DIEM

On my fundraising trips across the United States, Europe, and Asia, I developed many friendships with large donors who often presented opportunities to speak at their churches and Bible study groups. In so doing I also got to know the missions' pastors of several mega churches. Stella was with me on one such trip when we had an interesting experience that imparted a lesson we have never forgotten.

I had scheduled a lunch with the missions' pastor of a large church with two large campuses in a mid-western city. Their mission budget was over $2 million dollars annually. They had trained, sent, and supported 200 missionaries in 30 countries around the globe. This was a wonderful church I had attended several times while visiting some of its wealthy member donors. Here were great people, great pastors and truly one of the best and most extensive church outreach mission programs in the county.

Somehow the meeting schedule was miscommunicated. We arrive early at the mission's pastor's office and found a miscommunication had occurred and he had just left for lunch. So, we waited in the business lobby hoping to catch him when he returned. We walked to the main business office waiting area and there we noticed something we had never seen before: a Muslim woman fully clothed in her traditional black regalia, but without the burka covering her face. Now to us, this presented an opportunity. I struck up a conversation with her and offered to get her a cup of coffee.

In the course of our conversation, I asked her how it was that a Muslim lady happened to be sitting in the lobby of one of the largest mega-protestant churches in the Midwest. She explained that she came every Tuesday to bring her son to play basketball with the neighborhood kids. The church had a tremendous outreach program for neglected children from broken families in the city, and this Muslim lady sat in the church lobby every Tuesday for three hours waiting for her son. She had been doing this for several months. What astonished me even more was that no one in the office, sitting just 30 ft, from the waiting area, had ever bothered to meet her or share Christ with her. So, we did.

Stella joined us with her cup of coffee, a smile, and asked her, "Are you here because you love Jesus?" (That's my bride. Never beat around the bush.) Always go right to the heart of the matter. The Muslim woman was sincere in her response, "Yes, I love Jesus. He is one of our prophets and I love our prophets." Stella continued, "We believe that Jesus died for our sins to wash them away, was raised from the dead and gives us the assurance of Heaven." The woman raised her hands in the air and joyously responded, "Yes, I believe Jesus was raised from the dead." Thus, within our hearts, we prayed, Lord, your word says *"that if you confess with your mouth the Lord Jesus and believe in your heart that God has raised Him from the dead, you will be save"* Romans 10:9 (KJV) She tried to engage us in some theological talk, but we avoided it by asking her if she would like a Bible. She replied yes, and she would like to give us her Muslim primer in return. Several church staffers across the room had been listening to the conversation, so when I went to the counter asking for a Bible, they had one ready for me. When I handed the Muslim woman the Bible, her face was filled with joy, like she had just received the "pearl of great price." She embraced it to her bosom, closing her eyes as she received it with an enormous peaceful smile on her face. At that instant we knew God would do the rest. Sometimes, we can be so focused on "going to the ends of the earth" to share the Gospel we can easily overlook the opportunities God has placed in front of us.

I once read a study that found 80 percent of support staff on the mission field don't feel that it's part of their job to witness to the indigenous people they come in contact with on the mission field. They say, "I'm just support staff; I dig water wells. I build school buildings. I build small homes for people who have no homes but need a roof over their heads. To witness is the job of the missionary." Perhaps one of the reasons they find it difficult is because they don't know how to share the Gospel and consequently are just plain afraid to do so, with no confidence in the Gospel or the Holy Spirit's guidance.

Before I got involved in missions, I also had that fear of inadequacy, until it became a habit to always be on the lookout for opportunities to share Christ. Such opportunities are everywhere -- in the supermarket line, the dentist, the doctor's office, in making hospital visits, or when visiting with neighbors.

On one particular occasion, I missed such an opportunity. It has haunted me ever since. I was in the cashier line at the local K-Mart store when a handsome, very tall young black teenager was ahead of me in the checkout line. He was purchasing a few candy bars worth $1.56. He had five or six one-dollar bills in his hand but had absolutely no idea what to give the clerk, let alone what to expect back in change. I helped him with his purchase. He was a polite young fellow, smiled, thanked me, and headed toward the door. Obviously, the educational system had somehow failed him. I had compassion on him and the whole time I was thinking I should ask him if he would like me to help with his math and whatever other subjects he may have needed. It would have been a golden opportunity to introduce him to Christ. But the opportunity passed. I looked for him once outside the door but had already disappeared into the vast reservoir of humanity needing the Lord. It happened years ago, but the regret of that missed opportunity gave birth to self-made promise to never miss future opportunities.

SHOWING HOSPITALITY TO AN ANGEL

On another occasion, and somewhat different, Christmas was nearing, and I still had not made it to the mall to pick-up Stella's gifts ordered a month earlier. I was getting hundreds of Christmas cards ready for mailing to donors, but decided to run to the mall at noon, thinking I could be back in my office in less than an hour. Everything was going according to plan. It took only twelve minutes to get to the mall. Traffic was so light I wondered where everybody was. It took ten minutes to park, pick up the gifts and a few minutes later I was back on Foothill Boulevard heading west toward home. To my surprise, every car in Southern California seemed to be on the same street heading in the same direction. I could not believe it. It was if they had been hiding somewhere and all of sudden everyone decided to hit the road at the same time.

Everything was bumper to bumper. Stop-and-go as far as the eye could see. There was no way I would make it back to my office by 1 p.m. I was getting uptight. Blood pressure rising. Clock ticking. In reality of course, it did not matter. It was a self-imposed deadline. However, heavy traffic is one of the cracks in my armor. The impatience in my character can sometimes stand out like a giant redwood tree in a wheat field. Then I heard that quiet voice inside, *"Bob, relax. You have time. Stop and have a cup of coffee. Take a deep breath and enjoy the day, my creation and people around you."* It was that "people around you" which would turn out to be interesting.

I was almost home when I happen to notice the Big Texas Donut shop. It seemed like good advice, so I stopped for a cup of coffee and my favorite donut. (Well, okay, the donut was not part of the advice.)

While I was standing outside enjoying my treat, I saw a fellow walking toward me. He was not the typical poorly dressed homeless person you might see pushing a shopping cart filled with his possessions. Quite the opposite. He was a light-skinned black man, handsome, clean shaven with a short, neat haircut. He wore a clean white t-shirt, pressed brown khaki pants and his work type black shoes were nicely polished. I just knew he was going to ask me for money, and I made up my mind to say no. Sure enough, he asked. I replied with my pre-programmed response. He was very polite answering with a smile, "Okay, thank you and have a wonderful day."

As I watched him walk away across the nearly empty parking lot, I was filled with compassion. If you asked me how I felt at that moment, I would have said pretty low and cheap. I walked to the Subway at the end of the small strip center and bought a foot-long tuna sandwich, some chips, and a root beer. When coming back to the donut shop, I saw him at the far end of the parking lot, opening doors for customers at a Wendy's. He was apparently striking out there too. I yelled to him and we both walked toward each other, meeting in the middle of the parking lot. I apologized for my rudeness and said, "I hope you like tuna and root beer." He said he loved tuna and I handed him the sack of food and drink.

He graciously thanked me, and I told him he was most welcome. We both smiled, but there was something special about his smile. It was sincere and loving. I turned and walked away, taking no more than five steps before turning to say have a great day.

He was gone.

I stood there, scanning the empty parking lot. There wasn't a single car or any other obstruction for 75 feet in any direction. No one could have walked out of sight that fast. That's when two scriptures came to mind:

"Do not forget to show hospitality to strangers, for by so doing some people have shown hospitality to angels without knowing it." Hebrews 13:2 (NIV2011)

"They also will answer, 'Lord, when did we see you hungry or thirsty or a stranger or needing clothes or sick or in prison, and did not help you?' He will reply, 'Truly I tell you, whatever you did for one of the least of these, you did for me." Matthew 25:44-45 (NIV2011)

On a similar occasion, several months later, I saw a fellow standing in the entry driveway to another nearby shopping center. He was carrying a sign that read, "Homeless, will work for food." As I walked into the store, I turned around and watched him for a few minutes. He wasn't getting any takers, and I thought, "If I give him something, he'll just use it for booze or drugs. I'd be wasting money." But then the voice of compassion again spoke, and I knew it was the Lord. *"Bob, give him five dollars. It does not matter what he will use it for. It is a matter of obedience. His use of the gift is my concern."* I approached him and gave him the five dollars, feeling thankful I had been obedient.

When we know God moves on our heart to do something, we must do it immediately and with love. We can be sure that we will be blessed for our obedience. And, we can be sure that the gift will keep producing far beyond what we will ever know or imagine.

Jesus said in Luke 6:38, (KJV) *"Give, and it shall be given unto you; good measure, pressed down, and shaken together, and running over, shall men give into you...For with the same measure that you use, it will be measured back to you."*

31

PING GOLF

A key element of successful fundraising is networking. On a trip to Phoenix to see a donor friend, Bill, I asked if he knew the Solheim family and would he introduce me. He did and arranged a lunch at the Solheim Country Club with Karsten (Lou) Solheim, Jr., the oldest son of Karsten, Sr., who founded Ping Golf in the late 1960's.

On the day I met Lou, Bill joined us for lunch. We were all sitting at a large, round convention type dinner table that could seat eight people at the Solheim Country Club. Lou was sitting in between my friend and me. During our conversation, Lou kept falling asleep. Not wanting to embarrass him, I was able to keep waking him up by gently putting my hand on his forearm and kept talking. After this happened three or four times, he apologized and mentioned that he was extremely fatigued because the day before he had run a 100-mile race in the mountains near Payson. He had always been a Marathon runner and was competing in this annual race for some years. Runners actually make their way up and down a mountain trail course in the back country near Payson competing for the best time to run 100 miles in a 24-hour period.

I can't even imagine running a little over four marathon races in the span of a single day. At the time he was in his late 50's or early 60's, and I had to give him a lot of credit for even agreeing to have lunch with me after running such a staggering race.

He replied that he really did want to know more about what we were doing in China. I suggested we meet again in a few weeks after he was rested up, and he said that was a wonderful idea.

I had lunch with him a number of times over the next year, Stel and I also had dinner a few times with Lou and his lovely wife Bonnie in their home. A year later he and Bonnie became ministry partners after traveling with me to China to see the work of the English Institute.

ADVENTURE IN THE COCONINO FORREST

Six years later, Lou was contemplating moving from the Phoenix area into the shadow of Humphrey's Peak, the highest natural point in the state of Arizona, located just north of Flagstaff. When I called to set up a visit to give him a ministry update on the ministry, he invited me to meet him in Flagstaff. We would then drive into the Coconino Forest area to look at some property he was thinking about buying to build a new house.

We met in Flagstaff as he suggested and headed out to look at the property. I asked if he knew where the property was since we had been looking for a certain road number for nearly an hour. That's when he admitted we were lost.

Finally, after another hour of traversing hill and dale, we found our way back out of the woods to the Flagstaff area. We never found that property, so I assume it was extremely remote. But we had a great time laughing our way through the woods. I'll always remember that day fondly, and reminded Lou that it was easier guiding him across China than helping him navigate the Coconino National Forest in Arizona.

later he offered me the opportunity to come to Phoenix to be fitted for a set of golf clubs. It was tempting offer, but I could never find the time. Besides, any real interest in golf was still just future potential until there would be more time for it.

32

THANKS, BUT NO THANKS

D r. Ken was looking to hire a full-time Director of Development and asked me if I would be interested in taking the position. I thanked him but said I was having too much fun being on the road developing friendships with donors and could not imagine spending more time in the office. Things were going well, and he was pleased with my answer. I would however be willing to help find a development director and he consequently included me in the interviewing process.

The first fellow who interviewed told me that he had been successful raising money by threatening lawsuits against those who turned down his requests for money. In other words, he was a bully. We often think of bullying as a child's activity, but as we all know, politicians and governments use it as a powerful tool to dominate the weak, confuse and threaten those that are easily intimidated. I immediately relayed the story to Dr. Ken who quickly eliminated the candidate.

Eventually the job went to a man who was hired over my doubts. There was something about him that bothered me, but I could not put my finger on it. After he was hired, I found out verily quickly he was a womanizer.

He had a delightful attractive wife and two young children, but that didn't seem to make a difference. Several women in the office, both married and unmarried, told me privately he had "put the make" on them. I told them to report the details to their supervisors, who would forward their concerns to Human Resources.

Shortly afterward, knowing I was often on the road, this same fellow said he would be happy to look in on my wife while I was gone, take her to the store or appointments if needed. Yea! Right! It seemed like the fox guarding the hen house. I trusted the hen, but not the fox. My trust with him went as far as I could throw a bull by the tail.

Another issue was he jealous of me. I had become close friends with Dr. Ken, and we shared a high level of trust. This new development director had a controlling spirit and was determined to get rid of me. One day he told Dr. Ken that if I didn't follow his directions, he was going to fire me. Ken told him, "Don't interfere with whatever Bob is doing. Leave him alone. I don't care if he only works one day a week. I don't care where on the planet he goes to raise funds as long as he keeps doing what he's doing. End of story."

He never bothered me again, other than spreading untrue rumors which no one believed. He kept womanizing in the office. I mentioned it in passing to the chairman of the board. His liabilities caught up with him on a donor trip to China when the chairman saw firsthand similar actions and brought it to the attention of the president. His brief six-month tenure quickly ended after the trip. Nonetheless, he remained my nemesis and was still badmouthing me several years later. Eventually, his behavior cost him his career and he died from a heart attack. I take no delight in sharing the story, but it's another reminder that God protects His children and that we all reap what we sow.

"Many sorrows shall be to the wicked; but he that trusteth in the Lord, mercy shall compass him about." Psalm 32:10 (KJV)

33

HANGING OUT WITH
PRESIDENT GEORGE H. BUSH

As a fundraiser it never became a habit for me to take to many regular vacations. In dealing with people in countries around the world, it seemed like there was never a perfect time to take time off. I had been rolling along for several years without a vacation and finally decided to take a month of accumulated time off. A dear friend and ministry partner in Philadelphia offered to let Stella and me stay at her summer home along the river in Eastern Shore of Maryland. After a week spent enjoying some fishing off the boat dock on the Susquehanna River, the largest tributary to the Chesapeake Bay, browsing the small shops of the quaint town of St. Michaels and catching up on a few books, we decided to drive up to Massachusetts for a nice lobster dinner.

One of the things we enjoy most about our unplanned vacations is we can make spur of the moment decisions to see what's "over the next hill," taking the road less traveled. Such was the case heading for Massachusetts. We never did get that lobster.

We followed the Atlantic coast north until we reached the town of Kennebunkport, Maine. There, we saw several tourists pulling over and taking pictures of a large house across a small bay. Earlier that morning we had breakfasted at a nearby diner where the walls were covered with pictures of George and Barbara Bush having lunch with people who turned out to be tourists passing through just as we were. Ah! A light bulb went on. I had an idea.

That big house everyone was taking pictures of was surely the summer home of the Bush family. George H. Bush had visited China as vice president and before that served as a Liaison Officer in Taiwan. At that time, the United States did not recognize the government of the People's Republic of China. We had no embassy there and Mr. Bush did not formally hold the position of "ambassador", although he unofficially acted as one. The Chinese people always liked George H. Bush, and on one of his trips to Beijing he met a few of our English teachers, promising to call their parents when he returned to the U.S. to let them know he had met them and they were doing fine. He actually followed up on that promise much to the delight of teacher's families back home.

My thought was that perhaps we could use this link to invite him to lunch. After all, how many times do you get the chance to take a former President of the United States to lunch? Like everyone else passing through, we took a couple of pictures of the Bush compound while parked across the small bay. My suggestion to Stella was that we should drive up to the front gate and invite George and Barbara lunch.

Stella was horrified. "We can't do that. The Secret Service will shoot us. They don't know who we are and could take this as a threat."

"No!" I insisted, "there is nothing threatening about us and they don't shoot innocent citizens."

As I drove down the long winding driveway toward a gate-house, Stella was busy trying to look invisible by slinking under the dashboard as far as she could get. We stopped at the gate house, which was totally empty, but did contain several video cameras front and rear of our car. Immediately, a pleasant young man's voice came over a speaker saying, "Good afternoon. How can I help you?"

I briefly explained my work with the English Institute, saying the President had met some of our teachers, and added that my wife and I would be honored to take the President and Barbara to lunch in town.

He replied, "That sounds nice. Let me check with the President."

I immediately noticed two large black Chevy Suburban's with heavily tinted windows had pulled up behind us. Two fellows in dark suits and wearing sunglasses were in the front seat.

I turned to Stella and said, "We have company." She took a quick peek and said, "Oh Lord, help us!" and proceeded to slide back down to the floor. I told her she was making us look suspicious by trying to hide. "They're either going to think you are unusually short or wonder why you're on the floor."

The voice in the gatehouse came back. *"Can I have your name?"*

After providing our names he thanked us saying he would be right back. I knew he probably was checking some data base to see who we were. This didn't bother me because I was used to being checked out by various government agencies having taken several trips to China and a number of other Asian and Islamic countries.

A few minutes later the voice came back: "Bob, the President and Mrs. Bush would love to have lunch with you and Stella, but unfortunately, this being August, the whole family and all the grandchildren are at the compound for the entire month as they are every year. They rarely leave the compound as this is the only time the family can all be together."

I apologized for the intrusion and for my forwardness. He said it was not a problem as the Bushes often had lunch with tourists at the Lobster House in town, but just not in August. I thanked him, started the car and immediately the two black Suburban's behind us backed away and disappeared into the nearby tree line.

As a salesman, and now a fundraiser, I have a habit of never taking no as a final answer. We drove back into town, had lunch, and then visited a bookstore where we saw copies of Barbara Bush's newly released book. I bought a copy, skimmed it in our hotel room that afternoon and decided I should try again, this time inviting them to have breakfast with us the following morning.

After dinner that evening, I went to a phone booth outside the restaurant, looked up the number for the Bush compound and gave them a call.

The minute I said, "Hello, is this the Bush compound?" the same pleasant voice I had talked with earlier at the gatehouse answered, "Hello, this sounds like Bob Boomsma. You don't give up easily do you?" I replied, "No sir," and commended him on his voice recognition. He laughed and said he appreciated my tenaciousness, but nothing had really changed. "But now that we know you, I would guess that if you came any other month when the President is here, he and Mrs. Bush would certainly have lunch with you."

"Well," I said, "if we were here sometime other than August we certainly would try again. But since we're only here for a couple of days I guess we'll miss them this time."

He told me that we could most surely catch the former President at his office in Houston and gave us the President's private office number and secretary's name. I thanked him for the information and his kindness.

I actually had met Barbara once before at the White House when we took various ministry financial partners to Washington for briefings at the China Desk of the State Department.

Other venues at these events included various other speakers in D.C., such as Senator Lukens, Lawrence Eagleburger, who was at the time a Foreign Service Officer and also served as Secretary of State under George H. Bush, Senator Bob Dole and his wife Elizabeth Dole, who was heading up the American Red Cross at that time, as well as David Aikman, then a Senior Editor at *Time Magazine* concerning all things related to China.

On one such trip we had arranged a White House tour. We were passing through the main floor of the Whitehouse when Barbara came rushing down the stairs in her stocking feet, chasing after Millie, their Springer Spaniel. I knelt down and called to Millie and she came right to me. (Animals love me). I picked Millie up and handed her to Barbara. She was grateful. Apparently, Millie had been running all over the White House for the past twenty minutes, with Barbara chasing her. If we had the opportunity to have lunch that day in Kennebunkport, I would have brought that story to her remembrance. I doubt she would have recalled since the mischievous twinkle in Millie's eyes led me believe that probably was not the first time she had been a fleeing fugitive at the White House. Thus, ended my career as a White House insider and unofficial dogcatcher.

Bush compound Kennebunk port ME (Stock photo)

34
THE FUN OF NETWORKING

I was in Western Michigan to meet with a stockbroker for an early morning meeting. I had never met him before, but someone had referred him to me as a possible partner. It turned out he wasn't really a potential donor, but on the way to his office I passed a new, gorgeous sea-green glass building under construction. I made a mental note to ask the stockbroker if he knew anything about it. As it turned out it was a busy morning for the broker because Amway was issuing new stock as they prepared to enter the Chinese market. Our conversation was choppy as we both were constantly glancing at his computer to see what the stock offering would be doing. The broker had a piece of the action and I had recently met with Rich De Voss Jr., so I too was interested. It was fascinating to watch the stock move up and down as brokers and investors across the country bought in. At the end of our brief talk, I asked him if he knew anything about that new building on the beltway. He told me the owner was a local Dutchmen who had built a phenomenally successful cell phone company and I should definitely call on him. He even provided an office and private cell number.

Later that day I called the cell number and reached the owner, Ron on his private jet. After giving him my brief elevator speech, he said he would be getting back to town late that evening but would be glad to meet with me if I didn't mind the late hour. He suggested we meet for coffee at a McDonalds about 11:00

p.m. Naturally I agreed, and we talked until 3 in the morning. (Surprisingly, McDonalds didn't kick us out). It is always a good sign when you have a new prospect asking a lot of questions and especially when you sense a kindred spirit.

I made four personal visits to see him over the next year. He always made time to see me and we often spent a couple of hours talking and the same when I called him by phone. On one such call, I thought of something he might be willing to help us with. At the time, the ministry only had a $375,000 line of credit to help finance the recruiting cycle. It wasn't nearly enough. My thought was to find three major donors who would donate $500,000 each, for a total of 1.5 million to provide a larger credit line. Since we had an excellent record with the bank, always paying off the line of credit at the end of the year's recruiting cycle, these donations of $500,000 each from three donors would be gifts that would keep giving for many years to come.

The first donor I contacted was giving $18,000 per year. The year before he totally funded a project, I had asked him for, totaling $375,000 so he seemed a possible candidate for a $500,000 ask for the credit line. In our meeting I took with me all of our financial records for the past 12 years and our Director of Finance. He agreed to my request but would only write the check after I found another donor who would give the first $500,000.

Now was the time to ask Ron to be the first donor toward the credit line. I could safely tell him I already had the second $500,000 donor lined up. I had not yet contacted the third donor but knew who I would ask and felt sure that he would follow suit. I called Ron by phone, presented the idea. He said he would think it over. A week later he called me at home early on a Saturday morning to tell me he had thought about it but had something else in mind. He wanted to pay for the support for one hundred teachers in China for a full year. This gift was worth over $1 million! What a great surprise, even though different than what I asked for.

I learned early in my fundraising career that networking is a key to large gifts. The people who give large gifts are usually friends with others with a similar giving capacity. They like big projects, even though it may take years before any real results can be measured. Of course, gifts of all sizes are always great and a special blessing for both the recipient and the giver.

LISTEN CLOSELY

An important key to effective networking is listening closely to a potential donor. It has always surprised me to see how many fundraisers don't pay attention to the prospective donor's interest. Millions of dollars that could be used to help expand God's kingdom are lost every year due to miscommunication caused by a lack of listening.

In one such case I was making a joint call with a fellow fundraiser when I was with another ministry, who had been doing his job for over 15 years. We were calling on a major funder who was familiar with the ministry but had never funded a gift of any amount. Quite frankly, my fellow fundraiser talked too much and did not listen enough. After he finished, I asked the executive director of this major foundation for the key points that guided their giving purpose as written in their by-laws. I noted six key hot buttons. These were the crucial elements that would solidify a large gift, all of which we could easily satisfy with the many countries the ministry was operating in. After the meeting, I asked my fellow fundraiser what he thought it would take to get the grant. He could not name any of the six key points. He had not listened and didn't even ask the right questions during the meeting. I wrote a two-page proposal based on those six key points. The following month we received a first gift check for $500,000.

James 1:19b (KJV) "…let every man be swift to hear, slow to speak…"

35

PASTORING – AN IMPORTANT ELEMENT OF FUNDRAISING

During my years in missions, I discovered early on that a strong pastoring element is essential in fundraising. There are wealthy businessmen who often don't discuss their frustrations, fears and family issues with their pastor, but they would with me.

I think one reason is they knew I came from the business world before entering missions and thus were probably more familiar with some of their problems and concerns than a pastor who had never been in the business world. Secondly, they felt I was a safe, perhaps because in banking as in fundraising, you never disclose private information. In fundraising you never discuss donation amounts associated with any donor.

Often these pastoring elements within fundraising came from older men who had served in World War II, returned from the war starting and building successful corporations. I attribute this to several events I had where a donor called me asking if I could come and just talk. They had something of personal concern overlapping their business and personal family matters. At the time, there were only a few fundraisers who came into missions from business backgrounds. Many fundraisers had never worked in the business world and only in a mission's environment. Donors trusted my compassion for the pressures experienced in their daily business environments and were comfortable in sharing, knowing whatever they shared would remain a safe harbor for their distresses. I came to know these people as if I were a member of their own families, and often prayed privately with them over their concerns about grandma's gallbladder operation, grandpa's kidney operation, their daughter's marriage selection and their son's college and career choices.

More than once I received a call from a President and CEO of a corporation who asked if I could come for a visit to discuss a problem, they wanted advice on, most often a delicate family situation, but related to the business and wasn't sure how to handle it. A son-in-law involved in the business but having an affair with someone in the office. I would schedule a trip, always setting up meetings with other donors or potential donors in the same area of the country to maximize time and cost factors.

It was a special blessing to be raising money in a time when there were three generations with great wealth all at the same time. World War II area businessmen were aging, retiring and about to transfer several trillion dollars to their sons and daughters in the Boomer generation. The Boomer generation had also built huge fortunes, also totaling trillions of dollars which would someday be transferred to the Gen X generations. Every generation was motivated differently in their giving patterns. In a way, especially at first, it made fundraising more difficult, but once you found the generational motivation pattern it became easier. The World War II generation, the oldest giving generations at the time, was more emotional based in their giving and somewhat less interested in the numbers and rarely made donor vision trips abroad. The Boomer generation was much less emotionally motivated but did make many vision trips. The Gen X generation were much more hands on, wanting to be more involved, not so much in daily ministry involvement, but participation in actual missionary work in the field. Today the Millennials are considerably more numbers oriented than any previous generation, desiring a closer look and interest in the financial matters as well as participation in mission field activity. Definitely more hands on than previous generations.

Understanding these different generational motivations, let alone the many different personalities within each category --not to mention the specific interest of each donor -- made it somewhat like navigating a mine field. You had to be on your toes because it could be quite confusing, somewhat like playing three-dimensional chess.

36

EXPLORING WALMART

For anyone who does a lot driving around the country, they've surely seen Walmart trucks everywhere on the highway.
Many people know Wal-Mart gives to many worthy Christian causes, but I didn't know anyone who could help me get in the door. Hence, cold call time. I did my research, discovering that the company generally only gives to youth programs in areas where their stores are located. After collecting additional information, I learned Sam Walton, Walmart's Founder and CEO was rarely in his office. I decided to try the Chief Operating Officer, Don, who had been with Walmart almost since the beginning.

On the first phone call I spoke to his secretary, Pat, and gave her my short 90-second elevator speech. She was very receptive and a very pleasant lady, not in any way given to snobbishness as some in similar positions to key men of power. She knew her boss likes and dislikes quite well. She checked her calendar and said, "Yes, I can arrange a meeting on October 10th at 11:00 am. But as you would expect, he is a busy man, and I can only squeeze you in for 15 minutes. Would that be OK?" I told her that would be wonderful and thanked her for her help.

FIRST IMPRESSIONS

I arrived at the appointed time and walked into the main lobby of the largest retail organization in the world. The lobby was full of vendors waiting to sell their goods to one of hundreds of Walmart purchasing agents. They were sitting in plain, simple, molded fiberglass chairs, the kind you would find in most fast-food restaurants across the country, waiting for their turn to be called. The floor was simple, well-worn linoleum. In the center of the lobby was a large half-circle counter where three or four women sat answering phone calls and questions and calling the names of vendors who were waiting to see a purchasing agent. There were a few vending machines for soda's, candy bars, and chips. One wall contained photos of past and present board members, and that was it. The place was simple and plain. There were no marble floors, walls, squishy soft couches, or leather chairs. No frills of any kind. Definitely not what I expected for the largest retail company in the world.

I didn't have to wait long before someone behind the counter called my name and directed me to a lady standing at the front door entrance. It was Pat who greeted me graciously and then walked with me out the front door to a side entrance and directly into the executive offices full of administrative assistants, secretaries, and various support personnel, all in cubicles in the middle of a large room.

The outer offices were occupied with various upper level managers and senior officers. We walked past Sam Walton's office -- he wasn't in -- and into Don's office the COO.

I was surprised his office was so small. There were two chairs in front of his desk with barely enough room for your knees. He had to squeeze behind his desk and a bookcase to be seated behind his desk. I just had to ask him, "Is this a temporary office? I was sure you'd have a huge office with a sofa, a conference table, big easy chairs, etc."

He laughed and said, "You must be a banker." I laughed and mentioned, "Actually I was before getting into missions."

He wanted to know more of my background, so I gave him a brief overview of my banking history and now missions and rolled my conversation into what the ministry was doing in China. I wanted to keep within the 15 minutes allotted to me. Despite my effort to be brief, he gave me 40 minutes and confirmed what I had already researched about Walmart's giving interest. Nevertheless, I knew that since he had been with Walmart almost from the beginning, he probably had established his own personal foundation with his own particular giving interests. Before leaving, I asked if I could send him a two-page overview of our mission work, and also asked if I could visit him again in the future. He said that would be fine and he would look forward to it.

From that point on, Pat always got me right through to him whenever I called and was quick to arrange more time for me on each visit. When she wasn't there, Don answered the phone himself and always set a time for our visit.

A JOINT VENTURE WITH WALMART

On a subsequent visit six months later, I came up with an idea while in a meeting with Don. At the time, Walmart was just venturing into mainland China. Since we knew where the Christians were in various areas across China, I asked if it would be helpful if we could direct Walmart to Christians who might possibly be qualified for middle and even upper management positions in their stores. I had his attention, so I kept going.

"How about a joint venture with Walmart providing middle and upper managers from your headquarters here in Bentonville to serve in China for three or four weeks during the summer, teaching Christian Business Ethics to Chinese Christian businessmen? Would you be willing to cover the total cost for their time there, airfare to and from so they wouldn't have to raise their individual support from their respective churches? Also, if a team of your upper management could work with us, we could develop a curriculum together for the class relatively quickly."

I could see he was getting excited, so I kept going with another idea. Would he also be interested in helping us recruit Christian attorneys from within the Walmart structure, as well as their Christian attorney's friends across the country, to serve in China for a few weeks during the summer months? We could put a committee together with our curriculum specialist to develop a special course on Christian Ethics for Chinese lawyers.

Naturally, I had to emphasize that we currently had absolutely no infrastructure for either program, but we could work together to develop these two new concepts for sharing the Good News in an additional way to teaching English.

Don was so excited he stood up and quickly dialed a number on his speaker phone, asking me to repeat the idea to a fellow on the other end who was the vice-president with Proctor & Gamble, in charge of a large 400-employee facility just down the road from Walmart's Bentonville office, and one of the largest suppliers for Walmart. He was also a believer and a close friend who attended the same church as Don. I presented the same idea to him for the next fifteen minutes, asking if they would also consider sending their top executives to teach in the two programs for three or four weeks each summer and also work with us to develop the curriculum. I again stressed it was only an idea at this point as there was currently no infrastructure as yet for either of these two themes, nor had I even discussed it with the president of the ministry. But the possibilities for influencing key people for the future of China could be quite extraordinary. He said, without hesitation, "Count us in. We'd love to be a part of that. It would be a great opportunity." Now all I had to do was present the idea to the "powers that be" in the ministry.

When returning to the office, I couldn't wait to unveil my idea. It would give us two new avenues, besides the English teaching aspect, for recruiting additional professionals to share the Good News. It would increase the number of teachers sent every year and cost us almost nothing since two Fortune 500 corporations would pick up most of the cost.

I excitedly shared my idea with the new executive vice-president of the English Institute, a wonderfully kind fellow as well as a very gifted businessman who had sold his company and was looking to use his talents in missions. His opportunity came when Dr. Ken hired him to take over duties at headquarters when Dr. Ken moved to Beijing. His response was not what I expected.

He hit the roof, coming across his desk at me, red-faced and yelling that, "we didn't have any such program, let alone the financial means by which to build an infrastructure. How could you say such a thing?" He sat down and continued his rant for another several minutes.

I'm not one to let that sort of behavior intimidate me, and felt my idea was an excellent one, with the best interest of the ministry at heart. So, like a good Christian fellow, I stood up and came across his desk, nearly in his face, and told him he was not listening. "I told you that both Walmart and Proctor & Gamble know this is just an idea. I told them I'd have to lay it out to the president and board of directors. Nothing would be committed until then."

I left the matter on the table waiting to hear what the president might say and hoping it would soon present an opportunity to explain to the board of directors as well.

In the meantime, I had been planning and preparing for a vision trip to several provinces in China and Hanoi, Vietnam, to present the ministry's work to a group of donors. I also asked our Chairman of the Board, Bob Foster and his wife Marian if they would like to join us. Bob always had a heart for China and never turned down an opportunity to go there.

The trip was scheduled for three weeks later. But at the same time, I was having increasing discontent with one particular new leader in the organization who seemed to have jealous ambition. The ministry was growing and that was a good thing. I was delighted to have played a role in making that possible.

The downside of our growth was that it created less access to Dr. Ken. He and I had always bounced fundraising ideas off one another, and I missed that. My restlessness had nothing to do with the new and very qualified executive vice-president who took over operations at the home office after Dr. Ken moved to China. However, another new management hire created a clog in the free flow of ideas and vital information needed in my fundraising efforts. This fellow was put in charge of two vastly different aspects of the ministry, recruiting teachers and fundraising.

Everything related to fundraising had to funnel through him, creating a time-consuming bottleneck. The situation was further compromised by the fact that, in my opinion, he was not qualified for either position. To make matters worse, he actually was purposely obstructing my efforts by withholding ministry information at every turn. Several others in the organization also felt the same in their respective duties. The whole situation was becoming progressively frustrating for me. But for now, I was focused on contacting potential new donors and another donor trip to China and Vietnam in a few weeks.

THE STORY OF PETER COORS

I had opportunity to attend The Gathering, an event held annually in different areas of the country for many of the wealthiest Christians in the United States. The purpose is to share with one another what ministries they are supporting and why, but also as a tool to influence the next generation in giving responsibly.

One of the guest speakers was Peter Coors of the Coors Beer family. He began his talk by telling everyone he wasn't really interested in the family business and felt the Lord had something else he should be doing. He proceeded to show a short video clip of what his company produces. It was one of the most powerful presentations I have ever seen.

The opening scene has the audience looking through what is obviously a scope of a sniper's rifle, with the cross hairs clearly visible on an American soldier standing by his Humvee in full battle fatigues holding his M-16 rifle. He has no idea he is about to be shot by the unseen enemy sniper. Suddenly a shot rings out and the American soldier drops to the ground, presumably dead. The audience gasp and are stunned. A few seconds pass and suddenly the American soldier bounces back up and takes cover behind his Humvee. End of clip.

Peter stood up and said, "That's what our company makes and what the Lord directed me to manufacture, providing all the necessary contacts for raw materials and necessary technology to produce." The audience gave him a standing ovation.

Later that evening, I had dinner with him at his table and had an opportunity to hear more about how God had guided him in the development of this amazing technology that can save thousands of American soldiers and police officers.

His story reminded me of God's guidance at the time of the Japanese attack on Pearl Harbor. The Japanese assumed the Pacific Fleet would all be anchored in Pearl Harbor. What they didn't know was that our aircraft carriers, along with some battle ships and cruisers, were on maneuvers far out at sea and were delayed getting back to Pearl Harbor due to a heavy gale. If they had been in port that day, the war could very easily have gone in a different direction and taken much longer to end.

Isaiah 59:19 (NIV2011) *"From the west, people will fear the name of the LORD, and from the rising of the sun, they will revere his glory. For he will come like a pent-up flood that the breath of the LORD drives along."*

(Did you catch that? The Spirit of the Lord will put enemies to flight with His <u>breath</u>. Amazing! The Lord will just blow them away like dust.)

> *"The angel of the LORD encamps around those who fear him, and he delivers them." Psalm 34:7 (NIV2011)*

COLONIAL PENN LIFE INSURANCE

A couple years earlier I met Dick and Mary Ohman. Dick had been named President and CEO of Colonial Penn Life Insurance on an interim basis to take the company to the next level. I met with him a couple of times and found him to be a superb businessman who I thought would make an excellent board member for the English Institute. We could always use business executives to help guide the ministry's future. On one of my visits with him on the east coast, he invited Stel and me to have dinner with him and Mary at their home in Philadelphia. That's when I learned that he was considering getting involved in ministry after finishing his assignment with Colonial Penn. I suggested he consider becoming a board member for the English Institute. I connected him with the president, and shortly thereafter he joined the board of directors and made a trip with us to Hanoi to sign new contracts there for sending English teachers.

I always enjoyed visiting with Dick and Mary. They were warm and friendly, very professional, and extraordinarily well dressed no matter the occasion. In countries like China and Vietnam, the extreme summer months of humidity makes for uncomfortable situations, especially in formal situations like meeting with high government officials. Dick was always in a suit and Mary in a beautiful dress. They looked like they just stepped off the pages of a Macy's or Nordstrom's full-color catalog. Always calm, cool, and collected, even in humidity, never having a drop of sweat on their brows. Conversely, I'm always dripping wet in humid environments, looking like I just went through a typhoon. Humidity and I just aren't compatible.

After retiring from Colonial Penn, Dick became a gentlemen farmer of sorts, renovating and modernizing a beautiful country home, complete with a barn and a new tractor in the New Hampshire countryside. Knowing that I spent some summers on my paternal grandfather's farm as a boy, he invited me to come and spend a week driving the tractor during harvest time. It would have been so much fun, but unfortunately, I could never work out my schedule.

ARCHER DANIELS MIDLAND (ADM)

Every individual, foundation, or corporation I called on was always interesting. Some, more so than others. One of the scariest was ADM. (Archer Daniels Midland)

Having been accepted for an in-person meeting with the retired former President and CEO of ADM, I was looking forward to the possibility of developing a relationship with one of the largest international companies on the planet. Since it seemed nearly impossible to meet with the current leadership of such a conglomerate, I decided the best approach would be the former president.

At the time ADM has more than 32,000 employees world-wide, with annual revenues of over $346 billion. The company operates more than 270 plants and 420 crop procurement facilities around the world. Walk through any supermarket and you will pass hundreds of products that have ADM connected to them in some way. These include vegetable oils, flour from soybeans, sunflower seeds, canola, peanuts, flaxseed, palm kernel, syrup, starch, glucose, sweeteners, cocoa liquor powder, wheat flour, to name just a few. They also own a controlling interest in some railroads as well as several international food-product related companies. You get the picture. It's a huge conglomerate.

My meeting that day in the Midwest was with Dwayne Andreas Sr., then retired, but who originally became the CEO in 1970 and is credited with transforming the firm into an industrial powerhouse. He remained CEO until 1997, when his nephew was named to the position.

We met in his home, an exceptionally large three-story grand home built in the early 1900's. I was greeted at the front door by a well-dressed professional woman in her early 60s, most likely his personal assistant. She took me to his large office which featured highly polished mahogany walls with inset bookcases. The shelves were filled with books and manuals that resembled a public library. One wall was covered with awards, accomplishments, and pictures of well-known politicians. I call these "me walls." I have one too, just a lot smaller and not as impressive and without highly polished mahogany bookcases and ceiling.

Andreas, who I guessed to be in his early to mid-80's, was dressed in a three-piece business suit. He rose to greet me as I was offered a chair next to his desk facing him and his accomplishment wall. I thanked him for taking the time to see me and complimented him on his many accomplishments. I tried to get him talking about himself before getting into the broader points of the English Institute. For the first time in my career, I couldn't get this gentleman to open up. He just replied with one word, no or yes. So, I moved to an explanation of our work, doing my best to keep it brief and somehow tie our work to what his company was doing in China. It was during this time that I noticed his eyes were closed. There was no visible response and I thought maybe he was asleep. My second thought was that even though he was retired he must still be integrally involved with the company and was probably just overly tired. This was the second time a prospective donor had fallen asleep with my pitch. Not exactly a confidence building situation. After another five minutes I began to wonder if his heart had stopped and he had passed away right there in front of me. This was a well-known and high-profile man, always in the news for much of his professional life.

I began to think about what I would say to the police. There would be tons of questions. Would I be a suspect? I was about to get up and go look for the lady who had ushered me into his office when he finally opened his eyes. I was relieved. At that point I knew there was no real interest, so I quickly wrapped things up and asked if I might send him a short overview. "Yes," came the single word reply. And that was the end of the meeting. I did send him my overview, but never heard back after several follow up phone calls. Oh well! Not every call moves from hope to relationship to ministry support. As short as the meeting was, he seemed a like a nice fellow.

I later speculated that he might have been distracted by the pressure he was facing. A few years earlier, and probably still not totally settled at the time of my visit in 1998, was the U.S. Justice Department's investigation of price-fixing. Several executives were indicted on criminal charges for engaging in price-fixing within the international lysine market. Three of ADM's top officials were eventually sentenced to federal prison in 1999. In 1997, the company was fined $100 million, the largest antitrust fine in U.S. history at the time. It occurred to me at the time, how strange the government's position was on anti-trust criticisms when the government is unaccountable for similar actions and thereby also culpable. Whitacre, an informant for the FBI and whistleblower of the lysine price-fixing conspiracy, also found himself in legal trouble for embezzling money from ADM during his time as an informant for the FBI. Additionally, according to ADM's 2005 annual report, a settlement was reached under which ADM paid $400 million in 2005 to settle a class action antitrust suit. "The Informant" is a nonfiction book that documented the mid-1990s lysine price-fixing conspiracy case and the involvement of ADM executive Whitacre. The book was adapted into the 2009 film *The Informant*, played by Russell Crowe. *(Source: Wikipedia)*

RESEARCHING -BORG WARNER

When doing research, I always check "Who's Who" on various Director Boards, and then cross reference them via their biography and relationships with other companies they are associated with or involvements in. In one such case I came across a name remembered from my childhood at age ten. His name was Jim Bere` and he was President and CEO of Borg Warner Automotive (BWA). When uncovering his name, I remembered it well because he served with my Dad as a Deacon at the Arcadia Christian Reformed church. At that time, he was a salesman for one of Borg Warner's subsidiaries and now the President of Borg Warner.

Borg-Warner Automotive, Inc. is one of the world's leading developers and suppliers of automotive parts and systems found in passenger cars, sport utility vehicles, and light trucks. At the time of my call the company maintained 20 operations in the United States and about a dozen more elsewhere, including Canada, China, France, Germany, India, Italy, Japan, Korea, Mexico, Taiwan, and Wales. Known primarily for supplying powertrain components, including transfer cases and automatic transmissions to major automakers in North America, Europe, and Asia. BWA also made chain systems, like timing chain systems; air/fluid systems like intake manifolds, air pumps, vapor recovery systems, and turbochargers. The company had undergone significant changes over the years, but BWA' s manufacturing skill and reputation allowed it to not only weather the breakup of its corporate family, but to triumph first as a private, then as a newly public, independent company in 1993.

Jim managed the company starting in 1972, just four years after his appointment as president. He became CEO when the former CEO left the company to be the United States ambassador to Japan.

When Borg-Warner celebrated its 50th anniversary in 1978 the automotive profits had reached $98 million. Under Jim's leadership the company jumped to overall sales topping $2.7 billion with 75,000 employees worldwide. The company headed into the stormy business years of the 1980s with an unfriendly takeover by corporate raiders Jacobs and Heyman in the fast-and-loose leveraged buyout (LBO) haven of the 1980s. But Jim had already retired and was asked to come back to straighten out the situation. So, at age 65 Jim assumed the CEO role again to oversee the company's breakup and bring it back to the Private Company era between 1987-93. The task was a daunting one, made more difficult by the onset of Black Monday, a dramatic plunge in the stock market. It was November of 1991 when I called for an appointment which was set for early December.

In calling his secretary for the appointment, I mentioned he had served with my Dad on the Deacons Board of our church when I was ten years of age, and I was hoping to get an appointment with him to describe our work in China. She put me on hold, came back in a few minutes to say he remembered my Dad fondly and provided me with his schedule for a possible meeting date, but since he was always so busy it most likely he would only have 15 or 20 minutes. I said that would be fine and much appreciated.

My Dad and Jim were both in the automotive business but on very opposite ends. Back in those days we visited with Jim and his wife Barbara, who lived a couple blocks north of us across Huntington Drive off of Golden West and few blocks west of the Santa Anita thoroughbred racetrack. They in turn visited our home several times a few blocks south on Golden West. As a child I always remembered their big house because there were Peacocks all over their roof and front yard when we arrived. Those beautiful birds are protected under the law in Arcadia. There are hundreds of them in the area. As a boy, I never quite trusted being around those over-grown chickens.

As my research indicated, Borg Warner probably wasn't going to fund any Christian effort. However, I also knew that men in upper corporate echelons had large salaries with stock options and often established their own private foundations. My background research indicated he was on the Board of Fuller Seminary in Pasadena CA and that was another touch point as I knew some of the trustees and professors. Other serving areas for him revealed he was a director of Abbott Laboratories, where a cousin worked as a chemist, Ameritech Corporation, K Mart Corporation, Temple-Inland Inc., Time Warner Inc., and the Tribune Company of Chicago. He also served in various capacities at the Chicago Museum of Science and Industry, (one of my favorite places as a small child), the University of Chicago, Salvation Army, Chicago Symphony Orchestra and North western's Graduate School of Management, among others. None of these additional capacities would indicate an interest in our China work, except perhaps the Fuller connection, but then, I figured if interest did develop he could lead me to other Christian executives of large corporations within his sphere of influence who also had their own private foundations.

When I arrived at the Borg Warner corporate headquarters in downtown Chicago, I was given a special badge needed for a separate, secured elevator to the top floor overlooking Lake Michigan. The first thing noted when stepping out of the elevator was, I was entering a completely empty large room with travertine tiled walls and floor, a few potted vicus benjamina trees, and not a single chair. There was a massive floor-to-ceiling glass wall. Behind that glass wall was Jim's administrative assistant. Beyond her desk were several huge floor-to-ceiling windows with a sweeping view of Lake Michigan. When Jim's assistant buzzed me inside from the elevator exit area, I asked her about the glass wall that separated her from the elevator. She explained that it was constructed of bullet-proof glass and was there to protect her boss. She said, "Anyone trying to get to Jim would be trapped in that chair-less lobby with only the fichus trees." She mentioned "The elevator returns automatically to the first floor once you stepped out and we have a secret and secure fire stairwell and private elevators from our offices inside here." So essentially, anyone stepping off that elevator with wrong intentions would be a captive until the police arrived up from the hidden secret elevator.

I had an extraordinarily wonderful meeting with Jim who told me that his private foundation was run by his wife. We talked about the Christian Reformed Church in Arcadia, who the pastor was now, and how Arcadia had changed from back in the day.

He said, "I remembered you and your brother because you both were always so well dressed in full suits as were your parents, in both Sunday morning and evening services, and always so attentive to the sermon." I told him I also remembered wearing those suits, especially in the hot summer months. The suits were made of coarse unrefined wool, the kind of prickly trousers that nearly drove me mad with itching. I told him we sat still because any movement on our part was like being stung by a hundred "wool" bees. He went on to remember, "Your Dad worked on my car a number of times, and like all mechanics got dirty with grease under his fingernails; but on Sunday he looked like he just stepped out of a cab on Wall Street."

He gave me almost an hour of his valuable time. After I explained a little about the English Institute, he asked me to send him a two-page overview of our accomplishments over the last twenty years and our vision for the future. The new relationship was however short-lived. I sent the overview as requested but never heard back. Jim died on January 3, 1992, just two weeks after my visit.

Ameritech Chairman William L. Weiss remembered Jim "as a good friend, a remarkable citizen and an astute business leader. As a member of Ameritech's board of directors and, before that, on the Illinois Bell's board, he was generous with his counsel and time with a deep understanding of the community's needs and a strong sense of social responsibility. Chicago will miss his wisdom and energy. I'll miss his friendship and good sense." (Source: Wikipedia). I thought, "Me too," and wished I could have gotten to know him better in my adult years.

Remembering Jim reminds me of another Christian business leader associated with automotive parts that I also came to know and called on who became a donor for the ministry as well as a board member.

CARDONE INDUSTRIES

Cardone Industries is the world's largest privately held and leading supplier of automotive remanufactured replacement parts. Their commitment has always been to deliver the right parts at the right time when offering a full range of products and services.

I was drawn to them in my research by their core principles: *"Servant Leadership is a way of life that influences, models, supports and encourages people to serve others first. It is a way to personally develop and pursue excellence in every area of life."* Cardone Industries uses this model because its people are at the heart of the company. "We believe our Factory Family Members (FFMs) is our greatest resource." Their "corporate objectives" also made a tremendous impression on me:

> To honor God in all we do.
> To help people develop.
> To pursue excellence.
> To grow profitably.
> Value our people.
> Value our work.

I would like to have introduced Michael Cardone, and many others I met during my career, to that first professor I met in college, the one who told the class there was first and foremost, nothing more important than making a profit in the world of business, more than any other consideration. I thought of him as I heard Michael Cardone Jr., expound on his principles of doing business. Most of the company owners and corporate executives I came to know during my 20 years in the business world, and all those I met during 23 years of calling on Christian Corporate leaders have adhered to the similar principles and Biblical guidelines.

Cardone Industries, was founded in 1970 by Michael Cardone Sr. It began in a Philadelphia row house, reconditioning only one product, windshield wiper motors. The company is now being guided by Michael Cardone III. I've never met him but got to know his dad well when introducing him to the ministry. He eventually became a board member and was always a great asset to the ministry. I had the pleasure of staying with him and his wife at their beautiful home a couple of times and always enjoyed the first special tour of their Philadelphia remanufacturing plant. It was, and is, a most impressive operation. (Michael Cardone Sr. was inducted into the Automotive Hall of Fame in 1994 for his pioneering excellence in remanufacturing, having joined a list of others hall of famers and industry leaders like Lee Iacocca, Carl Benz and Eiji Toyota. Source: Wikipedia)

Don Soderquist, former COO of Wal-Mart

37

VIETNAM REDUX

I was getting ready to embark on a vision trip to several provinces in China and Vietnam. As vision trips go, the donor group was smaller than normal. But it was a great group, including one of the heiresses and her husband to the Johnson & Johnson family of products. I had stayed with them for an overnight visit in their stately home where we walked a block to the Bay for fresh caught Lobster for a home cooked meal in their massive kitchen.

Since it was to be the first trip out of the U.S. for two other ladies in our group, I suspected they would have far too much luggage, which is why I wanted to meet with them at the hotel near LAX the night before our departure. They were close friends with one another, and one was V.P. for the company's foundation funded by a large Steel manufacturing company.

I loved these two ladies dearly. They became donors several years earlier when I first visited them, but this would be their first opportunity to see the work firsthand. Before leaving on the trip my suggestion was, they make sure they always have a safe place to carry their passports, cash, and Travelers Checks. Since this would be their first International trip to see the mission work firsthand, my additional advice two months earlier, was to make sure they would travel light. I met them at their hotel the night before our flight and took them to dinner. During dinner I asked them how many suitcases they had taken. They each had two huge waist-high wheeled suitcases and two smaller ones – for a total of eight suitcases. There was no way they could handle all those bags, especially on shorter flights on smaller aircraft. Sometimes, we would have to climb a ladder mounted on the back of a pickup truck to get onboard smaller prop driven aircraft in remote areas, so it was absolutely imperative that we kept our luggage to a minimum. I had nightmares of being a baggage handler on the whole two-week trip. I suggested they sort through their luggage discarding all the fancy evening dresses, any extra sweaters, blouses, but keep one nice pair of dress shoes and especially keep the tennis shoes. By the time they were finished sorting there were six large full boxes which we shipped back to their home on the east coast. God Bless them.

The trip went well. We visited several teachers in various provinces across China and also made time to visit specialty venues like a handmade Koysina Vase factory, as well as a factory where expensive handmade rugs were made. One of the ladies bought a beautiful handmade rug for her formal living room. The cost in the U.S. would have been around $50,000- $75,000 for a 16x24 rug. The cost in China was $6,000 U.S. dollars.

Later, when she arrived home, she had a notice that the rug had been shipped and had arrived in her state. However, U.S. Customs denied ever receiving it. We saw it being made in the factory and it was the most beautiful handmade rug I have ever seen. Knowing that other donors on previous trips had never had trouble receiving similar shipments, I smelled a rotten fish in the U.S. Customs claim. There must have been someone working there who sabotaged the delivery. She never did receive the rug.

At the check-in counter at the Hanoi Metropole – the same hotel President Trump would meet with the President of North Korea many years later -- the check-in clerk asked to see and record our passport information. What I did not know was that they had hidden these items in some sort of strap holder underneath their blouses which had shifted location on a bumpy flight by the time we arrived in Hanoi. They stood there digging deep into their blouses to find their pouches. The eyes of the young

Vietnamese check-in clerk were as big as coffee cup saucers. He looked confused trying to figure out what they were up to. I was standing next to them and couldn't stop laughing as they dug and floundered around in their blouses to find those pouches. They also realized it was surely a comical commotion and couldn't stop laughing at themselves either. Twenty years later these dear ladies and I still have an intense belly laugh when we remember the incident.

A few years earlier I had told them about my bungie-jumping experience. While driving from Vancouver Canada into the Canadian Rockies to visit donors in Kelowna and the Lake Okanagan area, I saw a sign that said, "Free Bungie Jumping." On a whim, I took the short detour of a few miles on a side road to watch people jump from an 800-foot high bridge over a river. On a dumber whim, I let them harness my ankles and I jumped. My heart stopped. I know for sure my brain did because on the way down I was asking myself, "WHAT WERE YOU THINKING?" From that point on, whenever I made a phone call to them, I rarely gave my name, and instead always said, Hellooooooo, this is Bungie Bob…," as if I had just jumped and my voice was disappearing as the bungie cord took me down. There is never a doubt in their minds who was calling, and they immediately started laughing.

On another visit to their home on the east coast, I slipped off the pavement while taking a walk down their long-wooded driveway after a rain and injured my ankle. By the time I made it back to the house some 50 yards up hill my ankle had swollen to the size of my calf muscle. The pain was excruciating. The ladies helped me put an ice pack on it and provided a guest bedroom for the night. By morning not much had changed, except that the pain was more intense and more swelling. They drove me to the nearest hospital where X-rays revealed a small broken bone. A temporary fiberglass cast was put on and crutches provided. I had just started out on a three-week fundraising trip, but now had to cancel the trip and reschedule everything for another time. It took me two days to cancel appointments and reschedule flights home. Back in California, an orthopedic surgeon put on a permanent cast with instructions to stay off my feet for three weeks and keep my ankle elevated. He mentioned that the break was probably one of the five worst he had ever seen. He also recognized my name and said he went to high school and graduated with my brother. It is a small world after all.

I expected that my healing would take several weeks, but my dear older sisters in Christ called and prayed for my healing. The very next day the swelling had gone down so much that I could stick my entire hand down into the cast.

In revisiting the surgeon, the following day, a new cast was put on with the same instructions. By the end of that day, the swelling had again diminished to where I could stick my hand down into the cast. The third day the doctor took the cast off again and told me I could start wearing my shoes. After rescheduling the original trip, I was back on the road within a week. Prayer works.

Jeremiah 17:14 (KJV) "Heal me O Lord, and I shall be healed; save me, and I shall be saved: for thou art my praise."

A FAITHFUL MAN

Although we had some light-hearted moments on the trip to China and Vietnam there were also some hard times.

Bob Foster Sr., our chairman of the board, was already in his late 70's. His wife, Marian, was dealing with Alzheimer's and not in the best of health. Her doctors suggested that it would be best for her if they continued to live life as usual, and since she had made several prior trips to China with Bob, he brought her along instead of leaving her home. During the Vietnam portion of the trip, she became more ill and Bob never left her side, often being up all night looking after her. I suggested he change his plans and head for home as this surely had to be grueling for him. I was getting genuinely concerned for his health. He thanked me for my concern but stuck it out and even continued on after our trip, going on to Thailand and Singapore to visit friends there.

I admired his strength, fortitude, and faithfulness to his wife of 50-plus years. They eventually made it home and Marian passed away a few months later. Stella and I were on vacation in the panhandle of Idaho and drove to Denver to attend the funeral.

Bob went to heaven in May of 2016 at the age of 96 several years later. He was a special friend, a mentor, and godly man as well as a role model for many. He served on the board of Navigators for many years as well as Wheaton College, and was an excellent writer and Bible teacher who shared Christ with top executives of Fortune 500 companies across the United States. He also was one of my advocates and mentors for many years. I greatly miss our talks and his weekly one-page biblical devotions.

On our trip we met with several teachers stationed in various locations across China and everyone had the opportunity to teach at least one English class and test their creativity in carefully sharing the Good News. After two weeks, we concluded our trip in Hong Kong with an enjoyable dinner overlooking the Hong Kong Harbor at the Shangri-La hotel, discussing our experiences and how much they were willing to increase their donations now that they had seen and experienced the ministry's work.

For me it was an exhausting trip. I called Stella from Hong Kong, suggesting we rendezvous in Hawaii for a relaxing week at the Turtle Bay Hilton on the Northshore of Honolulu. This would be our second trip to Hawaii. We both arrived in Honolulu an hour apart. Stella floated in the Bay. I slept for nearly 24 hours straight.

Soon after returning home an opportunity presented itself for another challenge that greatly interested me. It also presented interesting varieties of assignments far beyond what I could have imagined.

First trip to Hawaii. Couple we met from Idaho. Bob suggested
we rent the catamaran & sail to the north shore of Maui.

The Catamaran had just won 1st place in an International Race
from Australia to Hawaii & rental came with a crew of three,
sleeping quarters, two bathrooms, galley & all the food we could eat.

Our helicopter for exploring mountain tops, valleys,
lava tubes and lunch on the black sand beach.

Para-sailing. Bob was reeled out to several hundred feet above
the boat while watching killer whales swimming below.

38

LOOK TO THE SKIES.

Within weeks of returning from Vietnam, I received an invitation to interview for the position of vice-president of development with Mission Aviation Fellowship (MAF), then located in Redlands, California. I've always been interested in airplanes and MAF's operations on three continents fascinated me. Sensing it was time to move on, I accepted the interview. The Chief Operating Officer had been looking for two years for someone with my qualifications and mentioned at the end of our two-hour interview that I was the one he was looking for. Nice to hear, but I wasn't sure about making a change.

Consequently, an internal conflict came into focus. On the one hand was my loyalty to the English Institute and the marvelous time I had there as well as the love of Chinese people that developed. On the flip side there was the excitement of a new challenge and the opportunity to join a worldwide ministry that would enable me to meet many other peoples and cultures where I could share the Good News of the gospel. The scripture below convinced me.

"Enlarge the place of my tent, stretch my tent curtains wide, and not hold back; lengthen my cords, strengthen my stakes. "Isaiah 54:2 (NIV2011),

A few days after my interview, MAF made an inviting offer detailing duty that would be expected. I prayed and sensed that after eight wonderful years at the English Institute, the time for a move had come. I accepted their offer with conditions that included a start date of six weeks later in September of 1996, a private office, not a cubicle. The six weeks would allow me time to complete other projects at the English Institute. The conundrum for me was that I had just completed my annual income projections for the coming year at the English Institute and didn't want to leave them with an income shortfall for the year due to my leaving.

Stella and I prayed about the situation, and over the next six weeks God was faithful and fulfilled my desire to finish well. In that six weeks, I was able to raise the entire yearly income amount I had projected and thereby avoided an income shortfall of nearly $3 million for the ministry.

The day after I accepted the MAF offer, Dr. Ken offered me a new position as Executive Director of a new sub ministry of the English Institute to develop and run with my original idea with Walmart and Proctor and Gamble to enlarge the scope of the English teaching across Asia. I would be recruiting their upper and middle level managers and attorneys to teach business ethics in China and across Asia. I was excited to hear the offer but saddened to have to decline having already given my word to MAF. It just would not be appropriate even though I would like to have accepted the offer.

My secretary at the English Institute was Kathleen. She was an outstanding and especially qualified assistant who had been working with me for nearly as long as I had been at the English Institute. She is the kind of assistant that many wish they had. Always a step ahead of me in knowing what was needed before I asked. In realizing this I mentioned to her several years prior, that if I ever left English Institute, I would offer her the opportunity to come with me if she wanted to, and if it could be arranged to everyone's satisfaction. I had already discussed this possibility as part of the conditional arrangement with MAF.

Six weeks after beginning my tenure at MAF, I called her and asked her to join me. She was ready to move on too. I wanted to do this in an orderly manner since she held a knowledgeable key position for the development department. It seemed fair for her and the Institute, to give a six-week lead time notice to help them find her replacement. My suggestion was once they found her replacement, she would be available one day a week for an additional month to train her replacement. It seemed equitable to me, but it caused quite a stir. It always amazed me that organizations sometimes think they own people. We eventually got past the "incident" and after I left MAF she stayed with them for over twenty years moving with them to Idaho. God indeed had a special plan for her life.

DID I HEAR THAT CORRECTLY?

The drive from my home to the MAF headquarters in Redlands took 45 minutes, a significant increase from the former three minutes to the English Institute. A positive factor was the drive was east, away from traffic, and opposite the traffic heading into Los Angles. This provided extra time for prayer and last-minute changes by phone to Kathleen for the day's schedule.

My first day at MAF started with an unexpected message from the Lord. I parked in one of the visitor locations not knowing exactly where employees should park. A few minutes later I would learn that "visitor parking" would be representative of my tenure there. Walking from the parking lot to the front door I heard the Lord's quiet voice tell me, *"Bob, your assignment here is for three years."* I was surprised, stunned, actually flabbergasted to hear these words just two minutes before starting the new job. I wondered why the Lord would tell me this now. Nonetheless I remained undaunted in the tasks that lay ahead.

My assignment was to build a REAL major donor department; tackle the massive task of replenishing the aging fleet of 84 aircraft stationed in various countries on three continents. This would require raising at least $60 million dollars or more just for the aircraft. I was also to oversee the other departments of fundraising like missionary personal support, radio advertising, Direct Mail, and all other fundraising/marketing duties. All of this with a budget that had just been drastically cut for the coming year, and to which I had no-input since arriving for duty six months after the budget process began and two months after the Board approved the budget. The only thing left to do was look within the fundraising department budgets for hidden or unnecessary cost and reuse recovered dollars for anything that could help generate income.

In the six weeks prior to my start date, I decided to meet for lunch with some of the other key players. Some were indeed key people who could and would be of great help. Exceptionally talented people. Others were "*supposed*" to be key players but really had only their own interests at heart. Sometimes, when people have been in a position for a long time, they consider it their territory and have the attitude that no one else should interfere with it. Yet, no one seems to know exactly what they are actually contributing and often there is a complete lack of accountability. These are the people I purposed to eliminate or reassign as soon as possible. It would be unpopular, but the ministry was under severe financial strain and had to be done. Bureaucracy is an unfortunate by-product in secular for-profit corporations and especially in government agencies. It exists in missions too. The dead wood – forgive the harshness of the term – can easily be overlooked in any growing company, or mission, and they are easily threatened when new players are introduced into the culture. The problem often occurs because upper management feels obligated to keep them because of long-developed relationships and often lacks the courage to release them for what God may have for them next. I have noted on several occasions that when these types of people are "let go" they grow beyond current sedentary levels to greater value in their next employment.

In one of my "pre-start get-acquainted lunch interviews" there was one fellow in particular who fell into this category. He told me he had 50 prospective donors who could give at least

$25,000 each as a first gift. I immediately sensed he was staking out his territory before I officially arrived. After asking how many he had brought into the ministry, his response was none. He was just collecting a list, had no plan, and hadn't brought in a single new donor into the ministry's since he had been there. He was supposed to be a manager so probably thought himself above hitting the road. I asked if he would pass them along by geographical area to the most appropriate territory manager for contacting. He said no because he wanted to do it himself. "Well how long have you been accumulating this list of names," I asked. "About two years," he responded, definitely not the correct answer. No wonder the budget was being cut. It was people like this I felt must be moved out. They should be thinking of the overall needs of the ministry not sitting on names of potential donors to seek his own glory. When I started a few weeks later, he was the first one I expected to get on the road calling his "potential" donors list. But he wouldn't, because he couldn't. He was either afraid or lazy; not a fundraiser and consequently the first to be relieved of his job.

At the time, they had 12 fundraisers across the country. Nearly all of them were former pilots who served in various foreign countries "flying in" everything from needed food, Bibles, and medical supplies, and "flying out" severely injured or sick people to hospitals hundreds of miles away. Some pilots fly into areas that are extremely dangerous, with landing zones and truly short mountainous runways in valleys between very steep mountainous ranges. I know, because in the months ahead I flew with them into several remote landing zones across the Indonesia chain of Islands surrounded by 12,000-foot-high mountains on all sides and landing on runways so short a seagull wouldn't try it. MAF pilots are considered by many commercial airline pilots to be the best they have ever seen. Actual experience confirmed it for me when sitting in the co-pilot's seat on some of these flights. A number of times I nearly saw my breakfast twice.

Pilots, especially those doing dangerous work under difficult treacherous flying conditions, like tribal wars, inclement weather, and aircraft mechanical issues certainly do form a "band of brothers" bond. All of them have invested tremendous amounts of time and effort, up to six years of additional education beyond college to prepare for Christian mission flying in remote areas, and all for a third of the income they could earn in the secular world. They raise their own support and most do a great job of doing so. I can't speak more highly of their commitment and dedication in their special calling in God's Kingdom work.

However, that does not necessarily mean they can or should be made fundraisers when leaving field operations. This seemed to me to be a built-in conflict of interest. How can they raise larger amounts of money for the greater needs of the ministry when their first interest would naturally be raising money for their personal support first? Additionally, most had no experience whatsoever with asking for a gift of even $10,000, let alone several hundred thousand or a million. Human resources were not going to hang them out to dry when they could no longer fly for medical or age-related reasons; and rightly so. This then, was my first challenge, a tight rope I was obliged to walk. I spent many hours in HR trying to find other options and positions within the ministry that would better suit them after being mustered out of the flying arena. In many cases there was not a suitable middle ground and consequently I was left to train them in major funding, raising their vision and confidence levels in asking for bigger donations for the ministry's larger operational cost; a significant number when considering the ministry had 84 aircraft scattered all over the globe.

The second challenge was being expected to be at all the directors' meetings held nearly daily on one subject or another. I understood this because every day's activities become important when a ministry operates on three continents. Wars, famine, natural disasters, and politics create fluid situations.

It was common for these meetings to last three hours or even most of a day. I told my boss we both knew I had not been hired to be sitting in endless meetings. "You hired me to take action on a number of issues not the least of which was raising $60 million for aircraft replenishment. Since there currently are not any field reps capable of asking for large capital amounts, do I have your blessing to 'get to it and hit the road?" Hopefully, I can raise some money to relieve financial pressure.

He whole-heartedly agreed. Over the next 6 weeks I made several internal department organizational changes, cutting out all projects and expenses that did not generate positive cash flow. There were several people capable for leadership who were fervently hungry for the opportunity to expand their horizons in leadership. I promoted them to project leader positions to increase their development and responsibility levels. Then, designated someone as my second in command to take charge while I was gone for three-week donor trip across the U.S in hopes of enlarging the other fundraisers vision by demonstration.

The trip was successful, producing over $2 million dollars in commitments and several new ministry partners. I often remembered a quote from President Eisenhower, one of the most capable American generals ever, who said, "Leadership is like a piece of string on the table. You can't push it; you have to pull it." Demonstration is, indeed, the better teacher.

Everything during this time had a sense of urgency, somewhere just short of panic mode. Budget constraints and declining income at the time of my entrance made me at times somewhat of a bull in a China shop. I justified this by viewing myself as a Beach Master. In World War II a Beach Master was given absolute control during the invasion of Normandy to establish the beach head. His word and directions were final and absolute, even above those of a five-star general. He was, in a sense, a temporary five star general. Once the beach had been secured, authority reverted back to the normal chain of command. Did I do everything right? I like to think so, but no, I made mistakes. But I did get us off the beach.

BANN AND BOEING AIRCRAFT

We received a call from the Baan Software Company, based in
The Netherlands. They were known for developing a special software for Boeing Aircraft in Seattle that could easily keep track
of the parts inventory at Boeing's worldwide service locations,
and thus save tens of millions of dollars for Boeing. They learned
that Mission Aviation Fellowship had 84 aircraft operating in
various countries around the globe. They were drawn to MAF
because they were strong Christians who were donating millions
of dollars to Christian organizations. While we were certainly
a much smaller organization than Boeing, they felt they could
use a version of their newly created Boeing software to also save
a great deal of money for us in our parts inventory and cost of
maintaining aircraft inventory in all our aircraft base locations.

A meeting was scheduled, and they flew into the Palm Springs
airport directly from Amsterdam in their Falcon 900 private jet.
I picked them up and drove them to our Redlands headquarters
for a day of meetings to discuss their idea. On our drive back to
Redlands it became clear they had done their research on us and
wanted to sincerely help. The meeting went superbly well, and I
felt this could be the beginning of a strong friendship that would
have great value to the ministry and for them. The software would
cost $900,000, which, with the needed software adaptations they
would donate. At the end of the day, I drove them back to Palm
Springs and decided to see how interested they really were. In our
discussion I learned they were also planning serious investments
at our Wamena air base in Irian Jaya near New Guinea

I mentioned that we too were planning to increase our presence and service to this remote area and needed to add a Cessna
C-208 to our fleet there. The C-208 is a larger aircraft that seats
six or seven passengers instead of the four passengers in a C-206
and with the seats taken out it would carry twice the cargo. The
only thing holding us back was the cost of $1.5 million for a
new one which was beyond our reach. They immediately said
they would also donate the $1.5 million for the new C-208. I
drew their attention to the fact that we had just one hangar in

Wamena to do repairs and service on our four C-206's based there. With the new larger wingspan of a C-208, we would need a larger hangar which would cost another $500,000. They simply said, "Not a problem. We'll cover the cost for that too." As the conversation continued, they learned we had four, four-bedroom homes directly across the dirt road from our Wamena base for our pilots and families. They wondered if they could have them for their increased personnel they would be stationing there, and if so, they would be willing to donate the cost of four new 4-bedroom homes a mile from the airport for our pilot and families. That gave me another idea to offer for a joint effort.

We have retired volunteers who have spent their lives in the trades; carpenters, plumbers, framers, cabinet makers, tile installers, etc., who are always looking to donate their time and talents for such projects overseas. What if we were to recruit them to come and train the local indigenous natives in these trades to build the new pilot's homes and we could also use local resources like wood and stone?

They were ecstatic and thought it was a great idea. They liked the way I was thinking -- and I definitely liked the way they were thinking. By the time we arrived at the Palm Springs airport, their gift of $900,000 for the software had turned into a total gift of $3.8 million.

When we got to the Palm Springs Airport, they welcomed me aboard their Falcon 900 for a "look see." The plane included a full-size bedroom complete with a queen bed, closet and two on-board bathrooms, one off the bedroom and one behind the pilot's cabin near the galley. This was definitely the way to travel. We continued to work out some of the details while sitting in the plane on the tarmac and that's when I remembered the added cost of preparing the new C-208, which wasn't done by Cessna's manufacturing in Kansas, but a special location in Montana for our special cockpit electronic needed equipment as well as the special logo paint job. I had no idea what that cost was and suggested I would get back to them if they were interested in helping with that too. They said the cost didn't matter. Just call us when you need the check, we will wire the money the same day. All together their gift came to $4.5 million.

Nine months later Cessna manufacturing in Kansas called to inform us that our new C-208 was ready. We sent two pilots to pick it up and fly it to our third-party paint company in Montana for Logo icon paint identification and special instrumentation. I called our donor in The Netherlands, and as promised, the money was wired to our account the following day.

COWS AND BOOZE?

Seven months later I made one of two trips to The Netherlands to meet with them on other portions of their gift for Wamena. I arrived at Schiphol Airport in the Netherlands at 8:00 AM on a Sunday. My administrative assistant arranged for a room at the Amsterdam Hotel, a block from the original Queens Palace and square. Like so many hotels in the older part of Europe, the lobby was small and crowded with people standing in line to register. The reception clerk wasn't able to assign any rooms since it was Sunday, and they were on a skeleton crew with maids and none of the rooms were ready. By the time I got to the counter the clerk asked if I had reservations. When giving her my name, I used the Dutch pronunciation of Boomsma (Bowms-sma).

She replied, "Oh yes Mr. Boomsma, your room is ready." Everyone in the lobby looked confused and surprised, but none more so than me. Nonetheless I wasn't going to question the windfall. Besides, I have this habit of never looking a horse in the mouth who is going to give you a gift. Oh! Wait. I have that old idiom reversed, "Never look a gift horse in the mouth,"

She also asked, "Would you like dinner and breakfast served in your room?"

I said, "No, I'll have meals in the dining room."

"Will you need a car tomorrow?"

"Yes," I said.

"What time would you like your car?"

"How about 7 AM."

A bell hop took my suitcase and led me to my tenth-floor room overlooking Amsterdam. I spent the afternoon exploring the canals of Amsterdam.

The following morning there was a brand-new Mercedes with a chauffeur, dressed in a traditional black suit, white shirt, and black tie. About now I'm thinking, "I wonder how much this extra is going to cost the ministry?"

I have to say the added service did come in very handy. My appointment was more than 100 kilometers south, and I needed to make several transitions to other major highways. If left to my own devices I probably would have wound up somewhere in Belgium, or even France miles from where I needed to be.

My meetings lasted all day. The chauffeur waited and took me back to my hotel in the early evening. Back at the hotel the clerk asked if I would need a car and driver for the next morning. Yes, I said, and added that I would be ready to leave at 7 a.m. The following morning a different driver complete with properly attired chauffeur suit and hat was waiting at the front entrance in a brand-new Volvo resembling something like todays S90 T8. Once again, he would be with me all day at the Baan company and I informed him it would probably be late evening as a dinner with the Baan company leadership was scheduled that evening. He said, "That will be fine, Sir." I was starting to feel like a celebrity business executive, Richard Branson of Virgin Atlantic maybe? After a day of meetings at Jon Baan's home the chauffeur was given instruction to the Baan Company headquarters as Jon had a conference call with a business partner in the Middle East. I was the first to arrive at Baan Headquarters.

The dinner that evening was prepared by the in-house world class chef for the Baan Company. I was met by a young pretty blond Dutch girl who would be our server for the seven-course meal in what was clearly not an average lunch cafeteria. The tables and general ambience modeled that of an exclusive restaurant in Paris. There would only be four of us for dinner in this huge well-appointed room. The young waitress asked where I was from and my name. At the mention of my name, she seemed delighted and said she had never actually met any of the Boomsma's. I asked her what she meant.

She said, "You are from the north in Friesland, yes?

"Well, yes, my paternal grandparents were originally farmers in Friesland, which I understand is basically all farm country. My grandfather was a farmer who had moved to America when he 21 or 22 and leased a small farm in Illinois about 80 miles south of Chicago. I'm second generation in the United States, born in Chicago and grew up and now live in a suburb of Los Angeles. I've never actually been to Friesland."

"Well" she said, "The Boomsma family makes what many Europeans consider is the finest beer, vodka, wine and schnapps in all of Europe. It's so special it's only sold in specialty shops here in Holland." Two thoughts entered my mind. Now I knew why I as getting such special treatment at the hotel, and secondly, I must be a family traitor because I totally dislike anything with alcohol in it, much preferring milk, which I always thought was the family heritage drink. Imagine my surprise to learn cows also produce vodka, beer, wine, and schnapps?

I asked her where I could find a sample bottle of one of those items with the Boomsma label on it. She had no idea as it was beyond her pay scale to afford such a luxury. I wanted to find a specialty shop before leaving Amsterdam but ran out of time. The airport did not carry the name in any duty-free shops either. I came home empty-handed. However, a cousin from Grand Rapids made a trip to Amsterdam the following year and gifted me with an actual crystal bottle of Vodka with the Boomsma label on it. It remains on my office bookcase as a remainder of "you never know what your family history may truly reveal."

I have stayed in touch with Jan Baan over the years and last communicated with him in The Netherlands in March 2021 wishing him a happy B-day to which he immediately responded. I enjoy staying in touch and keeping up to date on the lives of friends and past contacts.

MAF's President Meyers

The President of MAF at the time was Max Meyers. He was, and still is, probably the best public speaker and storyteller I, and many other people ever heard. If asked to speak on the spur of the moment he could talk for two hours and leave everyone spell bound. He never used notes. His stories were based on his many years as a pilot in Papua, New Guinea in the days when the local indigenous peoples were still cannibalistic headhunters, and any outsider was an enemy that would be killed and have his head swinging above someone's hut.

One evening Max and I flew to Dallas to attend the annual Dallas Prayer Breakfast the following morning at 6 am. Max was often asked to be a guest speaker at many such functions across the country. The room was filled with 400 of the wealthiest people in the Dallas area. I estimated the total wealth to be close to $20 billion knowing the companies they had started and operated. The night before Max and I talked in the hotel coffee shop until 3 a.m. That meant we got less than three hours sleep but he still spoke for 90 minutes the following morning. During the entire speech you could have heard a pin drop. It was the same wherever he spoke. Yet, like all of us, he had his gifting strengths as well as weaknesses. Speaking was his gift; his weakness was he just couldn't ask for money. His gift opened many doors for him with the wealthiest Christian businessmen in the United States, but ask for money, either in a group setting or a private personal setting just was not his inclination. But I could, and with absolutely no hesitation to do so. And therein was my plan; with his gift of getting in the door to see people based on his reputation and longstanding friendships with hundreds of wealthy people across the country, most of whom had not yet donated, I saw a gold mine of opportunity on how to combine our respective gifts for the Kingdom. We would travel together, he would tell stories, I would handle the ask and close.

The Board of Directors, however, thought it was time for a new leader and that would be the delete key that would obliterate my plan. One major donor, a close friend of Max who gifted

$500,000 plus each year, also thought it was a bad idea. I went to see this friend on the east coast because he was the largest single donor the ministry had. I spent the night at his enormous stately home, attended Sunday church services with him and his wife and had lunch with them after afterwards. He implored me to speak with the Board asking them to reconsider their decision to retire the current president, which I did when returning. But to no avail. Their minds were made up and I knew we were going to lose three valuable assets; the president with his natural speaking ability; the only large donor the ministry had; and my access to Max's vast arena of friendships with very high-powered wealthy men. In the end that's exactly what happened. A new President was chosen a few months later. The large donor withdrew his annual support. The new president was the first in the ministry's fifty-year history to come from outside the organization. His lack of understanding between the business world culture and Christian Missions culture would be quite evident.

On the Road Again

After my first six months on the job, the COO, Bruce Smith, my immediate superior, said I needed to see some of the field operations around the globe, starting with some of the major operations across the 15,500 islands in Indonesia where we had a significant presence on various strategic islands. These are mostly very remote locations where helicopters were originally used to lower a few men down with chainsaws to cut through the jungle canopy and begin building a base camp and eventually runways for Cessna 206's. They did this in the midst of hostile indigenous people who wore no clothing, carried long spears and 8-foot-long blow guns with poison darts and had never seen an airplane or a white man. If you have ever read the beginning stories of MAF with Jim Elliott and Nate Saint in Ecuador, you have a pretty clear picture of those early ministry days in many parts of the world.

In college, anthropology was always one of my favorite subjects. At the time, I never expected I would be visiting up close and personal with such a variety of indigenous cultures. Flying over these islands is like flying over broccoli for thousands of miles. Each mountain range has a different tribal group with a different language. Many of these tribes don't even know any other tribes exist. The jungles are so remote and dense that even if they did know, it would take three to four weeks of hacking your way through thick jungle to get to a neighboring tribal group. By plane, it's perhaps a 15-to-20-minute flight.

On this first trip to these islands, I decided to update the ministry's video collection of short films used for introducing the mission to potential partners. None of their videos had been updated since the late 1960's and early 1970's. What was available in their marketing library still had pilots wearing bell-bottom pants and wide shirt collars from the 1960's. I sent James Greenelsh and his wife Elizabeth (videographers) two weeks ahead of me to begin filming in various islands we had previously discussed in our planning sessions. I would follow two weeks later and rendezvous with them in Jakarta and continue our filming trip together. I was the first to arrive in Jakarta, three hours ahead of them. They had been filming in East Kalimantan for the past week.

WHAT'S THAT ON YOUR BACK?

A week before my scheduled trip to Jakarta, Stella noticed a mole on my back, and she wanted me to have it checked immediately. The following day, the doctor confirmed it was Melanoma on the lower left side of my back just above the waistline. He wanted to schedule surgery for the next week. I explained it would be difficult for me to dress the wound and stitches, changing band aids where I couldn't even see let alone reach, and could this be done three weeks later after I returned.

He didn't much like the idea but said he wanted to do the surgery the day after I returned. He was also a specialist in immunology and was always up on the latest vaccinations needed for world-wide travel. I used his talents a number of times for my remote travel itinerary, so while in his office he also took an opportunity to impart his collection of vaccines into my blood stream for such things as malaria and other diseases known to exist in countries I would be traveling in. The day after returning I went to see him.

He was a remarkable doctor with a great sense of humor. When he got me on his table, he mimicked moving his scalpel back and forth like he was sharping a butcher knife. I said, "You love this don't you?" He replied with a Frankenstein gleeful look on his face, "Ah, yes master, I love to cut people open," which he proceeded to do, cutting out a golf ball size hunk of flesh to make sure he got it all. I'm so grateful Stella noticed it and the doctor got all of it. If not, I wouldn't be here since that was 20 years ago. Thank you, Lord, for Stella's nurses training, sharp eyes and especially for your Grace and mercy. His Mercies are new every day.

"Through the Lord's mercies we are not consumed, Because His compassions fail not. They are new every morning; Great is Your faithfulness. "Lamentations 3:22-23 (NKJV)

39

ISLAND HOPPING
ACROSS INDONESIA.

The flight to Jakarta was one of the longest I ever experienced. LAX to Tokyo took 12 hours due to head winds. Spent 45 minutes in Japan's Narita Airport, waiting for our six-hour flight to Singapore, and then another three hours to Jakarta.

In Jakarta, I waited three hours for James and Elizabeth to arrive, flying in from other parts of Indonesia which afforded the opportunity to rent a room inside the airport hotel for two hours for a shower and a brief, sleepless rest. I hadn't slept for 23 hours. Unknown at the time, it would be another 34 hours before sleep would be possible.

After connecting with James and Elizabeth, we caught our three-hour flight to an island called Bima at the convergence of the Java and Flores Seas. We didn't see much as it was the middle of the night and the airport was closed. No drink. No food. We all were asked to deplane. For some passengers this was their final destination. An hour later the rest of us were again in the air, heading for Bengoi, a village on the northeastern coast of the Indonesian island of Seram.

By now I had not slept for 27 hours but wasn't really noticing it. It was finally daylight again so we could see the countryside just south of the equator. It was hot. With a temperature of 100

343

degrees and the humidity at 98 percent. The dirt floor airport was closed; again, nothing to drink. No food. No air-conditioning. In Indonesia, one does not formally enter the country and register your passport until you have reached your final destination no matter what island you're on. Bengoi was not our final destination, but it is for any commercial airline carrier. From here, we would be flying on MAF planes to even more remote islands.

In Bengoi we waited for the C-206 MAF pilot to meet us at the airport. He had been delayed, so while sweating it out in a dirt floor airport, I entertained some children who had been staring at us. I pulled out my small hand-held miniature battery operated fan, turning it on and off to show them how it worked. I'm pretty sure they had never seen one and having two with me I gave one to them. Since it had a small soft pliable rubber blades there was little chance for them to be injured. They ran off excited about their "cool" new toy. I'm sure it only lasted a day or two with no access to triple A batteries.

When our MAF pilot finally arrived the first order of business was to visit the local police chief to present our Passport and fill out customs paperwork. To find him we needed to walk through the jungle on a narrow path for nearly two miles to a small village in the humidity and heat. It was nearly unbearable dragging our luggage and several large metal protective camera gear suitcases. All the time, our eyes were darting back and forth, surveying the heavy undergrowth and trees for Tigers and Komodo lizards the size of a 1958 Oldsmobile station wagons. At the same time, our hands were busy swatting at swarming blankets of mosquitos. As Dorothy said, "We're not in Kansas anymore," and, I sure didn't remember falling down a rabbit hole, even though it certainly felt like it.

By the time we got to the village we were exhausted and soaked with sweat. Our MAF pilot set out to locate the Police station while James, Elizabeth and I headed for a small run-down motel which could be rented by the hour. It was air conditioned… sort of. A swamp box for air conditioning naturally only added more humidity, but it was better than nothing. Once inside, the air was indeed cooler, and it did help. James, Elizabeth, and I collapsed crosswise across the bed wiping the sweat from our faces with already humid damp towels from the bathroom. There was so much humidity in that room the brick walls looked like slow-moving waterfalls.

Meanwhile, our pilot had learned the police chief was in another village and he had to convince the assistant chief, who knew nothing of such matters, into doing the paperwork. Fortunately, our MAF pilot did an excellent job in convincing the naked assistant Police Chief that everything would be all right. Now all we had to do was walk back two miles back through the jungle to the little dirt floor airport with all our camera equipment cases and luggage.

Once we balanced the load in our small aircraft, we were off to another island three flight hours away for our first filming stop. The name of this island escapes me, but I'm pretty sure it was Ongi Dobo. It was 5,000 feet high with an uphill landing strip leading away from a large, gorgeous lake. The temperature was a consistent 70 degrees with fresh clean air and a slight most welcome breeze. Oh, how wonderful.

The villager's huts were made of two-inch diameter logs and raised 3 feet off the ground for water run off. I was invited into one of the huts and found that it was quite dark inside and difficult to walk on a small log floor with one-inch gaps even with shoes on. The natives don't have shoes, so I imagine they are used to the uneven hardness of the floors. Inside, in the center of the hut, a small fire burned in an open pit used for cooking and warmth for nights. Smoke filled the inside, most likely because the hole in the roof to let smoke out was far too small. It was a very unhealthy and smelly inside. No wonder these people have a short lifespan.

THE GERMANS ARE HERE.

The rest of the afternoon the pilot did take off and landings for us so we could film some of our "B" footage. It was here that I met a truly resolute couple of the gospel, Klaus, and Helga. They had been here for 25 years, learning the language and translating the New Testament into the language of this particular tribe. Klaus and Helga were born in Germany and were children when Hitler came to power.

At the end of World War II when Hitler was being pushed back to Berlin by the Russians on the eastern front, and the western allies were pushing in from the west, Klaus was drafted into Hitler's youth group. Germany was running out of manpower and was now forcing kids as young as twelve into the military. Thankfully, the war was over before Klaus could be forced into any battles. After the war he migrated to the United States, became a Christian, got his college degree, and with his natural gifting in languages joined SIM Bible translation ministry. Soon thereafter, he volunteered for service in this remote area of Indonesia.

Klaus had built himself a decent home out of lumber shipped in by MAF planes, containing a living room, two bedrooms, one bathroom with a shower, a cooking area and small office for his translation work. Water for drinking and bathing came from rainwater collected in a large outdoor gravity fed open tank which sat on stilts next to the house. They had a gasoline powered generator for lighting and a computer for translation work. Klaus had finished the New Testament three months before my arrival with printing done by Wycliffe and the Bibles delivered by MAF. During their 25 years on this Indonesia island they raised two children, who were now in the U.S. at college. Klaus also trained several tribal leaders to be pastors in their different villages. When they received their Bibles, Klaus said it was quite a celebration of praise and worship that continued for a week. After the celebration, these newly trained pastors carried 100 New Testaments each back through the jungle to their respective villages, often a two-weeks' walking journey through thick jungles.

I asked Klaus what happened after his work on the New Testament was completed. He simply said he went back to his hut and started at Genesis 1:1. A few months after our visit, Klaus and Helga retired and returned to the United States, turning their work on the Old Testament over to a younger couple.

While spending the afternoon with Klaus and Helga, our pilot received a message there was a medical emergency several mountain ranges to the east and was forced to leave us at our location. It was now late afternoon and we stayed in touch with the pilot via Klaus's high frequency radio. Our pilot was dealing with bad weather and didn't know if he could make it back to pick us up. We started making plans for a possible overnight with Klaus and Helga and sleeping on the living room floor. Two hours later the pilot radioed that he would arrive to pick us up in 30 minutes. Shortly thereafter, we were again in the air heading for another island two hours away across the Arafura Sea to Tual.

Tual would be our final stop for the day. After landing, we walked 100 yards up a steep hill carved out of the jungle to the home of our MAF missionary host for the evening. I didn't think the thickness of swarming mosquitos could get any worse than what we had already experienced earlier in the day. But it did. Walking up the hill from where the plane was tethered, the mosquitos were so thick it was like walking through a vail. Huffing and puffing with your mouth open would likely cause you to swallow 20 mosquitos with each breath. We covered our noses and mouths with large handkerchiefs, a travel tip I had learned years earlier. I had also learned to always carry some repellant; thank the Lord for DEET.

By now I had been sleepless for nearly around 53 straight hours. You can only live so long on adrenaline and my body was not producing any more. I needed a hot shower and a cold room. Our host had a nice small office. I asked our host if they had a lawn chair type mattress which I could put on the floor in their office, the only air-conditioned room in the house. They did, and after a hot shower was on the floor with two blankets and sleeping soundly. I slept for 13 hours, waking up at seven the following morning. After breakfast we flew to Wamena in Irian Jaya, west of Papua New Guinea, where the real adventure began.

40
NEW GUINEA

After an air-conditioned room and a sound sleep, the following morning we flew a few hours to the large island of Wamena, Irian Jaya, located about 500 miles south of Jaypura in the Jayawijaya Regency of Indonesia. It's in Papua's highlands, in the Baliem Valley part of West Central Papua, New Guinea and sits at 6,200 feet above sea level. No mosquitoes, no humidity, no heat; wonderful. For anyone interested in history, Jaypura to the north is where we would visit a few days later, and better known as the first location where General McArthur retreated during the Japanese invasion of the Philippines in World War II.

My first day in Wamena was a restful one. I wanted to see how the actual field operations worked in this remote location, how the planes were maintained, parts inventory organized and generally how everything flowed together.

Wamena is a large air base for MAF, with four aircraft and four families stationed there. They serve a large geographic area of Irian Jaya, encompassing thousands of square miles and countless different tribes, none of which speak the same language, and all of which still have one foot in the stone-age.

It's also a large operation base for the Australian government operating C-140 cargo planes. Their purpose there, as well as ours, is providing humanitarian aid to these remote peoples who had been suffering from extreme drought and fires that burned hundreds of thousands of acres of jungle. The prevailing winds blew the smoke across much of Asia, as far away as Singapore, the Philippines, and even as far northwest as central China. The fires had been fully contained by the time I arrived. From the air it was easy to see the damage.

The airport in Wamena at the time contained only a few small buildings and two hangars for our small C-206's Cessna planes. Native huts were scattered around the airport. There were only two roads, each a mile or so in length. One road ends just past the last few native huts. The other takes you up a hill to an Indonesian military base, where it also ends. I borrowed a Honda 175 cc motorcycle owned by an MAF pilot/mechanic to take a little exploratory ride around the small village. I first followed the slightly paved road that runs past the native huts. When riding back east toward the airport, I noticed about a 100 native people had gathered on the side of the road about 25 yards from the airport gate where a crowd was spilling across the road. Approaching closer they were all yelling and pushing each other. I thought it might be some sort of riot, perhaps a tribal dispute of some sort.

Since these people are only recently out of the Stone Age, still naked carrying spears and blow guns, I thought it best to approach with caution. From a safe distance away, I climbed a tree to survey the situation.

It turned out to be a trading frenzy. At any given time, there can be 25 or 30 different tribes who hiked two or three weeks through jungles and across mountain ranges to trade wild pigs, birds, spears, blow guns, vine ropes or any number of items. There was much yelling with arm and hand motions because none of them speak the same language. Trading looks rather chaotic, kind of like the floor of the New York Stock Exchange. In the middle of the circle, surrounded by a hundred naked men and women, the traders were attempting to unload their pigs or other goods for the best trades they could get. I was relieved to see it was a normal routine.

After hanging out in that tree it took me 15 minutes to divest myself and clothing of hitchhiking bugs like ants and other creepy crawly things. They were all over me, even in my pockets, and a small snake had wrapped itself around my right ankle. Fortunately, it was not poisonous, but I didn't know that at the time, so my debugging dance included a one-legged hop to shake him off. Maybe the snake was just lonely. I attracted some strange looks while doing my de-bugging snake dance trying to shake off all the excess baggage. But all was well. I had attracted the attention of 20 or 30 people in the trading frenzy, and they seemed to have a great laugh watching this peculiar, white-skinned blonde fellow jump out of a tree and do his bizarre dance.

MAF had four homes across the dirt road from the airport for pilot families. They leased them from a group called a Yayasan/ MAF which is basically a council of 9 to 15 local prominent village elders. The Baan company began building new homes a mile from the airport and the homes across the road would soon be occupied by Baan Company personal as the new pilot homes were completed. I stayed that night with one of the pilot families and their children and the next morning we began the next leg of our journey.

While there I had opportunity to walk through two of four homes completed by American volunteer tradesmen using trained local talent as originally planned. Two homes had been completed and two others under construction. They were beautifully done. The tile and cabinetry were superior to anything I'd seen in any-where. The MAF craftsmen volunteers had done a superb job in training the local natives in various trades.

THE SAD CONSEQUENCES OF JEALOUSY

Five years after my first visit to Wamena, Irian Jaya, James Greenelsh was back in Wamena on another project. What he found was distressing. A number of Christian ministries, foundations, and churches from different denominations discovered the area to be rich in opportunities for the spreading of the gospel. They poured millions of dollars into building large churches, some complete with education buildings with 20 classrooms. Everyone was excited about the possibilities and wanted in on an opportunity to spread the gospel. And that's where the trouble started. Fortunately, this situation is not the norm, but a good example of what can happen when ministries do not work together.

Jealousies abounded. Territorialism reared its head like a spitting cobra. "This is our territory. Stay out. Go to the other side of the valley." "Well, we were here first, so you move." And so on and so forth. While all this was happening, the secular world was also competing to win the hearts and minds of these remote people. Indonesia is rich in natural resources and there were many secular outsiders working hard to acquire control of them. Some of the language barriers had been breached and so they simply bribed them with free gifts. Cell towers were erected throughout the jungles. When James and I first visited, the people were still naked. Five years later they were still naked, but now men and women wore knitted cell phone holders around their necks. Everyone had small generators outside their huts for lighting, and flat screen TV's complete with VHS playback units. There were also stacks of porno movies that any vile sick mind could wish for. In five short years, these innocent peoples went from trading pigs, vine rope, spears, and blow guns to trading porno flicks. Rape became rampant. Women were being assaulted behind huts, even in the middle of dirt roads. The area was a scene carried forward from Genesis 13 and surely looking much the same as Sodom and Gomorrah.

In the meantime, the properties built by various denominational churches and mission organizations stood empty, boarded up, fenced off and surrounded by locked gates and chain link fences. Outside the gated fences, men and women lay naked, drunk, and addicted to drugs with needles hanging from their arms. Just thinking about it brings enough disgust to make one vomit and cry at the same time.

On my borrowed motorcycle I followed the only other road up a gradual hill to just outside the entrance to the Indonesia Army base, turned the bike around, shut off the engine and admired the view overlooking the beautiful valley and the airport. In my peripheral vision, I became aware of a soldier walking toward me from the entrance of the military base. A couple of feet away he pulled a .45 caliber semi-automatic pistol tucked in the back of his trousers, cocked it, and pointed at my forehead yelling something in his native tongue. My immediate reaction had a number of possible scenarios flying through my mind on how I could overcome him still seated on the motorcycle. I could do this, or that, or maybe both. All possibilities passed through my mind in nanoseconds but seemed like several minutes. Everything seemed to move in slow motion. None of the possible solutions seemed plausible. I could not be sure, considering how close that gun was to my forehead and still being seated on the motorcycle. It was all so surreal. The only remaining thought was to surrender my life into the Lord's hands. There it was again. Surrender and trust. If this is where it all ends, then so be it.

During those nanoseconds, my eyes were focused on the end of that .45 caliber barrel. I never realized how big the end of .45 caliber barrel actually was. But then, who looks at the end of a barrel even if they own such a gun. My eyes refocused to the eyes of the soldier holding the gun. I did not see anger, but pain, deep emotional pain. My heart immediately filled with compassion and somehow seemed to sense his pain.

That is when I noticed another soldier, who from his uniform looked like an officer, came up behind him. He was speaking calmly in his native tongue. Tears began running down the soldier's face as the officer relieved him of the pistol and un-cocked the hammer, telling him in a calm soft voice to return to the base. The officer spoke good English, explaining the soldier had just learned his wife, ten-year-old daughter and eight-year-old daughter had been raped and killed in the Indonesian uprising in Jakarta a few months earlier and had just received the horrifying news.

I remember hearing about the uprising some months earlier before my trip. The Indonesia people were upset that the Chinese, representing 3% of the population, owned 90% of the country resources and they wanted their fair share back. The discrepancies led to the uprising across Jakarta where gangs went through high rise apartment buildings working their way to the top floors, forcing their way into apartments, raping women, and children, and throwing their bodies off the balconies.

I had compassion on the soldier and certainly understood his deep grief. I thanked the officer. We shook hands, and I slowly rode down the hill thanking the Lord. I had enough excitement for one day. Ten days later, God's Grace and divine protection, by way of the Indonesian Army, would save my life once again thousands of miles away in the Jakarta airport.

41

CLOUDS - "LORD WE NEED A HOLE IN THE SKY"

"For He shall give His angels charge of thee,
to keep thee in all thy ways."

Psalm 91:11 (KJV)

The day after I had observed the traders in action from my bug-ridden perch in the tree, we flew off to visit another settlement village that isn't even on a map. There we would spend a few hours with another remote tribe that had given up cannibalism and headhunting just ten years earlier. I was excited yet could not help but hope they hadn't reverted back to their old habits of shrinking heads and eating people cooked in big black pots. I wasn't keen about having my head shrunken and hanging on some chief's pole outside his hut. I was fairly sure that wasn't a real threat, but nonetheless the day would hold another hair-raising adventure of a very different nature.

I shared the beginning of this story in Chapter One entitled "Clouds" in this small remote mountain village.

We were having a very pleasant visit, dancing arm-in-arm around the campfire, until our pilot saw the clouds moving into the canyon below. He had been watching their speed and density when he said, "We have to leave now, or we might be trapped on this mountain for who knows how many days?" We quickly said our goodbyes to the chief, his warriors and families, grabbed our back packs, camera gear and started running for the plane three miles back across the jungle mountain trail.

NOT A LONG-DISTANCE RUNNER

I had not done any running since the high school track team 30 years earlier, and that was as a sprinter for the 100-yard dash, the 220, 440, and the 880 relays. I was the first to hit the trail with the pilot, James, and Elizabeth closely behind. The chief and several of his warriors ran alongside us. Approximately one and a half mile into our race I was doing surprisingly well, especially considering my lackluster fitness of the past several years.

My legs probably looked something like my mother's electric bowl mixer stuck on high speed. Even though the temperature at 8,000 feet was a comfortable 60 degrees, I was dripping with sweat. The altitude and lack of oxygen in my lungs was starting to play tricks with my mind. I looked to my left and saw several of the warriors running parallel to me on the side of the hill just off the narrow path.

I noticed three things in my light headedness: One, they were smiling as if this was great fun or some sort of game. Secondly, they were not sweating or panting like I was. And thirdly, in their shortness of stature they seemed to be running in slow motion, almost suspended in air with each leap like the Impalas on the plains of Africa. Their short legs seemed to have twice the stride distance as mine. They looked so graceful in their strides. I'm sure their smiles were real, but surely the rest was my imagination. Lack of oxygen does strange things to the mind, and my lungs were quickly becoming oxygen depleted.

I stopped to catch my breath and turned around but didn't see my traveling companions or the pilot. They had all fallen significantly behind. I went back to see what was going on and learned that James had slipped on a wet log and was about to go down a 50-foot long slick rock water slide with a 2,000-foot drop onto the rocks and river below.

JAMES DON'T LET GO!

By the time I got to the scene, he was holding onto the log with one hand and his expensive shoulder-mounted camera with the other trying to save himself and the camera at the same time. The pilot latched onto one of his legs, and with Elizabeth's help was able to pull him to safety just as I approached. James was visibly shaken and later learned he was slightly injured and suffered from shoulder pain for nearly a year after the incident. But there was no time to worry about it now, only time to give thanks as we continued running toward the plane at least another mile or more away.

We finally reached the base of the runway. All that remained was 200 yards up a four-degree slope up to the plane.

James, Elizabeth, and the pilot still had some reserve air in their lungs for the climb. I did not and was bent over gasping desperately for air to re-enter my lungs. I motioned to my companions to go ahead while I tried to gulp some air. Several of the warriors stopped, dropped their spears, no doubt wondering what was happening to me. After three miles they had not even broken a sweat, but with looks of great empathy stood around me placing their hands on my back and probably wondering what they could do to help. It was very moving for me. These total strangers, warriors, and killers of a by-gone era with their head-shrinking past behind them just a few years earlier, were trying to help the best they knew how. And perhaps they did know how. Suddenly, I felt air filling my lungs. What a wonderful feeling. The warriors walked with me up the hill to the plane. I smiled, shook hands, and climbed aboard the plane. They seemed to understand my gratefulness.

James and Elizabeth were in the two rear seats with all the gear appropriately loaded. The pilot had the engine running with the necessary RPM's as I took my place in the co-pilot's seat. As I put on the headset the pilot's voice came across, "Are you OK?"

"I'm fine. Punch it." I closed the door and we headed full speed down the grassy runway. In seconds we were airborne. Thick clouds were now thinly blanketing the lowest portion of the runway and spreading quickly upward onto the lower end to the runway. Our pilot banked sharply to the right to avoid crashing into the mountain at the end of the runway and continued making tight right-hand turns climbing out of the canyon in a spiraling corkscrew maneuver.

The pilot kept looking back over my shoulder. When I turned back to see what he was glancing at, the clouds had moved in totally covering the runway we had left just seconds ago. Another few seconds on the ground and we would have been stranded for who knows how long.

The excitement was not over. Clouds had also descended from above as we climbed in a circling spiral pattern trying to avoid the canyon walls. In seconds, we were completely enclosed in a dense fog that made it impossible to see anything beyond the windshield. We were still surrounded by steep canyon walls on both sides and had thousands of feet up yet to go before we would be above the clouds. It was pretty much guess work and gut feeling trying to figure out exactly where the mountainsides were. The only option was to keep flying in tight spiraling circles. Our MAF pilot was incredible. He remained completely calm as we continued to spiral blindly upward. We were both looking desperately for some blue sky.

At 10,000 feet, he reached for his oxygen mask, a required practice in an unpressurized small cabin aircraft. I helped him get it firmly over his face. His mask was the only one on board, so James, Elizabeth and I prayed the situation was not going to last longer than the cabin's oxygen. I kept glancing at the altimeter as we continued our climb to 11,000 feet, 12,000, 13,000 feet. At 14,000 I finally saw and pointed to a small hole of blue-sky peeking through the clouds at 2 o'clock high and about 500 feet above us. Thank you, Jesus.

I was just starting to notice oxygen deprivation for the second time in the last fifteen minutes. Finally, we were out of the canyon and above the clouds. We could gradually drop our altitude below 10,000 once over the mountain range and could again breathe easy. We cruised back to the MAF base in Wamena delighted that we would spend the night in a comfortable bed and not rocky ground. That night we enjoyed a good meal of rice and roasted chicken cooked by the pilot's wife.

42

THERE'S GOLD IN
THEM THAR HILLS

A day or so later we were on our way back to Biak. Our pilot radioed ahead for clearance to fly over Grasberg, the largest open pit gold mine in the world and second-largest copper mine. What an impressive operation! In 2014 over 1.1 million ounces of gold were mined there, and that doesn't include the copper. It's owned by the Freeport-McMoRan Indonesian mine complex. It is now in transition from open-pit mining to the large-scale, long-lived high-grade underground block caving operations. Not sure what all that means, but from the air it certainly was an impressive operation and radioing ahead for permission to fly over was extremely important. Not radioing ahead means they will shoot you down with a ground to air missile. Even all commercial carriers, from any nation give this area wide birth as it has the same flight restrictions as a military base. Seems logical to me when mining a million ounces of gold a year.

After flying over Grasberg, we flew on to Biak, a small island which was first "discovered" by the Portuguese navigator Jorge de Menezes in 1526. Biak is located in Cenderawasih Bay, just northwest of New Guinea. Although small, Biak is the largest island in its small archipelago with many atolls, reefs, and corals. The rain forest which covers the island contains the largest number of endemic bird species of any single area in the New

Guinea region. There are also numerous rare reptile and amphibian species there. Among the many snake species catalogued during the last herpetological survey of Biak in the 1990s, the green tree python and the amethystine python are quite commonly seen.

During World War II, it was a strategic airfield for the Imperial Japanese Army. American forces eventually captured the island during the Battle of Biak. The captured airfield was later transferred to the Royal Australian Air Force. Biak was transferred from Dutch rule, along with half of New Guinea, in the 1960s.

We stayed with another MAF pilot and his family, but only for one night, as we were beginning to work our way back to Jakarta and would soon arrive at the farthest point where Commercial flights would be available back to Jakarta.

There was a large social hall which served as a church for Sunday services, and they also had three bedrooms and a large kitchen attached for use by special occasion. Attached to the quasi church was the pilot's family home. It was a relatively cool environment without air conditioning. I slept that night with only a sheet for covering and felt quite comfortable with no humidity or mosquitoes.

DINKY - THE GECKO OF BIAK

When I woke up the following morning, something was moving on my chest. I noticed a small, 2-inch Gecko staring at me, tilting his head from side to side as if trying to figure out who and what I was doing here. I was fascinated by the little fellow. His color was nearly that of light beach sand and he had somewhat transparent skin through which some of his internal organs could be seen.

We kept staring at each other while I tried to figure out what to do with him. I gently remove him, carefully placing him on the floor before heading to the washroom for a shower. I turned around and saw that he was following me. He went up the wall, across the towel rack and dropped onto the bathroom counter, continuing to stare at me while tilting his head from side to side. I was starting to enjoy this tenacious little fellow's company. After putting him back on the floor I took my shower. When stepping out of the shower, he was back on the counter, seemingly waiting for me. I put my hand palm down on the counter and he crawled on and scampered up my arm to my shoulder. I could not believe this little fellow. You would have thought he had known me and was a pet for years. I let him stay on my shoulder while shaving. He continued to scrutinize my every move as if trying to understand.

Apparently, I had a new friend and found myself talking to him as if he were a pet dog, but I didn't speak reptilian. Here I was in the jungles of Indonesia talking to a small lizard. Clearly, I had been away from home too long. I thought about putting him in my luggage and taking him home, although, I was fairly sure Customs at LAX wouldn't think much of the idea. I wondered if he was hungry but had no idea what he ate -- bugs, maybe? I looked around for bugs of any variety but couldn't find one. Amazing! I had seen billions of unknown bugs on this trip. Isn't that always the way it goes? When you need a bug, you can't find one. When you don't want bugs, they're everywhere.

I named him Dinky, got dressed and went for breakfast in the kitchen. Dinky followed me. I found some dead flies and a few moth's in the kitchen windowsill and fed him his breakfast. While I was eating breakfast, he climbed up my pant leg onto my shoulder and watched me have my eggs, toast, and coffee.

GOODBYE DINKY

We flew out an hour later. I have never truly understood what the Dinky situation was all about. Just a friendly lizard I guess, but one that reminded me of the many wonders of God's creation. I was almost sad to leave him behind. Admittedly, his company that morning was enjoyable.

The following day we boarded another MAF Cessna C-208 for a 400-mile flight to Sentani, where MAF has one of their largest airbases. It is situated on the most northern tip of Irian Jaya and was originally called Hollandia. Today, about 250,000 people live there. I was fascinated by the history of the place. On a plateau above the city is the original headquarters of General Douglas McArthur after his retreat from the Philippines. It remained a major American base until the re-conquest of the Philippines in March of 1945. During the war, over twenty U.S. bases were established with half a million military personnel moving through the area. The northern part of Dutch New Guinea was occupied by Japanese forces in 1942, but Allied forces drove the Japanese out after amphibious landings near Hollandia on April 21ˈ 1944.

After reviewing the MAF work there and meeting our personnel throughout the remainder of the afternoon, we checked into a hotel just below General McArthur's base camp on the plateau above. Our accommodations were clean but sparse. The hotel had a nice large dining room where we were the only guest and enjoyed a delightful dinner of American food. After going to my room, I discovered that thousands of ants invading the room via a crack on the windowsill.

I envisioned them taking complete control of the room by morning and probing everything in my carry-on in their quest for food. One of the things you learn by traveling to non-tourist destinations is resourcefulness. Like the U.S. Marines say, "Improvise, Adapt, and Overcome." I don't carry bug spray, only Deet for mosquitos. Earlier I noticed the small hotel store had some hair spray that would have to suffice. It's mostly alcohol and water, but perhaps I could drown them, or at least get them drunk. It worked. By morning they were still lying in the windowsill to stunned or drunk to move.

We spent the next day shooting B-roll footage for use later to be edited in MAF videos. The day after we flew back to Wamena to clean and prepare camera equipment and get ready for our return to Jakarta.

Chief – over my right shoulder with bone in his nose.

Chief (far right) & one of his warriors.

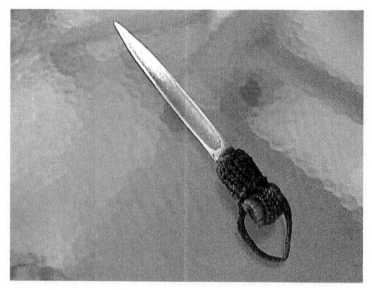

Shin Bone of former enemy once used as a dagger.

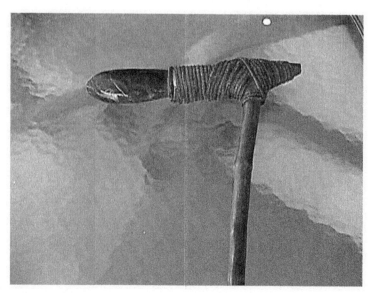

Stone age hatchet used by chief & warriors

Chief ran 3 miles to greet us when we first landed.

43

BOMBS AWAY IN JAKARTA

After spending three weeks on various islands, it was time to leave our base camp in Wamena New Guinea and work our way back to Jakarta, some 3,565 kilometers northwest across the Banda and Java seas; a trip that takes 12 hours flying time with several stops along the way.

The first leg was again with MAF in a Cessna 206. We flew over countless islands separated by various seas. On one remote island, we could clearly see the remnants of World War ll. Much of Indonesia was held by the Japanese during the war, and this particular island, now void of any humans, revealed an abandoned Japanese air base. We could clearly see Japanese Zeros still sitting on the runway, where they had been bombed and strafed, near what appeared to be an operations building with control tower totally reclaimed by the jungle.

One plane still looked in fairly good condition considering all the years that had past, with the rising sun emblem clearly visible. Others were riddled with bullet holes. I wanted to land and take a closer look but our schedule and pending bad weather wouldn't permit. We did however buzz the field.

Two days later I read an article in a Jakarta newspaper about an American B-25 bomber had been discovered on a mountain top on Biak Island. It was believed the aircraft had crashed due to bad weather or mechanical problems. The skeletal remains of the pilot and co-pilot where still seated in the cockpit, wearing their sheep-skin-lined leather flight jackets with Army Air Force crusher hats. There were eight crewmen on board. The article went on to report.

"On September 8, 1945, Sergeant Charles Bosler and seven other Army Air Forces servicemen left Australia on board a B-25 bomber, bound for Biak Island, Indonesia. Their plane never arrived, and there was no clue to their whereabouts. The debris was not discovered until 1995, and civil unrest in Indonesia hampered salvage efforts until 1999, when U.S. military helicopters began retrieving remains and personal items."

With the help of DNA from members of their families, the victims were officially identified and contacted, their bodies finally brought home along with personal items. The plane remained lost for over 50 years. The story can be read at: http://arlingtoncemetery.net/aircrew-09081945.htm

After researching the article to uncover details of World War II in the Japanese held Indonesia area of the world, it was shocking to learn how many other missing planes have been uncovered 50 plus years later, bodies recovered, and finally laid to rest. It surely would be a final emotional closing for families who never knew what happened to loved ones declared "Missing in Action."

Finally, back in the Jakarta airport, James and Elizabeth caught a connecting flight to another island to do more filming for our video. I quickly passed through customs and walked down a long corridor to the appropriate departure gate. This would be my third flight on Garuda Airlines, owned and operated by the Indonesian Government.

Like most major airports globally, the main terminal had many shops, but there were no retail shops the entire length of the last 100-yard-long corridor leading to my departure gate. The sides were lined with floor-to-ceiling glass with highly polished travertine floors. There was one small cart concession, the kind you see in the malls here in the States, with a small booth that sold jewelry, cell phones, purses, and other small knick-knacks.

This particular one also sold drinks and, fortunately for me, the vender had Coca-Cola. My flight wasn't scheduled to leave for another hour and this soda bar was very near my gate. Being extremely thirsty I ordered a Coke and peanut butter stuffed crackers.

After twenty minutes of enjoying my snack and a pleasant conversation with a Muslim fellow from Yemen, I headed for my departure gate. When I arrived, there wasn't a single person to be found. It made me think this might not be the right gate. Thirty minutes later, there was still was no gate agent to take boarding passes, no lines anywhere, no seating, not a single chair anywhere. A few minutes later I noticed there was no speaker system. I checked my ticket and boarding pass to make sure I was in the right area. I was, but I began to wonder if I had somehow missed my flight.

As I was about to leave the gate area to walk back to the main terminal, hoping to find out what's going on when two pilots came up the outside stairwell from the plane area, visible from a nearby window overlooking the tarmac. They placed their suitcases and briefcases up against the wall underneath the window, sat down on the floor and continued their conversation. I asked them if they knew what was going on. Fortunately, they spoke good English and they calmly said, "Yes, we are the pilots for your flight to Singapore. But there will be a delay because the maintenance crew found a bomb in the cargo-hold. The Army had been called in to help with the search." I felt much better now. **A BOMB! Great.** Am I ever going to get home?

They said the Indonesian army was taking care of the situation and that we should be on our way to Singapore in perhaps an hour. There was nothing to do but sit down on the floor with the pilots and chit chat with them. Still, I wondered where all the other passengers were. The pilots were very friendly and easy to talk to. After another hour, we were now two hours past departure time, one of the pilots received a call on his cell phone. I asked him, "Did you get an all clear so we can take off."

"No," he said, "They found another bomb."

I thought whoever planted the bombs wasn't taking any chances with only one bomb. I was amazed by the calm demeanor of the two pilots as if this were no big deal and something that happens all the time. Considering the social and political unrest in Indonesia at the time it very well could have been a normal occurrence.

By now I was quite sure, at the very least, my hotel reservation in Singapore would be lost and maybe I would be spending the night in the Jakarta Airport. Three hours later, the captain received another call, this time finishing his conversation with a smile on his face as he and his co-pilot said, "We are taking off now!" and made their way down the extension arm to the plane.

Finally, a gate agent showed up, almost out of nowhere, as did two hundred other passengers hurriedly scrambling down that last 50-yard corridor. The pilots invited me to follow them through the door and down the boarding ramp. Being first on the plane, I choose a seat up front just behind the first bulkhead.

It was now almost 11 p.m. I had been in the airport nearly 12 hours. It was a three-hour flight to Singapore and a dinner meal was provided. I declined. At this point my fatigue displaced any desire for food. I remember thinking that if there were any more bombs on the plane it didn't matter. I was going to sleep and if a bomb took us down in the jungles of Sumatra or the Straights of Singapore, I would wake up in heaven looking into the face of Jesus. I immediately fell soundly asleep.

My flight landed in Singapore at 2 a.m. By the time I got to the Intercontinental Hotel it was nearly 3am. My appointments with two wealthy Chinese businessmen was a breakfast meeting at 6. Because I was so late, the hotel had given up my room. They are used to delayed flights in this part of the world. The clerk felt badly but said he would give me a free upgrade. He re-registered me with a room on the 45th floor. I called my contacts' cell phone, leaving a message explaining the flight delay and asked if we could meet for a late lunch the following afternoon.

After the last three weeks of sporadic bathing across Indonesia's back country I was looking forward to an air- conditioned room, a hot shower, and a cozy king size bed. This was a 5-star luxury hotel located in the Bugis precinct close to Orchard Road and the Marina Bay area; definitely not the normal choice I would make when traveling by myself. On donor trips it is always better to have first class hotels for our investors who wouldn't be used to the harsher conditions in the back country. This type of luxury hotel would not be the norm when traveling alone for a Christian non-profit.

Booking airline tickets was much the same. It was my habit to always book coach and obtain an early boarding pass for a seat just behind business class so I could deplane relatively quickly on arrival. A number of times I was upgraded to business class without requesting it and I knew this first-class room upgraded was a special gift from the Lord. The young Chinese fellow at the check-in counter looked worried as he said the rooms were all filled, but he would upgrade me to a penthouse suite at no extra charge and further discount the normal rate by 25 percent. I would normally pay $120 per night in this hotel, nearly double what I usually spent. But with the additional 25 percent discount, $90 seemed like an exceptionally good deal for the spacious and elegant suite. I almost felt sorry for the young clerk behind the counter, but graciously told him that would be fine.

My room was on the top floor corner suite. It was actually more like an apartment. It took me ten minutes just to explore the place. It had a full kitchen, with a double door stainless steel refrigerator, a four-burner stainless steel built-in counter level stove, a table to sit eight comfortably, overlooking a full-size living room with two sofas, two easy chairs, with ceiling to floor glass and a breathtaking view of Singapore. Beyond the living room was a rectangular conference table that could seat eight. To the right of that was an open area library with a large executive desk surrounded by a full wood-panel library complete with the latest hard cover popular novels as well as many classics. Back towards the entry door and turning to the left was a wide hallway with two spacious bedrooms, also with ceiling to floor windows, a king-size bed with a walk-in closet and full bath with dual sinks and a huge shower. Across the entry hallway was a second master-size bedroom with views of the city to the south and east, another king-size bed with walk-in closet and another double sink bathroom with glassed-in tub and shower. By now I was wondering how I could extend my stay a few more days past my original reservation. What a blessing from the Lord after nearly three weeks of heat, humidity, snakes, and mosquitoes the size of bombers. The following day after my meetings, I grabbed a brochure from the front desk. My upgraded suite was normally $3,000 per night. Thank you, Lord!

I didn't have time to stay longer. My flight home was scheduled for the day after my meetings, but this would do quite well for a two-night stay. My flight home was also upgraded to business class, another special blessing. I was scheduled to be home for two days before heading off to Philadelphia for several meetings there, and then on to Atlanta, Chicago, Dallas, and Denver to meet with ministry supporters.

I have often wondered if there is such a thing as post cultural stress syndrome in our modern-day jet travel. If so, I never seem to have enough time to feel its effects. When finally arriving home after these trips, I usually only had time enough to get a briefing on what was transpiring in various ministry departments, make phone calls to donors I wanted to see across the United States and was back on the road within a few days.

44

REBUILDING THE FLEET

One of the most sizeable tasks for me to tackle was to raise money to replace the entire fleet of 84 Cessna 206 aircraft. The challenge was that Cessna had stopped making them several years earlier and had only recently begun producing them again. The question became, when the new models would be available, how much would be the cost per unit? I flew to the Cessna manufacturing facility near Kansas City to get answers and meet with the designers and heads of manufacturing. The news was not particularly encouraging. They were already taking orders and it would probably be two years before we could get our first one.

This meant we would have to continue the search for older used models to rebuild, which were getting as scarce as hen's teeth. I have to give a great deal of credit to the MAF mechanics whose job it was to recondition older used 206's. It can be likened to those TV shows where they find junk-yard cars rusting away and rebuild them from the frame up. When they're finished with improved modifications, they look like they just rolled off the assembly line, only better.

A few days later I was in Boise, Idaho with one of the fundraising field reps, Dave Voetman, a former MAF pilot in Africa. We were making calls on donors in the area. One evening we were having dinner and discussing the challenge of finding older aircraft for reconditioning when Dave mentioned he knew a fellow in

Sand Point ID, Tom, who had invented a machine that could do "compound bends" in the manufacturing of aircraft. As I understand it, compound bends are one of the most labor-intensive portions of aircraft construction and consequently one of the most expensive aspects of construction. Dave had known Tom for years and often discussed how great it would be to someday design a new aircraft specifically for Missionary pilots for use in remote locations around the globe. That sparked my interest so we decided to call him to and see if there would be any serious interest in such a massive project.

Tom told us he might be interested but he would have to really think and pray about it as this would be a massive undertaking for many years. He was hesitant because he felt it could mean too much time away from his family and children. Still, I was excited about the possibilities. I mentioned it to my superior, Bruce Smith, the Chief Operating Officer of MAF, suggesting that if Tom was interested in such project, we should arrange a meeting with him to discuss design issues, potential costs, and a possible timeline.

Tom agreed to a meeting, and two weeks later Dave, Tom, Bruce, and me met in Seattle to consider the cost of such an endeavor. Several questions came up about where the venture capital would come from, how much it would cost to build two prototypes, one to satisfy FAA regulations for crash testing, and a second to meet any needed new specs after the crash. One suggestion was $3 million, which I said would be more like at least $6 or even $10 million. In reality I had no idea of the true cost either, nor did anyone else, but having some experience in funding venture capital, I estimated $10 million would be the safer guess. Since MAF's business is assisting in spreading the Gospel, and not venture capital, the money would have to come from a separate outside source rather than the existing donor base needed for current operating expenditures and other new planned programs. I would throw some venture capital names in the hat.

So far, everyone involved was willing to take the next step into the unknown. I loved it. Take the leap of faith. Step off the cliff and believe God's hand is there to see you to the other side. However, not everyone at headquarters was willing to make the leap. When you've been doing things a certain way for a long time, change can be threatening. Several people wanted to stay with the C-206. I pointed out that was already a serious problem in not being able to find them anymore and new ones rolling off the assembly line in Kansas would take another two years and the final potential cost was increasing all most weekly. We really had no choice. Besides, the new potential "Missions" aircraft being designed by Tom was shaping up to be far superior to the Cessna 206 model having many more important features the older planes never had and thereby offering significant saving in operational cost. As the design unfolded on paper with the help of MAF pilots as well as other humanitarian mission relief agencies, the capacity and cost savings to operate became quite obvious.

Originally, the plane was called the Packer, but later was changed to the Kodiak under the newly formed company with the name of Quest Aircraft. The first advantage over the C-206 planes was the new Kodiak could use Jet "A" fuel instead of Avgas. Avgas is awfully expensive and was getting extremely difficult to find globally, especially in remote areas. Besides being cheaper, Jet A fuel can be found almost anywhere. Secondly, passenger capacity increased from 4 to 10, an important advantage when carrying injured or sick indigenous passengers or cargo to hospitals hundreds of miles away. Third, the useful load capacity, with seats taken out, would double from 698 to 1,259 pounds. Fourth, maximum flight distance jumped to 1,233 nautical miles from 618 nautical miles, with an average air speed of 170 nautical miles per hour compared to 120 miles per hour for the C-206. There were a number of other advantages as well indicating the new plane would save thousands of dollars in operating costs.

In short, the number of planes in the fleet could be reduced with the new Kodiak aircraft, and could easily double productivity by transporting twice the number of passengers and cargo at 50 percent less cost per cargo pound. With a wingspan only slightly longer than a 206 with a turbine turbo-charged engine, it could land and take off in half the runway distance of all the existing remote landing strips. If this new design could actually come to fruition and approved by the FAA, it would pretty much be a "no brainer" for our use.

As plans progressed, an old, abandoned factory in Sand Point was purchased and refurbished. On the beginning of this project, it was decided that for every third aircraft rolling off the assembly line and sold for full price commercially, the 4th would be a free plane for mission agencies paid for by commercial sales nationally and globally. I could see this probably would not work because of the escalating production costs that would surely come as the design further unfolded. Later, it was decided that every tenth aircraft would be held for mission work at a discount of 50 percent.

In the end, my $10 million development estimate was short by $50 million. I was also wrong about the existing donors not funding the cost. As it turned out, many major donors stepped up along with new donors to provide the capital needed and without affecting the regular ongoing ministry operational costs.

After several years, final approvals were given by the FAA. Naturally, there were times when cash flow was a major problem and payroll could not be made at the production factory. When enough aircraft were sold commercially, they managed to survive.

Today the plane is considered the finest "bush" aircraft ever made, is certified in 17 countries worldwide and serves key market areas including private owners, U.S. and other government agencies, humanitarian and missionary organizations as well as appealing to a variety of users from many foreign government operators to businesses and cargo carriers. Quest Aircraft said its backlog stood at more than 250 aircraft, worth about $600 million in sales.

Early in the project I stepped aside from any further involvement as I was needed for other regular on-going ministry fundraising venues. Besides, I didn't know a whole lot about designing aircraft and it surely wasn't in my job description. Dave Voetman took on the job of spearheading much of the fundraising for the project, and along with other missionary pilots from MAF, as well as other mission agencies such as New Tribes and Samaritan's Purse, all of whom helped with design characteristics that would best fit missionary pilots in actual remote field operations.

In 2014, the Japanese company Setouchi Holdings entered the aviation business when a subsidiary, Setouchi Trading of Tokyo, was named a Kodiak distributor for Japan and Southeast Asia. After the appointment took effect, the emerging relationship led to acquisition talks between privately held Quest Aircraft and Setouchi Trading's parent company, Setouchi Holdings. Setouchi Holdings bought Quest Kodiak in 2015.

The Kodiak price per aircraft in 2014 was $2.17 million fully equipped, and can fly into almost any remote and rugged region around the globe. It has the ability to take off in under 1,000 feet at full gross takeoff weight of 7,255 pounds and climb at more than 1,300 feet per minute.

Today, MAF has 15 Kodiaks in their fleet of 55 aircraft and increasing yearly, helping more than 1,000 Christian and nonprofit agencies share the love of Jesus Christ in countries all over the world.

Kodiak first FAA test flight.

Bob trying out the co-pilot seat.

Great talented people.
Bob's MAF fundraising Development staff at the then
Redlands CA, HQ (14 field fundraisers not pictured.)

MAF Directors L-R Dennis Fulton - IT Division, Tim Maxwell, Director Finance, Gary Barefoot, Personnel Director, (Far right) Bruce Smith, COO, Max Meyers, President, Dennis Hoekstra, Director of Aviation, Bob Boomsma, Director of Development

45

THREE YEARS AT MAF COMES TO AN END!"

On my first day at Mission Aviation Fellowship, the Lord told me I would be there for only three years. As time progressed, I was very much aware when my time was coming to an end. A new president had taken over a year after I started, the first to be chosen from outside the organization in the ministry's history. I could tell the minute I met him this was not going to be easy. He came from the corporate world with no experience in the missions' culture. That is not a bad thing. It can be an incredibly good thing. I had 35 years in new account development. He had none, but supposedly knew how to do it and often disagreed with me on fundraising matters. Disagreements flourished on how to develop friendships with new donors and how to maintain existing donor friendships.

The handwriting was on the wall. Not only for me, but for some others as well, including my immediate boss who had saved the ministry millions of dollars through his innovative thinking. My boss left six months after I did for many of the same reasons and became President of Wycliffe Associates (WA) in Orlando.

EGO AWARENESS

Let's face it. Many leaders have an ego. So do bad ones. I've worked alongside both. I recall reading somewhere there is healthy ego and negative ego. Healthy ego is good self-esteem filtered through your closeness and identity with Christ. Negative ego is an over-inflated view of self-importance without Christ, seeking to glorify self, rather than glorifying God. The motives are different: One seeks to glorify self in one's actions; the other glorifies God in actions and deeds. A negative egotist is detrimental because it has an overwhelming sense of the centrality of "me" – like a child who thinks that he or she is the center of the world.

I had seen this before with other mission organizations. The difference was that in some situations, a godly member of the board would call the offender on it, bringing it to his attention and giving him an opportunity to make a course change. At the English Institute, if things got heated in board meetings, Dr. Carlton Booth would stand up and start singing the Doxology or some great old hymn like, "There is Power in the Blood" or "Amazing Grace." I also had to ask the Lord forgiveness for my judgmental attitude. In judging, I was also guilty of arrogance and egotism for doing what only God has the right to do.

Having felt a release in my spirit to look elsewhere for another assignment. It did not take long to find it. A week later Stella and I were in Tokyo as guests, reviewing a ministry offer for me as vice-president of development. It spiked my interest. They were teaching leadership development and church multiplication techniques for pastors in Japan for the past 40 years and were now expanding operations across Asia. I was ready to move on and I gave my two weeks' notice to MAF.

Overall my experience at MAF was a special blessing. I met so many talented and gifted people who are wonderfully committed to their calling in sharing the gospel globally. I have stayed in touch with some of my closer friends there and they are thriving in a new location with new management. I'm most grateful for the experiences, the friendships and pray the Lord's continued protection and blessing over them.

"Thou preparest a table before me..." Psalm 23:5a (KJV)

46

ASIAN ACCESS

My time at Asian Access came about when invited to attend the first Asian Access International Leadership Conference in Osaka Japan. The purpose for the invitation was to determine if I would be interested in the position of vice-president of development. Stella and I flew to Osaka as guests of the President of Asian Access. Attending the conference were church leaders and influencers from Japan, Mongolia, Sri Lanka, Nepal, Cambodia, Myanmar (Burma) and China. The ministry was expanding its mission in leadership development to include the above countries. Its primary strategy was to train and develop emerging pastoral leaders from these countries and future countries to instill within them the vision for multiplying churches across Asia.

Our hotel in Osaka was traditional Japanese style, sleeping on futon mattresses laid directly on tatami mats kept folded in the closet during the day and set out in the evening after dinner. Meals were eaten at the traditional low tables with seating on tatami mats. For me, not being used to sitting on the floor, it was a bit uncomfortable, not to mention hard on the back and knees. I was hoping meals would be short, but they weren't. By the time meals were finished, I felt like a twisted pretzel. Nevertheless, we both considered it a great privilege to meet and socialize with these modern-day apostles during the week-long conference. After the conference we took the bullet train south to Tokyo where we spent a few days meeting with the President of Asian Access.

At lunch in downtown Tokyo, I accepted the invitation to join the ministry as V.P. of Development with a start date in two weeks. Naturally, there was a steep learning curve, but I was used to that and now having to catch up on the ministry's 40 years of operations in Japan and moving into these other countries using the same leadership model.

The president, was at the time, also involved as Executive Chairmen of the upcoming Third Lausanne Congress on World Evangelism, to be held in Cape Town, South Africa in 2012. He was extremely qualified to accept such a position, being a superb networker and personally knowing many evangelical leaders around the world. His global popularity did however amend the directional course for me. It fell on me to help lay out a rough plan for what countries the ministry would move into next, besides raising the money to kick start the expansion effort. It was not what I expected. Raise money, yes, but I was unsure of my qualifications as a visionary in setting the ministry's future course. I felt somewhat like Gideon, surprised in what God was inviting me to do and feeling inadequate for the task. However, unlike Gideon, I was not looking for a sign like a fleece, but instead undertook the task with enthusiasm.

The President in planning the Third Lausanne Congress on World Evangelism meant he was often unavailable for vision casting, and that was of concern for me. Nonetheless, I dove into the situation listening carefully to hear the Lord's direction for the ministry. The Holy Spirit surely guided because today the ministry is working in all the countries I first envisioned at the time, as well as several others all these years later.

In expanding the Asian Access ministry, it seemed a good idea to once again call on my videographer and friend James Greenelsh to travel with me to several countries where the planned expansion would take place for a video record and fundraising purposes.

YOU CAN ADOPT AND/OR BE ADOPTED.

One of the leaders at the Japan Osaka conference was a young fellow from Mongolia, Ariunbold, who was about 24 at the time. He quickly latched on to Stella and me, and before the week was over, he was referring to us as his American Dad and Mom. He was a self-assured young man who seemed to know exactly where he was going; taking the best of what there was to learn that met his vision and gifts and then going his own way. I liked that in him. We stayed in touch only a little at first, mostly because he knew little English and email connections were spotty in Mongolia at that time. Eventually, those conditions greatly improved, and his emails once again popped up in my inbox with much improved English composition.

In the interim he had found his gift and passion in Christian work after making a couple of misplaced steps along his journey. He kept in contact with me for advice and counsel on his various plans for the future. His passion and gift were evangelism. We heard stories from various mutual friends in Mongolia that when he traveled to various remote villages throughout Mongolia, he brought entire communities to the Lord, helped establish a church and would move on to the next settlement. This continued for several years before he married, had two children, and moved with his family to South Korea for more in-depth training. All these years later they now live in the Seattle area where there is a large Mongolian population. He is evangelizing there and helping a Mongolian pastor develop a Mongolian-speaking church.

GOD REDEEMED MY GREAT WALL

After my brother's death in Vietnam, there was no doubt in my mind that God was working in my heart to get rid of any resentment and un-forgiveness against China for supplying guns and ammo to support the Viet Cong during the war. The government was the culprit, not the people. But still, there was a great wall deep inside my heart. God removed my inner "great wall of China" when I got to know the people personally face to face in my many trips to China. They were humble people, friendly, and childlike in their growing faith. I quickly learned to deeply love and appreciate them. Especially so when meeting Catherine, her American name, whom I first met at an Asian Access donor event at the Four Seasons Hotel in Pasadena CA.

Catherine had been here only two weeks at the time, having received a grant from a Christian foundation to get her master's degree in Pastoral counseling at Biola University. She had been married only six months, and both she and her husband Tim felt it was a good idea for her to accept the offer for the next couple of years of her schooling. Pastoral counseling was certainly needed in China due to the astonishing Christian growth across the country.

Her English was excellent. She and Tim had met at a university in China. Tim accepted and became a believer through a Campus ministry at the university. Catherine became a believer because her Mom shared the gospel with her. Feeling Catherine would surely be lonely from time to time living in the girls' dorm in a strange new country, we told her she would be welcomed to spend the weekends at our house.

"Can I come tonight?" she asked.

Of course, we said yes. She spent that weekend with us, and the next, and the next, and the next. Because she had no driver's license or car, we drove to Biola every Friday afternoon to pick her up, taking her back to Biola after we attended our church together on Sunday. Within six months, a Christian Chinese sold her used car to Catherine after she purchased a new one, and she immediately obtained her driver's license. From then on, she often drove up to spend weekends at our house. A couple of months later we met her husband Tim, a music conductor teaching at a prestigious music university in Beijing. Before coming to the U.S., Tim and Catherine recruited the official Chinese Choir and orchestra, then rented the Tiananmen Square Music Hall where Tim conducted Handel's Messiah for the first time since 1949 when Mao expelled all missionaries from China.

The audience was comprised mostly of poor older people in their 70's and 80's who thought they would never again hear a live performance of Handel's Messiah. Tim and Catherine personally picked up the tab for the rented auditorium, the orchestra and choir as well as many of the entrance tickets for those who otherwise could not afford them. The crowd gave him a 20-minute standing ovation. Many in the orchestra and choir became believers.

Over the coming years, Tim also conducted several performances in Singapore where hundreds accepted Christ on each night of three performances. He has also done many concerts across Europe and is well known in the Chinese Christian community around the world.

Tim came to see his wife every couple of months whenever his busy schedule would permit. In the middle of her four-year master's program, Catherine became pregnant on one of Tim's visits. By this time, she was referring to Stella as "Mom Stel" thinking of her as her American Mom. Her real mother came for a six-month visit to help with her pregnancy, as did her younger brother.

Just before the baby was due, we had everyone over for dinner. As we sat down at the table, I looked at Catherine's face and just had a feeling she was ready to deliver. I said, "It's time isn't it?"

She shook her head yes. I jumped up ready to get everyone into the car for the drive to the hospital.

"No, No," she said. "In China we believe it's better to eat a full meal first to have energy in case of a long labor."

So, we had a full seven-course Chinese dinner complete with dessert. Catherine was calm. Tim was calm. Grandma was calm. Stella was calm. Everyone seemed calm and collected -- except me. I practically inhaled dinner and sat with my car keys in hand.

Joshua was born early the following morning. Tim called at 6 a.m. and asked if we could pick up Catharine's mom (Grandma) on our way to see the baby. It was charming to see Stella walking arm and arm with Catherine's mom, chattering and laughing with her as they walked together down the hallway to Catharine's room. Neither of them could speak the other's language and had no idea what the other was saying, yet both were laughing and excited about the new arrival. Six months later, Catherine graduated from Biola with a double master's Degree's, one in Pastoral counseling and a one in TESL (Teaching English as a Second Language.) How she managed while being pregnant is a mystery to me. Three years later son number two, Joseph, came along while Catherine was doing her internship at Chinese churches here in Southern CA.

In 2008 Tim wanted to do a concert at the Crystal Cathedral in Garden Grove. He asked if I could help secure the Cathedral to perform a concert for all the Chinese non-believers in the Los Angeles area where there is a large Chinese population. It would be the last stop of a four-concert tour beginning in Vancouver Canada, Seattle, San Francisco, and Los Angeles. The Vancouver Chinese community had agreed to pay for the entire Chinese Orchestra and Choir to be flown to Vancouver for a two-night performance there. Since they would already be in the States, Tim thought why not do three more concerts along the west coast in highly concentrated Chinese Communities. Tim contacted key Chinese leaders in each of the respective cities to have them arrange auditoriums that would seat at least 2500 to 3000 people. I would be in charge of the Los Angeles area, and the best location would be the Crystal Cathedral.

Knowing Dr. Robert Schuller's uncle was a missionary to China and a significant influence in Dr. Schuller's life, I visited the ministry's CEO to present the possibility. They not only agreed to host the concert, but to pick up the entire cost, including their complete film crew, with all the camera's, sound technicians, ushers, and parking lot attendants. Everything was set when the Chinese government discovered the plan and decided not to issue travel visas for the choir and orchestra. The plan for the entire west coast tour abruptly ended. But God had a different plan.

Three years later in 2011, when the Cathedral was having financial difficulties and in preliminary talks for being sold to the Catholic church, Tim asked me to find out if it would be possible to hold a concert at the Cathedral. Like three years earlier his purpose was for existing Christians to invite their non-Christian neighbors. After visiting and discussing the possibilities with the church leadership, I was able to negotiate a contract for the use of the Crystal Cathedral, and as before, all of their camera crews, sound technicians and organ. Through Tim's contacts to the Chinese Christian community in southern California, the choir and orchestra would be comprised of members of several Chinese churches across the Los Angeles and Orange Counties areas. The Cathedral granted permission, but this time it would be expensive. Tim was not able to raise the money but was able to get travel visas from the Chinese government to take with him to the concert the two best soprano's and tenors in China, who were now also believers. I was able to meet with the senior elders representing the consolidation of all Chinese churches in Southern California. They agreed to pick up the entire cost for the event, also providing parking lot attendants and ushers. I was greatly relieved since it was my signature on the contract thus making me the guarantor. The night of the concert, 4000 people attended, filling to capacity the main Cathedral with standing room only, as well as the original "drive-in" church with the overspill crowd who watched on closed circuit large screen TV. Four hundred Chinese accepted Christ at the alter call.

Today, Catherine is working on an advanced degree. We have two god-grandsons ages 15 and 13. Both the boys can play a number of classical piano pieces with or without sheet music and are "A" students. In March 2017 both boys made the decision to be baptized at their church. On Sunday, April 9th Tim had flown in from China a few days earlier for this special occasion, and the boys wanted Grandpa Bob and Grandma Stella to also attend their baptism at their church. We attended enthusiastically feeling humble and privileged, giving Glory to God.

"And all thy children shall be taught of the Lord; and great shall be the peace of thy children." Isaiah 54: 13 (KJV)

Baptism Sunday for Josh & Joey

Tim conducting Handel's Messiah in Beijing,
Tiananmen Square Concert Hall.
Photo-Tim's wife Catherine

Joshua 1st Recital at Azusa Pacific University - June 2019

Catherine using Bob's home office for study on
weekends while attending Biola University.

Tim conducting concert for Southern CA Chinese community
in 2011 at the Crystal Cathedral in Garden Grove CA just before
Cathedral was sold to the Catholic Church.
Photo: Bob Boomsma

47

SECOND LEADERSHIP CONFERENCE: CHIANG MAI, THAILAND

A year after starting at Asian Access, we held the second leadership conference in a semi-jungle setting near Chiang Mai, Thailand. Several mission agencies hold their mid-year meetings in this same location. It's a beautiful area with top notch accommodations, great food and free from prying eyes and ears found in other parts of Asia.

The ministry was growing and there were now several national leaders present to discuss enhanced methods of evangelism and curriculums that allowed for cultural complexities.

National leaders came from Japan, Mongolia, Sri Lanka, Cambodia, India, Nepal, and Australia. Our international teaching staff was also in attendance, as well as two of our twelve board members. One such International leader was Bishop Miawa who was in charge of all Methodist churches across Asia. When the United States is the host for annual International Methodist conferences he would call and ask me to pick him up at L.A International Airport. We had many good talks during our commute time.

National Leaders-Japan, Mongolia, Sri Lanka, Cambodia, Australia, India, Burma, & a few board members – hosted by Asian Access.

Bishop Miawa – National Director overseeing all Methodist churches across Asia & Southeast Asia.

Unexpected visitor, a Princess traveling with her entourage.

48

THE SPIES IN CHINA

By the time I made my third trip to China I was familiar with the feeling of always being watched. That is to be expected when you are known to be working for a Christian organization; but even more so when you're met at the Beijing airport by someone who has always been openly outspoken for Christ and against the Chinese government.

Such was the case with Dr. Chao. I first met him in Osaka Japan at the first annual Leadership Conference. We became good friends and since he lived near my home, we often got together for breakfast to discuss what was going on within the growing church in China. He was instrumental in learning firsthand what was really occurring in China before it became general news. This was most valuable for me when charting a course of possible action for the future in my current assignment.

Dr. Chao was the founder of China Ministries International, an institution dedicated to the research, development, and growth of Christianity in modern China. He received his B.A. from Geneva College, a Master of Divinity from Westminster Theological Seminary, and a Ph.D. from the University of Pennsylvania.

He ministered in China for 25 years, teaching his faith and tracking the development of Christianity in a country under Communist rule. Beginning in 1978, he traveled to China more than 100 times to train ministers to lead the Christian "house church" movement. He also served as director of Chinese Church

Research Center in Hong Kong and was the founder of the Chinese Mission Seminary. At the time of his death, he was considered the leading expert in the world on the church in China.

In addition to his extensive research, Dr. Chao helped establish several training centers near China, including the Graduate School of Theology in Hong Kong, where he taught courses in Theology and Chinese Religious History.

Among his publications are numerous articles and books including *A History of Christianity in Socialist China, 1949–1997*, *China Mission Handbook*, and *Wise as Serpents, Innocent as Doves: Christians in China Tell Their Story* (interviews by Dr. Chao). *Source: Our Daily Bread Christian University*

This trip to China would be considerably different because Dr. Chao was always watched so closely by the Chinese government. I had asked him if he could arrange a meeting with the leaders and some of the founders of the House Church Movement. He did better by arranging a sit-down dinner with five such leaders representing 25 million underground church members from across China.

He knew how to reach and secretly communicate with all of these leaders while government authorities didn't, but very much wished they could. And therein was the danger in meeting with them privately. The government had been looking for them for several years to "dispose" of them or send them to hard labor camps for the rest of their lives. These men had left their families more than ten years earlier and had not been home to see their wives and children since. They were always on the run constantly moving from one place to another. We would have to find a safe location where I could interview them and get their personal stories about their work to advance The Good News.

I stayed at the Beijing Holiday Inn as did James and Elizabeth who flew in from another location in Asia where they were filming for the ministry. The day after my arrival in Beijing, Johnathan had arranged for me to meet a Chinese believer in the lobby, a guide who would take me across town to the International Church for Sunday service.

Having not visited this church for a couple of years, I remembered how moved I had been the first time and wanted to attend again. Many Americans attended there for Sunday services when in Beijing. As it turned out, my contact was more than a Christian. He was a Christian spy, and I was about to learn something I was unaware of.

I knew that the Public Security Agency (PSA) has tens of thousands of spies following known Chinese Christians and International Christian visitors everywhere they visited. But what I did not know was that Christians also have their own network which tracks the PSA spies to provide intelligence to church leadership. In China, Christians are observed to see what they might say about God, especially from a church pulpit. Proselytizing is strictly forbidden. As most everyone knows, Christians are considered subversive to the Communist anti-God government.

I had no idea what my guide looked like and was sitting in the lobby waiting for him to find me. That's when I noticed a rather tall Chinese fellow who looked directly at me as he passed my location several times. His unusual height made him stand out. I thought, "This must be my guide." I was wrong! A few minutes later, another non-expressive fellow passed by me and winked. My spirit told me this was my guide. On the other hand, a wink could mean something entirely different. But I felt a peace about following him out the front door of the hotel to a waiting taxi. He got in and motioned me to do the same. He said nothing. Neither did I, guessing he may not speak English, or he already knew that the taxi driver probably was connected to the PSA.

As mentioned, my first trip to the International church had been deeply moving. What moved me most of all was that the worshippers were singing the same hymns that I had sung when

I was a boy in my church a world away. None of us knew each other, all living on opposite ends of the globe, yet here we were worshipping the same God, singing the same hymns, them in Chinese, me in English. It imparted to me an incredible sense of unity in the body of Christ. I wanted to experience that again.

Our trip to the church seemed like we were driving through a maze. We stopped and changed cabs three times before arriving a block away from the church. My guide pointed in the direction I should go and told me in broken English to walk one block north and take the first alleyway on the left to the church. He would meet me after the service at this same corner to get me back to my hotel. I was surprised. He had said nothing throughout our rambling travel all across the city to the far side of Beijing in getting to the church, yet he now spoke verily good English. By this time I felt assured my guide was in fact a fellow believer, who was not only protecting his Christian anonymity from anyone who might be following us, but more likely anyone keeping tabs on me as an American who had been met at the Beijing Airport by Dr. Chao the day before.

The Sunday service was again uplifting and very moving, much like my first visit. After the service, I walked back through the alley connecting to a main street and back to the same intersection. In the alley a short distance from the church, I saw a teenage girl sitting up against a chain link fence. She was alone, wearing dark round sunglasses, had no legs, and holding a tin cup. In China there were no government agencies or aid for anyone the government considered "defective outcasts." I do not know if it is any different today. I thought about the lepers, the blind man, and the cripple at the pool of Siloam and how Jesus always met people at their point of need. My heart went out to her. I knelt down in front of her and told her, "Jesus loves you," and put the equivalent of $20 American into her cup. I don't know how much English she knew, if any, but she did give me a big smile.

I waited at the intersection where my guide had left me two hours earlier. I scanned the massive crowds passing by me but didn't see him. However, I did see that same tall fellow who had passed me several times earlier that morning in the hotel lobby. *Ah Ha*! He was a PSA spy, and not a particularly good one at that. As he walked toward me, I looked directly into his eyes as I did in the hotel lobby that same morning to let him know I was on to him. Since my guide was still absent, I decided to play the game and turned to follow him, making sure he knew I was now tailing him. This was fun! A James Bond kind of excitement washed over me. I know, it was kind of silly, but if I missed my guide I knew how to get back to my hotel because I always carried a few hotel business cards often printed in both English and Chinese. Any cab driver would be able to drive me back to the hotel.

My "undercover," not so uncover PSA agent, walked down the first flight of stairs leading to the subway. At the first landing he turned left and headed down toward the subway. Before I could follow him, someone intentionally brushed by left shoulder and kept walking back up the opposite stairs leading to the street. It was my guide. He said nothing but I got the message and followed, being careful to stay about ten feet behind him. When we got to the top of the stairs again on street level, he walked about a block and boarded a tantrum city bus through the middle doors in the second portion of the bus. I followed, and we sat a few seats apart, neither one of us acknowledging we recognized each other. A few miles away he suddenly exited the front doors, paid for two seats, as I went out through the middle doors, again keeping ten feet or so behind him on the street.

After we had walked several blocks, he hailed a taxi and motioned for me to get in with him. Not a word passed between us. We drove several miles finally stopping and standing on the street. He made a cell phone call and another cab picked us up. That's when he finally spoke freely telling me he watched me leaving the church and giving money to the blind girl. At the same time, he said six different PSA agents were watching and following me. He was now talking freely because the cab driver was a fellow believer and this whole exercise had been pre-arranged earlier that morning. The cat-and-mouse games weren't over yet. There would be another hour of several taxi rides, walking down alleyways, through basements and underground passageways -- and then more taxis. We finally arrived back at my hotel late in the afternoon; and that girl with no legs in the alley leaving church? She was not blind. I only assumed she was because of the dark glasses. While she truly had no legs, she was a Christian plant working for the good guys. I was totally impressed with their counterspy and strategic organizational capabilities. It took a lot of coordination and timing to pull this off. It was an excellent dry run for what would take place over the next three days.

Back in my hotel that evening I noticed several flashes coming from somewhere in the room, like a flash bulb from a camera. I first thought it must be my imagination. After inspecting the room and finding the phone was bugged, which didn't surprise me since any American known to be working for an NGO in China would also have their hotel room phone tapped. Still, I could not determine what the flashes were.

I stepped out of my room and looked out and down onto the inside hotel courtyard seven floors below. There were only a few people in the restaurant area. Then I noticed a tall Chinese fellow stepping out of his room adjacent to mine. Well, well. Guess who? Yep, the same tall fellow who had been following me all over Beijing. I walked over to him and bluntly asked why he was following me. He looked nervous and replied, *"No speak English,"* and then headed back into his room. I thought, *"Hah! Caught you three times today. You must be an apprentice spy and you're terrible at it!"*

His room was next to mine and had me thinking about those flashes. Perhaps that tall mirror was a two-way mirror with a camera behind it. Returning to my room, I pulled the full-length mirror off the wall mounting hook and sure enough, there was a small camera peeking through a hole in the wall. I smiled, blew a kiss, and covered the peep hole with a post-it and replaced the mirror. This became a daily habit every time I returned to my room.

The following day the game began all over again. By now I clearly understood the risk involved for the pastors I sought to meet with and was giving serious thought to abandoning the whole project so graciously arranged by Dr. Chao. For the next three days we followed the same routine in setting a possible meeting location: changing buses, subway trains, and a number of taxis, through alleyways, building basements and underground tunnels. After three days a safe location was finally decided on. A private dining room in a well-known tourist restaurant in downtown Beijing; hiding in plain sight. Our meeting lasted nearly four hours.

I recorded their stories on my small Sony camera which stored everything on a small blue memory stick. As they shared their stories, none of the leaders concentrated on the sacrifices they had made over the last ten years, instead focusing on how the Lord led them by His Holy Spirit, blessing their efforts for the Kingdom, and how their work is always directed at glorifying the Lord. All the leaders knew about each other – a few had even met each other many years earlier – but most had never met. For these selfless men it was almost like a reunion; a special time of great fellowship in sharing the Word.

I was scheduled to leave the country the following day on a flight to Sri-Lanka. That's when it hit me. I had been so fixated on getting those interviews I totally forgot about getting the recorded material safely out of the country. Since I had been followed from the beginning of my arrival, and only comfortably able to "shake off" the PSA agents for this meeting, it was a given the PSA would know my departure date and therefore stop and search me at the airport. If they did, they would surely find the Sony memory chip containing the identities and other information about these apostle leaders, and worse yet their identities. This would undoubtedly be devastating and most-likely life-threatening for these men. My last night in Beijing was a sleepless one as I pondered how to avoid the potentially dreadful situation.

I contemplated various options. One thought was simply to erase the memory stick. Or, if detained at the airport, I could swallow it. That was not a particularly pleasant thought for me, or my colon.

By morning, after much praying, I felt a peace about taking the risk. While dressing, I placed the chip in one of my socks down near my angle. I would arrive few hours ahead of my scheduled flight and stay out of sight in a corner somewhere. As a frequent flyer and concierge service member with United Airlines, I found a perfect location in their concierge section. I waited there in a small alcove away from the food area until the last minute before going to the gate with my boarding pass. I took my seat in coach and finally dared to breathe a small sigh of relief.

That's when a flight attendant approached and asked me to follow her. Now what? Did a PSA find me after all? I started to reach for my sock but abandon the effort because she was watching me. Besides, where was I going to put it. After retrieving my carry-on from the overhead bin, I followed her asking where we were going. She replied with a smile, *"We're upgrading you to Business Class,"* I slept soundly on the flight to Singapore and on to Sri Lanka.

A Man Named Moses

It was on this same trip into China that I had an opportunity to meet a hero named Moses who I had known about for years, which added concerns for the memory chip even more important. I wanted to meet and honor him for his tenacious and sacrificial work toward advancing the Good News. He had just been released from 22 years in prison for preaching the Gospel. To be caught meeting with an American, who was already being watched, could be detrimental to him and maybe even put him back in prison. It was a courageous undertaking which he did willingly.

He agreed to meet at his home. I was guided there by Dr. Chao's wife who, like her husband knew him well and served as our interpreter. As usual, we took a number of taxis, alleyways, subways, trains, and hidden tunnels under various buildings. I had my trusty small Sony movie camera with me which I held in my right hand close to my right leg, film running as we walked down the last ally to his home; one final check, looking in both directions down the alleyway before we knocked on his door. Moses' wife smiled and graciously greeted us. What an amazing woman of faith to have raised their two children while her husband was in prison all those years. She was financially supported by her house church for the entire 22 years. As one might expect, Moses looked tired, having been released only two weeks earlier. He did however appear to be relatively healthy and in good spirits.

He started his prison sentence on the rock pile making small rocks from big ones. He was told he could reduce his sentence if he confessed his crime and turned against his God. He refused and consequently spent ten years on the rock pile surviving several serious beatings over the years. The government finally abandoned the torture routine and pretty much left him alone to finish out the remainder of his 20-year sentence. He shouldered no animosity toward his tormentors, considering it a privilege to stand firm for the Lord and pray for his captors. He told me, "It strengthened my faith and love for the Lord Jesus Christ, and for that I can thank them." While in prisoned he led multiple prisoners to the Lord.

During our visit there were a few anxious moments when a commotion was heard outside in the alley. It sounded like it might be the PSA agents angrily turning over trash cans as they made their way in our direction. There is really no place to hide in a one-room apartment just slightly larger than the average family room in America, but just in case I hid behind a curtain that separated a double bed from the rest of the room. I would have liked to hide under the bed but couldn't fit. In the end it would not have made a difference. It would have taken only seconds to search the room. I was more concerned for Moses. The situation could possibly be used as a reason to send him back to prison. And then, there still was that blue memory stick I was carrying in my sock because I dared not leave it in my hotel room. The alley commotion turned out to be nothing, so we continued our talk for another hour.

L to R Mrs. Chao, Moses, Moses wife.
(Face blurred for safety concerns)

49

KATMANDU NEPAL AND
MAO TERRORIST

Kathmandu Nepal is snuggled against the Tibetan Plateau. It's the largest Himalayan state in Asia with a population of 1.4 million in the city proper and sits at an altitude of 4,600 feet. The city is the gateway to the Nepalese Himalayas and the Mount Everest climbing expeditions.

Hinduism is the main religion with 90 percent of the population as adherents, but Buddhism is more visible. The two religions have existed side by side in Nepal for centuries and have become closely interwoven.

However, the Christian church in Nepal has also grown from 10,000 believers just 20 years ago, to over 500,000 at the time of my visit. Today the entire country has 3 million, approximately 10% of the population. The fast growth led to a severe church leadership crisis among many pastors. My videographer and dear friends James and Elizabeth rendezvoused with me in Bangkok and the following day we flew to Kathmandu to film "B" footage for a fundraising film and meet with a church leader.

A significant portion of the church growth in Nepal has been due to the efforts of one talented couple, who for safety reasons I'll refer to them as Barnabas and Sara. Over the last 25 years they have planted over 300 churches, thus pastoral leadership training would significantly help move things forward for the growing church.

We were met at the Kathmandu airport by one of their oldest adopted daughters who drove us to the only Holiday Inn in these parts, a short distance from their home. The hotel was the nicest one in all of Katmandu, for which I was grateful -- a safe island surrounded by beautiful gardens, free from the uncollected trash that gathered in the streets.

At the time of our visit, bombings occurred nearly every day, many of which could be observed across the city from our hotel rooms. The Chinese Maoists had invaded the northernmost portion of Nepal a few years earlier and the Nepalese National Army was having little success in controlling their advances. The Maoists were working their way south into Kathmandu with random bombings and killings of innocent people.

To help us acclimate to the cultural climate of Nepal, Sara first took us to the Swayambhunath Monkey Temple. There were hundreds of Macaque monkeys who made their home there. As I would learn later on a trip to Sri Lanka, you have to be careful around free-roaming monkeys. They'll steal anything they think they can get away with that isn't tied down.

It was at the Monkey Temple where I saw a woman scraping kernels from ears of corn. It was explained to me this woman did all the cooking, washing, and food preparations for over 100 monks living at the temple. She was also the Temple prostitute for all of the monks ranging in age from 10 years old to 80. She looked up at me while sitting on the outside steps to the inner living quarters. She seemed so sad, lost, forlorn, empty, and void of life. She was around 25 but looked much older. I waved and smiled in the hope of getting her to smile back, but she didn't.

As I turned and walked away, tears formed in my eyes with a heavy heart. I wished there were something I could have done for her. Prayer was the only option.

The following day we drove to Bhaktapur, one of the outer areas surrounding Kathmandu, a poor area where street children are raising other street children as young as two years old. They all seem to look after one another as they beg in the streets. The church there is doing their best to look after them, but with so many it seems an impossible task.

There was only one narrow road to Bhaktapur with an equally narrow bridge crossing a wide rushing river. A cow decided it was time to sit, rest, and chew its cud, thereby blocking the entire bridge. The driver of our old four-wheel Toyota Land Cruiser turned off the engine and we waited. To just sit on that bridge until a cow made up its mind to move seemed totally ridiculous to me. Other vehicles were stopped behind us blocking any retreat. We could be there for hours. I remembered that cows are considered sacred in Hindu culture and it's against the law to harm them. Nonetheless, I decided to take the chance, get out of the car, and kick it in its hind quarters to hopefully get us our way. I was only here for a week and had a busy schedule, and wasting time waiting for a cow to finish her lunch and nap was not on the itinerary. Sara shouted, "Brother Bob, no, no, no. Don't kick the cow; you will be put in prison for what could be year. The only way out is to pay a heavy fine." We had driven past a Kathmandu prison that morning, and it was appalling to see prisoners peering out of ground level barred openings the size of laptop computers. It was not a place I wanted to visit. So, we waited, and waited, and waited for nearly an hour before the sacred cow sauntered off to block traffic elsewhere.

Our visit to Bhaktapur also afforded the opportunity to meet and visit with the oldest known Christian in Nepal at the age of 102. We climbed a winding, old, wooden staircase to what would have to be called the Nepal version of an upstairs flat. It was four floors up a stairwell so narrow I had to climb it sideways.

He had only one small room with an old saggy twin bed, a table, one wooden chair and one exceedingly small window the size of a checkerboard with wooden bars across it. He considered himself a rich man because he had the Lord and the Lord had him. I don't remember his name, but it was a great pleasure to meet and talk with him for a couple of hours learning about his life's journey.

My visit with him stirred feelings of guilt. I was ashamed for all the complaining I had done in years past because I thought my house was too small with two thousand square feet, a three-car garage, two cars and a large cross- country motorcycle. Additionally, I had been known to complain when we ran out of milk and had to drive two whole miles to buy a gallon at a drive-through diary. I repented.

I also thought about the American college students rioting in the streets because they want the government to pay for their education. Young people would benefit from a trip to a country like Nepal. We can be so spoiled in our western culture of excess. I would direct them to 2 Thessalonians 3:10 (NIV2011): *For even when we were with you, we gave you this rule: 'The one who is unwilling to work shall not eat.'*

Since I was going to be in Nepal, another donor asked me to investigate an orphanage located a couple hours' drive south of Kathmandu. He had been donating money and now had reason to believe that everything was not on the up and up. I rented a jeep and driver to take me there. On the way we crossed a couple of rushing rivers that had water seeping onto the floorboards. Thankfully, the jeep had one of those air breathing extension pipes that came up above the windshield.

It turned out that the orphanage had over a hundred children from age 5 through 18 with large classrooms for each grade through high school. I sat in for a short time on several of the classes. They were well maintained. Teachers were disciplined in their methods. The students were orderly and respectful, and all wore neat clean uniforms. The dorms were also clean and well-maintained. After my tour, I asked to see the executive director who started the orphanage and who was raising all the money and supposedly lived in a big house on the grounds. The house was quite large and nicely decorated, but I was told he was seldom there and actually lived in Texas when not in Nepal. I wondered how much donated money was actually going to the orphanage and how much was being spent on his Texas home.

After collecting all the information possible, my driver took me back to the hotel.

When I arrived home a month later, I did further research on the executive director's ranch in Texas and discovered that he had several quarter horses and thoroughbreds. I then submitted a written report to the donor. I don't know what their final decision was, but our mission received a generous donation. I have since heard the orphanage was still doing well.

The following day my back began to stiffen, perhaps from too many hours spent bouncing around in that jeep the day before. We were scheduled to visit a group of pastors further south, near the border of northern India, but I opted out of the trip and spent part of the following morning and afternoon soaking in a tub of the hottest water I could stand. It was the right decision. By nightfall, my back was 100 percent better.

James went ahead with Sara and one of her staff but were delayed near the India's northern border due to serious rainstorm and had to spend the night on hard ground in the home of an indigenous pastor there.

On their way back, a fatal traffic accident backed up traffic for 20 miles in both directions on a treacherous narrow mountain pass. To add to the chaos, heavy rain caused a landslide that washed a portion of the road over the edge of a 1,000-foot cliff. According to Nepalese law, especially when there is a traffic accident involving a death, all traffic stops until the family of the deceased party arrives on the scene to settle for compensation and payment by the party at fault. It can take hours, even days for the bereaved family to arrive due to the remoteness of these mountain passes. The police become the investigators, judge, and jury at the scene. To make the situation worse for James and Sara, the accident occurred in front of the landslide nearly closing the road.

Remembering that our flight back to Bangkok was the following morning, James knew he could not wait. He has never been one to let long lines bother or delay him for any reason, especially in foreign countries. He instructed the jeep driver to move forward in the opposite lane along the cliff's edge for the full twenty miles where they found the landslide caused by the pouring rainstorm. After surveying the situation James told the driver to engage the four-wheel drive and punch the accelerator to power through the sliding mud and water coming down at a 10-degree angle and falling over the 1,000-foot cliff. It surely was a very intense maneuver to say the least, leaving everyone breathless. One slip of the tires and you are destined to make an impromptu visit to the rocks below. Thankfully, they made it through. James showed up at the hotel just in time to load the rest of his camera gear and we all made our flight as scheduled the following morning. I was glad I stayed behind to nurture my aching back.

THE CHILDREN OF BHAKTAPUR

You see so many heart-breaking scenes when traveling in poor countries like Nepal. I'll never forget the poor homeless children of Bhaktapur. They lived in the streets, surrounded by trash with no parents to care for them. The Nepalese government has taken steps to improve existing health facilities, diseases such as cholera, malaria, tuberculosis, typhoid, and leprosy still occur frequently. The infant mortality rate is high, and the average life expectancy is less than 54 years for the poor.

A common scene in Katmandu – Nepalese Government
troops patrolling - Communist Maoist troops
from China were penetrating the country.

Children of Bhaktapur – homeless children
taking care of children.

Prostitute at Monkey Temple

Oldest Christian in Nepal at 102 – Sara – far right

Not many people have cars in Nepal let alone trucks. These serve as transportation of farmers food to street markets in Katmandu.

50

GOD'S PEOPLE IN SRI LANKA

"Therefore, if any man be in Christ, he is a new creature: old things are passed away; behold, all things are become new." (2 Corinthians 5:17)

This verse well describes the men I met on my first trip to Sri-Lanka. The purpose of the trip was twofold: 1) to observe the first Asian Access Sri Lanka leadership class and 2) to follow up on potential international donors in Singapore. After fruitful meetings in Singapore I caught the only flight available at midnight to Sri Lanka.

I arrived in Colombo, Sri Lanka, at 2:30 am on a Sunday. I rendezvoused with Dr. Gary Parrett, one of the Asian Access faculty members from Gordon Conwell Seminary, who was arriving from a teaching assignment in Seoul, Korea. We shared a cab to downtown Colombo, where we were staying at the Gallinari Hotel. The General Manager there is a Christian, and our accommodations were arranged by our Asian Access National Director, Pastor Adrian De Visser who was able to get us excellent rooms at a reduced rate.

On Monday morning, Adrian had arranged a breakfast meeting at the hotel for nearly every Christian leader in the Colombo area. About 45 leaders attended, including Ajith Fernando, who was national director of Youth for Christ for 35 years.

We wanted to tell them about our mission and share our desire to work with them in training leaders for the Kingdom. The group was very receptive, gave us their blessing and asked how they could help. I received an open invitation from Rev. Canon Lakshman Peiris to preach at the Anglican Church the next time I was in Colombo, as well as an invitation to counsel and advise fundraisers working for the area Director of Habitat for Humanity in helping them to understand that raising funds is really about relationships and connecting God's work with God's people. I would also tell them that friend raising is the realization that donors are a gift before they give a gift, even if they never give a gift.

During my time in Sri Lanka, I was most impressed by Pastor Adrian. He started over 60 churches stretching from Colombo to the southernmost tip of the island. He started his home church some 20-plus years earlier and was still the lead pastor. He and his church quickly became a training ground for new young pastors. I was privileged to meet many in his 250-member congregation and also observed a Sunday morning dedication of 39 new pastors who were being sent out to villages and small towns to start new churches after their two-year training program. Over the course of a week I had an opportunity to meet some of the pastors in these surrounding towns, many of whom had sacrificed much for the Kingdom.

Pastor Adrian has a true pastor's heart and has an entrepreneurial gift. He has performed wonders when it comes to discovering ways to fund the growing church in Sri Lanka from within, rather than just seeking funding from Western sources. He has trained many of those not called to ministry in how to run a number of businesses to fund church planting endeavors. The people he trained run successful chicken farms, an egg farm, banana farm, pig farm, coconut farm, a coconut fiber mill making rope, fish farm, tea plantation, with their own water pumping station for crops, an orphanage, and a sewing school for young girls.

There is much persecution of Christians in this part of the world and it comes predominantly from the Buddhists who are extremely fearful of Christians. The Buddhists were, at the time of my visit, quite influential with the parliament and were constantly putting pressure on government leaders to close the Christian churches. I met pastors who, along with their wives and children, had been dragged out of their homes in the middle of the night, their homes and churches burned to the ground while the local Buddhist priest tied the pastor to a tree and whipped him nearly to the point of death. The following morning after the burnings and beatings, the congregation showed up to tend to the needs of the pastor and family. Church members immediately began to clean up the rubble and start construction of a new house and church next to the ruins of the old one. The bodily scars were deep, but these Christians seem to ignore emotional scars. There can be only one reason; the love of God is shed abroad in their hearts and they understand what Jesus said on the Cross, "Father, forgive them for they know not what they do." They are completely focused on God's Word, the mission of discipleship and glorifying Jesus.

CAREENING THROUGH SRI LANKA MOUNTAINS WITH PASTOR ADRIAN

On Tuesday morning, Pastor Adrian came to pick us up at our hotel for the drive to Kandy in the Central mountains of Sri Lanka where a week of leadership training would take place.

We stopped at his home to meet his wife and two young children. We enjoyed tea and sweets his wife had prepared after which Adrian, Dr. Gary Parrett, Pastor Rich Brohier, a member of our teaching faculty from Australia, and myself, loaded our luggage into his small Toyota and headed out on the mountain road to Kandy.

In Sri-Lanka they drive on the left-hand side of the road as in many other countries, which is always unfamiliar and strange to those of us used to the right side of the road. Personally, I'm convinced the left side is the wrong side, but that's just my opinion. The roads through the jungle areas are quite narrow, especially in the mountains. I can't say I was worried, but concern became an operative word, especially when riding in the front seat with Pastor Adrian. Being the wonderful kindly man of God that he is, would not be considered a good driver here in America on similar roads, but then they don't have interstate highways in Sri Lanka. By Sri Lankan standards I am sure he was an outstanding driver. Driving there seems to consist of taking chances in aggressively overpowering other traffic when any opportunity avails itself; and sometimes there is little opportunity. I quickly learned that there seemed to be a vast difference between what Adrian, and I would consider an opportunity for passing. We were zipping at high speeds around slow-moving trucks on narrow mountain roads, darting back into our lane just in time and nearly leaving our rear bumper on the front of the truck we had just passed. I'm pretty sure if Adrian had the opportunity to observe my driving on southern California freeways, he would probably have a similar feeling about my driving.

We were scheduled to start classes in Kandy at 6:30 that evening. This gave Adrian extra time to show us some of the sights, sounds and foods that were available in small villages on our journey over the mountain pass. One especially meaningful stop for all of us was a pit stop for a new set of brakes on his car. I noticed Adrian did a lot of down shifting after accelerating to pass and sneak in between trucks. I understood why when noticing the brake pedal was nearly all the way to the floor. Adrian is very well known across Sri Lanka, which explained why the mechanic in a small garage in the middle of the jungle dropped everything to install a new set of brakes. As his passengers, we too were grateful.

We took seven hours to cover what would normally be a three-hour drive to Kandy. We considered it most generous of Adrian to make the extra effort for us, especially the new set of brakes. We made two other stops on our expedition, one for some delicious fruit, and one for the fresh cashews that had just been harvested and were still warm from the sun.

Oh, how I love cashews! I had never tasted anything like these. I bought six small bags thinking that four of them would be for office staff back home, one for my wife and one for myself. Regrettably, none of them made it home with me. I rationalized they wouldn't fit in my suitcase, so it was much easier to carry them home in my stomach. And besides, customs agents at LAX might confiscate them. I'm pretty sure they would love them too. After a week all the cashews had disappeared.

When we finally reached the conference center, we discovered there weren't enough accommodations for all of us. I was pleased to find a room in a nice hotel a mile away. My room was beautifully decorated, featuring mahogany-paneled walls with a large walk-in closet and one entire wall of glass with a large walkout balcony. Gorgeous lacy jungle trees overflowed onto the balcony. It felt like being in a large tree house.

Kandy is in the mountains; the temperature is cool and there is little humidity. I thought nothing of leaving the sliding glass doors open while I unpacked my suitcase. That was a mistake. The jungle is full of Toque Macaque monkeys. They most often live in troops of up to 20. They're a medium-sized monkey with males usually weighing from 9 to 18 pounds, but they can occasionally attain much larger sizes. This particular species is only found in Sri Lanka. They're omnivores, eating mostly fruit, seeds, nuts, mushrooms and tubers, but occasionally do eat some animals, including reptiles and birds.

As I was about to learn, all are expert thieves wherever humans have encroached on their habitat. While I had my back turned, a Macaque quietly dashed into the room, grabbed my sun-glasses, bolted out the open sliding glass door jumping on top the railings and across 5 feet of open air to the nearest tree branch. I yelled, "Hey buddy, those are a $300 pair of prescription sunglasses," as if he understood and would remorsefully return them. I watched him for a full ten minutes as he tried to eat the earpieces; taste-tested the frame and licked the lens. He then did what I thought was amazing. He actually put them on. He looked pretty cool -- for a monkey. If they look good on him, they surely must have looked fantastic on me. For the rest of the week, I made sure the glass door was always closed behind me when stepping out on the balcony. I have often wondered if somewhere in the Sri Lankan jungle there's a monkey floundering from tree to tree looking drunk because he's wearing the wrong prescription sunglasses, and with bifocals no less.

THE FAMILY WE NEVER KNEW WE HAD.

The conference kicked off that evening with a get-acquainted dinner. Some of the 21 pastors in attendance had never met one another, but you would not have known that after the first hour. The common bond of Jesus Christ quickly cemented everyone. *"Wherever two or three are gathered in my name, there am I in the midst of them."* (Matt. 18:20 KJV) I do not believe I've ever seen unity develop so quickly among such diverse backgrounds and experiences.

I took a place in the food line, scooped up a pile of, I am not sure what, nor did I care. Hunger had arrived and it didn't matter. Cashews only go so far. Taking a seat at a picnic-style table with all the pastors, I quickly noticed there was definitely something missing. Where were the utensils? Everyone was eating dinner with their fingers. Sooooo.........when in Rome. There were some mosquitos joining us for dinner, and surely wound up in our stomachs for needed extra protein.

The first session taught by Rich Brohier, lasted from 8:30 to 11:00 p.m. The rest of the week was as follows (I mention the schedule just to provide cultural flavor, and to remind myself, I was eating dinner about the time I would be getting up for breakfast at home): Devotions from 7:00 to 8:00 am, breakfast from 8:00 – 8:30, class from 8:30 – 10:30, Tea Time from 10:30-11:00, and class from 11:00 – 12:30. After that, we had lunch from 12:30 to 1:30, rest time from 1:30 to 2:30, and Tea Time from 2:30 to 3:00, followed by sports from 3:00 to 5:00. Then, worship was held from 6:00 to 6:30, class from 6:30 to 8:00, with dinner from 8:30 to 9:00 and prayer from 9:00 to 10:00 pm.

The busy schedule made it somewhat difficult to get together with pastors to hear their stories, but I did capture some wonderful testaments of how God had and was working in their lives.

ROHITHA

None of the pastor's present had ever met me before. They viewed me as somewhat suspicious because they had been hurt once before by a ministry from another country came, took movies, and recorded their individual stories for the purpose of raising money to help build additional churches in Sri Lanka. The ministry did raise a lot of money with their movies, but the Sri Lankan pastors never saw a dime of it. The pastors felt used, betrayed and understandably suspicious of strangers since then. Things changed when Pastor Adrian had a special session with them, explaining that our ministry was the real deal. After that I had no trouble gaining their trust when asking them to share their personal stories.

When leaving a week later I felt a special connection with these new-found friends as true brothers in Christ. They freely shared their life stories with me during any free time we had, and that was often well into the late hours of the evening and early morning. One such person was Pastor Rohitha.

Rohitha was severely burned on his ankles and legs when he was six years old. Living in a poor family, with little access to appropriate medical care, his third-degree burns became infected and would not totally heal for the next 16 years. The burns created a foul odor causing him to be ostracized by other children, adults and even his parents. In his young life, love was replaced with anger and hate. By the time he was 10, he began stealing from anyone, anytime and anyplace, small things first, then larger items. With every "successful heist," his boldness increased.

The police eventually caught him and threw him into prison where he was savagely beaten with a baton for five days. He was so gravely injured that he had to be hospitalized for a full month. He escaped from prison more than once, and kept stealing, but also increased his boldness by ambushing policemen and beating them. He even burned a police station to the ground. One day a local Christian pastor held a crusade in Rohitha's town.

Rohitha responded by throwing stones and bricks up on the stage. Later, he attacked and severely beat the pastor, then burned all his Bibles. His purpose was to stop the crusade.

Shortly thereafter, he became discouraged and depressed. One day the same pastor came up behind him at a bus stop, hugged and kissed him on the cheek, and asked him to come for tea and cake at his church and to hear him preach. Rohitha was so astounded he didn't know how to respond. He attended the service and felt the sermon on Isaiah 9:6 was directly aimed at him. He was embarrassed and fled from the church. The pastor came and found him, took him back to the church, locked him in a room and preached the Word of God to him. Rohitha could hear many people outside the door praying for him, and he felt like his heart was melting within him. He accepted Christ later that same afternoon -- and within 24 hours, the burn scars on his legs disappeared. After a four-year training program under the pastor's tutelage, he became an associate pastor. Today, he is just as fearless and bold for the Lord as he once was for Satan. At the time I met him, he had already started six churches throughout central Sri Lanka. He is a devoted husband and father of two girls, and a recognized and respected Justice of the Peace.

PASTOR GAMINI UDALAWELA

Pastor Gamini Udalawela came from a Buddhist family. He is a talented singer, musician, and vocalist, but because there were not many jobs open in the music industry, he wound up working as an accounts payable clerk for a biscuit company. He made good money, but always spent it "living the good life."

In 1981, a friend invited him to attend a YFC (Youth for Christ) camp meeting. He wasn't the least interested, but eventually changed his mind. The pastor spoke about how Satan captures people and leads them down the road to hell and he wondered if maybe he was on that same road. He had many questions and was referred to a young YFC worker by the name of Adrian De Visser who became our Asian Access director there. The police began raiding homes and Gamini was arrested and placed in a "line up" where he feared he would be misidentified as a rebel. He wasn't and was eventually released. Still, he had compassion on these misguided rebels and led several of them to the Lord.

Then, in 1994, Buddhist radicals launched a wave of persecution against Christians. By this time, Gamini had started a church, which grew to 150 people within a few months and spawned several house churches. One night, while he was holding a meeting with his leaders in his home, several Buddhist priests burst in and dragged him outside, demanding he renounce Christianity and return to the Buddhist religion. He refused, saying he could not as he now belonged to Jesus Christ. He was tied to a tree and beaten with whips and batons. But Gamini said he was not afraid because he had a vision two days earlier when an angel appeared and said, *"Be of good courage and do not be afraid."* He was sustained by these words as he was being beaten, feeling no pain throughout the ordeal. But the physical scars remain on his back today.

The words of the angel continued to give him courage when he moved to another area, bought some land, and started a second church in 1996. But the Buddhist persecution followed him. He held praise and worship services every night where God confirmed His Presence with many miraculous healings.

Within a year the Buddhists bought the adjacent property and filed a complaint that the singing at Gamini's church was too loud and disrupted temple activities. The police told Gamini to move his church, but he proved to them that his church had been there longer than the Buddhist temple. He did however offer to have more quiet Sunday services. The Buddhists responded by burning down the church in the spring of 2000. Gamini would like to rebuild, but the Buddhists have now proven they own the easement that leads to Gamini's church property and have refused him access. The church remains a burnt-out pile of rubble, but

Gamini continues with his church growth plans and has established a series of house churches throughout the area. Jesus said, *"And I say also unto thee, that thou art Peter, and upon this rock I will build my church; and the gates of hell shall not prevail against it."* Matthew 16:18-19 (KJV)

Pastor Mahesh

Mahesh grew up in a mixed background. His father was a Catholic but became an atheist and Communist. His mother was a Buddhist. At age six he developed an eye infection which eventually cost him the sight in one eye. About this same time his mother ran off with a servant. His father became depressed and moved the family to a remote area where medicine for Mahesh's eye was not available.

His mother returned ten years later, but by then his father had drunk himself to death. His mother had no way to support the family, so Mahesh and his youngest brother were sent to a boys' home, run by a "Christian" headmaster, who turned out to be a homosexual and soon was abusing Mahesh.

His mother remarried a young man not much older than he was. Soon, Mahesh's anger toward his mother began to pour out in various uncontrolled rages. He called the Criminal Investigation Department and reported the headmaster who had sexually abused him and the other boys. The headmaster was arrested, but eventually released and immediately set out to kill Mahesh who then fled the area.

He began to drink and use heavy amounts of drugs and became obsessed with the thought of killing his mother and stepfather. He attempted to kill them on four separate occasions. On his birthday in 1984, he decided to make one more attempt to kill them. He planned to take his own life with poison after they were dead. Fortunately, his mother and stepfather saw him coming and fled for their lives.

Sensing that he had failed once again in his attempt to take revenge on them, he went ahead and drank the poison. He would have died if not for an Aunt who realized what he had done, took him to her house and induced vomiting to save his life.

One Saturday night not long after this, he decided to "go out on the town." On the way, he passed a church he had attended when he was a small boy. He went in and discovered that a childhood friend was now the Sunday school superintendent. He shared II Cor. 5:17b (NKV) and told him that anyone who receives Christ is *"...a new creation; old things have passed away; behold, all things have become new."* Sadly, he found that hard to believe and continued his drinking and wild living.

One day his childhood friend asked him to deliver a letter to the Anglican priest across town. The priest invited him in, prepared tea for him and listened intently to his story. He was gratified that the priest seemed to respect him, and he began attending the church. It was there, in December of 1985, that he discovered what it means to be a "new creation" in Christ. He also got a job working for the church and began to pray in front of the altar for three hours every day. He forgave his mother and immediately had a warm feeling for her and was compelled to reconcile. His mother didn't believe him for a year and a half, but they were eventually reunited and now enjoy a true, loving mother-son relationship.

After this, Mahesh started and directed several projects for the church, including a house prayer meeting program throughout the area. He eventually went to work for the Margaya Missionary Society, training missionaries to go out among the rural people. He married in 1993 and, with his wife, started a ministry among the 6,000 young and mostly under-age garment workers who labor 12 to 14 hours a day in the "sweat shops" of Sri Lanka. To support their ministry, Mahesh accepted a position a few years ago as the National Missions Coordinator for the Evangelical Alliance of Sri Lanka. He has since developed a five-year church growth plan, which he is now implementing.

I have met many modern-day apostles across many areas of Asia, and I am constantly reminded of their dedication and commitment "to be and do" what God wants for them. They are examples of the humility that St. Therese wrote about in the late 1800's: *"You wish to scale a mountain and the good God wants to make you descend: He is waiting for you low down in the fertile valley of humility."* In other words, as Psalm 23:2a (NKJV) states, *"He makes us lie down in green pastures."* It has been a great privilege to know and work alongside these powerful and humble men and women of God.

SPIRITUAL FRUIT IN SRI LANKA

Our first leadership training in Sri Lanka was bathed in prayer for months prior and the Lord provided abundant fruit. There were 21 delegates representing 9 growing churches, with many other churches attached to their leadership. It was truly gratifying to see so many young people in leadership positions, with the average age of the delegates being 35.

Dr. Gary Parrett, one of our Asian Access faculty teachers from Gordon Conwell seminary focused on theology, and Rich Brohier, one of our faculty and also pastor of a large church in Australia, taught on church growth, while Adrian dealt with local issues relevant to the church of Sri Lanka.

The pastors came from many rural parts of the countryside where they have been faithfully pastoring small churches and, in some cases, planting new churches, for the past few years. Seeing how they loved each other reminded me of the unity spoken of in the 17th chapter of John. When I began meeting and hearing their testimonies, I was also reminded again of how blessed we are to participate in the lives of these modern-day equivalents of the early apostles. Seeing what they do is almost like stepping back in time to view the early church in Rome after Pentecost. They worshipped, shared, and learned as one unit as only those who are totally focused on Christ can do. It brings tears to my eyes every time I think about it. Unity can develop much quicker when the pure word of God is not bogged down with denominational baggage. Jesus is the only thing that matters, and Him glorified.

There was also a unity between Gary, Rich and Adrian who had never met, let alone co-taught before arriving in Sri-Lanka. None of them brought any denominational baggage, no demands, and only expectations that God would deliver His Word and truth through them. Since that first session many years ago, the delegates have been meeting for prayer and now meet together monthly with their wives and families.

EAGLES IN SRI LANKA?

As my visit ended, I hired a driver to take me back to Colombo. Along the narrow mountain road, I noticed what looked like a flock of eagles flying overhead. I remember thinking how rare this seems. Eagles don't usually fly in flocks and I didn't know Sri Lanka had eagles. I asked my driver if those huge, winged birds were eagles, or perhaps some sort of vulture. If they were vultures, there must be something dead nearby, as about 100 of them were circling overhead.

The driver laughed and said they were bats. I said, "No, that can't possibly be! They have a wingspan of at least three or four feet." He told me, "That's true, but they are also known as Indian Flying Foxes." He wasn't kidding. I had heard of them, but never seen one. They look like a flying fox, with a foxlike head and nose. They live in rain forests and swamps where a large body of water is nearby and can be found in Bangladesh, China, India, the Maldives, Nepal, Sri Lanka, and Pakistan. I'd been to some of these countries, but this was my first time to see them. Of course, small bats can be found in almost every country, along with the old wives' tale that they like to land in your hair.

Of course, that's not true, but if it were, these flying foxes landing on your head could easily cover half your body with those large wings. Now there's an unpleasant thought.

THE VESTIBULE OF HADES

Buddhism is the dominant religion in Sri Lanka, but there is also a Hindu presence. I had an opportunity to visit a Hindu temple while there but wished I hadn't. I stepped through the first door into a large, very dark room, with no lighting whatsoever. The floor was wet, as if someone had sprinkled it with a garden hose, but actually the dampness was probably due to the extreme humidity. Directly in front of me 20 feet further was another door leading inside the temple. Someone approached me and told me I had to take off my shoes when entering. I thought, "Not a chance." It was filthy in there and smelled absolutely awful. What struck me most was the oppression I felt the moment I stepped inside that first large door. It was like I had entered the vestibule of *hades*, and on the other side of that second door was *hades* itself. I couldn't make my exodus fast enough. It was without a doubt the most oppressive and horrifying spiritual sensation I had ever experienced. It's hard to think of the millions of Hindus around the world who suffer spiritually from the many demonic chains that hold them in bondage.

A REBELLIOUS TEENAGE ELEPHANT

On the way back to Colombo, my driver nearly hit an elephant who was being guided by a mahout. A *mahout* is a person who rides and guides the elephant. Usually, a mahout starts as a boy in the *family profession* when he is assigned an elephant. They remain bonded to each other throughout their lives. It is estimated that Sri Lanka has the highest density of elephants in Asia. Human-elephant conflicts there are increasing due to conversion of elephant habitat to growing settlements, villages, and towns.

This particular elephant must have been a rebellious teen. He decided to walk more toward the middle of the road. The mahout could not seem to control him, and the elephant wasn't equipped with turn signals. The audacity of some elephants can sometimes be rather agitating to other vehicles and possibly to other elephants as well. Living in California, being T-boned by a

2,000-pound elephant had never occurred to me. A small Nissan 4-door sedan isn't much of a match. We avoided a collision by the thickness of a credit card. But this was not the closest I have come to waltzing with an elephant.

On another trip to Sri Lanka a year later, I borrowed a 175 cc Honda motorcycle for a ride down a narrow trail through the jungle. I lost track of time and headed back toward the small settlement too late in the day as it would soon be dark. As one would expect, there are no streetlights in a jungle. The motorcycle actually had a headlight that worked, and for that I was most grateful.

At night elephants move through the jungle on feeding excursions and they often cross small roads when they forage. They don't seem to like the sound of a motorbike putt-putting through the jungle, and as I discovered will sometimes chase after them led by the matriarchal female leader of the group. I can't blame them. I wouldn't like a motorcycle in my living room either.

When I heard a large female trumpeting and running behind me, I shifted into a higher gear and throttled to 35 miles per hour. I can't be sure how close she actually was as I was too busy looking straight ahead to be looking over my shoulder. All I can say is, based on the thundering footsteps and trumpeting sounds behind me, it sounded like she was gaining on me and she wasn't happy about my territorial intrusion. There may have been little babies in the herd, and I knew elephants can run up to 25 or 35 miles per hour, so I quickly throttled up to 50 hoping there were no elephants ahead to block the trail. Thankfully, there weren't.

After surviving the encounter with the wavering teen elephant, I had some time before leaving Colombo, so I asked my driver where I might do some fishing to fill in a few hours. He suggested that I try the Pundul Oya River, not far from Colombo. The Pundul Oya is a tributary of the Kotmale River which, in turn, is a tributary of Mahaweli River, the longest river in the country at 208 miles. The river flows through traditional areas of ancient villages and tea plantations.

I'm not really an avid fisherman like some, but I find it quite relaxing -- usually. A couple years earlier I had been invited by a dear indigenous Christian brother from Sumatra to fish with him at Lake Toba. It's the largest volcanic lake in the world, about 100 kilometers long, 30 kilometer's wide, and 1,666 feet deep. The fish there can be as big as 300 pounds or more. I wanted to give it a try but could never find time in my schedule. It probably wouldn't have been a relaxing adventure with fish that big, although, it certainly would have been an exciting challenge.

My fishing record has always been less than glamorous. As a boy on a camping trip to Yosemite with my parents and Uncle Gordon and family, I discovered a beautiful clear pool full of the biggest rainbow trout I had ever seen. After baiting my hook with salmon eggs, I watched with great anticipation as several of the trout swarmed all around my baited hook but never took it. I got so excited I accidently knocked over the uncapped bottle of salmon eggs. Horrified I watched them roll down the boulder I was sitting on and into the pool below. The trout immediately gulped up every one of those salmon eggs. I never understood how they knew what to grab and what not to. As an adult, I tried many times and have all the fancy equipment for fresh-water fishing, including an expensive fly rod and all the accessories. Even when going deep sea fishing far into southern Mexico with the guys to catch 100 lb. Yellow Fin Tuna all around the boat, I was the only one on the entire boat to catch a 10-pound fish with long spiny back spikes that were full of deadly poison.

Despite my not-so-illustrious record, I looked forward to trying my luck in a foreign country. Besides, I was fairly sure these fish did not get the memo about my dreadful fishing record.

I borrowed a fishing poll, and a local man suggested the best bait to use. I sat on a rickety old wooden pier extending out into the river. This was delightfully relaxing. After 30 minutes, several fish had graced my hook: two Silver Carplets, three Rasbora and two Swamp Barbs, all between 20 and 30 lbs. each. I had guessed correctly. They didn't get the memo. My luck had apparently changed, and the fun of fishing had returned. I hung them on a tie line fastened with a small twine rope to one of the wooden posts a few feet behind me allowing them to dangle in the river to keep them fresh.

A small outboard motorboat passed by on the far side of the river and the wake caused the old pier to begin swaying. At least, I thought it was the wake. The elderly man in the boat was motioning to me and shouting something in his native tongue. I don't speak Sinhalese and had no idea what he was trying to say but noticed that his right arm was moving in a circular motion, leading me to look behind me. The old rickety pier was moving, not because of the boat's wake, but because a six-foot long monitor lizard had shuffled onto the pier within arm's reach behind me. I froze as he looked at me and then the fish dangling in the water. His two-inch claws quickly snatched the save line as he pulled up my fresh fish from the water, biting through the line like a hot knife through butter with his razor-sharp teeth. He scurried back down the pier into a small open area near the river's edge to consume his catch. Well, actually my catch, but the operative word here was definitely "his" fish. It seemed wise to let any lizard that big keep them – and with my blessing. That was enough fishing for one day. It was one of the last times I fished. Fishing just isn't the same. Even now, years later, while sitting at any lakeside anywhere, for some reason I can't stay focused on fishing. I keep looking all around to see if anything is sneaking up on me. I had the same thing happen in Savanah Georgia once, only with an 8-foot alligator.

BOMBING AT THE SRI LANKA AIRPORT

Especially on international flights, I always travel as light as possible. On this occasion, I had two carry-ons, one regulation size and one about the size of two bowling-ball type bags. The larger one contained the usual change of clothing. The smaller one was for backup in case the main carry-on was delayed or lost along the journey through the many rural "back country" airports. It has happened many times. My back up case contained an extra one change of clothing, shaving essentials and other related items, and a camera. In every country, this combination of both cases was always allowed as a carry-on with the smaller one on the floor between my legs. The luggage handles easily and looks light and easy, which is the idea. Don't draw attention to yourself by lugging what looks like a heavy load. If you do, you'll be asked to check one or both of them. The smaller case carries nicely and compactly on top of the wheeled carry-on, always allowing one arm free at all times while passing through airports. Another advantage is it allows me to breeze through customs without having to wait in baggage claim lines -- except in Sri Lanka.

After passing through all the check points on the road to the airport, plus the "in-airport" military check points, I finally arrived at the gate area. We were due to board in 15 minutes when I noticed a uniformed army soldier talking with the gate agent. Both appeared to be looking at me sitting at the end of the row nearest the boarding ramp. I got that funny feeling in the gut that my normal comfortable travel routine was about to undergo a modification. I was right. The soldier and the gate agent strode over and asked me to follow them.

I thought, "Now what? I'm a good boy. I don't have a gun, although I did have a small Swiss Army pocketknife in my trousers (you could still carry one on a plane in those days). What is this all about? I obviously wasn't looking Holy enough.

I was asked to follow the desk agent outside. The soldier walked beside me as we made our way down into the belly of the airport and into the luggage area. The desk agent asked me to put my regular carry-on up on a table where she tagged it and placed it on the rolling belt leading outside. I breathed a sigh of relief and thought, *I guess I'll make the flight to Singapore after all, without an examination of my suitcase.* The desk agent smiled politely and the three of us walked back out onto the Tarmac, up the outside stairs and into the waiting area. The plane left on schedule ten minutes later and I wondered if my luggage did. I didn't actually watch where that rolling luggage belt was migrating. In Singapore, a few hours later the luggage arrived with me. Sigh of relief.

It's always somewhat stressful when you have a tight travel schedule and your luggage doesn't keep up with you, especially in foreign countries when you disappear into the back country where there are no hotels and consequently it becomes much more difficult for airlines to trace your steps.

The following morning in Singapore I turned on the TV and was greeted by scenes of devastation from the Sri Lanka airport. The Tamil Tigers attacked and bombed the Colombo airport two hours after my plane left, killing 25 innocent passengers and several soldiers. I always carry a small NIV travel Bible on my trips. I opened it that morning to Romans, Psalms, and Isaiah:

"What, then, shall we say in response to these things? If God is for us, who can be against us? Romans 8:31 (NIV2011)

"Because thou hast made the LORD, which is my refuge, even the most High, thy habitation; there shall no evil befall thee, neither shall any plague come nigh thy dwelling. For he shall give his angels charge over thee, to keep thee in all thy ways. They shall bear thee up in their hands, lest thou dash thy foot against a stone." Psalm 91:9-12 (KJV)

"So do not fear, for I am with you; do not be dismayed, for I am your God. I will strengthen you and help you; I will uphold you with my righteous right hand." Isaiah 41:10 (NIV2011)

These verses, and many others, have always sustained me in my travels.

Many times, I felt like a little kid in a candy store, taking in all the sights, sounds, smells and friendships of many cultures. But at the same time always being cognizant of what was around me and who was watching. In college, my favorite classes were always anthropology, the study of primitive societies. Never in my wildest imagination could I have envisioned having the opportunity to actually visit many of them.

FROM TRAGEDY TO TRIUMPH

I had met a lot of people in Sri Lanka devoted to the Gospel; wonderful Christians who had suffered greatly for the kingdom and were still suffering for the gospel. But they kept moving forward to change their world with Christ's love. I would not trade the experience for anything. Yet, I was glad to be heading home. The next trip to Sri Lanka would also be interesting, but more dangerous and especially deadly for many Indonesian soldiers as the Tamil rebels had intensified their terror.

Heading back to Singapore from Sri Lanka on a Triple 7, I found myself seated in the middle rows, near the rear of the aircraft surrounded by 150 Muslim women, all playing very loud Arabian music from what sounded like 40 different tape recordings. When our eyes occasionally met there was at best a courtesy smile, but not a word spoken to me on the entire flight. As far as they were concerned, I wasn't even there. Any attempt to socialize was met with only a polite smile and head tilted downward. They were all sweet looking young women dressed in their traditional Middle Eastern clothing with covered heads. They seemed to be together as one group, led by a man wearing the traditional white garb and head gear of an Arabian aristocrat. I wondered if these women were his harem. Maybe he had acquired his 70 virgins without dying. The women seemed to be having the time of their lives with all the varied blaring Arabian music. I on the other hand was hoping for the rapture. When we landed in Singapore my head felt like there were 20 jackhammers pounding inside. I had never been so eager to get off a plane.

Rohitha at leadership training session in Kandy

Pastor Mahesh & Rohithav

Pastor Gamini Udalawela

Flying fox bats

Stole my prescription sunglass

Ate my catch.

51

FIFTY CALIBER MACHINE GUNS

I've never seen or fired a 50-caliber machine gun. But I've had some pointed at me. My second trip to Sri-Lanka, a year after the first trip, was following up on how the leadership training efforts were progressing for needed reports to donors. Landing at Bandaranaike International Airport at 2 am it didn't take long to notice there were a lot more soldiers visible. Much had changed. I caught the first taxi available telling the driver what hotel I would be staying at in Colombo about 40 kilometers from the airport.

Before leaving the United States, I had checked the State Department's website to see what was going on in Sri Lanka and consequently had some idea of what to expect. But it wasn't enough to prepare me for the reality. Even on this second trip, my vision of Sri Lanka was still somewhat anchored in a report on Ceylon I did in a tenth-grade world history class. The pictures were of native people living in a paradise, harvesting their major export of tea.

Outside the airport, entering the main two-lane road to Colombo, and a few miles down the road was the first sandbagged machine gun nests blocking one side of the road. The 50-caliber machine guns were pointed straight at any vehicle coming toward them. On the other side of the road, a steel cross bar mounted in concrete pivoted up and down with a counterweight, blocking the one open lane across from the machine gun. Spike strips were laid across the road front and the rear of every car being stopped.

Sri Lankan soldiers armed with M-16 automatic rifles and AK-47's motioned for the cab to stop. A soldier with a mirror mounted on a wheeled dolly with night lights examined underneath the car. Other soldiers checked under the hood, inside the trunk and my luggage. Two other soldiers on either side of the car shined flashlights through-out the inside, asking for the driver's ID and my passport. They were all very pleasant in demeanor as they went about their search. The whole process took ten minutes, and we were again on our way headed toward Colombo. The narrow two-lane road through the jungle was pitch dark with the only light coming from the headlights of the taxi.

Three miles further down the road, our headlights revealed another sandbagged pill box, complete with another 50-caliber machine gun and another group of ten soldiers. The entire process was identical to the first check point and the soldiers were just as polite and complete in their search.

There would be four identical check points with the distance between them decreasing as we got closer to the city. I finally checked into my hotel at 4:30 in the morning. The hotel was directly across the street from the steps to the parliament building, where a suicide bomber had recently attacked and killed three parliament members. A couple of weeks before my arrival, a 12-year-old boy strapped with C-4 explosives dashed through the crowd, throwing himself into the arms of a parliament member on the steps of the parliament building and detonated the explosives strapped to his chest. Several government staff members were also killed as well as a news reporter. It was difficult to find a complete body of either the boy or his intended victims. Now I understood why there were so many check points.

COWARDLY TIGERS

Over the last few years, the Tamil Tigers, a communist group had taken root in Jaffna in the farthest northern tip of the island

and had been working their way south along the eastern side of the island. They are vicious killers, much like radical Muslims we are familiar with today in other parts of the world. They think nothing of brain washing teenagers and even small children to martyr themselves as suicide bombers. The Tiger leaders, like the radical Muslims, are at their core nothing more than cowards who mold young minds to do their deadly dirty work.

The goal of the Tamil Tigers is to force parliament into making concession of territories in the northeast and eastern portions of the island. Rational people know that any concessions parliament makes will never be enough. Sooner or later, depending on the degree or lack of degree, to aggressively deal with evil they will take the whole country under their dictatorial control. This vicious environment set the stage on which I arrived. The only way to stop the Tigers is to defeat them militarily.

The Bible clearly instructs us to deal with evil wherever we find it; not cower to it or appease it. Many times, in the Old Testament, God punished people and entire nations for the evil they had done. The New Testament tells us to purge it from within ourselves.

"To fear the LORD is to hate evil; I hate pride and arrogance, evil behavior and perverse speech." Proverbs 8:13 (NIV2011)

Notice, it does not say hate the individual, but the evil within, which we must lay at the foot of the Cross, and wait for God's supernatural Power, Love, and Sound Mind.

BODY PARTS FALLING LIKE RAIN

A week later while walking down the street window-shopping in Colombo, I saw a young boy, I guessed to be around 12 to 15 years of age, run across the street and jump onto the front bumper of a parked city bus full of soldiers. The soldiers were being transported to their shift at various check points leading to and from the airport. I knew immediately what was about to happen. The boy detonated his bomb. The explosion demolished the bus and blew out store windows for nearly a block in both directions. I ducked behind a parked city bus I was walking past and covered my head with my arms. Picking myself up and shaking off shattered glass from blown out bus windows and store front glass, I looked around to see the street and sidewalk strewn with body parts. Police sirens and armored vehicles with soldiers descended on the scene.

I saw no reason for hanging around to watch the gory mess and retreated to my hotel room to watch troop maneuvers from my fourth-floor window. Sleep eluded me much of the night. I had another day and two nights before my flight home and decided to spend the next day along a quiet beach south of Colombo on the west side of the island overlooking the Indian Ocean. It seemed important to be able to just watch and listen to the serene sights and sounds of the waves calmly rolling up onto the beach. It was very therapeutic and relaxing.

After a couple of relaxing hours, I walked up toward the jungle and found a small path leading into the jungle. Having once gotten lost in the woods near my Aunt Jeannette's house in Illinois, I knew how easy it is to get turned around. I told myself not to venture to far. After ten minutes of hiking my peaceful state of mind was again suddenly shattered. It was the kind of shock and fear that comes when you see those red and blue lights flashing in your review mirror when you didn't realize you were speeding, and the oversight was going to cost you. Instantly a bone-chilling fear invaded every fiber of my being.

I was stunned to see four of the most roguish looking heavily armed men appear out of nowhere. They looked like the kind of people you don't ever want to run into in any country. All of them were somewhat unshaven, wore bandanas over their heads and carried automatic weapons. One had an AK-47, another, an automatic rifle with a noise suppressor, the third carried an RPG rocket launcher and the fourth had what appeared to be a large-scoped sniper's rifle.

I thought to myself they just could not be Tamil Tigers, especially on this side of the island, hundreds of miles away from where the fighting was. Whoever they were I was shocked to see them. I'm sure they were just as shocked to see a white, blond-haired, blue-eyed guy standing in front of them. They made no threatening or aggressive moves. Neither did I. An inner voice said, "Don't turn and run," We stared at each other for what seem an eternity. Time seemed to stop. They were probably trying to assess the threat level. I, on the other hand, was doing three things; trying to stop my knees from knocking, my legs from collapsing and keeping my underwear from turning yellow.

Finally, one of them smiled. I smiled back feeling somewhat relieved. Then again, a smile may not mean much, but at least it was a good beginning. One of them asked me in exceptionally good English who I was and what I was doing here. After explaining a little about why I was in the country, the ministry I represented and that I was from the Los Angeles area in Southern California, the fellow with the RPG broke out with a huge smile. He told me he had attended USC for two years and asked how the Trojans were doing this year. Ha! Imagine that. Way out here on the other side of the world, a jungle warfare fighter was asking about the Trojan football team. Well, as far as I was concerned, we were now friends; and I'm not even a Trojan fan ... but I certainly was that day.

They told me they were part of a special jungle anti-terrorist warfare unit made up of several small squads spread across the jungles on the south and west of the island to make sure the Tamil Tigers were not infiltrating the southwestern portion of this tear dropped shape island.

Thankfully, they were very friendly guys. We talked for about thirty minutes about politics, college football, and NFL football. I shared some items with them from my backpack – peanuts and some power bars. They told me they were resupplied twice a month, but they gratefully accepted the chocolate power bars and peanuts, probably a special treat for them. I was also sure these guys knew how to live off the land.

Before going our separate ways, I asked if I could pray for them. No one ever said that to them. I told them there were hundreds of Christians in their country who were praying for their country and all the Indonesian troops even though most would not know their jungle squads even existed.

We smiled at each other and shook hands. They disappeared into the thick jungle brush as quickly as they had appeared. I retreated back down the path to the beach. It was reassuring to know they were out there, especially after the devastation I had witnessed the day before. They were an invisible wall of defense well prepared to fight and destroy any encroaching evil.

52

SEVEN CORE PRINCIPALS
TAUGHT TO EMERGING LEADERS

In my third year at Asian Access, we brought together a number of Asian leaders from several countries for our annual week of conference in Chiang Mai, Thailand. Once again, they came for prayer, planning, updating, and encouraging one another -- as well as introducing new potential partners to the work of Asian Access leadership development training.

This truly was a time of encouragement, unity, and edification. The scripture that best summarizes our time together would have to be Philippians 2:1-2: (NIV)

> *"If you have any encouragement from being united with Christ, if any comfort from his love, if any fellowship with the Spirit, if any tenderness and compassion, then make my joy complete by being like-minded, having the same love, being one in spirit and purpose."*

Our prayer for weeks before the gathering was based on Romans 15:5-6: (NIV) *"May the God who gives endurance and encouragement give you a spirit of unity among yourselves as you follow Christ Jesus, so that with one heart and mouth you may glorify the God and Father of our Lord Jesus Christ."* The teaching shared was based on seven core principles:

A Servants Heart – Luke 5:2-3 (NIV) *"He saw at the water's edge two boats, left there by the fishermen, who were washing their nets. He got into one of the boats, the one belonging to Simon, and asked him to put out a little from shore. Then he sat down and taught the people from the boat."* – **Jesus first looked for and tested the disciples' trust.** (One cannot influence people if you don't serve in some way)

Obedience – Luke 5:5 (NIV) *"Master, we've worked hard all night and haven't caught anything. But because you say so, I will let down the nets."* -- **God sometimes offends the mind to reveal the heart for obedience.**

Humility – Luke 5:8 (NIV) *"When Simon Peter saw this, he fell at Jesus' knees and said, 'Go away from me, Lord; I am a sinful man!' For he and all his companions were astonished at the catch of fish they had taken, and so were James and John, the sons of Zebedee, Simon's partners."* – **It's amazing what God can do with someone who finds out he is nobody.**

Seeing things other people don't see – Luke 5:10b (KJV) *Then Jesus said to Simon, "Don't be afraid; from now on you will catch men."* **Believe that what God says will come to pass, even if you don't yet see any evidence for it.**

Availability -- Luke 5:11 (NIV) *"So they pulled their boats up on shore, left everything and followed him."* **God takes ordinary people who make themselves available to Him in order that HE may do extraordinary things in them.**

Dependency on Jesus – "…they left everything and followed him." **You can entrust everything you have to Jesus – even your life.**

Faithful – With the exception of Judas, all were faithful to the end. 2 Tim 2:2-6 (NIV) *"And the things you have heard me say in* *the presence of many witnesses entrust to reliable men who will also be qualified to teach others. Endure hardship with us like a good soldier of Christ Jesus. No one serving as a soldier gets involved in civilian affairs-he wants to please his commanding officer. Similarly, if anyone competes as an athlete, he does not receive the victor's crown unless he competes according to the rules."* **The test of anyone's faith is what it takes to stop them.**

Our time together was both instructional and yet relaxing. The setting was a beautiful two-story hotel with several rooms and bungalows carved out of the jungle. At afternoon tea break a mahout came with her mother elephant, sister, and her baby for a snack of peanuts and a short ride around the hotel for those interested.

53

SHARING THE WORD
IN MYANMAR

The Union of Myanmar, known as Burma until mid-1989, is the land of the great Ayeyarwady River. Most of the country's people live in the fertile lowlands drained by the river. Myanmar, a land of more than 40 million people is bordered by China, Laos, Thailand, the Andaman Sea and the Bay of Bengal, Bangladesh, and India. The country is mountainous, and some regions receive up to 200 inches of rain a year, perhaps 30 plus years' worth of the wet stuff that ever succeeds in gracing the Southern California landscape. Almost 50 percent of Myanmar is forested.

Most of the ancestors of the current population came to Myanmar from southwestern China about 2,000 years ago. These various groups spoke different languages and had different customs, and as is true of China, it is believed that they are direct descendants of one of Noah's three sons.

Buddhism is the country's dominant religion. Each village has its own Buddhist temple, or pagoda. Millions of dollars are spent annually on these temples in what is otherwise a poor country. There are over 2000 Buddhist Temples in the country, all of which are covered in Gold leaf including many statues and especially of Buddha.

My flight from Los Angeles to Hong Kong and on to Myanmar would be a long one, again due to extremely strong headwinds. I kept checking the headwind speed in between short cat naps and noticed it was fairly consistent at 325 miles per hour. I wondered how much that would affect our gas consumption. As it turned out... a lot. There are just not many places to make a quick stop for fuel when crossing the Pacific Ocean. The headwind increased as we traveled further southwest of the Aleutians hitting and often holding at 375 mph for extended periods.

The flight to Narita, Japan, usually takes around 10 hours and we were already at 13 hours. All airlines naturally carry extra fuel for such conditions and possible holding patterns at airports due to bad weather and congestion. As I suspected, we were indeed running short of fuel and were forced to make a landing in Taiwan. It was a different process than I had experienced before. None of the passengers had visas for Taiwan and therefore not allowed to de-plane while they filled the tanks, a dangerous situation for all the passengers. In the U.S. this would be against FAA regulations and everyone would deplane while refueling. In many parts of the world safety is replaced with territorial protocols. After a 30-minutes of refueling we were again on our way, arriving in Hong Kong more than three hours overdue. Upon arriving a plane was already waiting to take us to Bangkok for an overnight stay with an early morning flight to Myanmar.

I spent the night at my usual hotel in Bangkok near the airport. By now I had been through this airport so many times for connecting flights to other parts of Asia, the check-in girls and even the maids knew me by name, always providing me with a nice two-bedroom, with kitchen, and two balconies overlooking the city. I don't need two bedrooms and balconies, but it was always nice to have extra elbow room for the same price. Within minutes of getting to my room, the maid always arrived with fresh bottled ice water, fresh fruit, and cookies. It wasn't exactly the Ritz, but it was always clean and friendly.

The next morning, I rendezvoused with James and Elizabeth at the airport for the two-hour flight to Myanmar to film the "back stories" of some of the church pastors and their congregations.

Since Myanmar is a military state, it's always good to carry a lot of good old American greenbacks. If you don't you may have to spend the night in the airport because you didn't have enough to pay the exorbitant airport tax. If you can't pay some gruff-looking soldier with a AK-47 won't let you out the front door, forcing you to spend the night sleeping on the floor or a row of hard molded plastic seats with no food, drink, or even vending machines.

It's not really an airport tax. It's basically forced bribery by the military and surely winds up in their pockets. The official Kyat exchange rate at the time averaged around 6 Kyats (MMK is the foreign exchange delineation for Kyats) for every dollar, but the black market-rate was ten times higher. Foreign visitors could only transact currency at FEC's (Foreign Exchange Rates) or could only obtain Kyats at the artificially high official rates. I paid $200 USD to get out of the airport. James and Elizabeth had to pay $200 each.

Fortunately, we all had the cash. The indigenous pastor I had communicated with via email was there to pick us up and take us to our hotel. The accommodations were excellent with a pleasant view of Yangon (formerly Rangoon) from the 12th floor.

NICE CAB, WRONG CAR

The same afternoon James and I decided to take a boat up the Yangon River to a small village to get some "B" footage of countryside life. As is the normal case with a cab, James and I would always sit in the back seat and place all the camera equipment in the trunk. But for the first time a Toyota station wagon took us from the hotel to the River dock. James placed one of his large camera back-packs in the cargo area behind the rear seat. After paying the driver, we inadvertently left the camera back-pack in the rear section of the station wagon, not noticing it until we were about to board the boat. The backpack contained all the needed equipment, not to mention a supply of expensive battery packs and fresh film cassettes that we would never be able to find, or purchase in remote back-country locations or even in a city like Yangon. Without the equipment, the rest of the trip to several Asian countries would be pointless. We ran back to the cab station, but our driver had already left with his next fare. Since there was no cab available, and the hotel turned out to be closer to the river than expected, we decided to walk/run back to the hotel in case we might see the same cab. As we walked, we prayed and wondered how in the world we would ever find that one cab in all of Yangon. But the Lord provided in an astonishing way. Never underestimate God's provision. "I will go before and make the crooked places straight. (Isaiah 45:2a (NKJV)

As we approached the hotel, we felt the Lord was leading us to first check with the concierge in the hotel lobby. It turned out that the concierge's brother was the chief of police in Yangon who immediately put out a radio call to all police cars to be on the lookout for the cab. The police also called the cab company, asking them to put out a radio call to all taxis for the one who had just picked up two Americans at the Park Royal Hotel.

James and I waited outside under the portico and 30 minutes later the same cab pulled up with a smiling cab driver retrieving the camera equipment from the rear of his station wagon. What a relief. The entire trip would not have to be canceled after all. James felt it was well worth it to pay the cab driver a large tip for his honesty and trouble. We gave him the equivalent of four weeks' pay. He didn't want to accept it, but we insisted. We felt it important to reward honesty. The cab driver went home happy that evening, and we all slept well. Thank you, Lord for guidance and provision. *"In everything, give thanks; for this is the will of God in Christ Jesus concerning you."* I Thessalonians 5:18. (KJV)

The rest of the afternoon, James and I continued shooting "B" footage upriver in a couple of villages north of Yangon. The following day was Sunday and our indigenous host pastor picked us up to attend his church service. He had a fast-growing church and after the service took us to see their new church building under construction. As a pastor in a small poor country, he had a number of other enterprises like buying and selling wholesale jewelry which helped finance his new building. He was definitely an entrepreneur and similar to pastors of smaller churches in the U.S. who take part-time jobs to supplement their incomes.

Every morning in Yangon finds Buddhist monks leaving their temples to canvas the city to "beg" for their daily bowl of rice. Since they visit the same shacks and crudely built homes of poor families every day, most everyone is expected to give a portion of their meager family food supply. It's basically a daily tithe so the monks won't have to work.

There is no caste system, nor is there true nobility in Myanmar. The hill tribes are under the rule of chiefs, and most of the tribes-men practice traditional beliefs, but many of the Karen tribe have been converted to Christianity.

The church in Myanmar has, of course, experienced politi-cal anti-Christian pressures in the past, but these days there are numerous churches scattered throughout the Yangon area. Many reflect colonial architecture and are quite beautiful. They are, however, not filled on Sunday as many people have left the "tradi-tional denominational" church for the many non-denominational charismatic smaller churches which abound throughout the city and country.

We spent the rest of our week visiting other pastors and filming the countryside, talking with pastors to determine exactly what their pastoral leadership training needs might be.

In the street markets we experienced many different delicacies. The **crickets** were crunchy and tasted fairly well if salted – but I much prefer Lays Kettle Cooked potato chips.

Durian fruit - Popular in Myanmar it's known as "the king of fruits" in South East Asia. It's also known for being large, having a very strong smell, and has a thorn-covered husk. The smell is so strong that often "no durian" signs are posted in hotels, airports and on public transport.

Pastor Philips new church under construction

Crickets – Needs some salt.
Nice and crunchy. Great
protein. Fritos taste better.

Pastor Phillips

Monks leaving their Temple going for their daily rice bowl.

Dorian Fruit

Traditional fishing & transportation boats on Yangon River

Burmese Python – not my kind of pet.

Yangon Street market

Ariunbold, Mongolia, wife & children

James, Elizabeth, Bob in Myanmar (Burma)

54

RETURN TO INDONESIA.

I heard about a fellow named Albert who had served as both past president of the Christian Businessmen Association of America as well as the International Christian Businessmen's Association. I was sure Al would be a great contact for learning the whereabouts of Christian businessmen who might be interested in funding ministry efforts in various Asian countries. What made him even more interesting to me was that he lived in a small town only a few miles from where I spent time as a boy on my grandfather's farm, and where my dad was born. Though younger than my dad, he probably also knew many of the large farmers in the area.

I set up a breakfast meeting with Al in Illinois and found him most helpful when it came to sharing the names of others in his vast circle of influence. He was still highly active in both Associations as well as being good friends with Carl, an Indonesian gentleman born in Sumatra and living in Jakarta. At that time his friend, Carl was the president of the International Christian Businessmen's Association.

Since Indonesia was one of Asian Access future target countries for teaching pastoral leadership and church growth planning, I asked Al if he would make an introductory phone call or an email contact on my behalf. He said all I had to do was call Carl directly and say, "Al said you should meet Bob when he comes to Jakarta." He gave me his direct personal phone number, and

I made the trip a month later. Carl said he would meet me at Jakarta International Airport.

After clearing Jakarta customs late in the evening, I waited outside the airport, but no one seemed to be looking for me. Finally, a young man dressed like a chauffeur approached me and asked if I was Mr. Boomsma. He said Mr. Carl had been detained in a late board of directors meeting but would join me at his home when the meeting was over and proceeded to take me to the limousine.

Carl's home was a beautiful hotel. He and his wife Kinta lived on the third floor. I met Carl and Kinta an hour later when they treated me to a light dessert and tea in the hotel kitchen. What a delightfully gracious couple. I immediately fell in love with both of them. The next morning, we had breakfast together in the hotel kitchen. I learned Carl owned the hotel. He was a wealthy and influential fellow, yet humble, down to earth, and without a doubt the most disciplined Christian I'd ever met. His daily routine was rising at 4 a.m. to spend two hours reading the Bible, then an hour of exercise, breakfast with Kinta at 7 and in the office at 8 a.m. ready to start the workday. He was 80 years old at the time, and this had been his routine for most of his life.

He would not think of eating his daily meals in his lavish hotel dining room, except when he had a special guest. Sunday dinner was always held in their private apartment dining room with the entire family where I was invited for Sunday's weekly family after church dinner. I already felt like a member of the family. Kinta immediately became like a devoted mother in her deeds and actions. They have three married daughters, all of whom are professional businesspeople, and their sons-in-laws are pastors and businessmen. The normal routine was to have Sunday family dinner together after church with everyone including grandchildren. It was a weekly family reunion and provided me the opportunity to meet all of them.

My arrival in Jakarta was late on a Friday night. The following morning after breakfast with Carl and Kinta, the chauffer took Carl and me to the headquarters of his large Life Insurance company he started as a young man. The company is located in the Jakarta business district, not far from consulate row, where various nations station their ambassadors and consulate staff members. His company owned several, hotels, several banks and container ships. Many items travel to and from Los Angeles to Indonesia on some of his ocean-going vessels.

Unknown to me, Carl had called a special board of directors meeting for Saturday morning and I was the special guest speaker. I had not planned on that, but it was a wonderful opportunity to share the ministry's mission having done so in other countries in Asia and Europe.

All these Christian men sitting around the boardroom table were dressed in business suits, which was never my habit to have with me on most international trips unless otherwise preplanned. Feeling out of place, I was asked to share the ministry and if we would be interested in possibly, at some future date, having a central location in Jakarta for training pastors across Indonesia. If so, they already had just completed a new building which we could use for offices and training free of charge.

I was then asked how to go about starting a Christian Foundation in Indonesia for funding ministry through various streams of income from their many corporate holdings and enterprises, all of which had been started by Carl. Our ministry would be one of the recipients funded from the foundation.

After making an upfront disclaimer, saying I had no knowledge of Indonesian tax law, but could give them starting points to consider later for evaluation with their attorney. One helpful factor was they all spoke perfect English. I stood up to speak and surely the Holy Spirit took control of my tongue because at first, I had absolutely no idea where to begin. But the Holy Spirit did and provided words and wisdom needed:

> *"But the Comforter, which is the Holy Ghost, whom the Father will send in my name, he shall teach you all things, and bring all things to your remembrance, whatsoever I have said unto you."* John 14:26 (KJV)

"But when he, the Spirit of truth, comes, he will guide you into all the truth. He will not speak on his own; he will speak only what he hears, and he will tell you what is yet to come." John 16:13 (NIV2011)

I spoke for two hours with another one and a half hours of questions and answers, using a white board for drawing diagrams. I love seeing the miracles that can and will happen when we let the Holy Spirit have free reign in our lives.

Carl's career began humbly, and he remains humble. As a young man he started out applying for a job at a life insurance company, actually several of them. No one would hire him. So, he started his own. Twenty years later he was the head of the largest insurance company in Indonesia, employing 10,000 life insurance salesmen, most of whom are Muslims. They are working for a Christian who openly states that when they are hired, they must attend a one-hour Bible study each and every morning at 7 a.m. before the workday begins. Imagine making that a prerequisite in the United States.

Carl is a man who knows how to get things done with his resources. He's well known in Indonesia and around the world. The United Nations asked him to run a program they had created to solve a major economic problem throughout Indonesia; farmers weren't making a profit.

The U.N. wanted to send hundreds of millions of dollars to guarantee that farmers could afford to buy their seed, harvest, and hopefully sell their crop for a profit. However, the U.N. interference would not solve the problem, only perpetuate a welfare mentality making the farmers forever dependent on U.N. intervention. Carl told them he would help but insisted he did not want the United Nations involved in any way shape or form, and especially didn't want to use their money which would only serve as a hook for control in the future.

After studying the economics of the situation, Carl approached the farmers and gave them the money to buy seed and further guaranteed to buy their crops at fair market price upon harvest.

If the world market price fell too low, he would personally underwrite the difference. At the end of that year, the farmers made a profit for the first time in two generations. The same offer was made the second and third years. The farmers were understandably grateful. The fourth-year normal economic supply and demand had kicked in and Carl's "hand-up" approach was no longer needed. Farmers were finally on their own making a profit and naturally they put their savings in Carl's banks. Most importantly, the UN. was not perpetuating eternal handouts.

Now for the first time the farmers could also afford to build and purchase their own homes. They understandably went to his banks for loans to build those homes, and also purchase planting and harvesting equipment, imported on his ships from the United States. He also owned a construction company which the farmers used to build their homes. The economy had taken a 180 degree turn in several sectors and salesmen were now traveling throughout many of the islands selling their goods to the farmers.

The salesmen were mostly Muslim in background, and all of them had to stay somewhere in their travels. That is where Carl placed additional hotels. Carl automatically thinks of opportunities to share Christ as part of everything he does in business. It's part of his DNA. All those hotels were originally designed with a closed inside courtyard, the purpose of which was for Sunday church services. Muslims may burn churches in other parts of the world, but not hotels they are stay in. The rooms have no radios, but Christian music is automatically piped into each room. There is an on and off switch, but that's it. The farmers love him. Salesmen love him. Muslims love him. The United Nations loves him. Thousands of employees love him. The system created without the U.N. grows and everyone is benefiting, unlike some governments and agencies that go on forever with tax dollars. Carl no longer has to jump start the economic engine. It runs on its own in a free market system.

A year after my visit, Carl and Kinta came to visit Stella and me at our home. One of the first things I noticed was how Kinta accepted Stella like one of her own daughters, treating her with the same caring and devotion she had bestowed on me a year earlier in their Jakarta home. Kinta presented Stella with some traditional Indonesian women's clothing.

It's always fascinated me how some people you meet, even those from very different cultures, so easily make you feel like you've known them forever. There is a kindred spirit that comes from the common bond of knowing Christ.

Company Headquarters

Carl & Kinta in front of their home/hotel

Sunday family dinner after church in Jakarta

My unexpected Boardroom Meeting at
Bumi Asih Insurance, Jakarta

Carl, Kinta, Stel, Daughter & her husband
assigned to the Indonesian Consulate in Monterey
Park California, visiting our home.

While in Jakarta, Carl told me about a doctor friend who had just left Indonesia a month earlier and was now living in America not far from my home. He suggested I visit him because he had an interesting testimony. I did, and in so doing met another amazing powerful man of faith.

In hearing his story, the Islamic Jihad had issued a wanted poster offering a huge reward for his capture, dead or alive and published it in a Jakarta newspaper. The posters and newspapers read:

WANTED
DEAD OR ALIVE

55

WANTED DEAD OR ALIVE

The sub-headline, along with a picture in a leading Jakarta newspaper conveyed to all readers the following:

Have you seen or do you know the whereabouts of this man? A $5,000,000,000 Rupiah reward is offered for him DEAD or ALIVE. If you know where he is, the Jihad wants you to notify them immediately.

These words, along with an article describing the false claims of this man against the Nation of Islam, along with the reward were published and syndicated in several newspapers throughout Indonesia and several parts of Asia in 2001.

His crime? He led thousands of Muslims to Christ; but if found, would get less of a trial than Jesus did. The Jihad wanted him dead. Period.

He is the first man ever to receive a death sentence from Indonesian Muslims.

The fact is, Muslims are in decline across Indonesia, and he has had a lot to do with it. He has led thousands of Muslims to the Lord, and thousands more have found Christ through Christian schools he established over 40 years ago. I was fortunate to spend an afternoon with him and meet his wife and two of his youngest children when I returned from Indonesia. Five other children are grown, married, and living abroad with his seven grandchildren. I cannot tell you where he lives now, but he fled Indonesia and now lives in the United States under an assumed name. For now, I will call him John. At the time I met with him, he had an attorney who was helping him with a request for political asylum in the U.S.

He told me that he was raised in a strict Muslim family, became a doctor, and served as a flight surgeon and personal physician to the Chief of Staff for the Indonesian Air Force. He came to know Christ at age 52 and later moved into his calling as an evangelist. When he became self-educated in the Bible, he started a school of evangelism, which has now been operating for over 18 years. The students came from every imaginable socio-economic background, doctors, lawyers, scientists, to factory workers and taxi drivers. All study together five nights a week to learn about Jesus and how to bring the Good News to Muslims.

He authored a book titled, "Personal Evangelism," which has been used for many years at his school. His approach to evangelism stands on the foundation of three main points.

1) Jesus is the Son of God and the Word of God is absolutely correct and true.

2) Jesus has power in heaven and earth and died for our sins.

3) Jesus will come again as a "just Judge."

He shares his faith with Muslims by using their Koran as a starting point by reminding them that Mohammed wrote of Jesus Christ and refers to him 90 times.

I personally remember quite well from news accounts what was happening during this time but had no idea of the actual extent of the lawlessness.

John's life was turned upside down in 1998 when Muslims ran wild across Indonesia, burning buildings, raping women and children in their apartments and throwing their bodies from the tops of tall apartment buildings. It was at this time that John went into hiding with his family. The Christian School of Theology, which he also helped found, was burned to the ground and several students were murdered while the police, many of them Muslims, watched and participated.

JEHOVAH JIREH (LOAVES AND FISHES)

The rioting continued for several months and the Rupiah began to seriously diminish in value, leaving many people without money for basic necessities. It was at that time John came out of hiding and again began living in his large home, which also served as his clinic. Like the Good Samaritan, he knew he had to do whatever he could to help the hungry. He only had enough rice and meat for three days, but he started to bring people in off the streets, giving them medicine and three meals a day of rice and meat. He continued this practice, feeding an average of 200 people a day, every day, 365 days a year for three years. Miraculously Stephen never once replaced the original small sack of rice that contained only a three-day supply. God kept filling the sack! Every day. For three years there was always rice in the sack for everyone he fed on any given day. Those coming to be fed were predominantly Muslim and he shared Christ with every one of them. Thousands accepted Christ as their Lord and Savior.

The story of the "good doctor" was reported in many newspapers across Asia, including the Reader's Digest, which presented him with a "Good Neighbor" award. Naturally, the publicity drew much attention, and not all of it good.

The Jihad comprised of hundreds of thousands of fanatic Muslim militiamen willing to die for Islam is fashioned after the fanatic fundamentalist Hamas group in the Middle East. The Jihad has been targeting indigenous Christians throughout Indonesia for many years, many of whom had fled into the caves and jungles away from the cities. When found by the Jihad, they are given two choices: Convert back to Islam or be killed. As John said, "some are thin of faith" and do convert back.

Meanwhile, John has continued his work in the United States. He has begun a ministry to Muslims here in the U.S. His outlook is the same as the Apostle Paul. In response to the death threat on his life, he says, "To live is to do ministry for the Lord. To die is gain." But, he says, "I will not die in vain. Jesus fled from the Pharisees many times. The only difference is I don't know when I will go to my Jerusalem to meet my Lord. Until then, I live to do His Work."

Stephen, wife, and daughter – faces have been distorted to protect their identity. I have not been able to locate them since 2001 and have no idea if the threat still exists.

I claim Psalm 91 for his protection.

56

SPIRITUAL PERSPECTIVES
FROM VISITING CUBA

"But we had the sentence of death in ourselves, that we should not trust in ourselves, but in God which raiseth the dead."

II Corinthians 1:9 (KJV)

As scripture says, a brother is born for adversity. Thus, through a friend, a surprise opportunity arose for a trip to Cuba. I was wondering if this was a new "open door" the Lord wanted me to go through. The trip became a solid encouragement for my spirit, fellowshipping with those of humble heart and pure motives. I remain grateful today for the opportunity. The humble pastors in Cuba gave me "a word in season to him that was weary", as Isaiah 50:4 promises. The message of their life and attitude was and is: *"While we look not at the things which are seen, but at the things which are not seen... II Cor 4:18a (KJV). "Looking unto Jesus the author a finisher of our faith... "* Hebrews 12:2 a(KJV)

The Christian church in Cuba was experiencing tremendous growth after fifty years of stagnation. I accepted an organizations invitation to see what they were doing in Cuba that was changing all that. This was a time when almost no one could get into Cuba. There were only two organizations allowed entry into Cuba, for reasons known only to God, who I'm sure moved on Fidel Castro's heart. One was the denomination of my childhood, the Christian Reformed Church (CRC), the other being my inviting agency which must remain nameless.

Our flight to Cuba was a special charter, an older B-727, which flew straight down to the Mexico City area and then east across the Gulf of Mexico to Havana. Apparently, there were only specific air approaches allowed into Havana. There were only five of us onboard.

Once inside the Havana airport, we were closely watched. The country director of the project, Edwardo, had made many previous trips and was strip-searched every time he entered the country. In his case, stripped meant totally naked right there in the airport in front of everyone. How humiliating. He naturally knew this would happen on this trip too. Consequently, he asked me to wear a money belt under my shirt since there would be much less chance of it being found. Hopefully, very hopefully, I wouldn't experience the same treatment. The money belt contained $10,000 in U.S currency which we would later distribute to several pastors in various towns across Cuba for entrepreneurial enterprises to help support the growing church. If the authorities found the money belt, they would, as they had done before, confiscate it for themselves.

I was the last to pass through the suspicious eyes of customs. Easily noticed, was that customs officials in Cuba were situated in booths that were significantly higher and raised above your head. I had never seen that in any other country I have visited. You had to look up, and reach up, to hand them your paperwork and passport. Most surely designed to intimidate people making sure they were always looking up to Cuban communist authority.

The woman behind the elevated class counter looked at me, looked at my passport, looked again at me and called for a supervisor. Everyone else, except Edwardo, who was still standing naked in the middle of the airport, had passed through the closed and bolted door were past customs. Admittedly, I was getting a little nervous. I was trying to look innocent but wasn't sure I was pulling it off. My concern was I might be the next one standing naked with a $10,000 money belt around my waist. *"Oh Lord. I'm already humble . . .Okay? Right?"* No answer! I'm worried.

The customs supervisor looked at my passport, looked at me, and gave his approval. The door unlatched and I walked through with a great sigh of relief feeling like I had dodged a silver humility bullet.

We waited outside the airport for another 90 minutes while Edwardo's humiliation continued as they took their time to search all his luggage.

Traveling with me again was my friend and videographer, James Greenelsh, and the vice-president of our host ministry, the son of a personal friend I had invited, and of course Edwardo, the country director of the host ministry.

Our driver in Cuba was Orlando, a pastor of a small church of about 75 members. What a wonderful young man. His countenance just embodied the love of Christ flowing out from deep within his heart. It was the same for all the many pastors we met as we traveled from Havana to just short of Guantanamo Bay Naval Air Station, the military detention camp referred to as GITMO.

Edwardo finally showed up, with all his clothes on, and we were on our way. At the time, Catholic churches in Cuba had been nearly void of parishioners for many years. I wanted to know what my inviting mission agency was doing and how the church had grown to hundreds of small churches with 5,000 members in only five years. It wasn't complicated. The leader made the decision to train 12 others for two years. After that, each man was expected to start a church wherever he felt the Spirit led him, with the first order of business to identify and begin training 12 others to do the same. Once they had established a church each of them would in-turn train 12 others. It seems like I read about a similar approach in the Scriptures.

What was additionally noticeable was the fact that the church growth paralleled the communist system in Cuba. Each small town has a communist overseeing one or two blocks. Any anti-government action or sentiment is automatically reported to his superior, who oversees several blocks of the town, who in turn reports to someone over the whole area, who in turn reports to an overseer at the upper government level in Havana. The church basically did the same. A pastor was trained to plant a church that covered a two-to-four block area. Another, the next two to three square block area until the whole town was sufficiently covered with small churches and overseen by a senior pastor for the entire community. In the process, many of the communist "spies" who attended these churches to spy on the congregation also became Christians.

By the time we left the airport it was getting dark, and we were driven to two separate host homes for the night. My hosts were a family consisting of a mother, father, their pregnant daughter, and her husband. We spent the rest of the evening visiting in their small living room. The Mom and Dad gave up their upstairs bedroom for me and slept on the hard floor in their living room. Even so, it was pretty much a sleepless night for me. There was no air conditioning and windows were left open with no screens allowing small armies of mosquito's easy entry. My bedroom overlooked the street, where there were all sorts of people making noise throughout most of the night, not to mention those incoming mosquitos looking for fresh foreign blood. Not many people seem to go to bed early in Cuba.

The following morning our host mother made eggs, potatoes, toast and coffee, and there was plenty of time to get to know each other better. Every host home we stayed in was the same, American food for breakfast and dinner. When I left after the second night stay with them, I gave them $60 U.S. which they refused to take, but finally accepted after I insisted several times. These are not rich people and those large meals surely put a burden on their meager finances and food supply.

Also noted was the concept of time in the Cuban culture. When everyone agreed to meet at 9 a.m., everyone showed up around 11.00 am. When we said we'd gather at noon, people showed up at 2 p.m. It was the same the entire trip. I've never been to Haiti, but I'm told it's the same there, so I guess it's a cultural thing and stems from going to bed so late.

We spent a day distributing Love Bags to unreached/ unchurched poor people living in mosquito-infested swamps. A Love Bag consisted of a 5-pound sack of rice, a large bar of Lava-type soap, 18 ounces of cooking oil, 18 eggs, and a sack of garlic.

For these extremely poor people the gift was like winning the lottery. In Cuba, one egg costs between $3 to $4, a small bar of soap $30, and most would be doing well if they could only afford one ounce of cooking oil and a half pound of rice. The Love Bag program has been phenomenally successful, with 75% of those receiving them visiting a church for the first time. Half of those become regular attending members. And one-fourth of those, after two years of training, become pastors and start another church which became self-sufficient within a year.

On the third day we traveled quite a distance to the town of De Holy Spirit to meet with pastors there. Along the way, I was incredibly thirsty, and we stopped at a roadside outdoor vending stand for some soda-pop. Everyone said the orange drink, which looked like an Orange Crush, my favorite, would be an excellent choice. It was a big mistake. I was so thirsty that I failed to check to see if it was bottled in Cuba with local water. It was. I received my bacterial reply an hour later on a large four-lane, mostly unused superhighway, without a single gas station for umpteen miles. My gut cramps felt like a volcano about to erupt with the velocity and pent-up power of the 1883 Krakatoa East of Java volcano explosion wanting to eject anything I'd eaten for the last three days.

Then -- there it was -- just as we came over a hill, a brand-new government-built gas station. Naturally, the toilets didn't work, but at this point I didn't care. It was better than the jungle wilderness that lined the road. I have this aversion to bending over in a snake ridden jungle. The new gas station was perfect for leaving behind what I thought of the communist government.

Fortunately, that was the only health related incident on the trip lasting only a couple of uncomfortable hours.

Coming back south on the same highway to Havana we were stopped by two overly aggressive soldiers who demanded to see our papers. We had no special papers other than our passports and we weren't going to surrender them to anyone, no matter how much they demanded it. We all knew never surrender a passport unless you are at an official location like an airport. They seemed determined to give us a bad time, but we all stood firm with loud objecting voices telling them we were special guests of Castro and any further delays would be reported to him personally. We were immediately allowed to pass. Sometimes in foreign countries one has to confound overly aggressive people who think they have real power. The exception might be if the leader is wearing four stars on their shoulders and has several soldiers standing behind him with loaded AK-47's. Presumably that's not going end well.

One afternoon we rendezvoused secretly on a small dirt road in the middle of a sugar cane field to distribute that $10,000 in U.S cash I had been carrying in my money belt. It was like a reunion for many of these pastors, who had come long distances on back roads in beat up 1940's and 1950's classic cars held together with spit, bailing wire and homemade fabricated parts. They're unbelievably resourceful people and have had to be for over 50 years. The cash would be evenly distributed throughout the many churches to help start businesses such as chicken and egg farms, as well as a variety of other small businesses to support the self-funded, growing church. Capitalism has been alive and thriving for quite some time in Cuba. The reality in Cuba is that behind the scenes there are hundreds of enclaves where capitalism has been slowly and surely choking socialism to death.

Nevertheless, there are still many dangers. When Castro took over the government, he took control of everything. This included everyone's livestock. Farmers no longer owned their cows or the milk, but still had to feed and care for them at their own expense. The government can take and kill them for their own bellies. But if you kill one for your own consumption to feed your family, you will be put in prison. I met the wife of a man who killed his cow to feed his starving family 12 years earlier. He was sentenced without trial to 30 years of hard labor. The church has been taking care of his wife and the children ever since.

In spite of hearing some of these sad stories it was a tremendously uplifting trip, and I made many new friendships. Because of Cuban government restrictions it has been difficult to stay in touch with these new friends. All of them were wonderful loving people filled with the joy of the Lord and doing the best they could with the situation they found themselves in. I like to think of them as people who took seriously Paul's letter to the Philippians on Joy. I was astonished how happy everyone always was considering they lived under such distressing conditions. Only a heart filled with the love of Jesus could produce such contentment. I hope someday to again see my friends there. Until then, I trust the Lord with their care.

While the mission work of this agency was and is outstanding, I sensed it was not a move I should make at the time. Thoughts of retirement again filled my head. But, most of all, the trip was a contemplative exercise in government philosophies and thereby compressing my views:

THOUGHTS ON THE FIVE BASIC PHILOSOPHIES OF GOVERNMENT – SIMPLIFIED

- Socialism—you have two cows. The government takes one and gives the other to your neighbor.

- Communism—the government takes both your cows and gives you back a little of the milk.

- Fascism—the government takes both cows and sells you the milk.

- Nazism—The government takes both your cows and shoots you.

- Capitalism—The government suggest you sell one cow, buy a bull, and start a herd.

The sad situation in this day and age is that over 50% of Millennials believe socialism and communism are valid ways of dealing with things. And yet, none of these philosophies has ever worked throughout man's history. They simply have no Christian Worldview because they do not know the Word of God or world history.

My host family for first two nights in Cuba.

Sunday church service - Tractor with sugar
cane trailer serves as a church bus.

Omar & family – the leader (center), who started the
entire church growth effort, his wife & children &
Edwardo, the country director helping from the U.S.

476

Love Bag – consisting of 18 eggs, large bar of soap, 5 lb bag of rice, 18 oz of cooking oil, sack of onions & garlic.

Passing the money belt baton in a Sugar Cane
field in the middle of nowhere.

L to R – Four of the original 12 Cuban apostles. We met and stayed with the other 8 in various towns across Cuba.

Jose & wife: We were honored to attend their commissioning as the first missionaries ever to be from Cuba, in this case to Mozambique. Significant because in 1975 several thousand Cuban soldiers were killed in Mozambique after Castro sent them to fight on the side of the Soviets. Tensions between Mozambique and Cuba have existed ever since. Sending Cuban missionaries all these years later was a significant effort toward reconciliation.

Spontaneously Sharing Christ

Shortly after returning home from Cuba, a fundraising event was scheduled in Boston for a weekend. Invitees started arriving in mid-afternoon on Thursday for the first introduction session starting at 7 pm. The event was scheduled for existing investors in the area and included some potential new investors like George Gallop. After breakfast on Sunday everyone headed for the airport for flights home. Stella and I decided to attend church services at the Kings Church across the street from the Omni Hotel where the event was held. It's one of the first and oldest churches in the U.S. first constructed in 1688. What I remember most about the service was how formal it was with seating for entire families in reserved boxes. Only 25 regular members were in attendance.

After the service we were invited for donuts and coffee. The church had no social hall; thus, coffee was held in a separate building a half block down the street just past the Trinitarian Church. While standing in a group of ten or so parishioners, we listened to the pastor make an interesting comment about those Trinitarians down the street. He plainly said he does not believe in the Trinity. I was standing nearby speaking with someone else when I overheard his declaration. I thought to myself, "Whoa," that proclamation was like waving a red cape in front of my wife. Before I could say anything my wife calmly, and with loving eyes, looked into his eyes and said, "But all of us are trinity. Just look in the mirror. We are made in the image of our creator: Mind, Body, and Spirit; like Father, Son, and Holy Spirit." Sullenly he said, "but you're one person." Stella replied, with her arms extended toward the heaven she compassionately said, "Yes, I AM, One Person." His face softened as he thought about it. The face of a lady standing nearby lit up with a big smile, came over to Stella, hugged her and said, "I am so glad you came today." No more words were needed. Hungry souls were fed and filled receiving the Light of Christ, that He, our Savior, is One with God. We could see she had received Christ's Spirit as Savior, just as she received us and the Lord's words of truth.

Kings Church – formal seating for families.
Photo by Bob B.

Kings Church - corner of Tremont & Beacon St.
(Internet Photo)

57

MATURING IN FORGIVENESS

Psalm 66:12 (KJV)
*"Thou hast caused men to ride over our heads; we went through
fire and through water: but thou brought us out..."*

It has been said that one of our struggles as human beings is
our difficulty with authority, more or less. When we seek to
mature inwardly, we exercise the spiritual discipline of submit-
ting it all to God and honoring those around us as best we can.

Perhaps because I was my own boss previous to entering
missions, I found it difficult when a few missions presidents I
worked with failed to provide accurate and frequent updates. Lack
of timely information can seriously disrupt fundraising efforts.
Without a continual flow of fresh information, a fundraiser is
out there on his own trying to guess where the ministry is going
and what the leader may be planning next. Information needs
to be reciprocal, flowing in both directions. Lack of information means a fundraiser has nothing new to share with donors,
let alone the needed information to write follow up reports on
the donor's investment. Hosea 4:6a (KJV) says, *"My people are
destroyed for lack of knowledge."* It is the same for a fundraiser.
When you cannot keep the investor informed, eventually the
money dries up. Hence, the only way to learn was to make trips
to countries the ministry was working in to learn firsthand what

was actually transpiring with their money. That was a great help for reports to investors but not much help in knowing the vision for the ministry's future.

During a breakfast meeting one morning with one president, he mentioned the cash-flow crises in the ministry. Out of compassion, I felt led to donate half my salary to help with cash flow. I had just made that contribution when he received a phone call from a "consultant." Right in front of me, the President hired him over the phone and told him he could now cover his fee (After I had just said moments earlier my donation was designated to the work on the mission's field). There are good fundraising consulting firms available, but I'm always cautious of "one-man" operations. In conversations with other Foundations and major donors over the years, many have the same cautious viewpoint. It is unfortunate many ministries are unwisely wasting time and money with "one-man" operations who have "no skin in the game" when trying to serve several organizations at the same time. The result is usually a negative ROI. Monies spent with no actual return. It surely has importance if Jesus cautions about serving two masters, in both Matthew and Luke. (Matthew 6:24 and Luke 6:13.)

The final straw of my discontent came a few months later when another fellow was named Vice-President of Development. Hum! That was interesting since I already had that title. I had never heard of two V.P.'s of Development in the same organization. Additionally, no one bothered to tell me about it and never has to this day. Thus, my thoughts of retiring became more consuming. I was tired of contradictions and lack of communication.

Like the secular corporate world, Christian organizations do not always do things correctly either. We would like to think our Christian leaders are perfect. We often think the same about our politicians. But of course, they are not! They are still human. No one is perfect and thinking otherwise is futile. I often pray Christ's prayer from the Cross: "Father forgive us for we know not what we do."

In his book, "My Utmost for His Highest," Oswald Chambers stated it so well in his May 31st devotion:

"Our Lord trusted no man; yet He was never suspicious, never bitter, in despair about any man, because He put God first in trust; He trusted absolutely in what God's grace could do for any man. If you put your trust in human beings first, you will end in despairing of everyone; you will become bitter, because you have insisted on man being what no man can ever be – absolutely right. Never trust anything but the grace of God in yourself or anyone else."

Chambers goes on to say,

"God's ultimate purpose is that His Son might be manifested in our mortal flesh. Many of the cruel things in life spring from the fact that we suffer from illusions. We are not true to one another as facts; we are true only to our ideas of one another. Everything is either delightful and fine, or mean and dastardly, according to our own idea. There is only one Being Who can satisfy the last aching abyss of the human heart, and that is the Lord Jesus Christ." (Source: Oswald Chambers in My Utmost for His Highest.}

We are all limited in our perspectives. We are all at different levels at different times. We all see through a glass darkly. (1 Corinthians 13:12, KJV) *"For now we see through a glass, darkly; but then face to face: now I know in part; but then shall I know even as also I am known."* Each of us sees only one piece of the puzzle. We must strive to forgive and release everyone to the Lord and see only His light covering and filling them. Romans 8:29 tells us He is conforming us, (and them), into the image of Christ. Proverbs 19:11 (KJV) tells us: *"The discretion of a man defers his anger; and it is his glory to pass over a transgression."*

Psalm 36:9b (KJV) states, *"In Thy Light, we shall see Light."* There are <u>two</u> lights in that scripture. There is "THY light" and when we come into that light we shall "SEE light." The first Light is the Light which belongs to God but is shed on us; the second light is the knowledge imparted by that light: we will come to know something; we become clear about something; and we shall see. When there is light coming from God then we will truly see.

When we see other people's imperfections, we too often turn our discernment into the sneer of criticism instead of intercession on their behalf. The Lord reveals things in order that we may take the burden of these people before Him and that we might have the mind of Christ about them. It is not that we bring God into touch with our minds, but that we reposition ourselves until the Lord is able to convey His mind to us about the person for whom we intercede. Is the Lord seeing the travail of His soul in us? He cannot unless we are so identified with Jesus that we are awakened to get His view about the people we are praying for.

I have not read everything Shakespeare ever wrote, but I do remember something from Macbeth that goes something like: "Give sorrow words; the grief that does not speak knits up the o're wrought heart and bids it break." As I recall, it was Christian Bovee, a contemporary of Emerson, Longfellow and Oliver Wendell Holmes, who also said it in a similar way: "Tearless grief bleeds inwardly." Perhaps that's what I'm doing. Venting grief! Forgive me. I'm not perfect either. All of my discouraging experiences of the past never bothered me as much as this situation did. Probably because I expected much more from someone, I considered a friend for 15 years before working for him.

The experience has always left me feeling betrayed, abused, shoved aside. Twenty years later, he apologized for being difficult to work with. I have forgiven him and have let it go with God's help.

Mark 11:25-26, (KJV) *"And when you stand praying, forgive, if you have ought against any: that your Father also which is in heaven may forgive you your trespasses. But if you do not forgive, neither will your Father which is in heaven forgive your trespasses."*

We learn to "bless and release" people to God at every turn in life, for our own freedom, and their freedom, so that God can work on us both.

Today, that ministry has a new President taking it to the next level of God's plan in its destiny. Most of the front office and field missionaries have been assigned to a larger international ministry while the new vision has broadened its mission in spreading church leadership training overseas. Pretty much what I had envisioned so many years ago. I am so thankful the ministry is moving forward in new directions with enhanced visionary leadership.

I feel humbly honored to have played a part in the early years.

58

MOUNTAIN HIGHS AND LOWS

I n a phone conversation with a friend in another state, I mentioned my thoughts about retirement. She said before I decided to retire, I should first check out what was happening at their ministry. I had worked with this young lady years before at the English Institute and knew that she had a heart for God and His kingdom. She worked hard to convince me to visit as they really needed a fundraiser. I had my doubts and hesitations about accepting the offer, having done some pro-bono consulting advice for them some years earlier which was never taken to heart. Now a few years later they were behind the financial eight ball.

Back then I originally cautioned them not to hire just any fundraising consultant, especially a one-man consulting firm. Such people often consult for several organizations at the same time. Consequently, they are too busy with their other clients to have any real skin in the game. Besides, they often charge an exorbitant fee. I told them at the time to bite the bullet and hire a full-time fundraiser, someone who will be in the trenches with them. I even offered to help them find the right person. Instead, they paid a $25,000 fee to a consultant who contributed nothing. Now, several years later they were telling me I was right; and now looking to hire me as Vice-President of Development. I was concerned they would again drift away from what really was needed, and I might be wasting my time and their money.

Over the years I had a several conversations with corporate missions' executives on this very issue. We could never figure out why so many ministries kept making the same mistake wasting donor money. Many corporations cannot always find the right person externally for a specific position, and consequently promote the best "possible" candidate available from within and mentor them into the position. It was precisely my plan for this ministry if I accepted their offer. However, since there was no one internally who could be trained, I developed a plan to amend the situation and decided to accept the challenge. I can't seem to let a challenge pass me by.

Hence, I caught a flight for the interview four states east, met the people and surveyed the situation. I liked everyone and all the key players, telling them I would give the offer prayerful consideration. It was then they told me they were talking with and contemplating a merger with another ministry in a Midwestern state which they felt would complement both ministries. After learning their potential plans, I advised them against the plan for several reasons.

I still wanted to retire but felt the Lord was calling me to accept the position of V.P. of Development being offered. After phone calls and discussion with the Human Resource Director to lay out my plan, we settled the details of my salary, etc. The Director and I quickly developed a lasting friendship.

I clearly stated my tenure would be for only four years. My plan was by the end of my second year, I would have hopefully located my replacement and hired him at an entry level fundraiser salary. I would spend my third year mentoring him, introducing him to all the existing and prospective donors, having him travel with me on all road trips. At the beginning of the fourth year, I would turn the entire job over to my replacement. My plan was to remain available to the end of that 4th year at half salary, the other half would go to my replacement and thereby bringing him up to a standard marketplace fundraiser's salary at which time I would retire.

The plan was agreeable to them. Stel and I packed our suitcases and car with as much as we could carry, locked up the house and headed for my new assignment out of state in mid-February. We had hoped to lease out our home to a missionary couple on home leave, but never had the time to find anyone.

Coming down the eastern side of the Rockies from the Eisenhower Tunnel we drove straight into 13 below zero weather and the worst winter blizzard in 30 years: a new experience for my California native-born wife. Not so much for me as a kid from Chicago. I remember only too well the winter wind and snow coming off Lake Michigan.

We started our adventure in the basement apartment of one of their part-time employees. It was a nice warm place with plenty of room, three bedrooms, bath, kitchen and living room. I showed up at the office the following day to get started, but the second day I came down with the worst cold I ever had keeping me in bed for a week. (I don't remember that part of the Chicago cold.) The second and third weeks were spent partially at the office and partially looking for a place to live. We found a beautiful condo with a 180-degree view overlooking a Lake below us. We signed a one-year lease for an unfurnished condo with two bedrooms, each with walk-in closets, two baths, living room, kitchen and two spacious outside covered porches, one on each end of the condo. The daily sunsets were unbelievably beautiful.

After shopping around for beds, chairs, sofa, eating utensils, towels as well as everything else needed for a completely bare condo, we were finally at home by the sixth week. Stel had great fun putting her nesting instincts to good use.

The plan was working. Two months into my tenure I raised $900,000 for a special movie project they had been working on. At the same time, I found an excellent young man who could easily be trained as my replacement. All I had do now was raise money for his starting salary and all ancillary costs, hire him, and begin the mentoring process.

"THE ENEMY GOD"

When arriving at my new assignment, a department of the ministry was working on producing a movie called *The Enemy God*, a story about a Shaman in the remote jungle of Venezuela, who unknowingly served the devil by leading his tribe into murderous and brutal killing raids on neighboring villages and tribes.

One day Jesus appeared to him in the jungle in a bright shining light from heaven. Jesus spoke to the devil and told him, *"Leave him. He belongs to me."* Like Paul on the road to Damascus, his life changed instantly. He got his hands on a Bible in his language -- another interesting story in itself, provided by a missionary couple who had been working in the nearby area for over 20 years. The Shaman was soon leading his people out of the darkness of the devil's bondage and into the light of the Gospel. In a couple of years, the entire tribe became Christians.

Ultimately the Shaman story was uncovered to the outside world and he was invited to Toronto where he shared his testimony in several public venues. Some Canadian newspaper reporters were so moved by his testimony they also became Christians. Eventually, the story made its way to the film makers who worked for the ministry. They made a trip to visit him in jungles of Venezuela. They became fast friends. The Shaman asked him to make a movie of his conversion to share with others around the world.

The movie producer and director raised slightly over $300,000 and began constructing movie sets in the Venezuelan jungle. At that time Hugo Chavez, a hardened socialist, was President of Venezuela and a sworn enemy of the United States. Unfortunately, a well-known TV evangelist made a striking public statement on national TV that the United States government should assassinate Chavez. The immediate response from Chavez was to expel all missionary organizations operating in his country, including the crew producing the movie. Nearly all of the money thus far raised for the project had already been spent and filming was about to begin. The remaining money was quickly being used up waiting for Chavez, who it was hoped would change his mind.

I realized we could not sit and wait for Chavez to change his mind because it probably would never happen. My question to the producer and director was, where else could we find a landscape that was similar to Venezuela with a more friendly government and shoot the movie there? It turned out the movie director was a missionary kid who had grown up in Belize and had stayed in touch with many influential government officials. I suggested he fly down to see if they would help with whatever governmental paperwork was needed to expedite a movie production. The Belize government not only gave their blessing, but also offered to cover hotel and food expenses for the entire crew while shooting the movie in the nearby jungle.

It seemed to me we should start our fundraising with the very donor who provided the first $300,000 gift and explain the situation, but not without a plan to complete the movie. Before going to the original donor, I worked with the executive producer and director to establish a timeline, as well as a complete budget for what they felt was needed to start from scratch in Belize. It was already early November, and we would have to start constructing movie sets immediately to finish shooting before the rainy season began in March. The next step was to call on the original donor to find out how he felt about losing his investment due to the political environment in Venezuela, establish his interest level, if any, in continuing with the production.

I had never met the original donor, a doctor by profession, but did know his father, one of his sisters and her husband quite well as they were significant supporters to another ministry where I served several years earlier.

During our visit we sat with him and his wife in their large living room in the mountains and explained the situation. His $300,000 investment had been totally decimated due to Chavez's actions, and we, as well as several other ministries were not likely to be allowed back in the country any time soon. I told them about our plan to shoot the movie in Belize, explained our timeline and it would take $900,000 to make the film. His response was that some years earlier he had donated $6 million to build

---

a new hospital in Cambodia to help people recovering from the Killing Fields of the Khmer Rouge. Because of political graft and corruption after the Pol Pot government the hospital was never built. His $6 million donation was a total loss.

He and his wife said they would think about our offer and get back to us. They took us on a tour of their newly constructed home, complete with multiple bedrooms and a 10-lounge-chair movie theater.

On our drive back to the office the donor called our cell phone and said they would donate the entire $900,000 to finish the movie. Back at the office several hours later, the news spread quickly. No one had ever seen a gift larger than ten or twenty thousand dollars in the ministry's history. To say everyone was elated was an understatement. I was happy for them but feeling more restrained. Something was troubling me. A feeling of foreboding I couldn't quite identify.

DO ALL THIS AND RAISE FUNDS TOO?

One of the many challenges I faced was helping the president understand how fundraisers work. He expected me to be at the daily one-hour prayer meeting every morning at 8 a.m. A cubicle had been provided as a workstation, but with all the other activity around, I found it difficult to focus on lengthy phone conversations with donors, not to mention the countless interruptions offered by a cubical office environment. Consequently, I opted to work from a small desk set up in the second bedroom of our condo, which was fine with the president.

The daily 8 a.m. prayer hour was nice, but my routine began on the phone at 6 a.m. reaching out to donors in the Midwest and Eastern Time zones. Going to the prayer meeting took nearly two hours of prime calling time out of my day. With so many people pulling at me with all sorts of questions and countless meetings, I often was not able to get back to my desk in our condo for the entire day.

I decided to attend one prayer meeting a week, but from the president's response you would have thought I was an unsaved heathen. He was adamant wanting me to attend daily. I stood firm on once a week, explaining that just those two hours a day equaled 10 hours a week, the equivalent of a full 40-hour work week per month. I told him "We're not going to make this work if you tie my hands." He reluctantly conceded but didn't like it much. As a fundraiser and even in banking, sixty plus hours a week was more the norm for me. I knew it wasn't healthy for the long run, but I always enjoyed my work, never really thinking of it as work. Fortunately, my dear wife understood and never once complained in all those years.

What the good people at this ministry didn't tell me before I arrived, was that they had already completed the merger with another ministry. Based on the information I reviewed at the time of my interview, I told them it was a bad idea. Nevertheless, both parties felt they had strengths the other didn't and together they would have a complimentary and more viable ministry. I pointed out several concerns, the first and most obvious being that no one from either ministry had a vision of what the combined ministries would actually become. No new name chosen, no new mission statement, no goals. Secondly, the ministry they were merging with had accumulated $250,000 in debt, which was not mentioned until the merger was completed. Seems to me I remember a scripture that covers that kind of thinking:

"Suppose one of you wants to build a tower. Will he not first sit down and estimate the cost to see if he has enough money to complete it? For if he lays the foundation and is not able to finish it, everyone who sees it will ridicule him, saying, 'This person began to build and wasn't able to finish.' Or suppose a king is about to go to war against another king. Will he not first sit down and consider whether he is able with ten thousand men to oppose the one coming against him with twenty thousand? (Luke 14:28-31, NIV 2011)

It was Seneca, the Roman stoic philosopher (c. 4 BC – AD 65) who said, "To the person who does not know where he wants to go there is no favorable wind." Proverbs 29:18a (KJV) states it quite clearly; *"Where there is no vision, the people perish."*

Other problems also surfaced. The executive committee, of which I was a member, was having a great deal of difficulty getting clean accurate financial statements even before the merger. Two key players in the organization seemed to be dragging their feet in providing accurate statements for us as the leadership team. This made it exceptionally difficult to plan anything regarding budget matters.

While this was going on, I hit the road for a five-week fundraising trip. The second week into the trip I learned from the rest of the executive team, via our daily late evening phone calls, that the $250,000 debt showed up on a makeshift balance sheet of the now merged Midwest ministry. To make matters more complicated, the designated money I had raised for the movie was being used to finance lawyer's fees and branding consultants to come up with a new name and vision for the newly merged ministries. My heart sank. It's not illegal to use designated funds for another purpose, if the board of directors has approved and entered it into the formal minutes with an understanding that it must be repaid within 12 months or sooner, and most importantly, with the donors permission. The problem was that the board knew nothing about the movie funds being used for these other purposes and neither did the donor.

Suddenly, the entire purpose of my fundraising trip had changed. After visiting potential donors all day long in various parts of the country, I was spending every evening on the phone until midnight discussing options and possible plans with the executive committee on how we could handle the situation. I clearly said, "I'm not out here to raise money for debt financing. Donors do not like financing debt. For them it's a sure sign there is bad management and they quite naturally think the organization must be poorly run." No argument there.

I began working with the vice-president of marketing on a five-year plan. Based on his research it could easily be determined a number of other ministries were using materials and publications produced by the ministry and would be willing to now pay for the same materials used in their respective ministries. We could demonstrate with very conservative projections that the ministry could be self-reliant and debt-free in 18 months if we sold these materials at a fair market price, instead of just giving them away. We polled all ministries nationally and internationally to learn if they would, and could, now pay for these materials they were originally getting for free. The answer was a resounding yes, even with some of the impoverished countries based in Central and South America.

This was especially good news; but only **If** we could get a gift of $500,000 gift to jump start the new self-sustaining income plan to pay off current debt. We would then be home free. Now that was something, I could explain to a new potential donor without raising money for debt financing. But there was of course, still the problem of that debt.

My trip now shifted to hopefully finding one person who could handle a $500,000 gift. One person came to mind. He was a current board member with substantial capacity and related to the president. If he would handle the debt and help us launch our self-sustaining plan, we could breathe new life into the ministry and within 18 months he would never need to be asked for another gift for the ministry. I could then use the rest of the trip to raise money for the "jump start" self-sustaining income plan.

I set up a meeting with the board member in Pennsylvania. Stella was with me and we spent the night at his home. He, his wife, and family took us out to dinner after which I laid out the entire plan with spread sheets at his home later that evening. He seemed intrigued by the amount of thought that went into the plan. But at 1:00 am in morning he still wasn't buying in. He'd apparently had enough of the ministry asking for money over the past many years.

STELLA'S TUMBLE DOWN A FLIGHT OF STAIRS

Shortly after finally getting to bed, Stel got up to go downstairs for a glass of milk. We were in the guest room upstairs and I had just laid down when I thought, "Stella doesn't know there is a light switch at the top of stairs." I bounced up to turn on the light switch at top of the stairs. I was two seconds too late.

To my horror I heard her tumbling down the stairs. Turning the light on she was sitting propped up against the wall on the first landing gasping for air having the wind knocked out of her. Everyone in the house heard her cascading down the stairs and everyone rushed to her aid. Half-stunned, then finally catching her breath, she looked around and quipped, "Anybody got milk?" Her comment was a good sign. She still had her sense of humor. However, I wasn't laughing. She could have easily broken her neck. As we learned later, she escaped with a severe fracture of one of the many bones in her left foot. An angel surely had protected her. I was most grateful and thanked the Lord for saving her life. We packed her foot in ice but neither of us got much sleep that night. The pain kept her awake most of the night. For me it was the thought of what her injuries could have been.

A FINAL "PITCH"

At breakfast I tried once more to convince the board member to support our plan. No deal. We thanked him for his hospitality and drove across from western Pennsylvania to Philadelphia the remainder of the day to stop for a quick visit with dear friends before heading further east to meet with new potential donors.

After a day of driving Stella's foot was quite swollen with sore and bruised ribs. She was a real trooper, insisting we stop to visit longtime friends of 40 years.

We met these special friends some 40 plus years earlier at our Christian Reformed Church in Arcadia. Dwight and Vangie had just moved to the Pasadena area and showed up at a church dinner held in the Social Hall. Stella and I joined them at their table when meeting them for the first time. I asked Vangie where she was from. She said, "Oh, a little small town you probably never heard of." I replied, "Well you never know, I've been a lot of places." She mentioned the town was Oostburg Wisconsin. I replied, "Oh yes, just east of Lake Michigan off Interstate 43 North. There are several beautiful homes on the left as you drive into town. There is a Presbyterian church on the left. Behind it on the next block is a beautiful Christian Reformed Church. Rev. John Olthoff is the pastor there. As you head into town there's gas station on the left and a grocery market across the street from the gas station and that's pretty much the whole town." Vangie's mouth dropped. Her eyes wide open in astonishment and asking how I knew that. My reply was we have been there a few times and attended church there. Your pastor at the Christian Reformed Church is my Uncle John, my moms' brother.

That was the beginning of a 40 year plus friendship. Her husband Dwight had just taken a position at JPL in Pasadena and also was a teaching assistant at California Institute of Technology (Cal Tech). Stel and I spent many fun times at their home and vice versa. At Christmas it became a tradition to decorate their Christmas tree by sitting around with a needle and thread stringing popcorn for the tree.

Several years later they moved to Salt Lake City where Dwight took a position at the University of Utah. It was quite a trip with their first baby Aaron. Kate coming along a few years later. Today both have two children of their own.

We helped them make the move. Vangie and the baby in their car, Dwight driving a loaded and overheating U-Haul truck, Stella and I with their cat, Max, in a cardboard travel box in the back seat of our car. Max was not a big fan of being imprisoned in that box and managed within a couple hours to pry open one of the breather holes, ripping it open far enough to squeeze his fluffy grey body through and then proceeding to make several revolutions around the car every couple of minutes. From Stella's shoulder, along the window rest, across the whole dashboard, around my window rest and shoulder and to the back window deck where the whole cycle began again. It took us nine hours trying to stay together with the overheating U-Haul, but we finally made it to Las Vegas arriving at 2:00 am. We chose hotels on the outskirts of town and slept till late afternoon to avoid the heat for the final push to Salt Lake. When arriving, Dwight called on a couple of friends from the University to help us move their upright piano to the second floor of their apartment. That was a struggle, but we got it situated nicely in the apartment. Back in those days, Dwight was already, and still is an excellent piano player.

They later moved to Eastern PA. We saved the front section of the cat box where Max originally made his Alcatraz escape, and sent it to them for an anniversary present. Whenever we were in Eastern Pennsylvania on business or passing through on vacation, we would always try to spend a couple days with them. They became like family. We are so grateful for their friendship and our times together throughout the changing seasons of life.

Our visit was cut short as her pain intensified. I rushed her to the nearest emergency room where there was a wait of several hours. We drove back west to another hospital on Route 30 where we found immediate help. A small bone had been severely fractured. A cast was applied, and we finally got into a nearby hotel at 3 a.m. The following day was spent lingering in the hotel room waiting and hoping for the swelling to subside, while I phoned ahead for more donor meetings and several more conference calls with the executive team.

Without the board member's help for the debt financing, I decided to go ahead with the post-debt approach of jump-starting the self-funding program to donors, but with the donors understanding that they would only come in with their gifts, after we had eliminated all debt. My explanation was, "if we can, eliminate the debt, will you step in to help us get started with the self-funding portion?" This was a big leap of faith as I had no idea how the debt could be taken care of at this point. During the remaining four-week trip, I was able to raise over $2 million in commitments for the post debt plan. I cut the trip short once having the commitments and we drove back to our condo.

By the time we arrived Stella's foot was somewhat on the mend, but it would take a lot of physical therapy and nearly a year before she could walk without a cane. However, the situation at the ministry had deteriorated even further with a number of horrifying revelations coming to the forefront.

After several attempts by the executive committee to warn the board of the looming financial implosion, the board labeled the executive committee as basically "Chicken Littles screaming the sky is falling." They dismantled the executive committee saying we were creating strife and division. They simply would not believe us. And, we still had not received any full financial statements and neither had the board.

THE FINANCIAL CAVITY

In the absence of the financial statements, the executive committee pulled some "all-nighters," and we were able to reconstruct a set of our own financials based on the limited information we actually did have. To confirm our suspicions, we hired a former Fortune 500 financial CPA, highly respected and of some notoriety, paying the cost out of our own pockets, asking her to obtain accurate financial records. The board ordered the vice-president of finance to provide them. A week later she confirmed what all of us on the executive committee already suspected. The ministry would be insolvent by March 30th and would need to file bankruptcy. She turned in her report to the board. The same day, 12 of the 18 board members resigned.

By God's grace, I have had the privilege of getting to know many godly men and women who gave freely of themselves for the sake of God's kingdom. At other times I have been disappointed by encounters with those who sought their own fame and fortune under the pretext of serving God and His kingdom.

I could write a small book on the incompetence of some Boards. Anne Graham Lotz summarized her brother-in-law experiences in one paragraph in her book, *Heaven, My Father's House* with his experiences in some Christian ministries, churches, and para-church organizations:

> *"After years of seeing behind the scenes, of being in boardrooms, reviewing spread sheets, listening to the aspirations of would-be Christian leaders, he had to make a conscious effort not to become cynical. So much of what he heard, saw and read was for personal promotion and self-advancement of those who masked their agendas in pious platitudes and spiritual clichés." (Source: p.101, Heaven, My Father's House, published in Nashville, Tennessee by W Publishing an imprint of Thomas Nelson.)*

Anne goes on to say that *"in heaven there will be no professional jealousy and no prideful ambitions, only humility and harmony."* Amen to that.

The situation left the executive committee with the challenge of how to protect the ministry from bankruptcy. If bankruptcy were filed, the intellectual property, used by nearly 100 ministries around the globe would be frozen in bankruptcy court and could not be used.

The financial devastation continued when missionary self-raised funds were also used for branding and merger cost, as well as funds needed to prepay rent five years in advance in various countries as well as college funds for kids just entering their first year of college in the states. None of these funds were available. It was an enormous predicament. A classic domino effect and the handwriting was on the wall. The ministry was essentially ruined.

As the executive team we were determined to do whatever possible to keep the ministry out of bankruptcy court, protect intellectual properties, get missionaries home from the field, and find new positions with other sending agencies for all headquarter staff and field missionaries.

Our executive committee chairmen set out to find another mission organization that was financially stable enough to buy the intellectual properties and absorb as many of the employees and missionaries as possible. I worked on raising money to purchase plane tickets home for the missionaries. Everyone on the executive committee had a specific assignment. Before it was all over, everyone found slots with other mission organizations. Another ministry which had cash reserves bought the intellectual property rights. Missionaries made it back home and were absorbed into several other missionary sending agencies. Truly a miracle guided by God.

Thank you, Lord. We are told by friends, as of this writing, they all seem to be happier in their new jobs than before. Praise the Lord.

Exactly one year after Stel and I had moved, our one-year condo lease was expiring. We hired a moving company to pack up our acquired furniture and other "stuff" and moved back into our home in California. We kept a few pieces of furniture and gave the rest away to others the Lord brought to our attention.

A CHANGE OF PURPOSE -- CHRIST REDEEMS

In reviewing the events of that year, I asked myself if it was a mistake to accept the offer? After reflection, my conclusion was, No. Through it all, God gave both Stel and I a special peace and wisdom to help others sort through their pain, grief, and loss. We had personally been through a much worse financial situation, but God's Love, Grace and Redemption brought us through, and that was our message to them. Christ redeems. God always brings us through and elevates us to a better place if we follow His shepherding hand.

In their heart of hearts, they knew that. But like Peter in a storm-tossed sea they needed to hear it from a calm, reassuring voice. We needed to be there for them in a vastly different way than originally imagined. Some of these dear people had sold their businesses to self-fund their work as far back as 15 years earlier. In any number of private conversations, we were able to calm their fears and assure them that the Lord could and would now use their gifts in multiple ways they had never before imagined.

And the Lord did just that. Everyone moved up to a higher level of ministry where their natural gifting's could be used with greater purpose. Their talents were multiplied, some thirty-fold, some sixty-fold and some one hundred-fold affecting many countries across the globe.

For me, it was yet another lesson in forgiveness. Jesus tells us in Matthew 18:18 (NIV 2011) *"Truly I tell you, whatever you bind on earth will be bound in heaven, and whatever you lose on earth will be loosed in heaven."* I forgave those at fault and released them, and in so doing broke my own chains of bitterness.

Another thought was driven into the forefront of my mind. A danger I had been wary of as far back as the Wells Fargo days. When the Lord blesses your work there is always the lurking menace of pride. It can slowly trickle into the soul like a small leak. Success can easily be a double-edged sword. It's wonderful to be publicly honored for your accomplishments but it can also be dangerous.

In my Wells Fargo days, I remember talking with Stel about how uncomfortable I was at the annual Christmas party when I received so much attention for successes. It seemed it could easily bring about a crack in the "anti-pride" armor. I didn't want to forget to give God the glory. If you are a good fundraiser, or at any endeavor of your gifting, your reputation will precede you. Other organizations try to acquire you. You are the rainmaker. You can make it happen. That's what happened in my assignment for that year. My friend who begged me to come, had spread the word before my arrival; "Our problems are over. We'll be rolling in dough now."

In some ways a successful fundraiser resembles the proverbial hired gun in a Hollywood western. My friend did not mean it in a bad way. She was filled with hope for a ministry she had spent years serving with equally high hopes. But spreading inflated expectations didn't help. It was like beginning a marathon with a 50-pound backpack. It created unreasonable expectations on everyone's part.

I like the way Catherine Marshall spoke about pride, *"Anything but praise, (to God) attributes more power to someone or something than to God." (Source: Something More, p. 32)*

Through most of my career, people have only known me for what I do, not for who I am. I would occasionally ask the same question Jesus asked his disciples, in the most serious tone I could, *"But who do YOU say I am."* Most would answer, "You're a fundraiser." No, that's what I do, not who I am. Who am I as a person? Most people have no idea, suggesting to me they never really knew me. Early on, I have come to the realization that can best be summarized by something Bobby Schuller, grandson of Robert Schuller, said many years later, *"I'm not what I do; I'm not what I have; I'm not what people say about me. I am, the beloved of God. It's who I am, and no one can take it from me."* (Excerpt from the Creed of the Beloved, © by Bobby Schuller.)

ONE MORE CHALLENGE

For Stella and me, our one-year investment in this project was pretty minuscule compared to other people's many years of dedication and sacrifice. One would think that after all of that, at age 62 and originally ready to retire before accepting that position, I would finally be ready to retire. But no. I went looking for another challenge, and easily found one.

A month after we returned home to California, I saw a Christian internet posting. A ministry in the Midwest was looking for a southwest regional manager. I sent a resume via email and received a call the next day. Can you come for an interview? I said yes, and three days later I was being interviewed by their then Director of Development. Thus, began the last chapter in my fundraising career.

> *"There is a time for everything, and a season for every activity under the heavens" Ecclesiastes 3:1 (NIV2011)*

Stella babysitting Aaron in Salt Lake while
guys carried piano & sofa to 2nd floor.

Bob's Impala cat transporter.

59

THE BIBLE MINISTRY TRANSITIONING TO RETIREMENT

"He changeth the times and the seasons:
He removeth kings, and setteth up kings..."

Daniel 2: 21a (KJV)

One would think after my preceding experience I would be ready for retirement. But no, with a lot of energy, fundraising knowledge, and desire to be of service, I answered an internet add from a Bible distribution ministry in the Midwest.

After my flight for the interview and picking up a rental car, I drove along Route 1 out of the suburbs. I was totally engrossed in childhood memories having traveled this same road in my childhood as a four-year-old. Every other weekend we drove this road to visit my paternal grandparents in the countryside, past countless farms and endless corn and soybean fields. As a child on Grandpa Nick's farm, I could run free in the fields and surrounding woods around his home.

As I approached the ministry headquarters, basically in the middle of farmland already being encroached upon by the flight of suburbanites fleeing urban claustrophobia; and there it was. An old, abandoned farmhouse I recognized at that bend in road used some 60 years earlier on our way to visit Grandpa Nick and Grandma Mary, directly behind and slightly to the right of the new ministry building. Nostalgia swept over me like the surging waters of a flood.

My dad told me as a young man of 15 on one of his visits to Grandpa Nick what happened on that same curve eight years before I was born. Dad and Mom purchased 1937 Chevrolet, two door Burgundy red coupe, and on a winter weekend trip going to visit his Dad and Mom in the country, that road was covered with ice. Going around that same curve they hit some black ice and lost control of the car, rolled over several times ejecting both dad and mom into an empty corn field covered with eight inches of snow. They both regained consciousness about the same time and found each other lying in the snow fifty feet apart. Other than being dazed, they suffered no injuries. The car was totaled. Dad could not find his glasses, his wallet and 87 cents in pocket change. Mom could not find her purse. The following spring, before the plowing and planting began, they stopped on that same curve to again give thanks for surviving the accident.

They walked into the field to the approximate location where they had regained consciousness. There -- Dad found his glasses and the 87 cents and Mom found her purse. God had saved and restored their lives. Insurance covered the car loss. Over a half century later, I was in the same area where the curve used to be, and which was now part of the sprawling front lawn of the Bible ministry on my way to an interview for my last job before retiring. Sometimes life seems to come full circle.

AN UNUSUAL INTERVIEW -- LESSON REVISITED

In my interview with the Director of Development for the position of the Southwest Regional Director, it quickly became clear he was one of those fellows who never actually raised any money by himself. Actually, it could more closely be described as an unfriendly interrogation. He had been there for over ten years.

Basically, I saw a bureaucrat masquerading in wolf's clothing, huffing, and puffing trying to blow everybody's house down with his great "supposed" knowledge. We have all seen these types of people. They need to tear other people down to make themselves feel superior. I felt sorry for him and found myself hoping to be a friend and perhaps release him from his insecurity. But I never got the chance.

In the interview, as graciously as possible, I determined to also interview him. After all, I also wanted to make sure I was the right man for the job. It was clear to me he saw himself as a gatekeeper for the ministry, and that was fine. But I was also a gate keeper for myself not wanting to make the wrong job selection, especially since feeling I was being attacked.

I believe it was John Maxwell who said, "There are two kinds of pride, both good and bad. Good pride represents our dignity and self-respect. Bad pride is the deadly sin of superiority that reeks of conceit and arrogance." That's the "pride" that goes before the fall" as scripture tells us in Proverbs. I had to remind myself not to point fingers, as is says in Isaiah 58:9-10 *(NKJV)*

> *"Then you shall call, and the LORD will answer; You shall cry, and He will say, 'Here I am.' 'If you take away the yoke from your midst, the pointing of the finger, and speaking wickedness, If you extend your soul to the hungry And satisfy the afflicted soul, Then your light shall dawn in the darkness, And your darkness shall be as the noonday.*

I had no ill-will towards him. If he didn't hire me, I would take it as a sign to retire. Behind his mask was insecurity. I had compassion for him and was convinced that underneath the facade he was a nice fellow. But I never got the chance to find out. I admit being somewhat sad when after I was on the job for a couple of weeks, I learned someone had liberated him to the job-seeking market.

It's a sad situation when people don't really know who they are in Christ Jesus. All of us can forget from time to time and in some respects we can all be "recovering Pharisees" in one area or another and covering up our own weakness.

The Bible ministry had been around for over 60 years before my entrance. I remember as early as eight years old listening to speakers visiting our church who came at least once or twice a year to tell us about their work around the globe. Most of their ministry's support in those days came from churches across America.

SINCERE ADMIRATION

I was astonished to learn how much the organization had grown. Their accomplishments over many years were exceptionally impressive. Outstanding is a is a better adjective. They had distributed Bibles and started Bible studies in countless countries, leading hundreds of thousands to accept Christ. They also planted thousands of churches, often in countries that were antagonistic to the gospel. I was excited and delighted to be a part of the ministry.

I was also extremely impressed by their new world headquarters. There were 10 interviews spread over a two-day process. The Executive V.P. of Development was out of town the day of my arrival but on the second day she made sure to take me to lunch before my flight home late that same evening. She was a pleasant woman who came from an EVP position in a Fortune 500 company a few years earlier. I liked her immediately. At lunch she asked a question, based on a problem she sensed the other sixteen fundraisers were having. She felt the other fellows seemed to be spending a great deal of time building relationships, which was fine, but had trouble getting to the actual "ask." I told her it isn't a good idea to fast-track building long-term relationships, but fear of asking was a common problem I had seen many times over.

I told her I personally always start from the position that the donor already knows the ultimate goal of my visit is to seek a donation, so my first order of business is encouraging a potential donor to talk about his business, himself, his hobbies, (most of the time noticing what hangs on his office walls that provides clues) and, most importantly determining his giving parameters. In other words, learning what really turns his "giving crank." I need to know what specifically excites him about the other missions he is currently supporting and why, before I start unloading tons of information on him about our ministry, I give the potential investor a longer version of an elevator speech, always trying to get him or her to do most of the talking at first. By doing this I've learned early on, either in a first phone call, or first visit, there is a good compatibility match in the research I've done before setting up any meeting. She mentioned that no one was doing much research. I would learn later she was right. No one knew how to research a potential investor before approaching them. It was more a toss everything against the wall and see what sticks, a dreadful waste of ministry resources and time.

I have always found that after doing your research you can more easily tailor your ministry information to match your donors' interest, and most of the time we have several points of common interest. I then asked her a simple question: "What's the one thing we all like to talk about?" The answer is that most of us like to talk about ourselves, our hobbies, our interests – and that is what I encourage the prospective donor to do.

By the time we have finished our first meeting the donor has done most of the talking and feels like I'm the conversationalist. I naturally give him enough information about the ministry so he will want to know more, and can share with him, based on what is already known about his interest. Before leaving I ask if it would be okay to send him a one-page review of what we discussed about the ministry, including additional specific points based on his interest, always mentioning a sentence or two related to our common personal interest. It always saves a lot of time and more importantly we've established the foundation of a lasting friendship. The second time I call him for an in-person visit, or a phone call, the welcome mat is out because he knows my primary interest is his friendship and not just asking for money.

I also mentioned the importance of leading the prospect into asking questions. This tells me how interested he really is. If he's not asking enough questions, or the right questions, it's probably because I haven't uncovered his true interest, or given him enough pertinent information, or, he simply isn't interested. If he's not interested there's no reason to waste any more of his time or mine; although always check back with him six months later to see if anything has changed. Asking the right questions based on in-depth research prior to that first call is a key to making the ask much easier. When the time comes for the "ask" it becomes a simple formality to follow up with a short written proposal because he has already made up his mind to make the gift and the proposal is basically a formality for his records.

I further explained there are four basic personality types and it greatly helps to know them when building friendships. I had learned many years ago when I met Gary Smalley and John Trent at a three-day conference based on their book *The Two Sides of Love*. They came up with a fun but accurate way of explaining personality types by comparing people to the basic constructs of four different animals: Beavers, Lions, Golden Retrievers and Otters.

- **Beavers** are deliberate, detailed, practical, precise, and scheduled. Like accountants.

- **Lions** are bold, take charge, assertive, goal driven, enterprising and thrive on challenge. Like Presidents and CEO's of corporations.

- **Golden Retrievers** are non-demanding, tolerant; avoid conflict, nurturing and good listeners that love the social aspect of relationships.

- **Otters** take risks, like variety, are energetic, verbal, and motivators who make friends easily, are spontaneous, optimistic initiators, enjoy change, but most of all just love having fun.

Each personality type generally falls into one dominant category and can easily have some of the other qualities as well. But once you know the dominant personality type, it's important to focus on it as your basic road map on how to approach them on first and subsequent calls.

As an Otter myself, I would want to be prepared to quickly identify the traits of each person on the first call. This method has saved me tremendous amounts of time in building relationships and overcoming any fear of rejection with the asking.

She asked when I could start. I replied, "How about the week after next?" So began another interesting journey.

Two weeks later I flew again to begin my five-day orientation. My new immediate supervisor said he had reviewed my capabilities and decided that instead of raising $250,000 the first year, he felt it should be $750,000. I remember thinking $250K seemed quite a small amount for a guy who likes to think much bigger, but I didn't say anything, instead asking what his decision was based on. He handed me a computer printout of 2,500 names in the southwest regional territory with their giving history over the last ten years.

He expected me to agree with his goal. I told him it has never been my habit to let anyone else set goals for me, especially on the first day of work, but I would take a serious look at the computer printout when getting home and come up with my own goal within a few weeks. I could tell my response went over like a screen door in a submarine. He didn't know what to say. I responded, "Don't worry. I always do my best to never over promise and under deliver."

The rest of my orientation was meeting different department heads and various EVP's of the different continents and the many country directors of each. I was impressed with all of them and felt comfortable about my decision to sign on, and especially about the ability to easily obtain needed information from EVP's and country directors in my fundraising efforts. This was important to me because I would apparently have less access to the president as this was a much larger ministry and my geographical distance from headquarters.

Unfortunately, I quickly learned that fundraisers were not supposed talk directly with EVP's or country directors, no personal meetings, no phone calls, no emails. All communications with any of these people had to be approved first by the EVP of Development. I started envisioning a bureaucracy bottle neck and a controlling spirit.

As an Otter, I ignored the rule and set up three-way and four-way conference calls between Executive Vice Presidents and large interested donors. It didn't take long before this tactic led toward two potential very large annual multi-million-dollar gifts. More on that later.

MANUALS, MANUALS, AND MORE MANUALS

On the last day of orientation, I was given a laptop computer, special modem, a 4-inch thick three-ring binder, a 3-inch thick three-ring binder, and one five-inch binder, detailing the software program needed to learn the reporting system for the multiple reports due at the end of every week. It was all packed in several boxes and ready to take with me on the flight home. I laughed and said, "You are kidding, aren't you?" They weren't. I travel light and suggested they ship it UPS.

On the flight home I wondered how anybody had time to raise any significant money. It would probably take six months to learn and use all those manuals, let alone time to call and visit new donors. I never did read those manuals. In analyzing the computer printouts, I quickly realized that 65 percent of the donors on my list had never given over $500 and the last gift was over three years ago. The rest were less than $5,000 givers and those had not given for nearly three years either. I concentrated first on the last category for the first few months and was able to raise their giving by an average of 50 percent simply by giving them updated information and painting a portrait of where the ministry was going and what their gift would accomplish.

In my heart, as usual, my attention was more focused on the multi-million-dollar giver. And there were only a few in my territory, all of which were Dutch dairymen who had set up Trusts with the proceeds to be disbursed to the ministry upon their death. Hence, I set about to do what I like doing best, pursuing new friends with larger giving capabilities. Large capital gifts are what moves ministry goals forward.

THE GOOD AND THE PERTINENT

The ministry had employed many excellent and superbly qualified people who had perfected an excellent system over time. Every system developed was able to track anything and everything. At the same time, all the rules and reporting associated with those systems deprived valuable time needed to pursue new and much needed larger donors, let alone the time necessary to build those relationships. Fundraisers all seemed to be stuck on the small donor treadmill, running for their lives to make assigned quotas. Most of the systems were based on "asks" from small donors of $5,000 to $10,000 or less. None of the systems in place were geared toward the large capacity donors.

In my second year I was quite surprised when great fanfare was made when one fundraiser finally hit a total of $1 million annually after ten years with the ministry. I rejoiced along with everyone else at the bi-annual fundraisers meeting. Internally I was thinking, taking ten years to finally raise one million annually just is not acceptable, but certainly understandable given the small donor mentality.

Additional shock came when one of the new donors I had brought in made their first gift to the ministry, received a thank-you letter, supposedly written by me, but which I never wrote. It was addressed "Dear Friend." Imagine spending nearly a year to develop a friendship who then makes a sizeable first gift and receives a thank-you letter that wasn't even addressed by their first name and you weren't even informed about the gift until you got the report several weeks later. It might as well have been addressed to "Dear Occupant." This is exactly what I meant by systems and policy that did not match large investors or even smaller investors. I saw it as a gaping hole in the bottom of the ship. It had always been my habit to make sure all donors, especially larger donors, not only received a personal letter and phone call from me, but also the President, the Chairmen of the Board and even another one or two board members.

The one thing that caused the greatest hindrance was having a donor in place for the ask and expecting the follow-up proposal to be based on the four to six points that most interested him -- then having to wait three months for the proposal to be written by one of four "professional" writers who had never met the donor. The writers were excellent, but it was the time element that created the challenge. I was used to writing my own proposals, but that was not allowed. If there were other proposals in the que ahead of you, and most of those "asks" were for small amounts, your $2 million ask would still be placed at the bottom of pile where it often took two or even three months for the "writers" to finally get to it. After that it still needed to be approved by the EVP of Development who often changed it, delaying the process another two weeks or three weeks. When I finally got a copy, the proposals would be 40 pages in length, 90 percent of which was redundant.

When a donor decides to give a gift, especially a large gift, he or she doesn't expect to wait two to three months for the written proposal. By then he has grown as cold and stale as last Thanksgiving's turkey dinner. It was just one of many bottlenecks.

After my experience with the proposal backlog, I began writing my own proposals, something I had been doing for 20 years in ministry. And, like most of the ones I had written over the years, they would be two or three pages in length, not forty. I also knew that most private Christian Foundations throw 40-page proposals in the trash unread.

Once again, I started writing my own proposals to circumvent the prolonged system. The first was written to a private foundation which had never given a gift over $25,000 to any one organization and never to this ministry. Based on my visits and additional research with them I knew they could easily fit into two project categories for gifts on two different continents. Since both projects closely matched to their giving interest, I requested their permission, could I send them two, one-page proposals for $25,000 each and let them determine which one they liked the best. The foundation board of directors applauded the clarity and brevity of both proposals and fully funded both of them. I was questioned by management how that happened. After explaining the details, I was reprimanded for dodging the standard proposal system. My response? If I used the standard proposal writing system, we would not have the gift. Many donors, and especially foundations, fund within certain time frames, often only once or twice a year, not to mention the nearly three-month delay of getting the proposal written. We would have totally missed their deadline creating a year-long wait before being able to approach them again.

I also continued to ignore the production report sent out weekly to all fundraisers. It made me feel like being on a treadmill. My list of small donors assigned to me always showed 50 percent behind the goal they had set for me. I spoke to the EVP of Development, saying I was spending my time finding the million-dollar-plus givers, not the $5,000 giver. She agreed with what I was doing, saying the organization just did not have enough larger donors. I asked her to please stop sending those weekly reports to me. It was depressing. Besides we both know ministry cannot move forward without showing the larger donor a greater vision than just a five or ten thousand dollar ask.

I asked her to give me the total budget needs projected for an entire country and also the whole continent. She said it couldn't be done because everything in the annual budget process was broken down into the smaller needs of each country. And that, I said, is obviously why we're lacking in million-dollar givers. They are big thinkers. They built their companies with lofty visions and they want to help ministries with large visions. It makes no sense to ask a mega donor for a $5,000 gift when you know he can give a million dollars or more. Hence the need for research before calling on them. In a way, you are actually insulting him by taking his time to consider making a small donation. It tells him the ministry does not have a substantial vision.

If the ministry's long-range plans for a country or continent call for $10 million or more, we should be asking him for at least a third or even one half it. My experience has been if the donor cannot do it by himself, yet fully believes in your mission, he will sell the idea to his closest friends who each take a piece. Multimillion-dollar donors most often socialize with like-minded givers who also think big.

I further revealed to the EVP of development, I had spent a couple days analyzing the records of all the fundraisers by comparing actual dollars raised with dollars spent to obtain the gift, and discovered that many were spending $100 dollars to get back $102 dollars in gifts, and many were only breaking even. They needed to be securing gifts 20 to 30 times the cost to acquire the gift, including travel expenses, salary, medical insurance, and all other administrative expenses. Was it any wonder there was stagnation? It was a vivid case of Lilliputian small thinking. Hundreds of millions of people in the world still did not have a Bible, Bible study or church in their area. We could reach many more when presenting a larger and broader vision.

Despite our conversation I kept getting multiple emails every week full of new rules about contacting smaller donors. I was getting conflicting signals and more importantly those same messages were tethering other fundraisers to the smaller gift mentality. She understood and agreed, but I don't think she knew how to make the transition. Since I had done it before several times, I offered to help teach the other fundraisers how to make the transition, but never got the green light. Sadly, as it turned out, her days as EVP were numbered.

MISHAPS ON THAT BEND IN THE ROAD

A new president and CEO had been chosen by the board of directors and the fundraising EVP's relationship with the new President/CEO was not equal to the former. The former president and CEO was terminated and shortly thereafter, so was the EVP of Development. Within a year under the new president some of the EVP's and country directors were dismissed or left. Once again, a new well-meaning leader, like once before, would throw a monkey wrench into all the gears.

The new President had been chosen from the business world and came with an outstanding record as an executive vice president of international sales for a major Fortune 1000 company. He was the first in the ministry's history to be selected from outside the ministry. However, he had no experience in the Christian missions' world and consequently understood little of the culture. He was given tremendous power by the Chairman of the Board, also newly appointed and who appeared to have total control over the full board.

In the new president's first address to the fundraising development staff, he admitted he didn't know anything about fundraising but said he would rely on our expertise to help him learn the ropes. He further said he would start by trusting us first, rather than feeling like we had to earn his trust. All the right things were said. I was impressed and hopeful. He also mentioned his wife noticed the first time she walked in the building she sensed a heavy spirit of fear and control. She was right. I too had sensed it when first taking this position. It didn't take long to realize a much greater spirit of control walked in the door in the form of the new President.

It was now a totally new ballgame and it was being run like a Fortune 1000 company with no understanding of a missions' culture and the differences between the two worlds. As it turned out, he didn't trust anybody. He chose another development director from the administrative staff who also knew nothing about fundraising, but also claimed he did. He lasted less than three months.

On our next semi-annual field rep meetings at ministry headquarters we would all see how little the new President/CEO really knew about fundraising when he came into the meeting ranting and raving, just short of profanity at everyone in the room about how everyone was now expected to suddenly raise $5 million a year. Anyone who did not, would be terminated. Not a very practical demand for a team that did not know how to do it having only concentrated on smaller donors for their entire careers. They could not possibly learn it overnight. It suggested to me he was operating in fear, perhaps from the new board of Directors Chairman who hired him.

Insecure people are often mean spirited, and they get meaner as their insecurity intensifies. The world's dictators have always been especially frightened men, and fear always exposes the tyrant within. I read somewhere, but can't remember where the quote came from, but if I recall correctly: "Fear unchecked is like a seed that becomes an amnesia tree, dulling the memory of Christ's love and goodness. When fear controls our lives, it undermines greatness because those who are fear-filled cannot dream passionately." Neither can I recall or fully remember who said it, but it read something like this, and I never forgot it:

"Fear of insignificance creates the ending it always dreads, attains the goal it attempts to avoid and consequently expedites the very outcome it disdains."

• • •

I would realize later that paranoia is also a by-product of the fear of insignificance.

It was near the end of the last day of the week of our bi-annual fundraiser meetings when the president unleashed his fury on the fundraising team and stormed out of the room red faced. I like to think the red face was because he was embarrassed for losing any manner of restraint, yet I doubted such was the case since his rudeness had already happened once before. He turned things over to the second new development director to finish the meeting, after which everyone would leave to catch their flights home. The new fundraising director didn't know much of anything about fundraising either but having just been promoted felt it necessary to continue his superior's stern tirade warning and continued the verbose outburst.

I had an appointment with a doctor to take out some stitches before I headed further east to the east coast for an extended fundraising trip. I left the meeting shortly before the Development Director finished his enraged yelling. I placed my hand on several of the fundraisers in the back row where I was sitting, said my goodbye and whispered my blessings to each of them. By now, everyone pretty much knew me and realized that I was not going to listen to this rage fest.

Another challenge was territorial protection for each fundraiser. This works well if the rest of the fundraising team is calling on significant donors with greater giving capacity. It doesn't work well if everyone is only concentrating on the small donors because that's all they know. Most of the really major donors I knew throughout the years were dispersed across the country and internationally. It didn't seem to matter that I already had a longtime friendship developed with many of them, management wanted the local regional development officer to work on the account to develop the friendship from scratch without my already known "value-added" friendship to help with the relationship building. Besides, many of the development officer didn't know how to develop a multimillion gift in the first place. Not their fault having no appropriate training, but I was not allowed to even help.

In one such case I had inside information on a major foundation. The principles had decided to close down the foundation, giving away their core principle with six final gifts of $6 million each.

I was quite familiar with the foundation having a relationship with them stretching back nearly twenty years and receiving significant gifts from them while with another ministry. As it happens, I mentioned the foundation in a conversation with one of my wife's cousins and she said she knew Mary, one of the significant influencers at the foundation, having attended the same church and been in the same Bible study with her for over 25 years. I asked her if she would meet with Mary, perhaps for lunch, putting in a good word on our behalf. She was delighted to do.

Their meeting went very well. Mary was pleased to learn I was related to her friend of 25 years. Beautiful! We definitely had an inside track. If given a probability of our chances of getting one of those last $6 million final gifts, I would have estimated it to be extremely high. But again, there was still the long proposal writing process so again I wrote it myself. I reported the details to the Director of Development and was told to wait for the proposal process. I waited several weeks to get an idea for what their proposal would look like even after providing detailed instructions based on my knowledge and friendship with the Foundation for the proposal's contents. Nobody at headquarters would give me even a hint of its contents. It appeared I was getting stonewalled.

By now we were on our fourth development director in nearly three years and this particular account was under one of the field reps who had been with the ministry the longest and recently named the newest development director, but had no inside track at the foundation. I had clearly stated two months earlier I didn't care who got the credit, I have an inside track, let's just get it done. We can work on it together.

STONEWALLED

I set up a meeting with the foundation for both myself and Director of Development to hopefully close the deal together. Two days before a scheduled meeting I still hadn't received the long-awaited proposal. All along I'm wondering what's in it, but at the same time prepared to use my own written proposal if needed. Additionally, there was no conversation on how we were going to coordinate the meeting.

Instead, I received a conference phone call from the new development director and the director of Human Resources. I knew instantly what was going on. He started the conversation by saying this just isn't working out. I responded, "You're absolutely right. Working here is a nightmare of rules, regulations and a tangled web of bureaucracy and territorialism causing nothing but confusion, not to mention lack of teamwork. I've had enough."

With that I resigned and, with a great sigh of relief hung up. I never heard if the foundation made the gift or not. My guess is the ministry never received a dime and consequently missed a potential $6 million gift.

NEW SEASON PRIORITIES

A quote from Drenda Keesee comes to mind in her book *"Shark Proof."*

> *"It's tempting when trouble comes to focus on the person who is responsible, to blame, or to become a victim. When criticized, it's a mistake to start doing what someone wants instead of what God said. You can't do it all. You must decide what season you're in and what's important in this season." (source: Shark Proof, pg. 42)*

I had reached my limit and was more than ready for my retirement season. In thinking back a couple of years earlier I had uncovered a scripture from Numbers 8:24-26. Many times, I heard a number of well-known pastors and mission agency leaders around the country say there is no retirement for those in God's work. That is a partially true statement. None of us should stop sharing the Good News of the gospel with anyone who needs to hear it and as we have opportunity to share. As Christians we are all considered priests according to scripture and ideally our responsibilities should lighten with age. I point to the instructions given the Levite tribe in Numbers 8:24-26 the (Amplified Bible) states,

> *"This is what applies to the Levites: from twenty-five years old and upward they shall go in to perform the work of the service for the tent of meeting, and from the age of fifty years they shall retire from the warfare of the service and serve no more. But shall help their brethren in the tent of meeting, [to attend to protecting*

the sacred things from being profaned] but shall do no regular or heavy service. "

It sounded great to me since I was already 64 and accustomed to 12-14-hour days, not to mention according to this scripture, already 14 years behind schedule on the matter. When I wrote my retirement letter to hundreds of donor friends, I was surprised how many called to say they never knew about that scripture and some said they had begun making more definitive plans to have their sons, daughters, and sons-in-laws take the reins of the company.

One week after my resignation, I received a phone call from a wealthy perspective donor I had been working with for the past year but had never entered into the bureaucratic computer system. When he was ready to make a substantial gift, I did not want him waiting a month for the written proposal. Consequently no one at headquarters knew about him. He said he wanted to provide a gift of $5 million, a multi-year gift toward the work in a major country. His gift would provide the distribution of thousands of Bibles that would have led to starting hundreds of Bible studies. The gift was to be a distribution of $3 million the first year, $1.5 million the second year and tapering off to $500,000 the third year. After that he said, "We'll see where I go from there."

Naturally, I had to tell him I was no longer with the ministry but did tell him I would be glad to refer him to the Northern California representative, who would take good care of him. He wanted to know why I had resigned. I said it was personal difference of opinion with management. He sensed I wasn't telling him the whole story and consequently became apprehensive about his gift. Two weeks after my resignation he called me back to say he had changed his mind and was splitting his gift into several smaller gifts to other ministries and offered me a job as Executive Director of his foundation. I was obviously honored, but respectfully declined. It was time to retire and do some of those things I always wanted to do but never had the time. We remain friends and have stayed in contact.

It was a distressing situation for me knowing that possibly as much as $11 million dollars had bypassed a ministry that had formerly accomplished so very much over the past sixty years and was now clearly in distress because of unsuitable leadership.

Many times, parachurch organizations, and even churches, can become conduits for self-serving egotists who have not yet matured into God's wisdom. After all, it is a "process." We all take different amounts of time to arrive at God's revelation that brings us His wisdom. I too am still "in process." Lord help me be "aware" of this human weakness and surrender it to You.

I am reminded once again of Nehemiah, a cupbearer for the King when Israel was in captivity under King Artaxerxes. A cupbearer in those days tasted the wine prior to giving it to the king to make sure it wasn't poisoned. Cupbearers were considered trustworthy and often lived in the king's palace as Nehemiah did.

Often the king sought advice from a cupbearer, sharing other intimate details about the kingdom as a result of this closeness. Nehemiah, as a trusted confident had favor with the king and would surely have heard news about Jerusalem during his twenty years in service to the king. When Hanani, one of the brethren, and his traveling companions came from Judah, Nehemiah asked them about the Jews who had escaped and those which were left in captivity. They told him those who had survived the exile were back in the province and were in great trouble and disgrace.

The walls of Jerusalem were in disrepair and the gates had been burned with fire. Nehemiah wept for several days at this news. But surely, he would already have known this being close to the king. The point is, it took time for the realization of Jerusalem's sad condition to move from Nehemiah's head knowledge to his heart, to the point of weeping and fasting for four days. It's the same for us today. It can take time for head knowledge to move to the heart and become true revelation.

BROKEN SPEARS

Not long after I left the ministry, one of the Executive Vice President resigned from the ministry because he felt the organization was quickly straying from its mission calling. Another EVP, overseeing an entire continent was discharged and given 30 minutes to leave the building with personal belongings. The organization was in turmoil.

Another EVP had a private collection of spears, bows and arrows presented to him by various chiefs and tribal leaders who had become Christians across an entire continent consisting of many countries. The private collection decorated his office walls. Because he was given only 30 minutes to leave the building, he would have to return the following day to pick up his collection of spears. It is easy to imagine this collection was a special remembrance for him. Before he could return to the office, the spears were removed from his office walls and destroyed. A paranoid leader was afraid his dismissal would cause the man to retaliate against him for dismissing him and perhaps throw the spears at him. This new leader certainly never knew the heart of the man who had devoted a significant portion of his life to spreading the gospel across an entire continent. Paranoia can be harmful as it creates blindness and obliterates truth. The fellow who was terminated was a humble man of God who I knew well and genuinely loved God and people.

Several months after my exit, the next scheduled semi-annual fundraising representative meeting was scheduled to be held at a hotel in Atlanta. This was uncommon since all previous meetings were always held at headquarters. Reps always had to travel with fixed airline tickets that did not allow for changes without hefty penalties for cancellations. Everyone showed up in Atlanta on Sunday evening at a designated hotel for their regularly scheduled semi-annual one week of meetings. As I was later told, at 8 am the following morning, they were all told they were fired and had to sign a non-compete clause preventing them from fundraising for another ministry for two years.

There were a number of issues related to this action. First, presuming this information was accurate, I'm not sure it was actually binding. Secondly, fifteen guys were stranded with no way to get home unless they personally paid the airline penalty for changing their tickets. There was no warning or even slightest indication they would all be out of work. With families to support, mortgages and bills to pay, not a very comforting situation. The shock wave in that room must have registered 12.0 on the Richter scale. When hearing about it, I felt sorry for all of them, but at the same time was thankful not to have participated in it. Thankfully, God had a better plan. And there is good news.

Over the next several years, I stayed in touch with a few people who were still there. In September of 2016 Stella and I made vacation trip to the East Coast. On our way we stopped to visit two steadfast people who remained. I admired their tenacity. Most of the people who built the ministry were gone. The place felt and looked like a ghost town. Most of what they once did around the globe had been subcontracted to another ministry. They were now essentially a job shop, a general contractor of sorts, sub-contracting mission work to other agencies. However, that was soon to change for the better with the hiring of a new president.

New Leadership, New Beginnings

A new president and CEO had been named and was due to arrive from his former position as head of the ministry in The Netherlands and due to arrive in a month. It is my prayer then and now, that he will be able to rebuild the ministry to what it once was and beyond. I'm sure he will succeed; after all, he's a Dutchmen and they're pretty good engineers having kept out the North Sea for decades, bought Manhattan for few beads, own Shell Oil, and Philips nuclear medical instrumentations used by thousands of hospitals around the world, and many other multinational conglomerates to name a few. (A little plug for my heritage.)

As of this writing, God is restoring what was lost on that curve in the road, as the Lord did for my Dad and Mom over 60 years before. God both saved their lives and restored their loss. I pray and believe it will be so for this ministry. My purpose is staying in prayer for them, standing in the gap and on the promises of God. My prayers are being answered.

I have stayed in touch with a couple fellows who were on the original executive leadership team as EVP's during my tenure there, and I was pleased to learn in December 2019, the ministry is on the mend and moving in the right direction. The new President and CEO has provided excellent leadership and built a new qualified leadership team. A new fundraising team has been chosen. The ministry is moving forward again, recouping lost ground and is gaining momentum. Glory to God.

As we learn from several scriptures throughout the Bible, sometimes God allows us, and organizations, to be pruned in order that it they may grow and flourish stronger than before.

"I will go before thee, and make the crooked places straight…"
Isaiah 45:2a (KJV)

"Trust in the Lord, and do good; so shalt thou dwell in the land, and verily thou shalt be fed." Psalm 37:3 (KJV)

60

ANIMALS

I have mentioned a few times in my life's narrative some uncommon experiences with extraordinary animals. For some unknown reason, I'm compelled to mention a few other interesting encounters. Perhaps because one of my favorite casual entertaining books many years ago was John Steinbeck "Travels with Charlie."

BOB'S ARKANSAS ARK:

For a couple of years, we took vacation trips to Mountain Home Arkansas where I fished Bull Shoals Lake and the White River below the dam. On this trip I rented a little rowboat with a 50 hp outboard Johnson motor. Pretty small for a lake that had high powered speed boats creating sizeable wakes. But I stayed close to the shoreline looking for just the right quiet cove to drop anchor. The boat rental manager said corn kernels were what Small and Large Mouth were taking. After purchasing a small bag of kernels, I headed out to find my nice quiet cove which was about 100 yards wide. I positioned my boat 25 yards from the west shoreline. After a few minutes I landed a beautiful 5 lb. German Brown trout. I was hopeful this would be a successful excursion with no alligators or water monitors. That's when I noticed a squirrel swimming across the cove from the far side of the cove. Behind him were eight additional squirrels, all heading towards my boat.

Behind them there appeared to be three and possibly four Water Moccasins or perhaps Cottonmouths known to be common in these parts. Both are in the pit viper category and dangerous if bitten. It was a time of drought and the squirrels perhaps were making the crossing looking for a food source. Whatever the case I was sure they weren't going to make it across and figured it would be my good deed for the day to help them if possible.

I placed an oar over the side and the first squirrel got the message. He climbed up the oar and huddled in the bow. The others also got the memo and scuddled up the oar with all eight of them shivering in the front of boat. Figuring they were hungry I threw some kernels of corn to them, which they quickly devoured. Since starting the motor might have frightened them, I rowed to the shoreline and place an oar to the terra-firma. All eight squirrels calmly climbed down the oar and seemed to know the free lunch and ride had ended. They all were last seen sprinting into the woods.

Having caught at least one fish for dinner and saved eight squirrels from certain death, I figured it was time to head back to the cabin with favorable karma winds behind me. I don't know the finale for the snakes, but I think one wound up pulverized by the propeller when I heard a thud and temporary engine grunt behind the boat.

Cat diplomacy

One morning while exiting the supermarket near our home, there was a young man with a box of kittens he was trying to find homes for. He had only one left, the runt of the litter. A light gun smoke color with a white diamond-shape chest and four white feet. I took him. Because of his color and ability to disappear so quickly I named him Puffer, just Puff for short, after a puff of smoke. He never got noticeably big, was always playful and incredibly smart. Like many cats they like to sharpen their claws on the corner of chairs and sofas. The first time I gently wacked him across his nose with the sport section of the newspaper (the sound being the deterrent) and yelled "No." We bought him a scratching post. After that I never had to worry about letting him roam the house. He got the message, and only used his scratching post from then on.

Outside, his small lean stature afforded him the swiftness to outrun his hunters that one time saved his life. I stepped out the front door one evening just in time to see four coyotes on his tail as he sprang five feet across open space to the tree trunk of a 75 ft. pine tree and scampered to the top. It took two days of encouragement and a lot of hunger before he finally showed up at the back patio sliding-glass door.

One morning I watched as our neighbors' cat from two doors down, Mickey, came for a visit. Puff, like most cats, was very territorial. Mickey on the other hand was a diplomat. The first meeting, Puff hunched his back, started growling and hissing ready for a fight. Mickey just rolled over belly up. Puff seemed to be confused and didn't know quite what to do. He was probably dumbfounded. The longer Mickey just laid there belly up, the smaller the hump and less hissing by Puff. As a result of Mickey's patience and kindness a great friendship soon developed. Both cats spent the night in their respective homes, but every morning after they had their breakfast, Mickey was the first to show up at our house looking for Puff. They spent the entire day, every day, playing and stalking each other and hunting birds and rabbits together.

One early evening Puff didn't show up at the back-door meowing to come in. The following day there was no sign of him, so I began to search the immediate neighbors on either side. Mickey was wandering around the yard meowing for him too. I found Puff later the second day in a neighbors back yard. His little body was already stiff as a board. I thought maybe a rattle snake had got the best of him, which he had dispensed once before, but couldn't find any puncture wounds. My guess was he had been hit by a car and in shock made it as far as the he could. I buried him in flower bed, along with a Red Tail Hawk that broke its neck flying into our sliding glass door not seeing his reflection while chasing a rabbit.

Mickey came every morning circling the house for Puff, with a forlorn meowing as he searched. I offered him some food, but he wasn't interested. This went on for two days until he finally found where I buried Puff. He sat on the top of his grave for another two days and two nights without food or water.

Mickey kept coming around everyday which became his habit for the next year. He often came from the same direction, over the south gate and would meow at the back-sliding glass door. I would sometimes let him in, and he would wonder around the house and finally want to go back outside the same door he came in. Perhaps he was still looking for Puff.

CUTE CORA: OOPS - BE CAREFUL WHAT YOU PET.

One evening I stepped outside the sliding glass door to the back yard for some fresh air. It was already dark with the patio only slightly lighted by the light from inside our family room. I heard a slight noise near the south gate and naturally figured it was Mickey. I reached down to pet his head and said, "Hi Mick." That's when I realized, in sort of delayed double take, his tail was considerably fluffier, longer and his head was smaller and more pointed. A second look indicated what my mind had already concluded. Yep! A skunk. And apparently a friendly one. It is said that skunks make excellent pets as they are very compatible once they've been de-skunked.

Not being ready for that sort of pet, I walked down the cement path to the back of the lot to the gazebo hoping he would follow so I could back track and get back inside the family room without him dashing in behind me. It worked. I had ditched him; or so I thought. The following day I was sitting out on the patio just after sunset when he came across the yard from the creek rapidly waddling right towards me. Not wanting to particularly encourage this new friendship, I retreated inside the house. A few months later and now fully grown with the most gorgeous large fluffy cascading tail I had even seen on a skunk (turns out he was she) came for a visit with six cute little baby offspring following single file directly behind her. Any one of them could easily fit in the palm of one's hand, about the size of a four or five-week-old kittens. She walked directly toward me, up the middle of the walkway from the gazebo, looked at me within a few feet from me as she passed. It was as if she was proudly showing off her family. I know that skunks don't have the best eyesight, but it was impossible for her to not see me. I named her Cora.

Cora leisurely meandered down the sidewalk paralleling the back of the house to the far north side and headed back towards the creek with three babies in toe. But the other three became frightened and huddled together by our sliding glass door after I took a picture. The flash from my camera probably scared them but not Mama and the other three. It was fascinating to observe how one of three stood firm with the other two trembling behind him. I reasoned he or she must have been the bravest of the three willing to defend the others. Probably the best I could do was leave them alone, figuring Mom would come back for them after stashing the other three in a safe place. I checked back after ten minutes just in time to see Cora collect the remaining three as I watched them amble off toward the creek.

Mickey's destiny became apparent one day a few months later when I found a lot of Mickey's fur along with a few large feathers from a red-tail hawk. I imagined Mickey must have hesitated a little too long on top of the brick wall, and the hawk, who was often perched in that 75-foot-tall pine tree in our neighbors' yard, swooped down and took him.

LITTLE FAT RALPH

On one of my weekly morning coffee and donut runs I stopped for a cup of coffee and a jelly filled. I knew the owner who had migrated from Cambodia and who I had led to the Lord few years earlier when I gave him a NIV study Bible and a children's picture Bible for his young son.

I sat by the window engrossed in watching a goffer pushing up dirt from several holes. It's a mystery to me how he ever got to this little patch of grass about five feet square when everything for two hundred yards in any direction was covered with cement, asphalt, building foundations and streets. The owner came over an asked what I was staring at. I pointed to the goffer and said, "That little fellow." I called him Fat Ralph. I made the owner a bet for a dozen assorted donuts that I could have the goffer eating out of my hand within ten minutes. He doubted but accepted the challenge. If I was wrong, I owed him for a dozen. Ten minutes later I drove away with my free dozen donuts and endeared myself to the local Police Department when I explained the story and gave them my winnings. The owner of the donut shop never made any further bets with me.

KIND KYLE

We first moved in our new home 45 years ago. Our home was the last one built in the middle of an orange grove, so we were the last on street. To the north and west across the creek there were only orange trees. The foothills were 100 yards to the north. The wildlife was, and still is abundant. Mountain lions, black bears, coyotes, rattlesnakes, bobcats, hawks, and even Golden Eagles have graced us with their presence. At the time, Racoons were particularly proliferous.

One evening I found Kyle, a racoon, (don't know why I called him that), but he seemed so lonely, forlorn and hungry. I knew it's not a good idea to feed any wild thing, but I couldn't help it. He just looked so sad. Every night it became my habit to provide him with some lettuce, a carrot, or some avocado. By the third night he was eating out of my hand and letting me pet him. I quickly grew fond of him.

Before long, about dusk every day, the back yard had four or five more coming from the creek. Maybe Kyle spread the word there was a sugar daddy in town. Realizing my mistake, I was forced to procure some cage traps from the Humane Society. After placing the first trap out just before sunset with half an avocado for bait, the first one was captured within ten minutes. It was Kyle. He looked so hurt. So unhappy that I would trick him. His sad eyes said, "Please get me out of this thing."

The Humane Society truck came and took him to be released into the wild by a nice lady who did this sort of kind-hearted thing. The second, third and fourth night were the same, trapping three more. The one difference was all three were fiercely mad, drooling from the mouth and most likely Rabid. It is most often found in raccoons, skunks, foxes, and coyotes. All three were huge, my guess would be 15 to 20 lbs. and so violent the humane society driver couldn't pick up the cage by the handle on the top without getting bit or clawed. We had to use a four-foot-long two-inch-thick dowel pole with both of us carrying the cage out to his truck. They would be euthanized the next day. I love animals but have been cured of feeding wild ones.

61

ON TOWARD THE PRIZE

I like to think, in spite of the difficulties of the last work experiences, I finished well, accomplishing what hired to do, even though in some situations my offers and knowledge fell on deaf ears and scaled eyes. I believe God placed me there for the purpose of encouraging others.

Overall, I would have to say, even with the trials, tribulations, the ups and downs over the years, I had a resounding good time having more fun than a man deserves. Met a lot of wonderful people and developed friendships in all walks of life, Senators, Congressmen, captains of industry and business. I have stayed in contact with many of them, as well as lifelong friendships since grade school. I'm rich in relationships. Most importantly, I've come to learn, rely on and enjoy a personal relationship with the Lord.

I can summarize my years in ministry by quoting a section of Henri Nouwen (January 24, 1932 – September 21, 1996) from one of the 39 books he had written, one of which I still have on my bookshelf. He was a Dutch Catholic priest, professor, writer, and theologian, teaching for nearly two decades at the University of Notre Dame, Yale Divinity School and Harvard Divinity School.

In his book "The Way of the Heart," Nouwen talks about the importance of solitude. "A time is coming when men will go mad, and when they see someone who is not mad, they will attack them." Does that seem relevant in light of what we see and hear going on around us every day in some of our major cities.

He goes on to say in his example that solitude can make a man compassionate. "Compassion is the fruit of solitude and the basis of all ministry. The purification and transformation that takes place in solitude manifest themselves in compassion."

I would strongly agree, since it is where we best hear the Holy Spirit in the inner man. Without that quiet still voice, as some call "the whisper," we can only guess what to do and where to go next. As a fundraiser, a minister, or any profession, this is critically important.

Nouwen answers his own question by stating why solitude gives birth to compassion. "Because it makes us die to our neighbor. At first this seems quite disturbing to a modern mind. But when we give it a closer look, we can see that in order to be of service to others we have to die to them; that is, we have to give up measuring our meaning and value with the yardstick of others. To die to our neighbor means to stop evaluating them, and thus become free to be compassionate. Compassion can never coexist with judgment because judgment creates the distance, which prevents us from really being with the other."

Jesus prayed to the Father, *"So that the mighty love you have in me, maybe in them, and I in them."* John 17:26 TLB

APPENDIX A

FAVORITE MESSAGES AND MOTTOS

❖ Sometimes we go through things just so we can help someone else with what we have learned.

❖ Never allow anyone to deprive you of your dreams and hopes. If you know in your heart, because you have sought the Lord, do it and don't look back.

❖ With God, it is not who is going to let me, it's who is going to stop me.

❖ There will always be someone who will stand against you, but there will also be those, if only a few, who will stand with you. Be encouraged and always encourage others.

❖ Try not to burn bridges; You would be surprised how many times you may have to cross the same bridge.

❖ Take full charge of your attitude. Do not let others choose it for you.

❖ Never over promise and under deliver.

❖ If your friends have to be perfect, you won't have any. Nobody is perfect.

❖ Great ambition and conquest without contribution is to have no significance.

❖ Life can be like a series of great adventures always launched from the secure base of God's Word.

❖ We need to BE the Gospel, pure in heart, before we can preach it or do it.

❖ The scriptural Old Testament Law condemns the worst of us. The New Testament Grace saves the worst of us. Give Grace to others.

❖ You cannot get the right results with the wrong people.

❖ "Vision without execution is hallucination." - Thomas Edison.

❖ Ronald Reagan said "It's amazing what can be accomplished when you don't care who gets the credit. He was right. The reality is that there are far too many people who like a Rooster take credit for the dawn.

❖ Answer the phone with enthusiasm and energy in your voice.

❖ Keep a note pad and pencil on your bed-side table. Million-dollar ideas sometimes strike at 3 am.

❖ Show respect for everyone who works for a living, regardless of how trivial their job. I once read that "everyone you meet is in some way your superior, in that you can learn from him."

❖ If there is one thing that stands out in both my banking and missions' careers, it's that far too many people don't think big enough. They too easily take up membership in the congregation of Lilliputians, joining the fraternity of Woe-be-me's and constantly worry about the "what ifs." By contrast, visionaries always think big. I don't remember who said it, but it's true, "Vision without action is a daydream. Action without vision is a nightmare."

❖ Limits only exist in the souls of those who do not dream.

❖ Society honors conformity over creativity, especially in this day and age, there is a time and place to conform, but don't let it take up residence in your heart.

❖ The scriptures tell us in Proverbs 29:18, (KJV) "Where there is no vision the people perish.' Zig Ziglar said it quite well; "*If you aim at nothing, you'll hit it every time.*" Zig Ziglar may have found that piece of wisdom from Michelangelo who said it this way, "The greatest danger for most of us is not that our aim is too high and we miss it, but that it is too low and we reach it."

❖ Go the extra mile, not just for the boss, not just for the mission purpose, but for the Lord. You will quickly notice, there are no traffic jams in that extra mile.

❖ It's easy for any fish to swim downstream with the rest of the school. It takes courage and tenaciousness to swim against the stream.

❖ KISS "Keep It Simple and Sincere" especially in this day and age when everything seems to be much more complicated than it needs to be. I like to reduce things to the lowest common denominator and go from there.

❖ Do your best to live life without too many regrets. You will surely have some. But God's Grace is unending. Repent, surrender it at the foot of the cross, and move on with renewed trust that Christ's Love will redeem it.

❖ Identify the "season" you are in and ask the Lord what priorities you should have in this season.

❖ And like the motto of the U.S. Marines, "Improvise, Adapt, and Overcome.

❖ "In everything give thanks for this is the will of God in Christ Jesus concerning you." I Thessalonians 5:18 (KJV)

❖ Change can surely trampoline lives. But choose to keep your eyes and heart fixed on Jesus, the author and finisher of our faith. Surrender to Christ:

❖ "I know the plans I have for you, says the Lord. They are for good and not evil, to give you a future and a hope. Jeremiah 29:11 TLB

❖ Eighty percent of the success in any position is based on your ability to deal with people. I have a plaque in my office entitled Great People. (See Appendix B).

❖ Let God's love for you make you smile.

Now, I admit that I have some regrets. We all do. The good news is that the Lord redeems. Grace abounds. God's Love has no limits. Our love shouldn't either. Our real work is keeping our eyes on Jesus and His assignment for us. This book and record of my life are like memorial stones of how God worked in my life for His Purposes. The Lord has charted my path ahead of me, where to stop, where to rest. Every minute He knew my location. He has a much better GPS system. *"You discern my going out and my lying down; you are familiar with all my ways."* Psalm 139:3 (NIV2011)

The opposite of pride is worship and that is why the devil does not want us to worship. Giving God the praise and thanking him is another form of worship. *"The angel of the LORD encamps around those who fear him, and he delivers them."* (Psalm 34:7, NIV2011)

APPENDIX B

GREAT PEOPLE

Great people are ready to help you
at the right time in the right way-
people you don't even know yet.

Never give up because you don't have help,
but trust God to provide, because
God has the resources to help
which you have not even considered.

There are multiplied thousands of persons
with all sorts of talents and skills
and concerns and contacts
that God can bring into your life
in order to fulfill His plans.

So, open your eyes and
see the faces around you.
Open your ears to what they are saying.
Today, tomorrow, next week,
you will meet someone - someone who is
just the right person you need.

And that right person will come along to
fill the right place at just the right moment,
and you will marvel,
knowing God arranged it so beautifully.
--Author Unknown

APPENDIX C

PSALM 23 PARAPHRASED FOR LEADERS

The Lord is my Shepherd and my ministry-developer, I shall not want.
He makes me lie down in green pastures of supply and provision.
He leads me besides the still waters of His personal Shalom, as well as supernatural supportive relationships.

He restores my soul, renews my mind, quiets my emotions, creates a right spirit within me.
He leads me in paths of righteousness, not for my ego's sake, not for my ministry's sake, not for my vision's sake,
but he leads me in right paths for His sake, His name's sake.

Yea, though I walk through the valley of the shadow of fear, uncertainty, change, limitations,
I will fear no evil, for THOU art WITH ME.
thy rod (thy Word), and thy staff (thy Spirit) comfort me.

Thou preparest a banqueting table of nourishment and provision before me, even in the presence of mine enemies of doubt, rejection, disapproval.

Thou anointest my head with healing invigorating oil of restful hope,

Not relying on ourselves but on Christ who Redeems all things.
My cup filled with your Spirit of Power, Love, and Sound Mind
runneth over in gratitude to You and refreshment to others.

Surely goodness and mercy shall follow me, chase after,
and overtake me all the days of my life.
For I trust Your Love Lord, to perfect that which concerns me
and to work all things together for good.

And I will dwell in the house, building, presence, family,
and ministry assignment the Lord has for me, forever. In
Jesus Name,
Amen.

Bob and Estella Boomsma
© Copyright 2021

APPENDIX D

DISCLAIMER

If anyone disputes how they remember what we mutually went through in any of these stories, I humbly apologize if my remembrance is different from yours. I have good will towards everyone mentioned, and I'm very grateful God brought us together. I pray for you 3 John 2 KJV *"Beloved, I wish above all things that thou mayest prosper and be in health, even as your soul prospereth."*

I give Glory to God for providing all these marvelous experiences. As we surrender each experience at the foot of the cross, and wait for Christ's Resurrection power to Redeem each, in His time, then we experience rich contentment. We learn from it all, and mostly we learn how to Love and forgive, as Christ forgave us, which then produces the fruit of quiet faith, trusting God's love.

"For I know the plans I have for you, says the Lord. They are plans for good and not for evil, to give you a future and a hope."
(Jeremiah 29:11 TLB)